PHOTO: DEBRA GOLDMAN

■ JON BOWERMASTER has journalism degrees from Drake University, Des Moines, Iowa, and American University, Washington, D.C. He was cofounder and editor of *The Planet* in Des Moines from 1977 to 1982. Since then he has worked as a film producer and as an editor for *Rolling Stone,* and he has written for *The New York Times Magazine, Playboy,* and many other national magazines. He currently lives in Brooklyn, New York.

GOVERNOR

AN ORAL BIOGRAPHY OF
ROBERT D. RAY

GOVERNOR

AN ORAL BIOGRAPHY OF
ROBERT D. RAY

JON BOWERMASTER

IOWA STATE UNIVERSITY PRESS / AMES

Jon Bowermaster has journalism degrees from Drake University, Des Moines, Iowa, and American University, Washington, D.C. He was cofounder and editor of *The Planet* in Des Moines from 1977 to 1982. Since then he has worked as a film producer and as an editor for *Rolling Stone,* and he has written for *The New York Times Magazine, Playboy,* and many other national magazines. He currently lives in Brooklyn, New York.

© 1987 Jon Bowermaster
Composed by Iowa State University Press from author-provided disks
Printed in the United States of America
Design by Susan Maher
TITLE PAGE: World Wide photo. Reprinted with permission.

First edition, 1987

Library of Congress Cataloging-in-Publication Data

Bowermaster, Jon, 1954–
   Governor: an oral biography of Robert D. Ray.

   Includes index.
    1. Ray, Robert D., 1928–   2. Iowa–Governors–Biography.   3. Iowa–Politics
and government.   I. Title.

F625.42.R39B68   1987   977.7′033′0924[B]   87–11223
ISBN 0–8138–0724–7

CONTENTS

ACKNOWLEDGMENTS **vii**

INTRODUCTION **ix**

GROWING UP **3**

THE YOUNG LAWYER **15**

FIFTH DISTRICT COMMITTEEMAN **26**

STATE CHAIRMAN **34**

THE DECISION TO RUN **48**

THE PRIMARY AND GENERAL ELECTIONS, 1968 **54**

THE FIRST TERM, 1969–1970 **76**

RAY VERSUS FULTON, 1970 **89**

THE SECOND TERM, 1971–1972 **99**

THE TJERNAGEL AFFAIR **107**

JEPSEN I **114**

RAY VERSUS FRANZENBURG, 1972 **130**

THE THIRD TERM, 1973–1974 **134**

RAY VERSUS SCHABEN, 1974 **139**

THE FOURTH TERM, 1975–1978 **151**

THE BOTTLE BILL **168**

KANSAS CITY **177**

THE GOVERNOR'S CONFIDANTS **188**

RAY VERSUS FITZGERALD, 1978 **201**

JEPSEN II   **215**

THE FIFTH TERM, 1979–1982   **224**

THE REFUGEES   **237**

THE 1980 CAUCUSES   **242**

THE ECONOMY   **253**

"I WON'T RUN"   **266**

RAY AND THE LEGISLATURE   **276**

RAY AND THE STATE PARTY   **290**

RAY AND THE PRESS   **300**

THE FINAL DAYS   **312**

THE FUTURE AND JEPSEN III   **318**

THE LEGACY   **329**

EPILOGUE   **343**

INTERVIEWEES   **349**

INDEX   **361**

ACKNOWLEDGMENTS

One of the reasons I considered it important to collect and assemble these memories was because none of us is here forever. Memories don't just fade, they eventually die. Unless someone gathers the recollections of the participants, much of history slips through the cracks of time.

One of the joys of traveling around the state and coaxing people into recounting their memories for this book was to watch their faces light up when they talked about those "good old days," recalling the hard work, the wins and losses, and, most important, the friendships that they had made. My hope is that this book will serve as a history of those times. I also hope that it may serve as a gentle reminder to each and all not to forget the importance of friendship and shared memories. I'm stealing from Hemingway here, but he summed it up best when he wrote that the only thing better than the best spring day is the best of friends.

One of Bob Ray's best friends was Bob Tyson, and I spent many hours in a corner office in the Lucas State Office Building listening to Tyson's tales. If anyone was a student of Ray's career, it was Tyson. They met in the late 1950s, when the future governor was 0 for 2 in political contests, and they worked closely together for almost three decades. Often during Ray's governorship when he'd find himself swamped with work, the call would go out for Bob Tyson's help. Without a second thought, Tyson would work his regular state administrative job (under Ray he headed the Office for Planning and Programming and the Energy Policy Council) and then head over to the governor's lower office to help sort out appointments, recruit candidates, or organize a special event. Most of my time with Tyson was spent listening while he, between the packs of cigarettes and pots of coffee always within arm's length of his desk chair, reflected and rambled.

In the spring of 1985, all those years of long hours and too many packs of cigarettes caught up with Bob Tyson, and his memories are gone but for the hours I have on tape and the hundreds of friendships he left behind. Bob Ray eulogized his friend on a sunny spring day. From the parking lot of the funeral home you could see the array of state buildings and the capitol where the pair had spent so much time together. "So many times I meant to call Bob, to see how he was doing, say 'Thanks for the help,' just talk. I didn't do it often enough, and now he's gone. He was a good friend," remembered the former governor.

Many people contributed to this project and deserve my thanks. First, and with no second, really, are Bob and Billie Ray. Not only did they allow me to question them at length over the course of what must have seemed far too many months, but they encouraged me to talk to their friends, occasionally chipping in with phone numbers and names that I'd not run across. And though I know they were curious, they never asked me how someone remembered them or an event. They fed me a few times, were always accessible and congenial, and easily won my respect and, I hope, friendship.

The same thanks follows for the over 250 persons who let me borrow time and memories from them. Most, be they Democrats or Republicans, friends or foes of Bob Ray's, enjoyed our talks about his governorship. It gave them the opportunity to reflect on years and issues that they had pushed to the back of their minds. For early encouragement, I must single out by name some friends of Ray's and some friends of mine: David Belin, Robert Buckmaster, Ron Briggs, Dick Gilbert, Carole Harder, Jack Hatch, Dan Hunter, John McDonald, Frosty Mitchell, Brad Morford, Dave Oman, Rand Petersen, Marvin Pomerantz, Vic Preisser, Bob Rigler, Marvin Selden, Mary Louise Smith, Dutch Vermeer, and Wythe Willey. For a roof over my head, I'll always be indebted to everybody at Busby Productions; for transcribing all those hours of tape with no idea of how it could ever be assembled, Tammy Morford; for legal and financial reasoning, Greg Kenyon; for allowing me to wade uninhibited through the *Des Moines Register*'s library, Vern Brown and Phyllis Wolse; and for lending design to the finished pages, Susan Maher. Obviously the book wouldn't be in your hands without the support and enthusiasm of Richard Kinney and his staff at the Iowa State University Press.

The biggest thanks of all must be reserved for a trio, my most loyal and enduring friends: Larry Vint, Ranja (in memoriam), and last, but never least, Debra Goldman. I'd like to dedicate the book to my mom and dad.

INTRODUCTION

I first sat down with Bob Ray in February 1984. It was a bright and sunny but bitter cold winter day. (I remember because when I stopped at an Iowa City truck stop to change into my blue suit, there was ice on the tile floor of the men's room.) The former governor had been ensconced on the sixth floor of Life Investors in Cedar Rapids for just over a year. The coffee table outside his corner office was piled, neatly, with *Leaders* magazine and copies of the insurance company's most recent annual report.

We walked into his corner office and stood before the expansive windows looking out over a picture-perfect Iowa landscape. Picture-perfect but for an unsightly tin shack a half-mile out. I, like most Iowans, I think, was not aware of Ray's privately renowned but publicly submerged wit. When I asked him what the shack housed, he replied without missing a beat that it was the local home office of his new industry's leader, Prudential Insurance.

Robert D. Ray. *Des Moines Register* photo. Reprinted with permission.

For a brief, though embarrassingly long, moment I was sucked in. The governor wouldn't be pulling my leg. Would he? How un-imperial. But he was, and like many who spent long hours with him, I quickly learned to appreciate if not to goad that razor-sharp humor, his love of a pun, a side of him the public rarely saw. It is an endearing, somewhat disarming, experience to be told jokes by a man who will go down in history as one of Iowa's most popular politicians.

He is a quick-witted guy, though that is not the description that would probably come to mind first if you were stopped on the street and asked to describe the five-term governor. Honest, maybe. Boy Scout, Jack Armstrong, all-American, perhaps. Even boring or dull. But probably not funny. He explained that he was always afraid to let the quips fly in front of the press or public for fear they'd be taken out of context. "Things have a way of looking a lot different when you see them in print," he confided.

Over the course of fifteen months in 1984 and 1985, I spent roughly seventy hours with the governor-turned-insurance-executive reflecting, theorizing, pondering his almost thirty years of public life. We talked in cars over Billie Ray's homemade ham sandwiches, poolside in his backyard on California Drive in Des Moines, in his spacious condominium on First Avenue in Cedar Rapids, in the dining room at the United Nations in New York, in restaurants in all three cities, but most often behind the gently closed door of his Life Investors office. Tie loosened, lounging back in his chair, he seemed to like the probing, the opportunity to look back on the memories, good and bad, and especially the individuals that peopled them. We were often interrupted by the ring of his private line — sometimes it was Billie, more often politicians — U.S. senators, state legislators, former staffers — asking advice, exploring rumors, keeping him updated. Some days, pressured by the dual responsibilities of a CEO and an ex-governor, he was short, terse, in his replies. He is, and forever will be, an intensely private man. His anecdotes reveal few names and little about his childhood. He is hesitant to hurt or embarrass anyone. Once, he decided it was okay to reveal the name of a legislator he'd argued with, since he was long dead.

To augment my own knowledge and prepare myself for our talks, I crisscrossed Iowa and traveled a few times outside the borders of the state to interview approximately 250 people who worked for or against, with or around Ray during his years as a Des Moines trial lawyer, state Republican party chairman, and governor. I've been in more Iowa county seats and met more Iowa Republicans than I ever imagined I would. I sat with bank presidents, lawyers, state officials, legislators, ex-governors, reporters, campaign workers, and captains of industry. I interviewed two-term U.S. senator Jack Miller in his opulent judge's quarters that boasted a view of the White House, and I spoke with five-term Michigan governor William Milliken on a deck outside his office overlooking Grand Traverse Bay. I also sat with an underweared politico in his tiny, cigar smoke–filled Des Moines apartment, our conversation interrupted by his repeated trips to the kitchen for a morning bracer. I collected almost 400 hours of tape recordings, over 7,000 pages of transcriptions.

People in Iowa love to talk about their "Governor Ray." I'll bet every Iowan who's lived in the state since 1982 and before possesses at least one Bob Ray anecdote–people who worked for him, legislated under him, were appointed by him, made mad by him, even people he met just once, and people who had never met him but who felt they had because of his intimate relationship with the state and its population. I am convinced one of the reasons he was so politically successful was because of the thousands of scrapbooks in thousands of Iowa living rooms that boast a personal thank-you note from the governor for everything from a fifty-dollar donation to an ice-cream cone. It is easy and true to say that during his tenure he touched every Iowan in some fashion.

This is a book crammed with anecdotes and opinions. I was never convinced that people would want to read a book about Bob Ray that detailed every piece of legislation, every proposal, every political machination of his tenure. Perhaps someday a historian or more scholarly writer will tackle "Robert D. Ray and the Reorganization of State Government" in a single tome, or investigate "Robert D. Ray and the Republican Party in Iowa" in 250 pages. Those stories and more are there for the interested. But this book details where he came from, how he rose to whatever heights he achieved, and why and how he stayed there. It is also a book about not just one man but the state government as a whole, which he helped to change and mold, and the political parties that supported and fought him through the sixties, seventies, and eighties.

This book is filled with opinions and memories, some of which are bound to run contrary to those of my readers. Fine and good. A public life is filled with controversy, and no one, not even Bob Ray, can expect to live such a life without feeling a few barbs of criticism. Some of the memories will make people laugh, some will make them mad. A few will likely do both for Bob Ray. Renowned for his perfectionism and thin skin, he will most likely want to correct his critics, explain the facts as he knows them to be. But he'll have to live with the 90 percent of them that laud his career and the 10 percent that thought he could have been better. (One note on logistics for the reader. As this is an oral biography, the participants will walk you through much of the text. If you are unfamiliar with who's who, just keep one finger in the Interviewees section, page 349. My own questions and comments in the interview segments are in italics.)

One problem I ran across regarding Bob Ray's transition to ex-governor is what to call him now that he has left office. He says he's comfortable with whatever other people feel comfortable with—Governor, Mr. Ray, Bob Ray, even simply Bob. But I found few who were able to refer to him as anything but Bob Ray, rarely Bob and seldom just Ray. Most often friends and foes alike refer to him as "Bobray," as if it were one word, an adopted Iowa-only addition to Webster's dictionary defined just as "governor." Many still prefer to call him by that title. The rule is that only heads of state—presidents, premieres, and the like—carry their titles for life. Senators, representatives, and even governors keep theirs out of respect, not privilege. But in Iowa, and wherever else Bob Ray touched people's lives, he will always be "Governor." Longtime state legislator Del Stromer explained the phenomenon most succinctly: "You know, in my mind you've got [*Harold*] Hughes and you've got [*Terry*] Branstad, and then you've got the Governor."

JON BOWERMASTER

Brooklyn, New York
June 29, 1986

GOVERNOR

AN ORAL BIOGRAPHY OF
ROBERT D. RAY

I:
GROWING UP

The year Bob Ray was born, 1928, there was a Republican, John Hammill, occupying the Iowa governor's office, Iowa-born Herbert Hoover was elected president, and the Depression was just around the corner. None of that mattered much at the time to the young boy born on September 26 to Clark Ray, an accountant, and his wife, Mildred. He was their second child and only son, and little did they suspect that he would one day hold his own in the annals of Iowa history.

During the decade of the 1930s and on into the 1940s, Bob Ray could usually be found in one of two places, either the big frame house on Twenty-sixth Street in Des Moines—a few blocks south of the Drake University campus and a mile from the Hubbell Mansion on Grand Avenue, two focal points of his later years—or hanging around Drake Park, ball glove in hand, waiting for the next game. That neighborhood and that house (taken by the MacVicar Freeway in the late 1960s) would be home to Bob Ray until he was married and in his mid-twenties. He went off to school at Grant, Callanan, and Roosevelt schools and Drake University from those steps, often with a basketball or tennis racket under his arm.

The neighborhood has changed since then. The butcher shop on Cottage Grove, where Ray worked as a young Roosevelt student, is gone. Reed's Ice Cream on Forest Avenue, where he stood in line for nickel ice-cream bars, sometimes returning to the back of the line immediately to

Japan, 1946–1947. Rev. Bill Sherman photo. Reprinted with permission.

wait for another, is long vacant. But the park is still home to kids with big dreams.

MILDRED RAY "Bob was a good kid, and he got along with other kids real well. Some little kids are fighters, but he never was. He didn't have a lot of buddies; he often just went into the backyard and played by himself while his sister Novelene was out front with a lot of other kids having fun. In fact he'd be in the back all by himself a lot. In high school he had some kids he ran around with, but didn't have a lot of little buddies hanging around. Now, Novelene was much more outgoing. She always had kids around her and would go and stay over at other kids' houses. But Bob wasn't like that. He didn't read a lot of books, either, when he was growing up, not like his sister. He worked after school for Mrs. Smith, who ran the meat department over at the market on Cottage Grove, and he carried papers. He was a pretty typical kid. And he loved sports.

"He never did get in any trouble. In fact, I can remember going by the school one day and his dad and I spotted him. Two kids were fighting in the schoolyard and Bob went over and broke up the fight. He didn't like kids fighting."

BOB RAY "We were financially very poor. It was during the Depression and opportunities were somewhat limited. My dad worked long hours at different jobs as an accountant and office manager, but it was a hard, hard time. We didn't have much in the way of materialistic things. I was fortunate to have a caring mother and father, and in grade school I can remember so well the desire to excel in sports. The one thing I always had was a bat and a ball and a glove. I thought when I grew up I'd hopefully play ball for a living.

"When we played softball I was always the captain and had to choose up sides. That's how it was whatever we did, starting in grade school. I must have wanted to be the captain. *Maybe it's something you're born with.* Or maybe your ego just starts a little earlier."

NOVELENE RAY GIBBONS "When he was growing up, he was always looking after the little guy. That was a constant concern of his. We're as different as night and day. I was always talking; I chatter all the time. He's the one that when he did speak, people listened.

"He was kind of a loner. I'd always be over at the neighbors, chattering to them, and he'd walk by, wouldn't even bother to say hi. It just wasn't his nature to stop and just chat. Not that he wasn't friendly; we were just different in that way. I was always in the middle of a crowd – he was often alone. But all through school, any office that came available, any honors, he had them. People seemed to migrate to him. It was funny, though. It wasn't like he was out pushing himself for them; he wasn't out selling himself. All through grade school and high school he was king of this or president of that, but he didn't brag about it. We would generally find out that he'd won something from someone else, or in the school paper. He wouldn't come home and brag."

MILDRED RAY "He wasn't a great student, though. I know in high school the teachers would talk to me and they'd say, 'If he'd just open his book and work hard, he'd be an A-plus student,' that if he saw or heard anything, he'd never forget it."

DOROTHY HALL "I first had him as a student at Callanan in ninth grade, and I expected good things out of him. He was capability itself, always had everything right at hand. He was always doing the right thing, but he wasn't a sissy. You could depend on him. Learning came easy for him, though, and very often it's those kids that don't crack their books as often as they might."

MARVIN POMERANTZ "Even in seventh grade I remember being amazed at his political skills. We had a pretty heated race for class president that year, and Bob prevailed. It was really a miniature campaign, with banners and posters and speeches. It was well run."

GARY LILLY "I nominated him for that first office, president of our class in seventh grade at Callanan. He was the classroom king – the basketball player, the track star, all-around good guy. Besides that, I knew he would win. He was always in the forefront of student activities, kind of an untypical kid. I wouldn't call him a loner so much as someone who was above the fray, so to speak. He was really too good to be true."

BOB RAY "I suppose I was a bit ego-driven even back then. I don't know. Some people are natural athletes, they can throw the ball well the very first time they throw it. But you have to work for votes. *Even in seventh grade?* Well, in those days I think you voted for your opponent and then went out in the hall and waited for the results."

MILDRED RAY "His dad was an accountant and his life was really lived for his family. He didn't like to go out and do a lot of social things. He was with people during the day, and at the end of the day he just liked to come home and be with his family. He was very interested in politics, though."

BOB RAY "My dad was a strong Republican. So was my grandfather on my mother's side. When I was a kid I would listen to the two of them talk politics. I was always curious – not very knowledgeable, but curious. I asked a lot of questions and I never felt I got very good answers. Often I felt like I got poor answers. They seemed to complain a lot about Roosevelt because he had been in too long, but I couldn't get a good, definitive response as to what could be done or who could do it better or different. I was never satisfied, and it was almost enough to make me turn Democrat or independent, because I really felt like there was a lot of anti-administration talk without very solid reason or a good alternative. I suppose I'm a Republican today because I grew up in that atmosphere, but they almost lost me."

NOVELENE RAY GIBBONS "We had this great-aunt, and when Bob was a little boy she took him to an inaugural of a governor, and that created an interest in him that I don't think ever died."

So the bug of politics got into Bob Ray's blood early, as did the friendship of his lifelong adviser, confidante, and future mate. Billie Lee Hornberger grew up not far from the Ray family, though hers was a more prosperous home. Her father was an IDS agent. Car trips around the country were annual adventures for Billie Lee and her twin brother, Richard.

MILDRED RAY "Bob met Billie at church when they were in high school. They both went to what was then University Church – it's now First Christian – at Twenty-fifth and University. They really spent more time together at church than they did at high school. He didn't have very many girlfriends; she was it."

BILLIE RAY "We went to the same church camp, and one year he was the king at camp and I was the queen. Even though we were the same age, we never had a class together all through high school, and we really didn't start going together until our last year in high school, 1945–46. Bob was kind of shy, cute, good-looking, and spent a lot of time with his sports."

BOB RAY "I don't think there was much direction relative to what our future occupations would be when we were in high school. There wasn't much effort in career-planning. They made a stab, but there wasn't a constant push. We did have a Career Day for a merchandising class, and I remember going down and selling men's clothing at Younkers."

MILDRED RAY "We really wanted our kids to go to college. The last year in high school Novelene got a job down at the Iowa Des Moines Bank and just kept on with that. I don't think she really wanted to go to college. Bob did, but he didn't study all that hard in high school. He just kind of goofed around a little, and I remember telling him that I'd policed him all the way through high school and after that he was on his own. 'And if you don't make it, you can just dig ditches or whatever comes along,' I told him. I think in a way it was the army that caused him not to care about high school, because he knew he was going to have to go, so why study? I think it did that to a lot of the boys back then."

BOB RAY "I had been a pretty good student and put some pride in that until about midyear in eleventh grade. It was a frustrating time. Lots of kids were graduating from Roosevelt and going straight into the service. Few really knew what they were going to do with themselves. I graduated in 1946, and it just seemed like that was what I was going to do, join up. When I did, my parents had to sign a consent form because I was only seventeen. That wasn't easy for them to do. But the war was over, so there wasn't the same kind of fear there had been before."

MILDRED RAY "He graduated from high school in June. He wasn't going to be eighteen until September, but he entered the service in July. That didn't make his mother very happy, but now I see it was the very best thing. He got it over with before he went to college. But, of course, I was afraid that he would come back and not go to college. There was never a thought that he would make the army a career.

"He went away as a boy out of high school and he came back a man. When he came back he said to his dad, 'Well, let's go down and get a drink of beer.' Well, my husband was very opposed to liquor. Bob just did that as a joke."

BOB RAY "We were the first replacement troops in the Pacific. Growing up in Des Moines, I was one of those who felt there were greener pastures somewhere else, anyplace else, and the sooner I could get out of Des Moines the better I would feel, the happier I would be. It didn't take long for me to realize that after going down to Texas for basic training and then that long ship ride overseas, that Des Moines didn't look so bad."

REV. BILL SHERMAN "There was nothing in my almost one and a half years in the army with Bob that would give a clue to the fact that he had political ambitions or that he possessed the remarkable leadership capacities which he would display in later life. There were about six or eight of us young fellows who met when we were sworn into the army at Fort Snelling in Minnesota. The friendships we made in those few days carried us through processing at Fort Riley in Kansas, through basic training at Fort Bliss, Texas, and then overseas. We hung together for support and protection during our entire army life. By hook or crook we got on the same ship, and most of us got into the same squadron in the First Cavalry Division. We were on the same ship coming home, and several of us toured the western states for a few days before heading back home to the Midwest.

"Bob Ray was part of the gang, a good friend, an old buddy. Frankly, none of us were outstanding in anything. We did our job, wiled away the days, saw the sights, and came home."

BOB RAY "The military made me grow up. I can't speak for others, but I think it's probably true with most. You only remember the good times. You remember your buddies, and you remember some of the fun things and even though you complained all the time you're in the service, it was a great experience. The traveling was a great experience, living away from home was a great experience. Witnessing the destruction of war was a lasting experience. The discipline is something that helps you grow up, too. You realize you have to depend on lots of people, that you just can't shoot out by yourself no matter how independent you think you are. I never quite subscribed to the argument that if you were old enough to serve your country you were old enough to vote and drink. When you're in the military you are told what to do. You think less, you are on your own less in the military, than at home."

BILLIE RAY "When he came back he knew he wanted to go to college. Before then he really didn't know what he wanted to do, and his family couldn't easily send him to college. He didn't want to burden them, and the GI Bill helped with that. The army gave him time to think about what he was going to do with himself. I give him credit. He came out of the service unchanged—he's not one to conform. He still didn't drink liquor or coffee, or smoke, and that would have been the perfect time to pick those habits up. In those respects he came back exactly the same.

"The devastation he saw in Japan also left quite an impression, and so did the ride over on the ship. There was a lot of homesickness and lots of seasickness, and it was hard getting him on a ship after that."

BOB RAY "When I first came back from the service I signed up for a couple night courses at Drake and went into the restaurant business with my brother-in-law. We had a little place on Locust Street for about a year. That made me develop a healthy respect for people in the restaurant business. We would get up at four thirty, five o'clock in the morning and we'd be there until ten at night. Neither one of us knew anything about the business when we started, and we did a lot of the cooking ourselves. We sold it and didn't lose any money."

BILLIE RAY "It was just a little hole-in-the-wall downtown. I only went down a couple times and had a sandwich. It was kind of cute, but I didn't ask him much about it. His brother-in-law was going to school too, and they thought they could just run this place on the side."

BOB RAY "After that I enrolled at Drake full-time. I don't know what the custom was then, but I didn't really look around at other colleges. Drake just seemed the natural place to go. I had grown up around the school, played ball on the fields nearby, gone to and even run in the Drake Relays as a kid. When I enrolled, the only thing I knew was sports, and I must admit I was still just kind of wandering.

"The GI Bill helped pay for my college. At the time, I think Drake's tuition was $250 a semester. In high school I had been a meat cutter in a store over on Cottage Grove, so I went back and worked there my first couple years at Drake. I lived at home on Twenty-sixth Street with my parents. I decided that I'd go to school for an education and not sports, so I enrolled in business administration. I'm not sure exactly why, but it seemed like the right thing to do. My father had been an accountant, had managed an office – that might have been an influence."

BILLIE RAY "He took enough extra courses to get his teaching degree and did everything but practice teach, and he thought he'd be a coach. But nothing had really struck him yet, so he got his business degree and still could have taught. At times he said he might even like to be a minister."

BOB RAY "I took the basic courses – English, history, social studies – and I remember taking one political science course. As a class project we reapportioned the legislature, and even though I didn't know anything about reapportionment, I got an A-plus on the project. I'm sure I didn't know what I was doing.

"I had played some football in the service, and one of the coaches was working at Drake, and he invited me to go to a rush party at a fraternity. I didn't know anything about fraternities, but I went and there were several people I had known from high school there. I liked the spirit and some of the people I met, so I joined the SAE's [*Sigma Alpha Epsilons*]."

BILLIE RAY "I dated while I was at Drake and Bob was in the army. I wasn't ready to get married. I always said we should have a lot more fun before settling down. But during my last two years in college, Bob was there. Then I graduated and started teaching."

BOB RAY "When I was in the service, Billie and I corresponded. We went together, broke up a couple times, but not for long. Then when she got a job and a car I decided I ought to marry her."

BILLIE RAY "Bob was very deliberate. We didn't get married until he was just about finished with school. We'd been dating for about six years, and I figured we'd end up together. One of the things I liked about him was his gift for leadership. That and he was pretty popular.

"He was also pretty shy. I used to tell him he should go out with other girls, but he didn't date many. I thought maybe he'd find somebody else. He didn't."

MILDRED RAY "They got married while he was still in law school, December 22, 1951. She was teaching. We duplexed our house and they lived there. We couldn't have afforded to lend them seventy-five or a hundred dollars a month for an apartment, so we invited them in. We saw quite a bit of them, but they were both really busy."

BOB RAY "At Drake I really just fell into politics. A fraternity brother was on the student council, and one day coming out of marketing class, he asked if I'd be interested in being on the convocations committee. He said it would be a great experience, and it was. We spent a bundle of money bringing in speakers and musical events. I got to be chairman of that committee when I was a sophomore. That got me some exposure, and one thing led to another. Pretty soon I was the one organizing things. I became the student council president, president of my fraternity, and president of Alpha Kappa Psi, the business fraternity. It was like rolling a ball down a hill, it just kept going faster and faster.

"I was president of the student body when Johnny Bright was playing football there. We had great sports teams. We used to fill up Drake Stadium. There were some moments when I envied the athletes. Admired them probably."

DICK OLSON "We competed in intramurals on the football field. The two big fraternities were the ATO's [*Alpha Tau Omegas*] and the SAE's, and I was president of the ATO's and Bob was president of the SAE's. We competed in everything, really—rush, intramurals—and our two frats won everything. He was the kind of guy in competition, even back then, who didn't say a hell of a lot when you crossed him, but he went click-click and somewhere along the line, when he had the chance, he got back at you."

JANET VAN NOTE "He later told me that he ran for office at Drake in part to get over his shyness. He forced himself to do it. He was an older student, and usually when you started school after being in the service you didn't get involved in all the functions and that stuff, but he did. He forced himself to run for office to get over being shy in front of people."

BOB RAY "Those experiences helped me later on. We would have splits between the faculty and students, and I would get great satisfaction out of getting them to work together to accomplish things, to head in a particular direction. That experience left me with the impression that people can work together. They don't have to be the same age, they didn't have to be from the same college or one career. We had business, pharmacy, and fine arts majors who worked together.

"But I was still at loose ends about a career. Nobody was exactly knocking on my door and suggesting one for me. I don't think I ever got much advice from any counselors. I decided to take a business law course one semester, and I don't know if it was the course or the instructor, but I have a feeling it was the instructor that made the difference. That was Garry Chinn, Mary Jane Odell's first husband. He didn't give me a good grade, but I really liked the course, so I decided to take the next step, which was law school. At that time you took your first year of law at the same time as your fourth year of undergraduate study, so I was able to get both degrees in six years."

DON ZARLEY "We started law school together in 1951, but I didn't get to know him too well until our senior year, 1953. I knew about him all through law school and was well aware that during his undergraduate days he was the big man on campus. It was generally known in law school that Bob was an important person on the Drake campus, but at that time he was working full-time and studying, which caused for a lower profile. Everybody worked as much as they could. It was commonplace then."

BOB RAY "By the time I started law school I was working full-time as a circulation manager at the *Register and Tribune*. It was a good job and I was fortunate to get it. It was the one job that I really sought, kept going back for, and finally got. All the other managers were older; this was their livelihood. It taught me a couple things: organization, and how to use time wisely. I handled seventy newspaper carriers and was constantly running back and forth between the *Register* and Drake. I needed the money, and they paid a bonus if all your carriers paid by Monday morning. Consequently, I made that bonus every week, which was not easy.

"The spine of my district ran up Ninth Street, from Grand Avenue all the way to the city limits. I assumed responsibilities on a Sunday, so on Saturday night I went out to check out the territory. My job was to recruit carriers, make sure they were schooled, and make sure that all the routes were carried and collected. I had been warned that whatever I did, I shouldn't lose the two brothers who carried the two routes by the river, because I would never find anybody to replace them, and if I lost those kids, I would be carrying the routes myself. Well, I was young and I just made up my mind that if they didn't do what was expected of them, they would have to go. They were supposed to pick up their papers at Ninth and Walker by five thirty or so, and that first evening they didn't show. All the other papers had been picked up and these kids still hadn't shown up.

"So the branch manager and I went down to their house, got their route cards from their mother, and delivered their papers. When we finished they showed up and couldn't figure out why we had delivered the papers. I made them show me their collection books, paid them what was owed, and fired them. I didn't think too much about it until a month had gone by and I was still delivering their papers. But we eventually found someone to carry the routes, and the kids in that whole district knew that you either carried the papers the right way or you didn't carry them. By the time I left, we had a good, clean district. *Sounds a little like recruiting candidates to run for office.* Yes, I guess that it was good training for that, too.

"The *Register* treated me well. When I finished law school they offered to find a job for me and move me inside somewhere. I thought that was very generous of them. But my boss said that even though he'd like me to stay, if he had a son just graduating from law school, he'd suggest that he practice law."

<u>DON ZARLEY</u> "We took the bar exam together in Iowa City in the summer of 1954. We'd take the exam during the day and then in the afternoon we'd head for the old Finkbine Golf Course. I don't think that Bob had great worries about not passing the bar. Most of us didn't in those days; most people passed.

"We all assumed that Bob would always be successful, but I don't think any of us had any idea that he'd go into politics. I suppose if it had been suggested to us, we would have agreed he certainly could have, but I don't think any of us envisioned it."

BOB RAY "Billie and I had decided to go to Europe after I finished law school. We figured we wouldn't have the time later, so we just took all of our money and spent about four and a half months there. At the time I guess it was kind of bold, but you wouldn't think much about it now. Matter of fact, the *Register* did a whole page about us going, showed us shopping for luggage and looking at maps. It would have been wonderful coverage if I had been running for office."

JIM TYLER "We were among the relatively few married couples in law school without children, and I think that's why they selected us to go to Europe with them. Bob and I were finishing up, and both Billie and Joann were teaching school and had the summer off."

JOANN TYLER "They wanted somebody to go along with them to help pay for the expense of renting a car, and we were the most likely prospects at the law school. But it was their idea."

JIM TYLER "Our parents thought we were insane. People just didn't go to Europe. We went on a boat because we couldn't afford to fly. Since then we've been there five times and haven't been able to afford to go on a boat. Our tickets were $630 round-trip, per couple. That was from Quebec."

JOANN TYLER "We waited until Bob and Jim had taken the bar. We left on July 2 and ended up traveling 11,000 miles. It was interesting at that time, because there just weren't many young people who picked up and traveled. We went to Spain just the second year after it was opened to tourists, and we were curiosities. We'd stop the car and a crowd would gather around us."

BILLIE RAY "We went low-budget and figured we could spend about ten dollars a day for everything—food, lodging, everything."

JIM TYLER "In southern Europe and Spain we were trying to have our evening meal plus lodging for a couple, all for five dollars. And usually did. It was also in southern Europe that we discovered Robert's propensity for bargaining. He just loved it. Every place we went where they had something to sell, he'd barter with the salespeople.

"At that time we still didn't know exactly how to treat Germans. But we had met a lovely German girl and her husband, and they asked us to their home for tea. It all went very well, and we got back in the car and Bob said, 'I sat on a bee when we first went in there, and it stung me.' He sat there the whole time, didn't move, didn't say anything. That's when I knew he was going to be a diplomat of some sort.

"Bob and Billie didn't have the cosmopolitan tastes they have now. They were pretty much into well-done meat and potatoes. We frequently ordered blind since none of us could read the menus, and in Marseilles they ordered something that turned out to be octopus. They didn't touch it."

JOANN TYLER "They were very, very close. Always supportive of each other. After their first trip to China, we went and saw Bob's pictures, which consisted of Billie in front of the Great Wall of China, and then Billie in front of the palace at Peking. She was a very important part of his photography. During the four months we were together, we must have talked about everything under the sun, but he would often make a statement followed by, 'Isn't that so, Billie Lee?' or 'Don't you agree, Billie Lee?' He would often bounce things off her."

BOB RAY "That trip [*to Europe*] gave us a great foundation for the other travels we have done since. I probably remember more from that trip than I do any of our other trips abroad."

II:
THE YOUNG
LAWYER

BOB RAY "We got back from Europe with about thirty cents in our pockets. Billie went back to teaching and I had to start looking for a job."

BILLIE RAY "He just started looking at law firms around Des Moines. I don't think he looked any other place in Iowa. But I started getting kind of antsy—I kept wondering, 'How come you don't get a job?' I don't think he started until the first of the year and we had gotten back from Europe in October. But that was typical of him, to make sure that what he does is what he wants to do and not just jump in and then jump to something else."

BOB RAY "I'd always had to work, whether it was cutting meat or at the *Register* or whatever. But I think Billie got a little anxious for me to get a job. I'd gotten interested in photography, and I can remember spending a lot of time with the pictures from our trip. For some reason I didn't seem to be all that inspired to rush out and start my legal career. I also don't think I knew exactly how to go about starting out. My dad wasn't a lawyer, I didn't have those connections, and in those days not many young attorneys just opened up offices. I'd heard of the Lawyer brothers. Verne had tried a couple of sensational cases and had been quoted in several of my classes by teachers. But I really didn't know them. So I just stopped

Marching from Ames to Des Moines for the polio drive. *Des Moines Register* photo. Reprinted with permission.

by to see them one day. They had just set up offices in the Fleming Building. They said they had a lot of people wanting to join them, but they weren't very anxious to grow into a big firm."

VERNE LAWYER "He came in looking for a job. He said he wanted to be a trial lawyer and a politician. I was in my office, and my brother Jim called me in and wanted to know if I wanted to meet somebody, a young lawyer looking for a job. Turns out he'd been sent down by a brother at the SAE house. We were all SAE's. My recollection is, although he says he doesn't recall it, that I was in a hurry—had somebody in my office—and I asked him if he wanted to be a trial lawyer and he said yes. I asked him if he wanted to be involved in politics and his answer was yes. I asked him if he wanted to run for office and his answer was he thought he did. My recollection is that I then asked him if he could be elected anything, what would he like to be elected, and his answer was immediately governor. He claims he doesn't remember that."

JAMES LAWYER "We'd had several people who wanted to join us, but we didn't have any particular interest in the ones that approached us. At the end of December, early January, my wife, Marge, told me she knew someone she thought would make a super lawyer. She had known Bob Ray since high school. About a month later, Bob came into the office and there was no question; he passed, so to speak. As far as we were concerned, he was in the right place at the right time. We didn't even invite him back for a second interview. We just told him right then that if he wanted to work for us, he could."

VERNE LAWYER "He was a very unusual human being. Even as a young man he had a charisma about him that was sort of a self-sell thing. He didn't really have to work at it. Kind of seductive. That's one reason he got along so well with women jurors.

"I never had any doubt in my mind whatsoever, from the very moment I first met him, that he would eventually be governor of Iowa if he wanted to be, and my big project was to keep him enthused—you know, encourage him and so forth. *Why?* For one thing, he looked like a movie star. A very, very charming first impression, which was one reason he was so successful with juries. He had that crooked smile and was clean as a whistle, didn't smoke or drink or swear or chase women. He was a clean-cut all-American boy with a lot of smarts, a lot of drive, and a lot of desire."

BOB RAY "To this day I don't know why they hired me. I certainly didn't run the fast social pace that Verne did, and maybe I was good for the firm in that respect. I wasn't that much like either Jim or Verne. We were a pretty good team; we complemented each other."

BILLIE RAY "Verne is a playboy, in a good way. He liked to go out and have a good time, spend a lot of money, fly around the country, mess around. Jim was an eight-to-five guy, stayed at home, more conscientious, and a big family man. They're completely different. But Verne would be out getting all the clients and bringing in the money. Bob didn't mind Verne going out and doing his thing because he knew that Verne was making contacts, bringing in business, and keeping the firm's name out in front. Jim was plugging away at his desk, and Bob was kind of in-between, kind of a buffer.

"Bob admired Verne's great ability at law, his great mind, and his spirit. I don't think their values are the same, but Bob likes to do things. He's not content to sit at home and watch television. Verne ran around the country, did things, had friends like F. Lee Bailey and Melvin Belli.

"Being around Verne was fun. One day he called—this was after Bob was governor—and wanted to know if we wanted to attend Lee Bailey's wedding. He married an airline stewardess out at Johnny and Kay's on Fleur Drive. It wasn't very publicized, but Verne invited some friends, and Leo Oxberger came out and performed the ceremony. They had a bar set up, and that was the first time I had ever been to a wedding in a hotel room, and they served drinks before the wedding."

BOB RAY "I started trying lawsuits along with them. We never wanted the firm to grow very big, because we really wanted to practice law and not manage a big office. Verne had developed quite a national reputation, was very active in the Academy of Trial Lawyers, and his contacts were tremendous. Because of that, we tended to go the direction he was going, because that's where the business came from. I suppose if I were still with him, I'd be joining him on his airplane crash suits.

"I was doing a little bit of everything—criminal work, some divorces, bankruptcies. I defended a sodomy case one time and then a bunch after that. Once you get a reputation for winning a case like that they keep coming back, even if you don't want them to."

VERNE LAWYER "He was eager to learn. When we tried cases together he would undertake any task that was assigned him. No argument, no problem, just do it. I think the first case he participated in was a murder case I defended. Luther Glanton was the prosecutor. It wasn't very long before he was handling them on his own. He had a lot of talent and a lot of

personality—the kind of guy who attracted people. He'd only been practicing law a year when we ran him for county attorney."

JAMES LAWYER "In the early 1950s there wasn't much big news, so what
would be in the back pages of the paper today was often on the front
pages. As a result, Verne and I had a lot of name recognition. We'd done a
lot of criminal work and gotten our names in the paper. We encouraged
Bob to pursue office in part because we felt it would help establish his
own name. He was a born politician; we didn't have to encourage him
much."

DRAKE MABRY "When he was in the Lawyer Lawyer and Ray firm he
was really an oddity. Verne Lawyer was a flamboyant trial attorney—he
owned his own airplane and raced around the country. After a while it
was pretty obvious that the law firm was just a political base, an income
base for Ray. Verne spent a lot of time covering his ass while he was out
politicking."

BOB RAY "I liked practicing law. If somebody else didn't want a case, I'd
do it. I had just gotten to a place where I felt fairly comfortable in the
practice when I got mixed up in politics.
    "I didn't really plan to run for county attorney in 1956. A lot of people
came to me. I suppose they thought I was so naive that I wouldn't ask
why Republicans didn't get elected in Polk County."

FROSTY MITCHELL "In those days it was not ethical or legal for a lawyer
to advertise, so the best way to advertise was to run for county attorney.
And lose. Because a Republican running for county attorney in Polk
County was almost a kamikaze mission, but win or lose, your name got
around."

VERNE LAWYER "He had to get some name recognition and get involved
in up-front politics. You can't come out of obscurity and run for governor
and expect to get elected. He had to become a recognized name in Republican circles, and one way to do it was to run him even though we
knew he wasn't going to get elected. He didn't have a ghost of a chance,
but he got some experience."

BOB RAY "I had been active in politics on campus, and I think that colored
my thinking. I hadn't really experienced much politics outside of that. I
didn't know what to expect. But there was a feeling that maybe it was
time to elect a Republican county attorney. I didn't do my homework very

well. I didn't go out and try and find why the county was Democratic or what had happened in previous elections, but it sounded like an exciting thing to do, so I agreed. Afterwards I was kind of bitter, because a lot of the people who had encouraged me to run weren't around to help after I said yes.

"My mom was kind of ambivalent about it all, and I don't think my father was very enthusiastic about me getting into politics. But he was a strong supporter, nonetheless, and I think he was proud, even pleased at times, especially when I didn't make a total fool of myself. He would have been a proud daddy ten, twenty years later."

TONY CRITELLI "I think Verne and Jim saw him as someone who had public acceptance. They thought he added some class to their operation. He was more valuable to them in that respect than he would have been in the work he did for them. They'd been representing some pretty despicable people, and this was a way to get some class in the operation. They saw that early on.

"In that campaign, Bob popularized those small signs which we'd go out and put up on telephone poles. They were red and yellow. Someone had told him that those were very visible colors. That was a first. And he had some girls dressed up as the 'Bob Ray Girls' or something, and even at that level he kind of innovated local politics."

BILLIE RAY "Bob is not one who sticks to tradition. He's not a maverick, but he's innovative and willing to try something new if he thinks it's good. We had the Bob Ray Girls from the very beginning. Their costumes changed, but they were always dressed in red and yellow. The first ones had 'Bob Ray' stenciled on the back of their jackets, then we went to red skirts and yellow jackets or sweaters, then after that we went to yellow skirts and red jackets, and once they had red-and-yellow cowboy hats."

JANET VAN NOTE "Leo Oxberger was the one that got me involved in the first campaign. He was the head of the Young Republicans at Drake, and I was working for the health department, right after I got out of high school. He called me, just out of the blue, and said he was looking for some girls to work at the state fair and I said yes.

"The first thing we [Ray Girls] did was work out at the state fair. Bob Ray was running for county attorney, and Billie and some of her friends made outfits for some of us and we became Bob Ray Girls. I think it was probably Billie and her friends' idea. I didn't know that much about politics at that point. We rode in parades and passed out little leaflets. It was fun, my first exposure to politics."

<u>LEO OXBERGER</u> "Bob and I would go out every night and post signs on telephone poles and trees. We just plastered the town. One of my fondest memories is one cold night we had been out for a couple hours and we were very cold, and we stopped at a service station out on East Thirty-third Street and University to warm up. A policeman pulled up, and he came in with an armload of posters and handed them to us. He'd been following us and tearing them down as fast as we put them up.

"We continued, though, putting them on vacant lots, on trees. We had a crew of lawyers that would go out every night with us. We thought if we could get his name around, we'd have some luck. In 1954 the Republicans had come very close to winning several offices in Polk County."

<u>BOB RAY</u> "We ran a good race, a colorful race. We did some things then that people hadn't done before. Gene Kieffer did the advertising for me and for the county Republicans in those days. In the past they would put black-and-white posters on the telephone poles all over the county, with just the candidate's name and picture on them. We took all the money we had and ordered some red-and-yellow placards that were long and narrow and wrapped all the way around the poles. Gene tried to explain that those were great colors, that they would catch people's eyes. They were distinctive."

<u>LEO OXBERGER</u> "We also held some dances out at Connie and Lou's Sky-liner, across the street from the airport. At ten dollars a ticket they were fun fund-raising events. I didn't have much to do with the fund-raising, but I know that most every lawyer in town was given the opportunity to contribute, and we spent more money than anybody else did that campaign. We had sixteen billboards, multicolored posters, things that hadn't been done before."

<u>BOB RAY</u> "It was mostly college friends who helped during that campaign. Jim and Verne were supportive, but they were doing the office work that I wasn't doing."

<u>TONY CRITELLI</u> "I remember being out until four, five in the morning, putting up signs, sometimes climbing poles and trees to get them up. We were kind of political pragmatists, in large part because he was an unknown commodity. I was personally impressed by the fact that he was able to cut the winning majority in half—first time out of the chute and he gets beat by only 10,000, when the Republicans were used to getting beat by 20,000."

JACKIE DAY "He wasn't taken too seriously as a candidate, but he was young, handsome, and brash—which was a lot different than most of the rest of the Republicans, who were rather stodgy. Everyone knew that he was going to get clobbered."

TOM WHITNEY "Ray Hanrahan was his opponent in that race, and his best line of the campaign was when he referred to the Lawyer Lawyer and Ray firm as Felony Felony and Misdemeanor. The Lawyer brothers were the older, more experienced, more prominent attorneys. It was a delightful line, but he paid the price later on when he was nominated for a judgeship three times. Bob Ray has a long memory." [*Bob Ray finally appointed Ray Hanrahan a District Court Judge in 1976.*]

RAY HANRAHAN "I'm glad I didn't have to try and beat him again. It was pretty simple back then. There were more Democrats than there were Republicans in the county, and we were better organized. I never thought I won because of my personal popularity."

BOB RAY "Those were good years, despite the loss. I can remember being in a parade with Ike [*Dwight Eisenhower*], meeting him. He was a national hero; everybody loved him. But I didn't exactly ride in on his coattails."

LEO OXBERGER "In 1956 everybody was somewhat encouraged because the Republicans had run well in 1954, but the organization was not in very good shape. Bob Ray lost by 10,000 votes. The sheriff candidate lost by 13,000. The others lost by much worse."

BOB RAY "No one ever told me that Republicans didn't win in Polk County. I was really green, and when we lost I decided that was enough of that. I just wanted to practice law. Then Jack Schroeder, the state senator from Davenport, offered me a job as the law and reading clerk in the senate. I really questioned whether I should take it, because it would take time from my practice, which I thought I'd better concentrate on. But I took it.

"In those days the legislature didn't have all the research capability they have today. There was no Legislative Service Bureau, just a couple of people to help draft bills. Part of my job was arranging a lot of that research. Sometimes I think I learned more from that vantage point than if I had been a senator, because often a senator is not in on all aspects of writing legislation. I got to be on the edge of a lot of good thinking and saw how and why it would be done. And I got to see a lot of great legislators work—Jack Schroeder, Bob Rigler, Dave Shaff, Bill Stuart were in that session. They were really strong, strong people and great persuaders. I made some lasting friends out of the experience."

JACK SCHROEDER "I was the majority leader that session. I thought the job would be interesting for him because it would give him an opportunity to see how the legislature worked. He did a great job, and then Leo Oxberger and Tony Critelli followed him in the job."

BOB RAY "During the sessions, I worked at the capitol, and every day after I finished I would go to the office and practice law, often until after midnight. I was putting in long hours. Then the next session, in 1958, I ran for the House of Representatives. I shouldn't have done that. I didn't want to, and if you don't want to, you shouldn't. Leo Oxberger was the Polk County Republican chairman, and he was really stumping around trying to do a good job and just couldn't get candidates. He came to me and said if I ran he could fill the ticket, and if I didn't he'd have trouble. I felt loyal to Leo, who had helped me so much and had helped the party. I did it, and I didn't do a very good job of marketing myself. I worked at it, but I didn't have my heart and soul in it, not as much as when I ran for county attorney."

LEO OXBERGER "My first job in 1958 was to get candidates to run. It looked like it was going to be a big year for the Democrats, and nobody wanted to run. Bob Ray had made the biggest splash in 1956, and everybody thought he was the future of the party, so it was important to get him on the ticket. Well, Billie didn't want him to run, and Verne Lawyer wasn't going to let him run, so I scheduled a luncheon at the Standard Club and invited 250 of the top Republicans. Charles Iles, soon to be the mayor of Des Moines; C. Edwin Moore, who would become the chief justice of the Iowa Supreme Court; and Floyd Burgeson, the president of the school board got up and gave testimonials about why it was so important that Bob run. I made sure Verne and Billie were there too.

"Bob had told me he'd run for the good of the party. He knew he couldn't win and it wouldn't help his career, but he understood the party needed him and so this luncheon was staged with his approval. The upshot of it was that they agreed, and we got a flood of candidates.

"The other thing I did was line up a sugar daddy to finance the campaign, because Bob didn't want to spend the time out raising the money, and he didn't want to put in his own money, and Verne wouldn't finance it. So George Faul, who was general counsel for American Republic Insurance and was fairly well-to-do, said he'd underwrite the campaign. We worked to raise money, but whatever we needed to spend, within reason, he said, 'Just go ahead and spend it, and I'll foot the bill.' And he did. But it wasn't a very expensive race. We actually spent more in the county attorney's race.

"We did do some television advertising in that campaign, which most candidates weren't doing. We had a union electrician come on and talk about why he was for Bob Ray, things like that. After I'd talked him into running, I couldn't very well leave him out on a limb, so I used all the power of my office to try and get him elected. But there wasn't much money that the state and county organizations could give individual candidates. Most of that went to selling the whole ticket."

BOB RAY "Leo was aggressive and eager and really believed in the party and liked the challenge. He was so dedicated that I really wanted to do it for him. But that wasn't a good enough reason. I just never got in the swim of that campaign. We ran at-large then, with the two top vote-getters going to the house to represent Des Moines. Howard Reppert and John Andrews, both Democrats, won.

"Losing was a valuable experience. Since then I've watched a lot of candidates, and no matter how far behind you are or how impossible it is, somehow you think the votes will fall in place and you'll win. It's a terrible letdown—just an awful feeling—to lose, and after having lost the first time, throughout my whole political career I was prepared to lose. I knew it could happen, and I knew what the feeling was when you lost. I didn't want to, I was really committed to winning, but I was also always prepared for the worst."

LEO OXBERGER "After that 1958 election we had a meeting of the central committee and only 16 out of 225 eligible people showed up. The party was ready to throw in the towel, and Bob and I decided we wanted to make an effort to keep building. We either had to quit or we had to have some new techniques to bring new people into the party. So Bob and I joined fifteen to twenty organizations. We joined the Eagles, the Moose Lodge, the March of Dimes and went to all the meetings. It was awful at times, but we did it because we could make new contacts and hopefully encourage people to join the party. We were also trying to identify precinct workers, which really came into play when Bob ran for the state central committee."

BOB RAY "I wanted to join those clubs not so much because of the politics but because I knew that if I was going to be a successful lawyer, people had to know who I was. I just decided if you're going to be active in business or law or politics, whichever, you really needed to know what was going on and who made things happen. But one day I went home and my oldest daughter, Randi, who was just a baby in the crib, was calling her Mickey Mouse doll 'dada'. That made me think my priorities were a little mixed up, so I started fading out of some of those activities."

LEO OXBERGER "As Republican county chairman, I was able to pick people to head up any program we had going on and get publicity for it, and Bob always got appointed to anything he wanted. He was the finance chairman whenever there was a neighbor-to-neighbor fund-raising drive. Anything that was going to get his name in the paper, I appointed him. It was a very conscious effort. Bob also became chairman of the March of Dimes, and that's how we met Frosty Mitchell."

BOB RAY "When I chaired the March of Dimes we were the only organization that was going into the public schools to raise money. I'd go out and pitch the March of Dimes, and I developed a group of students that helped me map out how to raise money in the schools. We decided we needed to get local personalities to show up at school assemblies to help fund-raising, and they decided they wanted the hotshot KIOA disc jockey Frosty Mitchell.

"So we asked him to put together a show for the assemblies. He put together a show and told jokes that were considered off-color, especially in those days. At the last assembly, at Lincoln High School, they wouldn't let Frosty onstage because they'd heard about his previous shows, and here I am smack in the middle, working free for a charitable organization, giving the kids what they asked for."

FROSTY MITCHELL "We went on to do several stunts for the March of Dimes. One time I stayed on the air twenty-four hours, broadcasting from the window of the old Sears and Roebuck building in downtown Des Moines. Then we did a couple walks from Ames to Des Moines. One year I had to push a wheelbarrow with a barrel in it all that way, and it got down to twenty below zero."

LEO OXBERGER "All this time Bob was still trying to develop his law practice, and I think if he hadn't been so bitten by the political bug, he would have been a first-class trial lawyer. He just had a flare for it, and people loved him. He wasn't tough, really, but he was firm.

"I'll give you an example of his loyalty to a client. We were both very active in the Junior Chamber of Commerce. He was the vice-president and I was the recorder. That meant I was the publisher of the Jaycees' newspaper, and he was one of the directors, under which fell the obligation of putting together the soapbox derby. Well, one day Bob has this client come into his office who had won the soapbox derby but had been disqualified because the Jaycees' judges ruled he had too much antifriction substance on his axles. He didn't get a trophy and didn't get to go to Akron for the finals.

"He felt he'd been wronged, so Bob convinced the Junior Chamber to change their decision."

III:
FIFTH DISTRICT
COMMITTEEMAN

In 1960, after two resounding defeats, Bob Ray, not accustomed to losing at anything, figured his fling with politics was over. He was going to devote those eighteen-hour days strictly to practicing law, hoping to start making some money and spending more time with his wife and daughters. His partner Verne Lawyer was a little disappointed – his role as kingmaker wasn't working out so far – but also somewhat relieved. He needed Ray around the office.

But instead of being able to give up politics, its stranglehold on his psyche and his time only tightened. Perhaps he couldn't get elected himself, but he was smart enough, organized enough, to get others elected. He recognized the problems he'd had in his own campaigns, and harkening back to those early snatches of political talk he'd overheard as a boy, he recognized the need to elect Republicans.

As a young lawyer, Ray had displayed a respect for freedom of choice. His societal values, though he seldom publicized them, were fairly liberal, and many of his friends were Democrats. But it was fiscal responsibility, at the county and state levels, that encouraged his fight to help elect Republicans. "The only solution Democrats ever have is raising taxes" was an early and heartfelt Ray theme.

Also, despite his later protests to the contrary, his ambition and ego

Des Moines Register photo. Reprinted with permission.

were hardly ordinary. Yet he insists that, skillfully as he may have plotted and planned for others to get elected, he never set out a plan for himself, never possessed any long-range goals. Maybe, but remember, this was the same fellow who had been "king of everything," as Marge Lawyer, a high school classmate, remembers. Political ambition dies hard, and in 1960 Bob Ray better understood the ladder of Iowa politics and what it took to climb to the top.

LEO OXBERGER "In 1958, right after Bob was defeated in the legislative race, he told me he wanted to try and be a delegate to the presidential convention [*in Chicago*] in 1960 and wanted me to support him. I said I would, and as the race neared I was out working on his behalf, making calls and visiting with people. Then I got a call from Art Donhowe, who was the Fifth District representative on the Republican central committee, who said they had already picked the nominee for national delegate from Polk County, John Keith Rehmann. I told him that I was going to continue supporting Bob Ray and that we'd just have a friendly fight. But he told me I couldn't support Bob Ray, because the central committee paid my salary and that he'd take my job away. Well, I went back and told Bob, and he said, 'I'd rather be on the state central committee, and rumor is that Art is not going to run for reelection. So why don't we get Art to support me for his old job as long as I don't oppose John Keith for the national delegate job.'

"I made the mistake of meeting with John Keith to pitch that deal, instead of with Donhowe, and he assured me that Art was going to retire and that they would support Bob for district chairman, so Bob withdrew from the race against Rehmann. That seemed like a good deal, in part because Bob was getting a lot of pressure from Verne to spend more time in the office tending to business."

BOB RAY "Leo was trying real hard to develop a Polk County organization, and he talked to me, like he had before, and convinced others to talk to me. He was scared because they didn't have a viable county organization. They needed some new blood on the state central committee, and he wanted me to run for Fifth District chairman.

"I knew Art Donhowe, who held the position, and considered him a friend. But he was a big banker and I was just a little old struggling lawyer. The problem I had with bankers being in politics was that in those days the banks really had a strong hold on local politics. While I had no objection to them doing business with the state legitimately, I never favored them being able to hold state funds without paying interest, and that was then the practice supported by both parties."

BEN WEBSTER "Leo was the one that talked Bob into running. I ran into Leo one day on the street in front of the Hotel Savery, and he told me he'd convinced Bob Ray to run. I said great, I'd support him. Later he called me and told me he was getting some pressure from the establishment Republicans, which included my dad. So I had lunch at the old Des Moines Club one day with my dad and two other guys. The purpose was for them to tell me to tell Leo to lay off, but I assured them that Bob Ray was going to run against Art Donhowe and that we were going to elect him."

BOB RAY "I didn't really have a problem with Art, but there was a feeling that the Republican party statewide, and especially in Polk County, was stagnant. There used to be a saying around Republican circles that it was better to control than win. I'm not sure I understood everything that was going on, but that didn't have a very good ring to it.

"But I wasn't the one generating all the interest in 'getting some new blood' on the central committee. I thought I'd done my thing, was a little disenchanted and a little bitter. I think Leo really had a better fix on what he wanted. He felt rather hamstrung, that the people on the central committee were not really helping the party. They weren't getting good candidates, they weren't giving the party a new outlook, they weren't giving Republicans a good image. It was just the same old stuffed-shirt, reactionary approach that we thought was killing the Republican party."

LEO OXBERGER "When it came time for Art Donhowe to retire as we expected him to, he didn't. I knew we shouldn't have trusted them. Well, I wanted to take on Art, but Bob wasn't sure there should even be a contest. He said, 'I've got to make a choice either to stay in politics and make a career of it or get out and just practice law.' So he wouldn't allow me to do anything on his behalf.

"After the county convention a week went by and he still wouldn't make a commitment one way or the other. The delegates to the state convention had been selected, we knew who they were, who we would have to work on. So one day I saw him on the street, between Walnut and Locust on Sixth Avenue on the east side of the street. I stopped him and drew a line with my foot and said, 'If you don't step across this line and tell me you're going to run right now, I won't be there to help you if you decide to later on.' He thought for a minute, then said okay. We got right in the car and took off, started visiting all of the delegates to the convention. He really just needed to be pushed.

"We also drew up a paper that said, 'We the undersigned candidates, believing that for the future of the party we need a change, endorse Bob Ray for district chairman.' We took it to all of the Polk County candidates to sign, since I had recruited them all—Al Couppee, Garry Chinn, Bill Babcock. They all signed it, and then Bob and I drove over to Art Donhowe's and showed him our manifesto.

"Bob went in and confronted him, showed him the support we had, and Art told Bob he was going to withdraw from the race. We thought 'great' and drove back over to my house. As I pulled in the driveway, my wife came out and said, 'Harold Brenton is on the phone.' He told me that if I didn't get Bob Ray out of the race, he was going to destroy me—financially, politically, socially, economically, whatever way he could. Art had been his full-time campaign manager when Harold ran for president of the American Bankers Association, but more than that the Republican party was then controlled by the bankers, the Farm Bureau, and the Iowa Manufacturers [Association], and that was the group Donhowe represented.

"They all belonged to a club called the Lincoln Club, and Donhowe was the only officeholder. He was their contact man, and Brenton warned me I didn't know who I was playing with. I told him I did know. At the time, Central National Bank had in their deposits $16 million of state money that they paid no interest on. The bank got the interest, not the state. We knew this, and I told him so."

BOB RAY "Art worked for Central National, and we knew the bank wasn't paying any interest on the state's money. I don't know how much politics played in it, but we all thought it did, and I still think it did. In any event, I didn't have anything personal against Art.

"When I went out to Art's house south of Grand on Thirty-fifth Street to clear the deck with him, he surprised me and said, 'Well, if you're interested in doing it, maybe I won't run.' I told him if he wasn't going to run, then I'd consider it. I asked him when he was going to decide for sure. He said 'give me a week.' I told him I didn't want it to linger, and why didn't he call me the next day with his decision. He said he'd have to check with some of his political friends.

"So I went home. We were living on Fifty-seventh Place, a couple miles away, and by the time I got home Leo was on the phone for me. He said, that he just got a call from another banker who told him if I ran, he would never practice law in Des Moines again. I told Leo that if that would happen, I wouldn't run. But he said, 'No, I want you to run.' [Ray *resolutely refused to name many names throughout most of our conversations, though he confirmed later that the 'other banker' was in fact Harold Brenton.*]

"I hung up and got Art Donhowe on the phone. I said, 'Art, I know you planned to call me tomorrow afternoon and tell me your decision, and I'm not going to say anything publicly until then, except that no matter what you decide, I'm running.'"

JOHN REHMANN   "Art Donhowe, Harold Brenton, and Bob Goodwin controlled things in Polk County up until that time. They were hardheaded, tough, conservative, and they controlled the money in local Republican politics. I know of a couple times they made loans to people in the party, people they knew would be voting in the state convention."

LEO OXBERGER   "The next day Art comes to my office and says, 'I know you guys are unhappy with the way we raise money and the way we divvy it up, and I'll make you whatever deal you want if Bob will get out of the race, and I promise to support him next time. I just want two more years.' Well, we said yes, but he couldn't deliver. Bob and I had talked about it already, and I agreed with Art that if we in Polk County could divvy up whatever monies were left over after the state party had raised a certain amount, $50,000 or $100,000, Bob would stay out of the race. Art said okay, then went to Harold Brenton and Bob Goodwin and I don't know who else, and they told him no.

"So Art had to come back and report that to me. I really loved the guy, he was a nice guy, but Bob was my better friend and I had to stick it to Art, and he's never forgiven me to this day.

"It was just the two of us against the world. We did everything together. I had the title of Polk County chairman, but my real goal was to build Bob Ray. I never had any ambition to run for anything, and I thought he had the charisma to be elected."

BOB RAY   "Leo and I spent a lot of time driving around the district, talking to delegates to the state convention. We worked our tails off. It was hard work and I was really beat. I had hoped that all I had to do was tell them we needed some change and that would be it.

"Leo had a beautiful convertible—I think it had been Verne's at one time—and to make our day a little more interesting, we'd put the top down and go scooting down to Warren County or up to Marshalltown. But before we called on anybody, we'd stop and put up the top. We didn't want to look like the couple brash kids we probably were. We tried to pull those votes out one by one, but it was tough. Dallas County wouldn't even talk to me. At the convention they literally turned their backs on me, didn't have the courtesy to let me talk to them."

The two young lawyers, Oxberger and Ray, worked the Fifth District hard all summer as the state's Republicans headed for a late-July convention in Des Moines. The central committee in 1960, whose job was and still is to encourage and elect Republicans at all levels of government in the state, was run by the state chairman, Verne Martin from Newton, and eight powerful district representatives. In those days each district representative was always a man, and he was joined on the committee by a woman from a neighboring county.

Art Donhowe and Ray squared off at Veterans Auditorium on a Wednesday in one of the few fights of the convention, and their lobbying for majority votes from contingents from Polk, Story, Marion, Dallas, Warren, and Madison counties lasted into the early-morning hours.

BOB RAY "I really didn't know how involved the whole race was until we got into the state convention. There were six counties, and I won Polk and Story, and Art won Madison, Dallas, and Mahaska, and we split Warren. Winning Polk County, though not by a big margin, helped. I really was better known than he was, but there were a lot of people that owed Art something, so it wasn't easy."

LEO OXBERGER "I had done some things early on to make sure that if Bob ran, I could deliver for him at the convention. As county chair I had the power to pick the standing committees of the county convention – chairman of platform, rules, and so forth – and by tradition the vacancies of the delegates that go to the state convention were filled by a committee that was composed of the county chairman, the vice-chairman, the chairman of the platform, the rules committee, and so forth. Traditionally, each precinct was entitled to one delegate at the state convention. That meant there were a lot of delegates that were not elected at the county convention, and this committee filled those positions. It turned out to be a substantial block, 70 of the 230 delegates.

"When I appointed the chairman of the rules committee, I said, 'You can be chairman of the rules committee, but I want your cooperation when it comes time to fill those seventy seats at the state convention.' One of the reasons we won was because there wasn't one Art Donhowe vote among those seventy. We were going for the jugular.

"But the other side was vicious too. Art Donhowe went over to Elmer Miller, then president of the Des Moines Savings and Loan, and told him, 'You have eight employees who are going to the convention. I want their votes.' Jim Crosby, a good friend of Bob's and mine, called me and said 'I want you to take me off the list of delegates. I support you and Bob, but my father got a personal visit from the bank officer at the Central National Bank that loans us money to operate the business, and my dad was told that they wanted my vote to be for Donhowe. Dad called me in and said, "You vote for Art Donhowe." " That kind of story was repeated many times.

"Darwin Lynner was one of our supporters at the convention. His wife was my vice-chairman. He came into Vets and I asked him if he was still with us. He said yes. Five minutes later he got up on the convention floor and spoke in favor of Art Donhowe. I stopped him after the meeting and asked him why. He said 'After I saw you Art Donhowe stopped me and reminded me that my financing for my development projects was through Central National Bank, and it was a very clear message that my loan was in doubt if I didn't get up and speak for Art.' That was the kind of political or financial pressure used to keep Art in office."

JIM CROSBY "I was a little naive about politics at the time, but Leo had a lot of alternate delegate slots in his hip pocket that he handed out to people like me. I went to a number of conventions as an alternate just because Leo appointed me. *Which made you somewhat indebted to Leo?* That's right."

LEO OXBERGER "We went to bed that night thinking we had lost, because Story County was going to caucus the next morning and we figured we would lose that. But we won 41 to 20 and with that, won the election. Bob Ray was elected."

BEN WEBSTER "That same year, 1960, Leo Oxberger started what we first called 'Buck Night' and later 'Neighbor-to-Neighbor,' where we'd go house to house on a given night and pick up a dollar or two on each stop. We were able to collect $6,000, $8,000, $10,000 that way. And when we had that $10,000 in the bank we didn't have to call up Mr. Donhowe or Mr. Brenton with our hat in our hand and say, 'We need some money to operate headquarters today,' and they'd say, 'Alright, boy,' and give you a check. That was the way it had been run.

"By coming up with some independent financial resources, we were able to have a bigger say, and that really changed how the party was operated. No longer would four or five businessmen call the shots."

LEO OXBERGER "We set that 'Be a Buck Republican' fund-raising up just like we had at the March of Dimes. We knew how to organize that type of a house-to-house campaign. We picked up $16,000 in one night. With that $16,000 on top of the $25,000 we had picked up earlier, we knew we had really won. Bob Ray then had some clout on the state central committee that he would not have had if we hadn't raised it. That's when people started talking about him as a state chairman candidate."

MARY JANE ODELL "My impression of him at that time was that he was always in motion, because he was dashing. I know that his hair wasn't literally flying, but that's kind of the impression I have in my mind. Just constantly on the move, always accessible."

PAT BAIN "One night Ben Webster, Bob Ray, and I were driving back from a meeting in Fort Dodge, and he started talking about running for attorney general. I asked him if he would consider running for the state chair instead. I said maybe that's the route to governor. Of course, at that point there was no precedent for it; a state chair had never gone on to be governor. I don't remember exactly how he put it, but he said, 'That's something I hadn't thought about.' "

IV: STATE CHAIRMAN

As a member of the central committee, Bob Ray set out, somewhat unintentionally, to modernize Republican party politics in Iowa – unintentionally simply because it was his nature to challenge the stodgy process he found himself working under, not necessarily because he possessed any far-reaching vision or plan.

His ascent to the state chairmanship came at a time when the Republican leadership in the state was mixed. One-term Republican governor Norman Erbe had been unceremoniously shunted into oblivion by the party after losing to Harold Hughes in 1962. The rest of the executive branch was filled with Republican holdovers – Lieutenant Governor W. L. Mooty, Secretary of State Melvin Synhorst, Auditor C. B. Akers, and Treasurer M. L. Abrahamson. Both Secretary of Agriculture L. B. Liddy and Attorney General Evan "Curly" Hultman, were Republicans. The GOP controlled both houses of the legislature, led by Bob Rigler, Carroll Lane, Jack Schroeder, and David Shaff in the senate and Robert Naden, Marvin Smith, and John Mowry in the house. But the party lacked the cohesive voice, the moderate voice, that Bob Ray felt was necessary to regain the governorship. Ray wanted to move the party organization into a more substantive role in writing the party's platform. Up until then the party doctrine had been drawn up the night before the state convention by a half-dozen people, and the outcome generally amounted to little more than flag waving and grandstanding.

The party was obviously willing to let Bob Ray lead the way, because there was no struggle in this election, and on December 7, 1963, Ray was elected Republican state chairman, the youngest person to hold that posi-

Janet Van Note astride the party mascot. *Des Moines Register* photo. Reprinted with permission.

tion in over a century. One of his first acts was to commission Central Surveys in Shenandoah to conduct a public opinion poll on the issues of the day, a first, which he previewed for Republican legislators at the newly opened Des Moines YMCA. Several legislators refused to attend. But the biggest concern among party regulars was how this young lawyer would handle the party's finances.

BOB RAY "I never wanted to be just a member. I think there's something kind of challenging about running something, and it wasn't long after I got elected to the central committee before I knew I'd like to be the chairman. I let people know of my interest, and there were some great qualms about me doing the job. I had two good friends on the committee, Ben Gayler and Fred Benson, who really helped me, but I wasn't all that shy about getting that particular job.

"The state chairmen during the period I was on the central committee were Verne Martin and George Nagle. Verne was a big, dynamic guy, pretty much a one-man show. I liked him very much, but it was a little hard to get very close to him. And I don't know how much influence the central committee had with him. That was a stage where the committee didn't involve itself much in the issues. Then George Nagle came along and was a wonderful, wonderful state chair. He looked the part of the typical Republican. He was a banker, a businessman, always dressed impeccably in grey flannel suits and wore a little white mustache. He was a very moderate thinker and raised a lot of money, which was his forte. He was an entrepreneur, a successful businessman, owned a lumber company in Iowa City, was into construction. He was a modern thinker and didn't hesitate telling people who kept trying to turn the clock back what the future held and how we had to be part of it. His one great concern when they were talking about me replacing him was that I might not have the necessary fiscal responsibility because I had not been in the money part of the party. When I took over, there was $22,000 in the party's bank account, and I was absolutely determined that when I left there was going to be $22,000 in the bank.

"My law practice suffered during those years. I was working all the time. It wasn't like I was totally removed from the office, but I couldn't do some of the things I should have been doing. Jim and Verne had to pick up a lot of slack for me. I really planned to get out of the state chairmanship after 1964 and back to law. It's kind of funny how things unfolded."

BARNEY DONIELSON "Bob Ray would not have been as successful if Verne

Lawyer hadn't supported him. He would go in and try lawsuits for Bob, because Bob was totally consumed with politics when he was state chair. You'd go over there and by ten o'clock in the morning he'd have a stack of messages two inches thick."

BILLIE RAY "I figured he was probably working as hard at the law business as he could or wanted to and was doing well enough, still trying to get established. I guess neither one of us felt the pressure to be more financially secure. He was just doing what he wanted and enjoying it. And Verne was always very supportive and very proud, even though he thought Bob was crazy sometimes. And from a business sense it didn't hurt to have Bob's name in the paper and on Verne's door. So it was kind of a mutually acceptable arrangement."

While Ray ran into some resentment from the Old Guard, his open, fresh approach to a previously back-room process was appreciated, especially by younger party members. Bob Tyson, then executive director of the state party and a future Ray adviser and confidant remembers, "He was a good idea man. I don't know if they were always original ideas, but what in politics is? And he sure knew one when he saw one." But Ray's early renovations, begun during a heated LBJ-Goldwater presidential clash, were not without some thumb smashing by his own political hammer.

BOB RAY "I wasn't cut from the Old Guard Republican material, and I don't think people knew quite what to expect. They knew that things were going to be different. I wasn't part of the old clubs, I was kind of a rookie, the kid. Longtime Senator Bourke Hickenlooper, for instance, didn't know quite what to make of me. I tried to communicate with him, but I always felt like a kid being lectured. I thought I never would really get close to Bourke, because he was from the Old Guard, he was from Washington, and I was just a kid who had come along to work for the party for a while.

"When I took over, the party was a pretty class-type structure. We needed to come into the twentieth century, and we weren't getting there. I didn't plan to be the one to be the leader of that movement, but it kind of developed that way. Of course, it started badly when I went to the national convention in San Francisco and voted for Bill Scranton.

"I took over right in the middle of the presidential warm-ups. I saw my job as one to produce winners and that's what I was going to do. Surveys were becoming popular, so I watched the six o'clock news, watched the polls closely, and it really frightened me that the more exposure Goldwater got, the more the polls showed that even Republicans weren't supporting him."

BOB TYSON "One day Bob came into party headquarters and said that about five that afternoon Nelson Rockefeller had announced he wasn't going to run for the presidency, and it didn't appear there was anybody else with a chance. We had done a survey earlier in the year down at Central Surveys that showed that 12 percent of Iowa Republicans were for Goldwater, 12 percent for Rockefeller, 24 percent for Nixon, and 24 percent were uncommitted. Bob felt that Goldwater just wasn't strong enough to be a good candidate, so he wondered out loud if he shouldn't support Bill Scranton, the governor of Pennsylvania, who'd recently surfaced as a potential candidate.

"Bob sent him a telegram that afternoon, urging him to run. I typed the letter, called up George Mills [*chief political reporter*] at the *Register,* and it was front-page news the next morning.

"Bill Scranton was flabbergasted, and he called us for a meeting shortly after that in Chicago. Some other midwesterners were there and we convinced Scranton to run."

BOB RAY "I really liked Scranton. I didn't personally dislike Goldwater. I wasn't an ideologue, I was just trying to do my job – elect Republicans. I wasn't trying to change things because of personalities or issues, I just wanted to win. The polls showed that Goldwater couldn't get a very high percentage of the Republicans, much less the Democrats. And worse than that, he wasn't making any headway. So I thought I could, with good conscience, vote for Bill Scranton. I liked his approach, I thought he appealed to the people and was the kind of leader the party desperately needed. My recollection is that when we went to the national convention ten of the twenty-four-member delegation were behind Scranton.

"But I was torn once we got out to San Francisco. I knew Barry Goldwater was going to be the nominee. I knew if I voted for Scranton, people would ask why I wasn't playing on the same team. The fact is I thought if I voted for Scranton I'd vote for a decent person, and I really thought I'd be exercising what I thought Republicans back home were saying. But Goldwater was nominated and I went home saying we had our chance, our man didn't get nominated, and let's work for the nominee."

BOB TYSON "That was when Maurie Van Nostrand and Bob got into a shouting match in the lobby of the Mark Hopkins Hotel. Maurie came thundering in, Bob was standing there, and Maurie screamed at him, convinced that Bob should be thrown out of the chairmanship for supporting Scranton. Maurie said he'd get Bob Ray, and Ray was up for reelection in two weeks."

BOB RAY "Maurie really got angry with me. He was kind of a self-appointed chairman of the Iowa Goldwater group. Even before the convention, he stormed into the headquarters one night about 11 P.M. He shouted at me, couldn't understand what kind of chairman wouldn't be supporting the leader, Goldwater. As a result of that conversation, just before we went into caucus in San Francisco, I thought I'd pay him the courtesy of letting him know that I was going to vote for Scranton. I had wrestled with the decision. I really liked Scranton. I said, 'Maurie, before we go in there I've got to tell you that I made a decision that hasn't been easy. I know that Goldwater is going to win, but I feel obligated to cast a vote for all those Iowans that say they're not going to support him.' He just got livid. He was so angry he ran over and grabbed George Mills and ranted and raved and said, 'One thing is for sure. Bob Ray will never touch one dollar of Goldwater money, never ever.' "

MAURIE VAN NOSTRAND "The point was that those guys had gone from Lodge to Rockefeller to Scranton, and I said, 'If you've got a guy, you had every right to be for somebody other than Goldwater.' But they were just against my guy, Goldwater. I resented what they did very much at the time, but it didn't make any difference. The good Lord himself couldn't have beaten Lyndon Johnson in 1964."

BOB RAY "I knew I was going to catch some heat, but all through my career I would evaluate each situation first, and only after that would I think about how it might affect me politically, because sometimes you can help soften that blow, sometimes you can't. But I've always taken the position that they could find themselves another boy if they weren't happy with the job I was doing. I knew the consequences of voting for Scranton, especially since Goldwater's supporters were likely to have the most clout after the convention.

"When Goldwater was nominated, I said it was up to us as Republicans to work for him. It was a good theory, but it didn't work very well. I really worked hard on that campaign. I never worked so hard politically in my life, because I felt if I were going to be state chairman, it was my responsibility to do everything I could to elect our candidates.

"We moved the Goldwater headquarters right in with the state head-quarters, down in the old Sears building, where J. C. Penney's is now. And I appointed John Burrows from Davenport the state Goldwater chairman. I remember at 11 P.M. on election night I called him and he said he thought Goldwater still had a chance."

BOB TYSON "We had done a cross-section survey of the five largest cities in the state to see if we could uncover anything to help congressional candidates and the statehouse campaigns. Fifty-two percent of the Republicans favored Harold Hughes for governor, and 52 percent of the Republicans favored Lyndon Johnson for president. We concluded immediately that there wasn't much we could do to save anybody, so we just held our breath and watched it all go down the tubes."

BOB RAY "We got whomped. The party was in disarray. Everything that could go bad, went bad. The Sunday before the election our lieutenant governor candidate denounced our gubernatorial candidate, Curly Hultman. We lost control of both houses, lost all the congressmen except H. R. Gross, who won by three hundred votes. I had really planned on getting back to the full-time practice of law after that campaign. I knew I couldn't be a part-time state chairman. But I stayed because I finally concluded that we didn't have the leadership in the party at the moment to stop the slide. There might have been leaders, but there wasn't cohesive leadership."

BOB TYSON "Bob's stand against Goldwater really got the conservatives in the state madder than hell. But in 1965 he got them back, in large part because the press proclaimed the Republican party in the state was dead. Bob went out and gave them hope.

"It was a funny election. Half the Democratic ticket that got elected to the statehouse didn't know whether they'd been elected to Washington or Des Moines. I ran into Lex Hawkins, the Democratic state chairman, on the street one day, and I said, 'You know, I wish you'd have been a little more careful about your selection process,' and he said, 'You ain't the only one.' "

BOB RAY "That loss really gave me a golden opportunity. We had a couple meetings, let people come in and tell us what was wrong with the party. They were blaming everybody, including me. Anyway, I just decided I wasn't going to get out, no one was asking that I be thrown out, and we were going to rebuild the party.

"Between 1964 and 1966 we really did some innovative things, things that sound very ordinary today. We created the 'Party-to-People' hearings. That's when people said I was going to tear the party apart by letting people chip away and knock the party. We invited anybody, everybody, to come and talk to us about what they thought our party ought to do, where we should stand on the issues.

"We also decided that we were going to fill the entire ticket. We were going to have a Republican candidate for every spot on the ballot state-wide. That hadn't been done before. We made that a goal, and we flew around the state trying to convince people, good people, to run. We had the first school for legislative candidates. We invited lobbyists and people to come in and not just state their position, but we made sure we had the pros and cons of the position, and we were committed to letting people make up their own minds based on the facts. What I had found when I ran for the house was that legislative candidates got themselves locked into a position, and then they had to defend it no matter how wrong it was or what they thought about it. I wanted them to really get knowledgeable about issues, to know the different sides, the arguments, and also hope-fully to try to get them from being locked into a position from which they couldn't maneuver.

"I was full of vim and vigor and loved the excitement of the challenge."

JOHN McDONALD "I felt a little uncomfortable moving in on the establish-ment of the party, but I think we were generally well accepted because they knew we were willing to work. I think Bob Ray was perceived as someone who wanted to do something. I don't think we were seen as troublemakers or that we wanted power or to be governor."

DICK REDMAN "Bob Tyson was the executive director of the party, I was the organization director, Bob Ray was the chairman, and we were pretty much the 'A Team.' I remember one day the three of us went down to the Kirkwood Hotel to an Iowa Republican Women's meeting to just stick our heads in and watch. When we got there Pat Pardun, who was the vice-chair of the party, came out and said, 'Don't go in there now.' They were entertaining the motion on a resolution to get rid of the three of us."

The saving grace of the Ray-Tyson-Redman operation was that they couldn't do any worse in the upcoming elections of 1966; they could only go up from the party's trouncing in 1964. They expanded the scope of the central committee, brought in more staff, raised more money, and never hesitated to spend it. "What good does a fat bank account do if your people aren't elected?" queried Ray. The party made spending on advertising and promotions a priority. They launched "Ideas for a Better Iowa" to spark public debate, continued the "Buck Night" fund-raisers, held schools for candidates. Their slogan was quaint but new: "Being a Republican Is Fun!"

GEORGE BROWN "I had gone back to work for the St. Paul newspaper, had quit the UPI in Iowa, around the middle of November 1964, and in the middle of December I got a call from Bob Ray asking if I'd be interested in coming back to Iowa and helping rebuild the party.

"I'd been a longtime newspaperman and a registered independent. I'd been pretty well tapped a liberal, but I'd run a Republican's campaign once. It struck me as an interesting job opportunity, and I kind of liked Bob Ray, so I went to work for the party as a researcher, writer, and lobbyist. The office consisted of me, Redman, Tyson, and Jackie Day. Cooper Evans came in at one period to be a full-time fund-raiser."

BOB BURLINGAME "I'd had no contact with Bob Ray, barely knew who he was, then one day I had a call asking me to meet him for lunch at the Des Moines Club. I knew him so little I wasn't sure who I was looking for as I came off the elevator.

"He was then the state chairman, and though he didn't tell me this, I assumed at the time he was going to run for governor. I deduced that he wasn't interested in my part-time services as a researcher and writer simply to tout the Republican party, so I felt he probably had some other motive down the line. For the next few years I did occasional speechwriting for him."

BOB RAY "I took it upon myself to lead and decided that if the central committee didn't like my approach, they'd get themselves a new state chairman. That was always a possibility. But I don't think anybody ever seriously entertained that. I had good support. They were full of questions and opinions, and even if they didn't always agree with me, they'd tell me to go ahead and try. I couldn't have been a state chairman like Steve Roberts in the late 1970s, who always had a split 9 to 8 committee under him. I don't know how you can operate like that."

DICK REDMAN "We didn't approach the rebuilding as if we were going to reinvent the wheel; we'd have never made it. We just wanted to take what existed, tune it, and make it fly. And have some fun.

"It was fun, and we had a zinging operation. We had the first hundred-dollar-a-plate dinner ever held in Iowa, that kind of thing. Ideas for a Better Iowa. Instead of a bunch of party hacks sitting around writing the platform, we went out around the state, held hearings, tried to find out what the people wanted. We did dog and pony shows around the state, had district meetings. Instead of just having people come in, get drunk, and have dinner, we had workshops, work sessions.

"When I was the finance director we had county finance directors. We put together a state finance committee. There hasn't been anything original in politics since the day of the early Romans, but these were things that weren't being done in Iowa. We had the Party-to-People hearings, where we scheduled a series of meetings around the state and would invite people to come in and testify in their area of expertise and make suggestions on what needed to be done. That was all recorded and transcribed and used as the basis for building the party platform.

"The challenge was to just see how many seats we could get back. We had the shit kicked out of us in 1964, and none of us were much used to that. This gave us the opportunity to build from the bottom up and put together an organization.

"Another thing we did was work like the dickens to recruit candidates. I remember one time all three of us—Tyson, Bob Ray, and myself—all went out to the Des Moines Flying Service and got on different planes going different places around the state. There were good candidates out there that went down in flames in 1964, and they didn't see much hope for 1966. We knew that if we were going to get back, that was the year to do it.

"One of the problems when a bunch of people that aren't too bright get elected, which were a lot of the Democrats in 1964, after a couple weeks of being called Mr. Representative and stuff they begin to think they got there on their own merits. And they started thinking they ought to be doing things, so they started hassling Governor Hughes, and whenever we would see a little breach, we'd try and drive a wedge in.

"We did another innovative thing by hiring George Brown as the news and research director for the party. We did radio actualities, where we would get our legislative leadership to address a certain subject, whatever was hot or whoever was in the midst of something, and send out a Republican point of view for the radio stations to use. At that time most radio stations didn't have reporters at the capitol.

"Frankly, if you don't have the governor nor control the legislature nor hold any state offices, then the party is in perfect position to do new things."

HARRY RASDAL "Bob Ray was probably the most active lobbyist on the hill during those sessions. He got tossed out of the house and senate often because he was up there pumping away for what he felt were Republican interests. Of all the state chairmen I have known, he was by far the most active lobbyist on the hill."

ART NEU "The central committee had hired a guy to go out and encourage Republicans to run for the legislature, Bruce Bradley. He was trying to recruit more moderate Republicans, I had decided to run, and so he took me down to meet Bob Ray. They were trying to fill the legislature with a certain kind of candidate. A lot of the legislators up until then tended to be older, maybe retired or quasi-retired farmers or businessmen, and they were looking for something else."

JOAN LIPSKY "Polk County Republican politics had always been a little different from anywhere else in the state, and Bob had had a lot of opportunities to learn how to play the game, so he came to the chairmanship with a lot of experience and knowledge. He put together an excellent staff, guys that knew how to raise money, how to get publicity, how to take the pulse of the public. They knew how to campaign and had the skills helpful to a novice.

"They put together a seminar for the successful candidates after the primary which for me was one of the most important aspects of my campaign. They brought in experts, without regard for their political thinking, really, to bring us up to date on current and important issues."

CHUCK GRASSLEY "After that 1964 election there were only 23 Republicans in the legislature, out of 124, and I was one. Bob tried to bring a lot of grass-roots people into the party—party workers, business people, farmers, all kinds of people. He brought them together into weekend workshops and then broke us up into some work groups. We tried to chart ideas for the party and what we should be pursuing."

RALPH McCARTNEY "I had run in 1964 and was beaten, but I ran again in 1966 and participated in several workshops that Bob Ray had organized or suggested. They also had some research on issues, and if you were running against an incumbent, they had research on his votes. It wasn't in any sense a smear campaign, but the state party provided us with this information. I won in 1966 and was part of a freshman class of legislators that included Betty Shaw, Joan Lipsky, Del Stromer, Dick Welden, Andrew Varley."

FRED SCHWENGEL "When he took over he was able to get me to run for Congress again. After ten years in the job I'd pretty much decided I'd had it. But he prevailed on me to run again, and they used leaders out here in Washington as well, particularly Jerry Ford, to get me and others back into the picture."

BOB RAY "There were some, I think, who didn't know what to think of our new approach, and there were some who welcomed it. The only one I really had problems with was Bill Scherle. Bill had his own reapportionment plan, and even after it had lost he wouldn't give up on it, and we had some words out in the rotunda of the state capitol. If I had to do it over, I'd probably just walk away, but I said, 'Bill, get away from that railing, because if you don't, I'm tempted to push you over it.' We weren't exactly friends that day. My reapportionment plan, with some modification and Dave Belin's help, was adopted. But I really didn't want my name attached to that. I really didn't want to be out front on the issues. *Of course all those things with your name attached to them didn't hurt down the road.* No, eventually they probably helped. Some of the things that hurt the most at the moment did me the most good in the future, but you never knew then if one of them might topple you and you wouldn't have any future."

BILL MURRAY "One thing about Bob, he was always fair. When I went to the central committee and announced that I was going to run for governor in 1966, I don't think he was too happy about it. But he was very fair. He took no position, didn't say, 'No, you shouldn't do that.' And when Bob Beck announced the next spring, Bob didn't support him over me, either. And I just squeaked out a primary win over Beck. He was very popular around the state."

DICK REDMAN "Bob Ray got a lot of unanimous help (from the central committee) at that time. If you've got a bunch of people at sea clinging to boards and other debris, like the Republicans were in 1965, and somebody comes along and says, 'This is the plan and this how we're going to get from here to nice, dry land, a warm fire, and something to eat,' you do what the guy says.

"And it worked out in our favor. The only thing we lost in 1966 was the governor's race. Bill Murray lost to Harold Hughes by 100,000 votes. We ran a full slate of legislative candidates, but for one district, and Iowa led the nation in recoveries, just like we'd led in defeats in 1964."

CLARK RASMUSSEN "[*The year*] 1966 was a disaster for us. I took over [*as head of the state Democratic party*] in June of 1966. I had worked under Lex Hawkins as executive secretary of the party. Lex was pretty smart, pretty perceptive, and he picked a good time to get out. Times for Democrats weren't real good.

"One of our biggest jobs was to get all of our legislative candidates—statewide—in order. Our congressional candidates were no problem because of our success in 1964. We had incumbent congressmen Stan Greigg, Bert Bandstra, John Culver, John Schmidhauser, Neal Smith, everybody but the Third District, which was H. R. Gross's seat. We had 101 house members who had been elected in 1964, out of 124.

"Obviously what had happened in 1964 was an aberration and wasn't going to happen again. We knew we'd be lucky to maintain all those seats we'd won. We had elected legislators in Allamakee, Bremer, Muscatine counties and, you know, Democrats just don't do that in Iowa. We don't do it today. *Had the Republicans and Bob Ray done a good job reorganizing?* Well, they surely hadn't done a bad job. I think what happened, though, is that on a graph, in 1964 we'd just shot way up, and in 1966 things kind of leveled off."

BOB RAY "Dick Redman, Bob Tyson, and I had really done our job recruiting candidates. I think we filled the ballot except for Dubuque. The local Republicans didn't want to run anybody. My feeling was that you fill every slot. We were told we had the greatest gains in 1966 of any state in the country. I think we picked up eighty-eight house seats. We got all the congressmen except two and took all the state offices except the treasurer and the governor. That's when I started hearing from people about running for governor. But I really wasn't thinking about running for office. Gee, I hadn't even been able to get elected to a local public office. I might have considered the attorney general's job if the governor's seat had been my goal, because Leo Hoegh had come that route, so had Norm Erbe. Curly Hultman had tried. It seemed to be kind of a stepping-stone for Republican candidates. But I still wanted to get back and practice law."

BOB TYSON "After the 1966 campaign he thought maybe he ought to retire as state chairman. He was trying to do two full-time jobs. So I went to Washington and worked as an administrative assistant to Fred Schwengel. No sooner do I get out in Washington and Bob Ray decides that maybe he'd like to be governor, but just for two two-year terms."

GEORGE BROWN "We were a pretty tight-knit group, and I don't recall anybody sitting down in early 1967 and saying, 'Okay, now we've got the guy ready to run.' That never happened. But I think Bob did pull together some people like Rand Petersen, Frosty Mitchell, Walt Shotwell and started talking about the possibility that he would run and that we should, as a party, really put our best foot forward."

Bob Ray realized he was that "best foot." He'd led the rebuilding, introduced some innovations, he was young, attractive, a good family man. His weaknesses in a statewide election would be that he was a lawyer from Des Moines, which made him a tough sell to many rural voters, and he was too liberal, which rankled conservatives in the party, young and old.

At the same time his gubernatorial ambitions were heating up, they were forcing him out of another passion: football broadcasting. Every fall weekend since 1960 Ray had hooked up with Frosty Mitchell to broadcast University of Iowa football games over Mitchell's statewide radio network. But if he were to become a statewide candidate, the color commentary he added to Frosty's play-by-play could lead to requests for equal time from his opponents. Bob Ray did not intend to give any opposition three or four hours of free radio time every week, so he gave that "career" up.

BOB RAY "Frosty was the pro. I was just a hack, the color man. And the engineer. In those days they played nine games a season, so on nine weekends Billie and Joanie, Frosty and I traveled to all the games, all across the country."

FROSTY MITCHELL "He had taken up football in the service and got pretty knowledgeable about the game. He did a good job; he's fluent and knowledgeable. They'd save all the newspapers and I'd send him things; he'd come prepared. He did the whole pregame show. When I used to introduce him after he was governor, he used to say, 'I've come a long way since Frosty Mitchell used to introduce me by saying, "Now here's the pregame dope." '

"The most memorable halftime interview he did was with Forrest Evashevski, Iowa's coach. You've got to realize that Bob's interview style was that of a trial lawyer, not a broadcaster. Bob asked Evy a question, and he gave him a rhetorical answer that most sports journalists would just accept. But Bob said, 'Did you or did you not?' and everybody looked at me, wondering what kind of a sidekick was this?

"Most of this time Bob was the state chair, and I remember landing that small airplane in airports we hadn't planned on stopping at so Bob could call someplace to find out what was going on in this race or that. We'd just go up and down, up and down between these small airports across the country."

V:
THE DECISION
TO RUN

Bob Ray was ready to be governor, so he stepped down from the state chairmanship in December 1967. Two formidable candidates, former American Legion commander Don Johnson and Centerville publisher Bob Beck, were rumored to be in the running, and a tough primary lay ahead.

Ray's law partner Verne Lawyer had long-figured his protégé could be governor but was surprised it had taken this long. His partner-for-life, Billie, finally gave in to his running: "One day I finally said, 'I think if you don't do it, you'll always wonder if you could have gotten elected, and I'm not sure I can live with that.' I knew he had the spirit, he wanted the challenge. I said, 'I'll vote for you, but don't ask me to campaign. I don't want to make any speeches.' I think that's when he decided to run."

BOB RAY "Verne Lawyer was actually the first person who suggested the governor's office to me. We were down in West Palm Beach [*in early 1967*], where we had been at a trial lawyers conference. We were standing out in the ocean and he asked me if I'd ever thought about running for governor. I said, 'Not really.' He said, 'You can be governor if you want to.' That was sort of the beginning."

VERNE LAWYER "Larry Scalise had gone to the convention with me and as I recall had flown in my plane. Bob had come down later, and when we

1967. *Des Moines Register* photo. Reprinted with permission.

started for home the weather developed very rapidly, thunderstorms, so we stopped and decided to stay in Palm Beach.

"We were standing there in the surf, waves just beating on us, just he and I. I just told him that as far as I was concerned the next time was the time to go. He agreed. I also told him at the time that if he wanted to, he could be president. I also laughingly told him that if he got to be president, he could put me on the Supreme Court."

BOB TYSON "He was concerned that his only support would be in Polk County. But Bob had a friend, Bruce Bradley, who had been an advance man for Nelson Rockefeller and had access to a national WATS line and was then making calls for Dave Stanley to see if Stanley had any support for a try for the U.S. Senate. Well, Bradley was very loyal to Bob Ray, so he asked in the same phone calls whether they thought Bob would make a good candidate for governor. He quickly discovered there was more support for Bob Ray out around the state than for Dave Stanley."

MAURIE VAN NOSTRAND "I was the editor of the *Nonpareil* in Council Bluffs, and I got a call from this young guy in Denver, Bruce Bradley. He said a friend of mine was thinking about running for governor and wanted to know if I would help. I said, 'Well, no friend of mine would have some guy from Denver call me. He would call me himself.' About five minutes later Bob Ray called and said, 'I'm thinking about running for governor, and I just wanted to know how you felt about it.' We set up a meeting for the next night in Avoca. We met there probably six or seven times during the course of the year, and I decided to come out for him hard and strong and, man, I worked my fool head off for him."

DEL STROMER "One day during the 1967 legislative session, the party's lobbyist, George Brown, told me the boss would like to have dinner with me. I said fine, so myself, Earl Yoder, Don Voorhees, Ralph McCartney had dinner with Bob Ray. He had done his homework real well, asked us what our concerns were, what we thought of the session thus far. But you could kind of see that he was trying to build a coalition that would be available to him later in the year, when it was obvious that somebody was going to emerge as the Republican gubernatorial candidate.

"In November he sent up some smoke signals that he was interested in being the party's candidate, so I wrote him a note saying I was impressed with him, I would like to support him, but I needed a firmer commitment than I had that he understood agriculture. Well, he wrote me a handwritten letter, hand addressed, two pages, of his beliefs, his philosophies, affirming that Iowa was an agricultural state. So I became a Ray Republican, as did several of the people in my county who were prominent Republicans. And this was a county where his future primary opponent, Don Johnson, probably had a lot of inroads – in fact I had a brother-in-law who was Don Johnson's county chair. And I was a close friend of Bob Beck's, so it was a tough decision, but I was cognizant that we were losing elections because we couldn't sell our candidate to the urban population. Even the Bill Murrays couldn't carry Des Moines, and I knew Ray would have that advantage. I was convinced that he would either be a good student of agriculture or already understood a lot of the problems. I found out later he wasn't quite as knowledgeable as I'd hoped."

L. B. LIDDY "One time we were having breakfast – Bob Ray, Bob Tyson, Dick Redman, and I – and Bob Ray said, 'Luce, do you have any aspirations to run for governor?' I said, 'None whatsoever. In fact, I'm farther now than I'd intended to be.' He was obviously testing the waters, but I don't think that had I come out it would have scared him any. But they were trying to figure out if there'd be any obstructions in his way."

CORRINNE HUBBELL "We gave some parties to introduce him to people – that's the name of the game, get them started, get them launched. We took him to parties all over town, all over the state. There were certain people my husband Crawford and I thought he should touch base with. We knew some people that would be helpful down the line."

JOHN McDONALD "Rand Petersen and Bob and I got together for a meeting in my travel trailer at Lake Okoboji late in 1967. We sat around and talked for an hour, the three of us really hashing out the pros and cons of his running, and it was my impression that he came to his final decision then and there. We got up and got in the car and drove over to see Anna Lomas, who had been the immediate past Republican national committeewoman. We wanted her blessing and her support."

DEL VAN HORN "I remember sitting with Rand Petersen and Bob Ray in a hotel room, telling him he should run. Rand particularly believed in the guy. I remember thinking it was strange that while Rand and I discussed it, Bob Ray just lay on the bed. If I was thinking about running, I'd want to be in on the discussion.

"He was the only fresh face we'd seen in Republican politics since Rockefeller. He had different ideas, and he didn't go along with all the old party hacks. He was a fresh breeze. But it wasn't easy to convince him to run. We'd ask and he'd say things like, 'Well, can you get these guys to go along with us?' 'Can you get this district?' 'Are you guys willing to work twenty-four hours a day?' and so forth."

BOB RAY "I talked to Rand Petersen very, very early, because Rand, who was a political activist, had always supported me and new ideas. I remember John Rehmann, who was pretty active among the conservative wing of the party and had friends on the national level that backed Republicans, talked to me about running. I remember talking with Dutch Vermeer. We knew his support would be critical because he was well respected, from a farm community, and was conservative. We knew in a Republican primary we were going to need some conservative support. I wasn't exactly known as a conservative.

"I liked Dutch, but I didn't know him very well. He'd been friendly, but my experience with him went back to when I was state chairman and we were in the throes of reapportionment and I tried to talk to him and he brushed me off. I really didn't think he'd be favorable to me or my candidacy, but we went down and talked to him and he had no trouble making up his mind. He wanted to support me, which was a big plus."

DAVID BELIN "I was one of the first to talk to him about running for governor. I thought he would make an outstanding governor. He had very, very good overall judgment and very good political instincts. I thought he was a very hard worker, which is one of the ingredients of success. I thought he was a very likable person and could really turn the Republican party in this state around.

"His concerns were that he didn't know if he could get elected, and he was also concerned about the financial commitment that it would take to leave his law practice. He was not in any sense a wealthy man."

DUTCH VERMEER "John Rehmann first contacted me and asked if I would help. I told him I would and then made an appointment with Bob Ray. He decided he wanted me and Rand Petersen to cochair the campaign, so I went to work for a month or so before he announced, in January [1968].

"I might not necessarily have been in agreement with all his thinking. I was probably a little more conservative, but I also recognized that a conservative would never get elected."

BOB RAY "I wasn't sure that I wanted to take that big a chunk of life away from my law career, and I wasn't certain what the effects on my family would be. I had youngsters that I really did not want to mistreat, and I knew there would be some problems. Bob Tyson was one of the few people who talked to me seriously about not running, because it spoiled people, he said. He'd been around and was a good authority. He said people change when they become candidates, they change even more when they're in office, and he said you can destroy yourself. He was right. But I thought there could be exceptions. Of course, everyone who ever ran for office probably figured they were the exception. I don't think I disappointed Bob, though. He made me think seriously about it, because I believed what he was telling me and I knew he believed it. He was very politically astute."

MARY LOUISE SMITH "I don't think he ever questioned his ability to do the job. He has a sense of self and lot of self-confidence, so I think it was just trying to decide whether the timing was right – was it right for his family, was it right to give up the law practice.

"I suppose there are a lot of us that would like to think we had a part in his decision, but I think he would be the only one involved in that decision. With Billie's approval, of course."

BILLIE RAY "One time I was in the car with Mary Louise Smith and she said she thought Bob should run, and I said, 'Oh, I don't know if he'll do that.' I guess I thought it would take a lot of his time and he probably wouldn't win anyway.

"I think Rand Petersen really had a hand in talking him into it. I thought if he did, it would just be a continuance of what he'd been doing as state chairman. I didn't know anything about a campaign that big. I just figured he'd have to keep going to fund-raisers and meetings, that sort of thing."

BOB RAY "Billie really made the difference. She came to me one night, and she said, 'I see these people talking to you about running for governor. At first I saw you dismiss the idea and then I saw you, more lately, listen, like you're getting interested.' She said, 'I don't want you to run. I don't want you to get any deeper into politics, and I'd really like to have you get out of it. But the problem with that is if you don't run, all the rest of your life you're going to wonder if you could have gotten elected. And I'm not prepared to live with that thought. If you want to do it, then you'll have my total support.' That's when she made me promise if I did run, she wouldn't have to make any speeches.

"Once I made the decision to run I said I would run whether Harold Hughes ran or not, which was probably foolish. But by the time I announced, he had announced he was going to run for the Senate. I thought, 'This is going to work out great.'

"I announced on January 6, 1968, and I had always told the press it was going to be a cold day in Iowa before I ever ran for governor. George Mills had asked me a couple times if I was ever going to run, he'd give me big play. I saw George and reminded him of that, but before I announced, a press release was sent to some of the out-state newspapers so they could have it for their Saturday editions. I formally announced on Saturday so we could get the announcement in Sunday's *Register*, but George Mills was violently angry that these out-state papers had gotten the release first, and he blamed me. He said, 'Don't ever expect me to do anything favorable for you.' Needless [*to say,*] I didn't get much of a ride in that Sunday *Register*."

NOVELENE RAY GIBBONS "We'd lived in Omaha since 1960, and when I heard on the news that Bob was running for governor, I called him immediately and said, 'Congratulations. What can I do to help?' He said, 'Would you please move across the river?' "

VI: THE PRIMARY AND GENERAL ELECTIONS, 1968

When he announced his third candidacy for elected office from a podium at the Hotel Savery on a frosty January morning in 1968, Bob Ray was flanked by a trio of dissimilar supporters. Longtime friend Rand Petersen, a former central committee member from Harlan, introduced the candidate. It was announced that Dr. Harry Rasdal, a Marshalltown optometrist and a Goldwater conservative, would run the Ray campaign. But the appearance of Elmer "Dutch" Vermeer on the same stage as Bob Ray was the biggest surprise of the young campaign. A five-term Republican legislator from Pella and an ardent conservative, Vermeer was seen as Ray's link to the rural, more conservative elements of the party. The Ray camp foresaw, accurately, the danger in a campaign drawn on strict ideological lines – moderates versus conservatives – and hoped to head it off by bolstering their campaign leadership with a handful of well-known conservatives, led by Vermeer.

Vermeer's presence also demonstrated just how hungry Iowa's Republicans were to elect one of their own. It had been a long, hard six years for them enduring the decidedly liberal leadership of Harold Hughes. They wanted a Republican governor, ideology notwithstanding. Thus the mixed bag of conservative old pols, Young Republicans, and moderates who ended up on deck with Ray as 1968 got underway.

Gubernatorial candidate Ray on crutches following the airplane crash during the campaign of 1968. *Des Moines Register* photo. Reprinted with permission.

Before the end of January, two substantial, and more conservative, candidates had declared for the September primary: Don Johnson of West Branch and Robert Beck, of Centerville who had been narrowly defeated for the same nomination in 1966 by Bill Murray. (Two other minor candidates had previously announced: Colonel Henry, a Lawton buggy-whip manufacturer, and John Knudsen of Albion.) Ray had expected these entries. In fact, before resigning as state chairman he had counseled with each of them about their chances should they decide to run.

To get the Ray ball rolling financially, Petersen, Vermeer, and Rasdal each threw in $200, opened a bank account, rented some office furniture (on credit) from Storey-Kenworthy, and moved into a suite at the Hotel Savery, donated by the hotel's manager, Paul Lefton, a stalwart Republican.

KENT CRAFTS "It was a collection of fairly pragmatic people who were drawn to him as an individual. Bob Ray's appeal is and was as a pragmatic leader, and he appealed to people of all political persuasions. It was definitely not an ideological group."

DUTCH VERMEER "I was convinced we needed somebody who was more middle-of-the-road and could get elected. We'd had six years of Hughes, and that was more than I could stand. But Bob Ray needed some guys on board who were more conservative—John Rehmann was one, Maurie Van Nostrand was another. Bob Rigler and Dave Shaff from eastern Iowa were helpful, though they were a little more moderate. Harry Rasdal was an arch-conservative. But through it all I can't ever really remember having an argument with Bob Ray, on an issue."

JOHN REHMANN "Ray was known by the central committee and some of the rank-and-file Republicans, but we had to have the Farm Bureau, people like that. So I went out to Gary Lilly and he donated a red Cadillac and we gave it to Dutch and put him on the road.

"Dutch was out on the road, I was raising money, and Rand was the state chairman, doing a lot of promoting. It was hard to raise money for a guy who'd never held statewide office, and I'm sure Rand had more luck around the state than I did with people outside, and I don't think we got $150,000."

BOB TYSON "Rand is a pretty reserved guy, independent as hell. He usually said no to similar requests, but Bob really wanted him to chair that first campaign, to get on the phone not only for contributions but to build support. He was willing to do anything for Bob Ray, and Bob had confidence in him."

BOB BRENTON "I was working at the farms in Dallas County then, and Rand Petersen would come around again and again, asking for money, and eventually I'd give him some. Then I remember him coming around and bringing this new fellow with him, Bob Ray. And they'd both be looking for money. Rand Petersen made Bob Ray in those early days."

RAND PETERSEN "When he finally decided to run, which took a long time—you know, I always kidded him he'd be late to his own funeral—I resigned from the central committee to work full-time. I put about 30,000 miles on my car during that primary, traveling between Harlan and Des Moines and all over the state. When we weren't flying I often served as Bob's chauffeur."

BOB RAY "I'd watched a lot of campaigns, participated in the Curly Hultman and Bill Murray campaigns, but we brought out some people who had run Ted Agnew's gubernatorial campaign. They'd had a couple big successes, and I was aware of them because of Agnew's win. But they wanted some horrendous amount of money, more that we'd planned to spend on the whole campaign. But what really amazed me was that I honestly didn't feel they knew any more about campaigning than I did. I was pretty amateurish, but I'd had enough experience that they didn't convince me we needed them."

KENT CRAFTS "He was very demanding. He expected his staff to be the best organized, his events to be the most colorful and his speeches to be the best prepared, and so forth. And they were. He had the best staff, even though I don't know that he ever believed it. If he did believe it, he never admitted it, which is perhaps the second lesson he taught me. He wasn't a particularly supportive boss. Even when you'd done well he was able to point out something you could have done better.

"The first lesson he taught me concerned a battle between a couple of county chairmen. He taught me that you can't take sides in those things, because you're going to have to work with them both next Monday. That's a lesson I've used since, because there's always another Monday."

BOB BRENTON "Bob Ray worked incredibly hard in that campaign. He'd drive all over the state to give a talk, appear at a dinner. There'd be forty people at a home and he'd travel hours out and hours back. He'd wear his drivers out; they couldn't take the long days he'd put in."

BOB BURLINGAME   "While Robert had a mental sense of order, he was not very orderly as an administrator or an embryo executive in those days. Throughout that 1968 campaign he carried a suitcase with him full of mail and other materials. By November that suitcase was the size of a footlocker; it just grew and grew."

HARRY RASDAL   "This was before there were some of the stringent campaign laws you have today, and we went to various companies around Des Moines and got free use of their WATS lines after five. We had Drake political science students come in and make phone calls for us, and we were able to poll for pennies but very accurately.

"During the first months of the primary, Bob was still trying to put in full days at the law office, and he was often unavailable when decisions had to be made during the day. About 5:30, when I was ready to go home, Bob would be just coming to the campaign office and wanted to review the day. A couple times I told him, 'Hell with it. If you want to know what's going on, come over during the day.' Things could have been easier than they were."

MAURIE VAN NOSTRAND   "I had told the finance people they could count on me for $300 every Monday morning. That was quite an incentive when I'd look in the drawer on Thursday and find out I only had $100. But I never missed; the money was there."

BEN WEBSTER   "A couple times Rasdal called me up and said he'd run out of stamps. So I'd go out and get a couple guys to donate a roll of 1,000 stamps. They probably took them out of the drawer at their corporations, which was probably illegal, but I didn't inquire [about] that."

KENT CRAFTS   "We had some incredible supporters who remained very quiet. George Forstener over in Amana was a very major early supporter, and that was not known in the state during the campaign. Howard Hall up in Cedar Rapids was a good friend and supporter. But the campaign was largely based on relationships that Bob had built in his years as chairman. We started off the campaign with chairmen in all ninety-nine counties, which the other candidates never did match. And those were personal relationships. He could pick up the phone and ask for personal favors and they'd do them."

JOHN REHMANN "I had a Camanche airplane at the time, and I flew him quite a bit. He was a good candidate, but he still wasn't attracting a number of regular party people. I took him out to see Bob Goodwin one day, and he refused to support him. He claimed he was a businessman, and he didn't like plaintiff's lawyers like Bob, because they were always suing him. The old establishment, the luncheon clubs, were not for Bob Ray. Some of that went back to when he beat Art Donhowe, and some because they thought he was too liberal, he didn't come from the old clan. Many of them probably voted for Bob Beck."

JACKIE DAY "Jan Van Note deserves a lot of credit for the hoopla that went with making Bob a distinctive candidate. They stuck with the same colors—red and yellow—that he'd used in those campaigns in the 1950s, which was important in those days, when that kind of hoopla really helped.

"Jan was working another job full-time, but on her lunch hours and after work she worked for Bob Ray. She organized the Ray Girls, established a theme, which was important for a guy who was still a relative unknown in a lot of places around the state."

JANET VAN NOTE "After he announced we got a bunch of girls to start the Ray Girls again, because they liked to do it. People want to be involved in politics, and one of the biggest problems in politics is that there is not enough for people to do. So we had all these girls who wanted to help, and they couldn't stuff envelopes eight hours a day. So we had every parade in the state mapped out, made ourselves some red-and-yellow outfits, and went to every event we could. Once we were out at the airport with the Nixon Girls. There were probably about a hundred of them to our ten, but we stuck out because of our red-and-yellow costumes.

"We passed out buttons and fliers, two or three girls at every event. Some were girls in their twenties and some high schoolers. The governor's three daughters had outfits. I found out when all the conventions were going to be in town, when their breaks would be, and made sure somebody was there to pass out fliers. I worked at the Farm Bureau then, and lots of times I'd go out on my lunch break, whip on my little banner, and pass out fliers for a half hour.

"We figured that we might be the only contact some of these people in that first campaign had with Bob Ray, and we just wanted to be pleasant. It was not an informative job; we weren't to discuss policy and all that stuff. We just passed out our little fliers and smiled. After about three months you started seeing the same conventioneers again, saying, 'Are you still here?'

"Twice I rode an elephant in a parade. They asked me if I'd ride Candy in a parade for the Republican party. I misunderstood. I thought I'd be sitting in a convertible with all this candy, throwing it to the crowds. Two days before the parade I find out Candy is an elephant. I was scared to death, and it was fine until she stood up on her back legs. By the time the parade was over, I'd worn all the skin off my knuckles just hanging on."

KENT CRAFTS "A lot of us thought the Ray Girls were out of character, even for Bob Ray. But the goal of the campaign was to have the most colorful, flashy approach, draw the largest crowds at all times, get the cameras turned on you. I think we were the only campaign that had a float. One of my harder tasks was to make sure that that float made every parade in the state. My most onerous task was when I couldn't find a volunteer to drag that float, and I'd have to drive up to someplace like Mason City and put in a twenty-minute appearance in a parade, because we didn't want to miss any of them.

"Despite all the hoopla, I cannot recall any expression of doubt on his part that if elected, he was prepared. How he became so, I really don't know, but he was confident that he was the best man for the job. In later reading that strikes me as unusual, because I think there are dark hours in any campaign, moments of doubt and questioning and worrying on the candidate's part, and we spent a lot of hours together and he never questioned his competency to proceed."

JOHN MERRIMAN "I did a little bit of issues work in that campaign, and he had very definite and usually pretty well thought-out views on almost everything. He'd been the state chair and been exposed to the issues. That was the advantage he had in that contest. Since 1964 there had not been anybody who you could call a Republican leader in the state except Bob Ray. He became the spokesman, the focal point. A lot of people placed in that circumstance wouldn't have lasted, but he is a very bright man."

BOB TYSON "Bob Ray's experience showed. He'd been in Washington every month as chairman of the state chairmen, dealing with the national press. Those guys really liked him, were big boosters of him. He was candid with the press and they liked that."

BOB RAY "Everyplace I'd go I'd get introduced as the Des Moines lawyer. Don Johnson would get introduced as the agribusiness leader and past commander of the American Legion. Bob Beck would be introduced as the great, loyal, and faithful party worker who was the master editor from Centerville. I began to get concerned about this image.

"I finally decided there was nothing wrong with being a lawyer and we in Des Moines were Iowa citizens also. That helped me get over that hurdle. On several occasions people would be talking to Billie, and if she told them she was from Des Moines they seemed to turn off. One day, she decided to tell them where she was actually born, Columbus Junction. All of a sudden people would sit and want to talk about their gardens and recipes and farms and everything.

"One of the advantages Des Moines had was access to planes and pilots that neither Beck nor Johnson had from Centerville or West Branch. We operated out of the hub of the wheel, could get just about everywhere in the state with the same effort. Bob Beck wasn't going to get any votes in Missouri, so nearly every trip was long for him."

DICK REDMAN "Don Johnson one-on-one against Bob Ray would have made a very tough race out of that primary. I'm not so sure about Bob Beck. He had all the old war-horses, but Bob Ray had the state party, the organization. He succeeded not because he came in and took the party over but because he brought a whole bunch of new people in. That was very important. They saw a bright, young, dynamic leader that they could support. They came in, got involved, and then had some allegiance to this guy who had brought them in."

GEORGE BROWN "Was Bob Ray qualified to be governor? With the degrees of problems that you face in top political office, you elect somebody with the capacity to grow into it, because nobody is really qualified. Rather, you look for somebody with the kind of personality, the kind of mental ability, the wits to solve problems in the best possible way. I don't think Bob Ray was any more ready than the other two, but you could see his potential."

DON JOHNSON "The media pictured me as a strong conservative, on the basis of my Legion activity. And as the primary wore on, it was indeed true that Beck and I split the so-called conservative vote.

"It did help that Bob Ray was in Des Moines, the center of commerce, financial wealth, and transportation. And being a "professional" from Des Moines didn't hurt either, I don't think. From the time I got involved in politics, in 1946, it was like there was Des Moines and then the rest of the state.

"We spent about $60,000 in that campaign, got all of our polling information right from the *Des Moines Register.* Campaigning then was done much more on a person-to-person basis, getting to as many people as you possibly could, with the main attention being to the organized state party and its members. That's why you tried to drink more coffee, eat more cookies than your competitors."

FROSTY MITCHELL "We thought we recognized something in Johnson's campaign that had been done before. The governor in Nebraska then was named [Norbert] Tiemann and his campaign had been run by Bozell Jacobs, an advertising agency in Omaha. Johnson was friends with Chuck Peebler, who owned the agency, and they were helping him out. Well, I took a look back at the Omaha World Herald and saw what kind of advertising had been done for Tiemann. They were doing pretty much the same thing for Johnson. In fact, some guy had done his doctoral thesis on the Tiemann campaign, so I went down to Columbia, Missouri, and looked it over. Their main theme was going to be 'Don Johnson: A New Way to Spell Governor.'

"People were a little curious why in mid-June we bought half-page ads in the Des Moines Sunday Register proclaiming 'Bob Ray: A New Way to Spell Governor.' Johnson had already printed his brochures, though they hadn't been distributed, and they held some quick closed-door sessions. They couldn't figure out the source, but they figured somebody in their camp was leaking information."

GERALD BOGAN "I ran Bob Beck's campaign out of a little hole-in-the-wall office on Grand Avenue. It was a pretty polite campaign. We tried to make Beck out to be the 'real' Republican, modeled after that television and radio show 'I've Got a Secret.' "

BOB BECK "The primary in 1966 was quite close. I think Bill Murray beat me by only about 1,500 votes. I thought that was sufficient support to try again. Bob announced first, then Johnson, then myself. The Lincoln Club had paid for a survey by Central Surveys and found a carryover in name recognition which put me ahead.

"My campaign issue was the state of the Iowa economy, which seems a little ironic today. One of my main pitches was that Iowa had to diversify its economic approach and get more serious, because even back then the state had been enduring population losses and attrition. But that wasn't a very saleable commodity back in those days. It wasn't a very easy pitch to get people serious about. They were too content."

KENT CRAFTS "One time Mrs. Beck really let me have it at a joint appearance. Each of the candidates had ten minutes at the podium, and Frosty Mitchell, being the promoter that he is, had planned on filming Bob Ray's speech to be used in later television commercials. So when he took the stage all these bright lights came on for the cameras, and the impression was that the press was focusing on his speech. Mrs. Beck thought that was highly unethical.

"It was a primary where there was no personal exchange between the candidates, ever. They would arrive and they would depart with practically no exchange."

BOB BECK "Now, if it had been just Johnson or I, chances are one of us would have prevailed. Of course, the historic note on that is that we did get together, and I offered to have an in-depth poll taken, and whoever was lower in the poll would drop out. We both recognized that if we both stayed in, we'd both go down. But his advisers advised against that poll in May 1968, because they still thought they could put together a winning campaign. They turned me down, and thereafter we just couldn't see how we could win."

BOB RAY "We'd done some polling and felt that if Beck jumped out, I'd get the majority of his votes, because we were kind of second on everybody's list. If Johnson dropped out, I'd get a big chunk of his. There weren't a lot of people who disliked me.

"Two things Johnson and Beck might have done is to paint me as more liberal, because if a voter didn't know any of us, they'd vote against the liberal. They also could have claimed, although unfairly, that I was interested only in big cities and that I didn't know anything about agriculture. But neither one of them did that. I think Johnson thought that he could tell them what a great guy he was, that he was the national commander, which was a big, big accomplishment, and honestly not have to worry about us. Beck, though, had lost once. He approached things a little differently, a little scrappier."

JOHN REHMANN "We tried at one point to talk Johnson into getting out, very early on, before he'd officially announced. I had a meeting out at Crawford and Corrinne Hubbell's house on Park Avenue with him. It's probably a good thing we didn't. We tried to talk Johnson into running for the Senate against Hughes, instead of Dave Stanley."

HARRY RASDAL "At one point there was talk that Johnson and Beck were just going to flip a coin, and the loser would drop out. At that point Bob Ray was running with about 40 percent of the vote; they were splitting the other 60 percent in half. John Rehmann felt he knew Don Johnson well enough and that he could take some of our campaign money, even though we weren't that wealthy, and feed it into Johnson's campaign to help keep it alive. That was vetoed, but there was nothing to stop us from going out and saying to somebody who worked for Johnson that you had heard Beck calling him a lousy, no-good son of a gun. We relied a little on those tactics."

BOB BECK "Now when Ray had his airplane wreck, that was a definite turning point. His name identification then eclipsed ours, because we had better name recognition up to that point. But that was an overnight phenomenon, and from that point he grabbed the lead and stayed there. It attracted widespread attention, and being a newspaperman myself, I understood that."

DICK REDMAN "The best thing that happened to the campaign was the successful airplane crash in that field of nice, soft mud. It was nice that he got banged up, but not too bad. It was nice that nobody got killed, that there were no fence posts in the way. Those are the kinds of things that happen in campaigns that nobody has any control over."

KENT CRAFTS "I was supposed to go along in the plane with Bob Ray that night, but I had a French test I was studying for, so I sent along one of my friends from Drake. As it turned out I flunked the French test, because I got a call from Mason City and went immediately to the office and called Walt Shotwell. I spent the night calling people, coordinating the press, the campaign, and the family. Ironically, it was that same night that Rand Petersen really emerged as the leader of the campaign. He and Dutch were cochairmen. I called Rand that night, got him out of the shower, and he was immediately on top of the situation, suggesting who I should call, what approach should be taken, the communications that needed to be made, all while he was drying off from his shower. I called Dutch and he sent off a telegram to Bob Ray and then called me back to talk about the next campaign rally."

FROSTY MITCHELL "Kent Crafts called me at home. He knew how close Bob and I were personally, though I really wasn't much involved in the campaign at that stage. I got up and went down to the radio station in Grinnell to watch the wire service, called some of the media people I knew up in Mason City. I immediately talked to Billie, and we agreed not to go up to Mason City until first thing in the morning. The next morning Rand, Billie, and I drove up.

"Bob knew that no matter what areas of his campaign might need help—whether it was to raise money or help with speeches—I was there to help. I hadn't been involved in the day-to-day managing of the campaign prior to the plane crash. But necessity is the mother of invention, and zap, that plane went down and somebody had to come in and help."

BOB RAY "It was raining that day, April 22. Jack Linge and I had been out campaigning all day. We ended up in Boone in the early evening. Jack didn't like to fly, so he was going to drive back to Des Moines and the plane would take me on. I wanted to go to Oelwein and Fayette County, because both my opponents had campaign managers from Fayette County.

"I had done quite a bit of flying, and generally I never ever questioned the pilot. I figured the pilot wanted to live as much as I. But I remember that day several people had mentioned that the weather was pretty bad and that we probably shouldn't go.

"I had never flown with Gene Abbott. In fact, I'd only met him once before, and in those days you flew with whomever you could, whenever there was an opportunity. He had arranged to use his insurance company's plane. I told him before we took off not to take any risks, that I didn't have to make this meeting, I wasn't the main speaker. He said, 'Well, we'll try and get there, and if the weather looks bad, we'll turn around or we'll try and land somewhere else.' We were flying in a twin-engine Apache.

"Kent Crafts's friend John Lloyd was sitting on the passenger's side in the front, and I sat right behind the pilot. I dozed off pretty quickly and Abbott woke me up a little later, saying the weather was getting pretty bad and suggested we land at Mason City. I said, 'Fine, no problem, go ahead.' I dozed off again and I don't know what woke me, but when I looked out, even in the bad air, I saw lights. So I looked at the altimeter and it read that we were about 1,400 or something. I didn't know what the elevation of Mason City was, but I knew Des Moines's was 957 and I said, 'We're only about four hundred feet above the ground.' I leaned up and said, 'Hey, I don't want to be a backseat driver, but we're flying too low.' He had a map stretched out across his lap and I remember him pushing that map aside and grabbing the wheel. Had he not pulled the wheel quickly, we would probably have nosed right into the ground, but I think he must have pulled it back just as we stalled and immediately we hit.

"We hit so hard the fuselage right behind where I was sitting completely broke off, and then we slid in a mud field about a half mile. The wings came off, the gas tanks came off. Talk about God wanting something to happen, we didn't hit any buildings, we didn't hit any fences, we didn't catch fire. I was knocked unconscious. The next thing I remember was waking up in the hospital."

JOHN LLOYD "I don't recall ever losing consciousness. There was just a tremendous amount of racket, chaotic thoughts, and then quiet. Abbott and I were still in our seats. What was left of the front of the plane was in our laps. We had to get out of the plane on my side. I couldn't walk; I had a broken leg. We couldn't see Governor Ray, didn't know where he was. Gene Abbott went towards the back of the plane. I kind of hobbled along. Abbott just kind of reached in the wreckage and pulled him out through the back of the fuselage where it had broken off behind the passengers' compartment. He was not conscious. We quickly determined that Abbott was the only one capable of moving any distance, so he went for help."

Gene Abbott stumbled down the road, found help, and an ambulance was quickly at the site, though the muddy fields required that a tractor be called to pull the ambulance out of the mire. A nearby farmer, Don Payton, was the first to get to the plane and remembers Ray, always polite, apologizing, even though semiconscious, for being such a bother. John Lloyd tried to get to his feet, broken femur and all, and attempted to introduce his candidate for governor. Ray was the most severely injured. For two days after the accident he couldn't move. They stitched his face and his chest, cleaned the mud out of his nose and ears, and repaired a badly fractured ankle and lower leg. He remembers overhearing the doctor say they thought they could sew his ear back on. He was kept in the hospital in Mason City for a week until his transfer by ambulance to Des Moines, where Dr. John Kelley operated on his ankle, reduced the fracture, pinned it, and put it in a cast.

BOB TYSON "That was a hard way to get publicity, but he got a lot of it. I'll never forget the picture on the front page of the *Mason City Gazette* showing Bob Ray leaning forward on his crutches with the most angelic look on his face you ever saw. You couldn't have bought an ad like that, let alone get it on the front page. And, of course, he ran big in Cerro Gordo County because of the crash."

BOB RAY "Soon after the plane crash, Billie was asked to make appearances for me, and she went along with them. Remember, she had agreed to my running as long as she didn't have to give any speeches."

FROSTY MITCHELL "I didn't give Billie any choice, told her we were going to keep every date on Bob's schedule. Two days after the crash we made the first one in Waterloo. She quickly became his biggest political asset.

"There were those who said I milked the accident a little bit. Billie would go out and give a little speech and then we would have a tape-recorded message from the candidate in his hospital bed. It would get awful quiet in those rooms. I mean, how would you feel if you were Bob Beck or Don Johnson, sitting on a platform waiting to talk, and you've got to follow this little lady holding a tape recorder with a message from her husband, from his hospital bed?"

HARRY RASDAL "At the time of the crash we had piles of invitations for Bob Ray to speak, often three or four invitations for the same time, same day. After the crash we wrote to every one of them and said, 'Bob Ray had planned on coming to your event but because of the crash he will not be able to,' and every afternoon Frosty would go up and he and Bob Ray would cut tapes and they would send out four or five for the same night. Each tape would start out the same, 'I had planned on being here tonight, but . . . '"

Frosty Mitchell's emergence as the hands-on engineer of the Ray campaign after the plane accident introduced a new style into the statewide race. As a Des Moines disc jockey in the 1950s, Mitchell was known citywide as "Frosty the Showman." He knew the Iowa media, the personalities involved, and how to promote, promote, promote. Along with Walt Shotwell, a former *Register* reporter turned adman and longtime Ray friend, Mitchell lent a knowledge of advertising and public relations that most prior campaigns had not had access to.

LEO OXBERGER "The addition of Frosty Mitchell to the campaign was the best thing that could have happened. You just can't run a campaign for governor and be the candidate, which is what Bob Ray had been trying to do. And if that accident hadn't happened, that would have probably continued.

"Frosty was a take-charge guy. He's got more energy and more drive than most ten people."

BILLIE RAY "Frosty is temperamental and a perfectionist, so now we had two of them running the campaign. Frosty is the kind who likes to be begged to help. And Bob would be the last to beg anybody to help him. That's kind of why Frosty hadn't been involved before. But once Frosty got involved, you knew he would come in and save the campaign."

KENT CRAFTS "Frosty initially came in as an adviser, just a personal friend. Yet he and Bob Ray had some remarkable blowups. Our campaign was run out of a two-room suite in the Hotel Savery, and so any time there was going to be a little problem, whoever was having the problem would slip off into the other room, the door would be closed, and the rest of the staff would crowd into the remaining room. Boy, for the first few weeks after Frosty got involved there was a lot of staff crowding into the one room.

"They argued mostly about issues and mainly Bob's demand for high performance, as he saw it. Frosty was a very strong willed fellow, and he knew how to produce a great show. On the other hand, Bob felt he knew exactly what he needed in his campaign. But neither had a lot of experience communicating what they wanted to the staff. They were both perfectionists – they'd have these quasi competitions to see which of them could get along with the least sleep, and people like myself who were trying to schedule them would end up exhausted while they kept charging about."

DEL VAN HORN "Bob Ray and Frosty Mitchell got to a point during that campaign where they just plain would not speak to each other. Did not speak. Probably neither one of them will admit it, but that's the truth. But it never seemed to last for long. Frosty loves Bob Ray, but still today there's a little negative magnetism there."

BOB RAY "Frosty is a talented, temperamental entertainer. I had always wanted him to help on the campaign, but I wasn't sure if I asked him if he'd want to or not. Sometimes when I thought something was very logical, his reaction seemed to indicate otherwise."

BILLIE RAY "I got a girl to live in that summer. They had coaxed me into making some appearances for him. I guess I didn't really have much choice. But they did always send somebody with me – Maurie Van Nostrand, Rand Petersen. I'd go along and give a health report. I never talked about issues, nor did I intend to. Knowing Bob, no matter what I would say it would have been the wrong thing. But it was probably the best thing for me, because I did not like to get up and give a speech.

"Once he went back out campaigning, in late June, I went with him almost everywhere. He says now he went back five or six weeks too early.

It was a tremendous effort just to walk on the crutches for one thing, and then to have this big cast on during the heat of the summer. He'd break out in perspiration whenever he'd be speaking, and so many of the radio stations were up steep flights of stairs he had to learn to go down steep flights on crutches. Also, when he'd been in the hospital they had tubes forced down his throat, which bruised his throat muscles, so he had trouble talking afterwards."

FROSTY MITCHELL "After the accident I wanted him to be back on his feet by the state convention in June with a whole new campaign that said 'Bob Ray is Okay.' Here was a guy who walked away from a terrible airplane accident."

BOB RAY "I saw that airplane about a year later. The manager of the Mason City Airport said that he'd gone out to pick up the parts. He said most of the parts were picked up by hand. He also said he'd investigated a lot of plane crashes, and that's the first one he'd seen where there wasn't one reusable part. He couldn't believe we lived. I had a brand new Remington electric razor with me—I'd got it to use between campaign stops—and it was in a little container. When I opened it up I just shook out all the little parts. I always accused Frosty Mitchell of staging that plane wreck . . . and of going a little too far."

One other event of that 1968 campaign stands out, one that many pinpoint alongside the plane crash as bringing much-needed attention to Bob Ray's run for governor. It was a simple song, a campaign theme song, brewed up by an unusual foursome—Bob Ray, Frosty Mitchell, state party executive Dick Redman, and former Des Moines resident and singing star Marilyn Maye.

BOB RAY "I was driving down the street when I heard a Lincoln-Mercury commercial in which they used Marilyn Maye's song 'Step to the Rear.' I had not liked political jingles before. A couple years before, we had listened to them, and a lot of candidates were jumping for them. They were awful. I thought they did more harm to candidates than good and were a waste of money. But when I heard 'Step to the Rear' I thought it was the best tune for a political jingle that had ever been written, except perhaps for 'Happy Days Are Here Again.' So I talked to Frosty about it and he wrote some different lyrics for it.

"We decided we wanted Marilyn Maye to sing it for us. John Rehmann said he knew her, since she'd grown up in Des Moines. We found her in Kansas City and Frosty and I went down to meet her. She liked it and agreed to do it. They'd been asked by several politicians – Hubert Humphrey, George Romney, Bob Dole – and they had turned down everybody. But Frosty sent the publishers tapes anyway. They finally sold us the rights."

FROSTY MITCHELL "The Broadway producers' concern was that they didn't want some trite jingle ruining their Broadway show, *How Now Dow Jones*. But I finally convinced them to let me show them a sixty-second jingle. I got the choir director of our Lutheran church in Grinnell and we laid down a track with piano, then we dubbed in the vocals.

"They wanted me to wait until the show went off Broadway. I told them by then it would be too late. We convinced them we weren't going to harm their show, and they sold us the rights to the song for $1,500. Then I got ahold of Marilyn Maye, whose dad still owned a Super Valu in Des Moines. She was a little concerned, because she only wanted to be involved with a winner.

"We kept the lyrics 'Let a leader show the way' over Marilyn's protests. She wanted it to go 'let a winner show the way.' But this was during the primary, and I wasn't about to let the boys at the *Register* jump on that, reminding people that Bob Ray hadn't won *anything* yet. After the primary we recut it with 'winner' replacing 'leader.' "

MARILYN MAYE "They had heard 'Step to the Rear, Let a Leader Lead the Way,' which was the whole title of the song, which was a hit record for me. Bob Ray and Frosty came down and heard me perform, and we discussed how much it would cost, what the lyrics would be. It was pretty cleverly written originally, and I said I wanted some control over the lyrics. I had already done the song as a national commercial for Lincoln-Mercury, which ran for three years, but it was a perfect campaign song. Hubert Humphrey wanted to use it, but he wasn't of the right political party.

"One of Bob Ray's primary opponents later said, 'We have a purpose, not a song.' Another opponent, in a later campaign, had bumper stickers that read 'Don't Blame Me, Blame Marilyn.' "

Bob Ray became a winner on September 3, taking the primary with 43 percent of the votes cast. Johnson followed with 31 percent and Beck with 26 percent, not far off the public opinion polls that had been reported since June.

It's not stretching the point to say that the primary win was the biggest electoral victory of Bob Ray's long career. Without the attention and sympathy the plane crash had brought, without the split encouraged by the presence of Beck and Johnson, without Frosty Mitchell's bagful of then-progressive campaign tricks, like keying personal appearances to the six o'clock news, Bob Ray might have lived in anonymity, just another lawyer from Des Moines, a three-time loser. His friend Tom Stoner later summed up that win as an anomaly: "He got into office by virtue of a conservative split in a three-way primary. If there had been just two candidates, Bob Ray would probably not have won. He later told me that late in that campaign Beck and Johnson started picking on him as a Des Moines lawyer, and he felt if they'd started that earlier and gotten on him harder, they might have knocked him out. My point is that he was not elected on a great wave of moderate support, not on the basis of any great ideology. So I'm not sure that underneath it all, from 1965 on through, that there was ever a majority of Republicans in Iowa who were moderates. They just liked Bob Ray."

Only sixty days lay between the primary and the general election that year, and that worked to Bob Ray's favor. His campaign was on a roll, and he was coming off nine months of hard campaigning. He'd traveled all over the state, his name and picture had been in every paper, and he was more than ready to face Democrat Paul Franzenburg.

A two-term Iowa state treasurer, fifty-one-year-old Franzenburg was the sole Democratic candidate hoping to replace the seemingly irreplaceable Harold Hughes. Bob Fulton—a lawyer, former state legislator from Waterloo, and two-term lieutenant governor—had been favored by many Democrats to be their party's standard-bearer but had declined for "personal reasons." (Fulton's name lives in the record books, though, because he later stepped in to relieve Hughes as governor when the new senator left office early to gain seniority in Washington. For fourteen days in January 1969, Governor Bob Fulton led the state, but primarily in the dismantling of Hughes's office.)

JIM FLANSBURG "When Bob Ray won that nomination I was absolutely confident that Paul Franzenburg would win the governorship, because Ray didn't know the first damn thing about state government and Franzenburg knew quite a lot. Nevertheless, Ray was elected and quickly proved that first term that he didn't know a hell of a lot about state government."

KENT CRAFTS "The general election was a piece of cake compared to the primary. The mood of the state matched Bob Ray's moderatism. He was considered a very charismatic man and was very attractive to the majority of voters in the state. Franzenburg had never been able to capture any personal popularity and did not leave the clear impression that he was the pragmatic, moderate, problem-solving candidate that Bob Ray was. In the primary we had a lot more ideological divisiveness, much more personal animosity."

FROSTY MITCHELL "We never backed off. The day after the primary election Bob and I flew to West Branch and Centerville to smoke peace pipes with Johnson and Beck. In those days you were supposed to fall back and kind of let the state central committee take over the campaign, supply money and what not. But we had built an organization outside the state party like no other. Dave Stanley, who was running for the U.S. Senate, had a good organization out there too, and we talked about marrying the two campaigns, but he passed it up. They thought they were too big for us."

BOB RAY "I fully expected to be positioned as the challenger, but Franzenburg went on the defensive right away. I wondered why. He had been the state treasurer, he had survived in 1966 along with Hughes, and he had gone out and made speeches for Hughes for the last two years. I figured he'd be well prepared. But the day I got nominated he started taking off on me, putting me in a position I didn't think I deserved, as the frontrunner. I suddenly felt like I was the incumbent and I didn't complain at all." [*An October 13* Des Moines Register *Iowa Poll showed Ray ahead of Franzenburg 52 percent to 42 percent.*]

HARRY RASDAL "In our tracking, Bob was quite a bit ahead of Franzenburg just after the primary. But as November neared, Bob's numbers started slipping and Paul's were getting better. If the election had been held December 1, it looked like Franzenburg would win.

"I had known Franzenburg for a long time. He was from Conrad, and I used to check his eyes in Marshalltown. So whenever we would go to appearances I would try and pull Franzenburg off to one corner to visit about his mother or his dad, that type of thing, while Bob Ray was out shaking hands with the people at the meeting."

BOB FULTON "The main reason I didn't run was because I was absolutely broke. If it hadn't been for that, I would have run. Paul was an issue-oriented type, which I saw as a weakness in a campaign, especially against a guy as popular as Bob Ray had become.

"Paul would have done a good job as governor, but he was never able to draw a very distinct line between himself and Bob Ray. Bob had never been in office, Paul had been. Paul was a very good state treasurer; he understood the state treasury and state government. Bob Ray had never held office before."

FROSTY MITCHELL "We thought Franzenburg felt very equal to Bob Beck and Don Johnson but that he had a kind of inferiority complex about Bob Ray. Partly because Bob was a lawyer, partly because he represented the big city. I knew, having lived in Grinnell, that, gee, if you want to do something big, you go to Des Moines. That's where the state fair is, the basketball tournaments. That's a feeling you just don't lose if you're from a small town. You're a product of that environment.

"I also think that Paul always somewhat questioned whether or not he'd just ridden into office on Harold Hughes's coattails. Because of that perception, we never passed up an opportunity to get Paul and Bob on the same stage. I don't think we would have treated Bob Fulton the same way."

PAUL FRANZENBURG "I had announced January 11. I had to wait until Hughes decided what he was going to do. But it never really mattered to me who my Republican opponent was. I really thought things looked bright for me through the spring, but then a number of things happened. Lyndon Johnson decided not to run again, which of and by itself was not so critical, perhaps, but it established a tenor of the times. Then a number of dreadful things happened – Martin Luther King was assassinated, Bobby Kennedy was killed, the Democratic convention in Chicago erupted. It was a bad year for Democrats. All of that, plus Ray badly outspent me. They ran an ad in the *Des Moines Tribune* on election day, a real sign they had plenty of money. But I really felt confident up until a few weeks before the election.

"Ray's principal hue and cry in the election was that the Democrats had frittered away the state's surplus. I repeatedly tried to explain to audiences, especially when we were together on the stand, that if the surplus had been reduced, it was the fault of the Republican-controlled house and the senate, where the Democrats controlled by only three votes. It wasn't just the Democrats who reduced it. After he was elected he complained a lot about the Democrats leaving him with this deficit. Granted, we didn't leave him with a big surplus, but not a deficit. We had some pretty good joint appearances, but I always had to respond to that issue first before I could set out on my own views. I spent too much time putting him down, not being positive.

"Then there was that silly song. It was popular and well done. So some of my people came up with the slogan, 'Don't Sell Your Vote for a Song.' That was somewhat effective, but we dropped it. I got the impression that they were glad we did."

BOB RAY "Ours really was a great song. Every place we'd play the song, you'd hear people humming it when you passed them on your way out. It drove Paul Franzenburg crazy. He got so he never made a speech without talking about that song.

"I didn't hesitate talking about what I thought Hughes had done wrong or what his administration had done wrong. They had raised all the taxes and then spent all the surplus. But I tried not to blame it on Hughes personally. And I tried not to condemn Democrats, because I realized that a lot of Democrats agreed with me. I was going to need their support in the legislature, and at the polls, too."

FROSTY MITCHELL "It was kind of funny, though. Even though it might have looked like we were running this big campaign, oozing with money, I can remember sending Jim Callison down to see Harry Dahl and trying to get free potato chips and dips, or whatever he could, for events. Del Van Horn was always good at coming up with free booze.

"After the primary we pretty much only went into towns that had either a radio station or daily paper. I'm sure we were the first campaign to think along those lines. We were the first to have a daily news release go out, the first to do a fly-around press conference, where we flew into all the television towns in the state on the same day. The last ten days of the campaign we appeared only in towns with television stations. We wanted to be on the six and ten o'clock news. Meanwhile, Paul Franzenburg seemed to be back in Conrad or someplace, and we'd be in Sioux City talking with three television crews. We made great use of television and airplanes.

"We were real good about notifying the local media that our candidate was going to be in town. And while I knew it was important that Bob get over to the Methodist church basement in Creston to meet thirty-five people, I made sure we stopped at KSIB's newsroom about noon first. Hey, those thirty-five were going to vote, maybe raise a little money, but boy was that noon news important! I've got to give Walt Shotwell a lot of credit, too. He did a brilliant job of buying and placing our advertising. He was close to the campaign; it was more than just a job to him. Our billboard locations were better than anybody else's. Plus I knew enough about radio and television to know what the best buys were and when. One day we took out a half-page ad in the *Register,* statewide, and encouraged people to make their own yard signs. They sprang up all over.

"Because of the big media buys we made in the primary and general elections, I'm sure it was the most expensive campaign up until then. I had some fun with that Ray jingle, too. I sent it out ahead of time to the radio station people I knew who might lean toward the greedy side and said,'Here is a list of good Republican contributors in your county. Take this tape out, play it for them, and get them to pay a little for you to play it.' Let them sell it, make a little money. It helped us saturate the market.

"Verne Lawyer was also real important during those days. If I called him and said, 'Verne, I've got to have a plane and a pilot later today, because we're going to Council Bluffs and we're not coming back until midnight,' he'd find one, a good one. But Verne had mixed emotions about Bob winning, I think, just like Billie. They were seeing a part of their lives being sacrificed.

"Bob and Billie's perfectionism – and mine, I guess – really showed up during that campaign, too. They were both really conscientious and sensitive about getting thank-yous out. I'm not talking about 'Thank you for your great contribution to my campaign.' I'm talking about 'Thank you for picking me up at the airport in Hawarden,' or, you know, 'Gee I enjoyed the chocolate-chip cookies you prepared for me,' those kinds of thank-yous, and he cranked out a bunch of them. I'll bet they're still sitting in scrapbooks all over Iowa, a real key to his long success."

TOM WHITNEY "Ray beat Paul Franzenburg basically with a song and an impression that Franzenburg left, which was kind of a stodgy older man. There was no creativity in his soul, and as a consequence Ray was able to put Franzenburg on the defensive in regards to the surplus issue. It was a tough year for Democrats all across the country. Hughes only won the Senate seat by 6,000 votes, and Paul fell to a combination of things."

Franzenburg's admonitions on the stump, like "Ray is a nice guy, but that's no reason to vote for him," went unheeded. On November 5 Bob Ray won 54 percent of the votes – a 93,000-vote margin – to become the thirty-eighth governor of Iowa. He won 83 out of 99 counties, though he lost his home county, Polk, by 5,000 votes. His campaign against the former state treasurer had focused on a looming potential budget deficit brought on, he said, by the Hughes administration's spending of a $100-

million-plus surplus and raising "virtually every conceivable tax," leaving the state cash-poor.

The *Des Moines Register,* in the first of five editorial endorsements of Ray over the years, sanctioned Bob Ray because, they said, they "believed he has demonstrated a somewhat broader grasp of the problems of Iowa. He impresses us as a man with the maturity of judgment and courage to rise above sectional, industrial or partisan interests in considering the interests of the state as a whole."

On that same election day the country elected a new president, Richard M. Nixon, whose career would one day change the face of politics. The state had a new U.S. senator, Harold Hughes, whose liberal voice would become a rallying point for Democrats nationwide during his six-year tenure. Iowa also had a new lieutenant governor, Roger Jepsen, a former state senator who had run alongside Bob Ray for his first statewide office and who would soon become a major thorn in the new governor's side.

VII: THE FIRST TERM, 1969-1970

Iowa's thirty-eighth governor was sworn in by Chief Justice Theodore G. Garfield at Veterans Auditorium on January 16, 1969, before a crowd of 6,500. Bob Ray was the first governor elected from Des Moines in twenty-six years and the first since 1904 to be inaugurated outside the capitol's house chambers. The event was celebrated on live television, another first, and at four inaugural balls that evening. Roger Jepsen introduced Ray, proclaiming it a "sunny day in Iowa's future," and the fresh-faced governor proceeded to deliver the longest inaugural address in state history, over one hour and fifteen minutes, a sweeping dictate outlining Bob Ray's views on just about everything. He talked about the need for a state ombudsman, the potential for consolidating police radio facilities, tax incentives for training the disadvantaged, stiffer penalities for air and water polluters, and the equalization of property taxes. The epic speech—assembled by Ray, speechwriter Bob Burlingame, and Max Milo Mills, who had been helping the transitioning governor since Mills's primary loss to Jepsen—came from notes on scraps of paper and napkins and odds and ends of research collected over the prior two months. "There was kind of an internal struggle over what should be included," says Mills, "and I guess I lost in the sense that I would have preferred a forty-minute speech. I won in the sense that it didn't go on for three hours."

BOB RAY "We stayed up all night working on the speech. I didn't have a lot of professional help; we just had people who'd worked on the campaign and people I respected, and we worked and worked and worked,

The inauguration ceremony, 1969. *Des Moines Register* photo. Reprinted with permission.

night and day. It got to be the night before the inaugural and I was just beat, couldn't keep my eyes open. Max Mills and Bob Burlingame stayed at the office in the Savery to finish up. They said they'd shave it down and we'd have the whole text available at the auditorium and I'd just deliver a synopsis. I came back at eight the next morning and they had decided it just couldn't be boiled down. So I had nothing but the whole text. When I went up on the stage I knew it was going to be a bomb. Everybody went to sleep. I almost fell asleep myself. I could see my kids down in the front row, sleeping.

"But the address was done with foresight. Right or wrong, it served as my guide. I felt we had gone through a campaign and, like most campaigns, had not dealt heavily with many issues. So I thought I had some duty to let people know what my position was on the many, many issues. If I had to do it over again, I'd give a five-minute speech."

After the four inaugural balls that Frosty "The Showman" Mitchell had organized were out of the way and the new governor was ensconced in his capitol offices, Bob Ray had little time to sit back and dwell on his good fortune. The election had been good for Republicans statewide. They controlled both houses of the legislature, had five of the seven congressional seats (electing Fred Schwengel, H. R. Gross, John Kyl, Wiley Mayne, and Bill Scherle), one U.S. senator (Jack Miller), and all of the executive branch (with Melvin Synhorst, secretary of state; Lloyd Smith, auditor; Maurice Baringer, treasurer; L. B. Liddy, secretary of agriculture; and Richard Turner, attorney general). But that overwhelming GOP success resulted in one of Ray's biggest headaches during that first two-year term, because party leaders—especially those in the legislature, which was dominated by established conservatives—expected the new governor to fulfill their every wish.

BOB RAY "When I walked in the door that first day in office all we were left was the key to the place. There wasn't anything, not a pad of paper or a pencil, nothing. I had a secretary who'd been over and talked with her predecessor, and I had made an effort to visit with Hughes, but there really wasn't any transition. We had something like 30,000 notary public applications, bags of mail waiting, and I had four legal-sized pages filled with names of people who wanted to see me right away.

"I hadn't really had time to hire a staff, and the people we had hired I hadn't spent any time with, didn't really know some of them. We didn't have the trooper to help with the driving and scheduling.

"The first day in office I was inundated with appointments and a lot of people just walking in, wanting to see me. Finally I buzzed my secretary and told her to hold everybody for a few minutes while I caught my breath. That's vivid yet today; I've thought about it many times. I remember swinging around in that big chair, leaning back and deciding that at that moment everybody wanted me to do something their way, everybody had an idea of how I should be doing the job. I just couldn't please all the people – half of them at best. I was elected for two years, and the thing for me to do was the best job I knew how, using my best judgment, and if people didn't like it and I ran again, they could throw me out of office – that was their prerogative. And I'd be satisfied in my own mind that I did the job as well as I could and with my own judgment. I decided I would listen to anybody who wanted to talk to me, all sides of an issue, and I'd take the time necessary for me to make a decision based on what I thought was right. I recognized there would be times when I'd have to make on-the-spot decisions, but if I had some time, I was going to take it, so that I felt comfortable with those decisions, and I'd know why I thought one option was better than the other. After that I turned the intercom back on, people started flowing in again, and I felt very comfortable.

"But it wasn't easy. We had to thumb through the code to figure out which appointments were up, we had to figure out the best way to have news conferences, we didn't have any stationery. It took a long time to get the staff started. No matter who you hire, those people have different strengths and weaknesses. I hadn't even been able to sit down with them and explain what I expected.

"It was different than when I left office. You saw Terry Branstad traveling all the time. He was constantly here and there, every place, always on the go. I couldn't do that, at least I didn't think I could. Part of the reason was that I felt even if I didn't get reelected, I was elected to run the office and I was dwelling on that. That first term my job was my life. I slept with it, ate with it, did everything just for the office. I wouldn't go outside of the state except for governors' conferences, and I really stayed there to try to learn more and make good decisions.

"I was also trying to learn the budgetary process. I was determined not to increase the budget that first term. When I was elected I thought, 'Whew, one thing I won't have to grapple with will be taxes, because they raised virtually every tax just before I became governor.' But I learned very early that you don't raise taxes and really solve problems. You've got to couple it with something that honestly will do what you intend. Property taxes were killing the farmers and they were letting me hear about it, coming into my office and saying they weren't going to pay them."

Many legislators thought Ray was too detail-oriented, his decision-making process laborious. Many appointments were delayed and delayed again. His staff members, with the exception of Dutch Vermeer, who had signed on to be the governor's legislative liaison, were new to state government. Bill Ball, a Waterloo lawyer and Black Hawk County politico, was the governor's executive assistant. Midway through the first term he was replaced by University of Iowa public affairs specialist Clayton Ringgenberg. Bill Thompson, a Central College journalism professor, joined as press secretary, assisted by a young newspaperman, Dick Gilbert. Campaign worker Keith Peterson was the scheduler, Mike Sellers the governor's legal counsel. The ever-loyal, never-conspicuous Janet Van Note guarded the governor's door, helped by longtime Republican party worker Jackie Day, who had done the same job for the last Republican governor, Norman Erbe.

MAX MILO MILLS "His perfectionism was a little frustrating during that early period. It's what I call the 'freshman governor syndrome,' and I've seen it in other states. At first, before you start to get the perspective of the big picture, you want to read every piece of mail. You're a public servant, and if it takes forty-eight hours a day, you do it. As a result, you get tangled up in a bunch of details. But you can't run an organization the size of the state of Iowa without delegating a hell of a lot of stuff."

BILL THOMPSON "Bob had a horrible time with correspondence at first, because he wanted to dot every *i* and cross every *t*. Sometimes the letters were stacked up all over the place. One time he went on vacation or someplace, left me in charge, and we just mailed the letters out. That made him mad. They were already read and signed, but he wanted to look at them one more time."

KEITH PETERSON "I don't like the word disorganized, but there was a certain amount of 'feeling your way around' to do in those first few months in order to get organized and get a feel for how the governor wanted things done. There was a book of some kind that Dwight Jensen had put together, an outline of how they [*Hughes's staff*] had run the office. I read through it and thought it was helpful, but it was like anything else—a new adminstration was not going to do things the same way; we weren't going to divide up the responsibilities the same way."

One individual close to Ray who was not new to state government and who proved to be one of the governor's longtime allies was a holdover from the Erbe and Hughes administrations. Marvin Selden's job description, as state comptroller, was listed in the very back of the *Iowa Official Register* for this year, but if read closely it details very simply how important he would be to any new governor: "The comptroller controls the payment of all moneys into the state treasury and all payments from the state treasury, . . . prepares the budget document and drafts the legislation to make it effective, . . . [*and*] reviews requests for allotment as are submitted to the governor for approval." Many viewed Selden as the most powerful person in state government at that time.

MARVIN SELDEN "They used to accuse me of at least being the second most powerful person in the state government. What I tried to do was figure out what was important to the governor and then get it in the budget. When Bob Ray first came in I had to get to him awfully fast and find out what promises he'd made. And if he had said, 'Boy, I'm going to take care of the Conservation Commission,' then you better take care of the Conservation Commission or be able to explain why you weren't. When Hughes first came in he leaned pretty heavily on me, and his first budget was really mine. When Ray came in he had Dutch and Maurie Van Nostrand and they'd been through the process, so his first budget was pretty much a combined effort.

"I remember going home and laughing when I was indoctrinating Bob Ray on the budget, 'This is the last goddam governor I'm going to educate.' They are stuck with dealing with the budget, like it or not, and it did not come easy for Bob Ray, but he sure as hell learned it. I don't think he ever enjoyed it, though. In later years he'd do almost anything to keep from working on the budget—Dick Gilbert used to say he loved working on the budget because then they'd get appointments made. But Ray used the budget as a tool to get to know the departments, find out what they were doing."

MAURICE BARINGER "It's funny. I remember Marv saying to me after the compromises had been worked out in the legislature during Hughes's last term and the appropriations allotted for the new programs that he sure felt sorry for the guy who was elected to be the next governor, because he knew that the revenues were not going to be adequate to support the new appropriations. *So was it a fair criticism when Bob Ray would chide Hughes for leaving him with all the taxes raised, the money spent, and new programs to fund?* He was right."

BOB RAY "I made a point not to be critical of Harold Hughes, and I, whenever I could, tried to point out the good things he had done. But in the term before he left office the legislature had raised the sales tax, not numerically but had added it on services, and the income and property taxes went up. They had also allotted those increased revenues for new programs. But the revenue forecasts were discouraging, property taxes were high, farmers were having some tough times. I didn't know where to go for more money. That's when we started working on the school foundation plan."

In February 1970, Bob Fulton, Ray's eventual Democratic opponent in the fast-approaching election, accused the first-term governor of "the greatest buck-passing act ever conducted under the golden dome of the statehouse" after Ray had once again claimed that "Harold Hughes left this state with no money, all the taxes raised and all the money spent." Ray conceded that Hughes had gotten a good start on reorganizing an antiquated state government, including revamping the tax-collecting apparatus and the social service agencies, but he continued to complain that he had "inherited an empty treasury."

BOB FULTON "Bob just refused to do anything during that first term; he just sat there. Looking back, I think he just didn't know what to do to face up to the state's fiscal problems. Half of his party really didn't like him yet, and the Democrats knew he was hard to deal with, but they were out trying to make sure he wouldn't be around for two more years."

HAROLD HUGHES "I didn't intend for any fiscal problems to hang on past my tenure. We had had an economic feasibility study done, and I literally went down the line and tried to enact it completely and totally. After those guys [*the legislators*] went home it became a huge tax bill, and it was the greatest liability I ever had on my back in my life. Later on, some of it was declared unconstitutional. A lot of it was replaced. But we did rebalance the school aid, rebalanced the highway-use-tax funds, enabling the cities and counties to receive a bigger share in cuts. We got the community college system established. All of those programs were underway, with appropriate financing based on a rising economy, in the hopes that a new governor coming in would at least have time to breathe while he had a chance to get his feet on the ground, take a look at the system, and decide where he wanted to go."

DUTCH VERMEER "There were a number of things that made 1970 a tough year for us. The hog market went to pot. I think they dropped to 13 cents, which hurt the farmers, and they couldn't pay their property taxes. The schools were having a tough time getting by, the economy was going down, and our revenue wasn't coming in as expected. Fulton really started playing on this and gave us some anxious moments."

BOB RAY "After I got elected I think the farmers and commodity groups had some real qualms about how well I understood things, primarily because a number of things happened which I didn't have any control over. One of the commodity chairmen came in and said, 'Look, I want to be supportive, but all these things have happened and the farm community is really restless, uneasy.' "

DEL VAN HORN "Right after he was elected, I don't think a governor could have set out to make more mistakes than he did with regard to agriculture, and I'm not saying anything behind his back here, he knows that."

DEL STROMER "In 1970 we had pitchforks and hammer handles in the rotunda, farmers protesting their tax bills. Bob Ray wasn't as cognizant of the problem as he should have been. He didn't perceive how serious that property-tax issue was, but what you had out there was a net earning capacity for that ag land of fifteen dollars an acre, and you had six and seven dollars an acre property tax. Nearly half of our net was being taken away in property taxes. Now we've got the same problem, but it's interest and not property taxes. That lack of perception nearly got him beat."

DEL VAN HORN "When he appointed his first blue-ribbon committee to study the economy, he appointed a minister but not a farmer. I said, 'You've got to put a farmer on there. That's what this economy is all about.' He said, 'Well, there's more schoolteachers than there are farmers.' I researched it, told him he was wrong.

"At that time people's image of farmers was pretty bad. It was still the Ding Darling cartoon of the hayseed in overalls, a straw hat, and a piece of straw hanging out of his mouth. We tried to change that. We started from scratch, calling all the agencies, every commodity group, every farm union, anybody who had three initials, to get their ideas. I asked some guys from the Farm Bureau—Merrill Anderson and Dale Nelson—over to the IDC [*Iowa Development Commission*] and told them we were going to start promoting agriculture and I wanted to have their input. Anderson said, 'That's the first goddam time we've had the state of Iowa ask us anything.' Bob Ray backed that. He would make room to always be at the meetings and he could always spark them up, make them do things above and beyond what they thought they could do. He had fun doing it, too. He got a genuine kick out of farmers."

JOHN SOORHOLTZ "I met him after he was first elected governor, and at that time I had a different viewpoint of agriculture than he did. But by allowing me the opportunity to express my concerns and thoughts and worries, he responded in a very positive fashion and soon related to agriculturists from the right perspectives. He soon became accustomed to working with us, and his office was always open to us. We knew he was listening to us and that he respected us. Consequently, you gave him that respect in return."

Above and beyond any problems Ray was having with the Democrats, the economy, or the farmers, many of his biggest critics were Republican legislators. Lots of conservatives saw him as a one-term governor and started running against him immediately. As lieutenant governor and therefore the leader of the senate, Roger Jepsen worked on Ray's legislation, but he privately harped about the governor's lack of legislative experience. Ray stood up to the right wing of the party, led by Jepsen and Speaker of the House Bill Harbor. As Ray now says, "They thought they were going to just be able to tell me what to do. They were wrong."

BOB RAY "Republican legislators had historically been very powerful and dominant. I remember way back when Leo Hoegh lost [*in 1956*] several legislators said, 'We really didn't want him to lose, we just wanted to teach him a lesson.' That's a power they shouldn't have and don't deserve and yet tried to exercise.

"I don't think legislators as a group elect governors, though they can hurt a governor's chances. Their primary concern is themselves, and most of them have to run with the emphasis on their own campaigns. They don't have time to try to influence anybody else's.

"When I got elected there were some old-time Republicans that felt like they were back in the saddle again. They treated me like a youngster. The first thing that disappointed them was when I said we were going to bring back professionalism in government and I wasn't going to put people on the payroll merely because they'd been good Republicans or because they contributed to my campaigns. Early on I announced we were going to keep Bill Forst and Buck Harmon, the heads of the newly reorganized Departments of Revenue and Social Services. They'd been hired by Hughes and immediately my Republican friends in the legislature wanted them thrown out. They wanted their own people, Republicans. I understood that, but I also understood that either I was going to be in control of the executive branch and do something about maintaining professionalism, or creating professionalism, or I was getting out. They eventually left, but that was a real step in the direction towards having competent personnel running state government."

Through good times and bad, the new governor began what would become a long friendship with the statehouse press corps in that first term. He liked most of the regulars, understood their deadlines from his days in the press box with Frosty Mitchell, knew what was expected of them back in the newsrooms. For the first several years in office he held daily press conferences, an oddity then and now, but an effort that assured him of some sort of coverage every day, even if it was simply a paragraph in the *Tribune* announcing "White Cane Day."

JERRY MURSENER "We in the press were sort of used to having Harold Hughes around, who, if you asked, 'Governor, what kind of car do you drive?' he'd say, 'Well, it's a black Chevy, automatic, convertible, 1962 Impala.' With Ray you'd say, 'What kind of car do you drive?' and he'd say 'It's a Chevy.' If you wanted to know what color it was, you'd have to ask. He had a lawyer's mind and he only gave you what he wanted you to know. Of course, that wasn't always conducive to getting the best story, because he left out the facts which might have enhanced his own story. But as the years went by he got much better at telling his whole side of a matter. He learned those kinds of things, and I think his press secretary, Dick Gilbert, had a lot to do with that."

The late 1960s and early 1970s also witnessed an unusual amount of violence and unrest on Iowa's three state university campuses. On many campuses in many states, notably Ohio's Kent State, governors and their National Guard units used unnecessary force to deal with what some political leaders saw as the immoral conduct of students.

There were bombings in Ames, Des Moines, and Iowa City. One night in 1970 several hundred students in Iowa City marched out Highway 218 on their way to block Interstate 80. They were turned back, peacefully, by the Highway Patrol. Bob Ray, in coordination with the Board of Regents and the university presidents, kept the National Guard on alert but off the campuses. There were rumblings from the legislature about sending in the Guard and setting up machine guns on campus. Some wanted to cut appropriations because they didn't approve of the language used on campus. "That's an issue where the conservative stripe in the legislature really showed," says Ray. According to University of Iowa president Willard "Sandy" Boyd, "He seemed to respond in a way that made things better, not worse." University of Iowa student body president in 1970, Bo Beller, a Democrat, said, "I liked him, which many on campus found hard to believe. But he was honest, he had integrity. It was a volatile situation, and I thought Ray went out of his way to meet with the students, listen to them, without trying to get publicity for himself. You may not have seen his hand in things, but he was always tuned in."

One dispute with the local youth, in August 1970, did get the governor in some hot water, with election day just three months away. A Chicago firm, Sound Storms, Inc., had purchased a 220-acre farm near Wadena, in the northeast corner of the state, for $47,000. They were planning a rockfest and anticipating 20,000 to 30,000 people from around the Midwest. It wasn't Woodstock, but many in the state, including seven out of ten Iowans polled by the *Register,* felt it should be stopped.

The weekend came, July 31 through August 2, and the show went on as planned. Attorney General Richard Turner suggested calling out the National Guard and stopping the festival before it got "out of hand." Bob Ray flew to Wadena on Friday to observe the situation. He was not sure the state had any legal right to disperse a crowd attending a private party on private property. Late in the afternoon on Friday, he went out on the stage and addressed the gathering throng, which would soon number nearly 25,000. "I hope you leave here knowing you had a good time," he told them, a message he hoped would be calming but instead was interpreted as an encouragement by the media and opposing politicians.

BOB RAY "I had begged Dick Turner to get an injunction and try and stop it *before* it began. In Chicago the night before, they had a rockfest in a city park and it ended up with overturned police cars and fires. But I decided to go up there and see what it was like. There were thousands of people. We had it blocked off so that cars could not get close to the entrance and people were walking from all over. It was probably 100 degrees. The show was supposed to start at two or three in the afternoon and it was getting late and they hadn't begun.

"I hadn't intended to go on stage, but they pleaded with me because the crowd was kind of restless. I figured I'd better say something, because if there was trouble I would regret not trying to calm things down. I went out on this huge stage and said, 'Look, I don't want what happened last night in Chicago to happen here. These things can get out of hand, so you're here to have a good time, please have a good time, but we want you all to leave knowing you had a good time. Try and stay off the stuff.' There wasn't anybody there who didn't know what I was saying.

"We handled the crowd and all the associated problems without incident. Nobody got hurt, nobody got killed. There were a dozen arrests, but no riot. But the doggone *Register* shot pictures of some junkie selling drugs, hardly mentioned that only twelve people were arrested, and reported that the governor had been there urging these kids to just have a good time. So I became an endorser of Wadena. But I was the guy who had tried to get it stopped and then made arrangements for the Highway Patrol and the DCI [*Division of Criminal Investigation*] to be there.

"I really thought that was going to hurt politically. Three days later I went into the hospital; I'd had a gallbladder attack. So Roger [*Jepsen*], of course, was going around saying, 'I don't know why the governor does things like that,' and that he was going to take charge. It was a miserable time for me. I never apologized for what I said or did, but by the time I got out of the hospital Roger had had his say and it was old news. Nobody wanted to hear my side."

BOB BURLINGAME "That was also the summer of the notorious rock festival up in northeastern Iowa, at Wadena. It unquestionably cost him votes, not only with the right wing of the Republican party but geographically as well, because [*of the*] strong conservative Lutheran population in that part of the state. The first picture in the *Register* the following day was of Robert conversing with a scantily clad young gal."

DONALD KAUL "It was a good piece of work by Ray. There'd been a number of these huge rock festivals, and some of them had turned out rather badly. People in the area and around the state, . . . well, in Iowa they get pretty excited about motorcyclists, hippies, drug-crazed hippies. But he went in there and laid a calm hand on things. He came in very casual, without trying to be a hippie, and, I think, reassured people. That was a move a lot of governors wouldn't have made; they'd have been afraid, for political reasons. With a little risk, he did a good piece of work that day."

While in the hospital recovering from surgery, Bob Ray had time to contemplate the first eighteen months of his governorship. So far, he'd angered many in his own party while winning support from some Democrats by opposing capital punishment, vetoing a wiretap bill, urging the lowering of the voting age from twenty-one to nineteen, and endorsing the supplying of birth-control pills in mental hospitals. He'd spent a lot of time with the Iowa Development Commission planning how to spend the agency's $825,000 budget to encourage people and business to try Iowa. Legislatively, he'd not been a major force, and the state budget did not appear to be balancing. He was awaiting the results of the blue-ribbon panel he'd convened early on to recommend cost-cutting measures.

ART NEU "We in the legislature got to know him pretty well that first term, but I think the public perceived him as kind of a good-looking, genial man but not very tough. But those of us who had gotten to know him realized that underneath that smile he was just as tough as nails when he had to be."

BILLIE RAY "Those were really bad times. He was working really hard, never able to get away from the job, and still people were beating on him all the time. After that first two years I said, 'Forget it. You proved you could win. It isn't worth it.' But we agreed he hadn't accomplished much of what he'd hoped to.

"Bob was and is a perfectionist and very sensitive to criticism. I hated for the newspaper to come in the morning, because he grabbed it first thing to see what was said and how it was reported, and, of course, they were never accurate, according to him."

Governor Ray announced his candidacy for a second term in a speech to the Iowa Federation of Republican Women at the Hotel Kirkwood on March 6, 1970. He credited his administration with working with the legislature to enact several programs, including tuition grants for needy private-school students, bonding authority for state universities, elimination of the controversial sales-tax credit, and substantial increases in education and welfare programs. "But our most important accomplishment has been holding down spending and balancing our budget," he closed.

VIII:
RAY
VERSUS
FULTON,
1970

G ubernatorial elections came up hard and fast in those days and it was hard not to feel like the campaign never ended. A handful of legislators and party regulars had hoped that either Roger Jepsen or Congressman Bill Scherle would challenge Ray for the Republican nomination, but neither came forward. On the Democratic side, Bill Gannon, minority leader of the house from Mingo, and Bob Fulton squared off in a June primary. Fulton squeaked by with a slim 1,900-vote margin.

Although he wasn't winning the highest marks around the statehouse, Ray's public approval rating hovered around 60 percent. By October public opinion polls showed him substantially ahead of Fulton. But the farmers, propelled by the property-tax issue, continued to gang up on Ray, and Fulton was gaining.

Fulton was closely tied to the state Democratic party. He'd run Hughes's victorious 1968 Senate campaign and was acknowledged by friends and foes as one of the best minds in state government. One year older than Ray, he'd served in the house and senate before being elected lieutenant governor in 1964. He and his fellow Democrats were after Bob Ray to raise the state sales tax from 3 percent to 4 or 5 percent to help bring down property taxes and stave off potential budget cuts. Ray refused. Under Hughes, state sales and income taxes had been raised by more than $110 million, and a $112-million surplus had been exhausted.

Robert Fulton. *Des Moines Register* photo. Reprinted with permission.

Much of that money went to local schools in increased state aid, with the hope that it would help replace property taxes. But most local school boards had spent the additional state aid, increased their budgets, and raised local taxes. Fulton claimed that Ray was responsible for the increased property taxes because he didn't have a solution, and Ray argued that he didn't control property taxes, because they were levied by local governments.

In a September debate at the Hotel Savery, Fulton made a slashing attack on Ray. "We've got a Twentieth Century Pontius Pilate who looks at part of the problem and then dips his hands in water and says he's not responsible," he declared.

BOB FULTON "In 1970 Bob Ray had only been in state government for two years. He was still learning, his knowledge of state government still developing."

MARVIN SELDEN "Bob Fulton and I were close friends and I was probably closer to him than I was Bob Ray at the time, because if ever a guy was groomed to be governor, it was Bobby Fulton. He was talented and he would have made a good governor. The only thing about Bob Fulton was that politically he was lazy, and he didn't have that inner drive or killer instinct. But he was sharp as nails."

TOM URBAN "Bob Fulton could have beat him if we had just believed in ourselves. One of the difficulties was that the Democrats in Iowa at that point did not have leadership, and we didn't put up very good candidates. We had a couple good candidates for the [U.S.] Senate seats, and it was as if we said, 'Well, we've got the senate, we'll let Ray have the governor's seat.' "

TOM WHITNEY "I spent some time on the road working for the election of Tom Urban as governor in 1970 and still believe that if he'd run, Bob Ray would have been a one-term governor.

"Urban was interested. We traveled to the Quad Cities, met with a number of financial people who were willing to support him. Unfortunately, Pioneer Hi-Bred International was in trouble at the time, and my impression was that Tom had essentially been told by Pioneer, 'You come back to the company now and do what we need to have done or the door is closed.' "

TOM URBAN "I spent a couple months traveling around the state visiting with Democrats and Republicans, talking about the direction of the state, and went through that whole process. The issue was that I'd come to think that the problems of the cities and towns in the state were absolutely enormous, and it was clear that Bob Ray didn't think so. It was on that basis that I felt the urge to try and change the tone of the state's leadership.

"But when I went out there and talked, I found that I was tired. I'd been mayor of Des Moines for four years and it was a very, very difficult four years. I was pooped, and in retrospect I'm delighted I didn't, because it would have been a disaster for me. I was not ready."

BILLIE RAY "That first reelection was the hardest and closest. One reason was because people thought Bob ought to be more like Harold Hughes, and when he was more laid-back or his voice was less booming, they didn't consider him as strong."

BOB RAY "I was so involved in governing, and was being bombarded from every direction, that I wasn't doing anything about the campaign. John Murray had joined us, and fortunately he was astute enough to know that we couldn't wait until October of the election year to get something going, so he went out and got us a campaign manager."

DUTCH VERMEER "Bobby Fulton was a sharp politician and a good man, probably the most competent of anybody the governor ever ran against. We had some problems in that first campaign, too. Our first, and part-time, campaign manager, Joe Flatt, had a heart attack during the first couple months of the campaign. John Murray was on board as the governor's executive assistant, and he decided we really needed a full-time campaign manager."

JOHN MURRAY "One of the things Bob Ray wanted me to do was take charge of the campaign; he said that to me over and over. He was spending all his time on the governorship, and while he considered himself an expert in campaigning, he was too preoccupied to get anything done. By the time I arrived in June, the campaign was in awful shape, and it was getting late.

"I quickly assessed that the executive assistant from his office was not the person to be running the campaign, so I contacted Mike Getto. He had worked for [Nelson] Rockefeller in Kansas, and that's how I knew him."

MIKE GETTO "John called me up in August of 1970 and said, 'I'm working for Bob Ray and we're having some troubles. In fact, he's in the hospital with gallbladder problems right now. Can you come help?' So I drove up to Des Moines from Kansas City and went to see the governor in the hospital. Next thing I knew, I was the campaign manager. I don't think Ray had a lot to do with it. John just decided.

"I had never even been to Iowa before. I'd never had total charge of a campaign before. I came up in August, state fair time. But John knew the players, the county chairmen. We moved into the Hotel Savery, where the campaign headquarters were. I had a secretary and we just went after it."

JOHN MURRAY "I knew my own limitations, and one of them is not loving the hoopla of a campaign, but that was important, especially in a Bob Ray campaign. Mike was highly organized and he structured a campaign, almost from zero, within weeks. All of a sudden there was activity, it was organized."

MIKE GETTO "We had two full-time secretaries and one volunteer from Drake who was real good, Tom Thoren. Once in a while Bob Burlingame would come in—we had a desk for him—and write stuff for us, do research. We didn't have any paid field staff; we just relied on county coordinators. You can imagine the shape they were in when in August they didn't even have an office, no campaign staff."

JOHN MURRAY "There was a residual amount of support out there for Ray, but he had developed a reputation as a vacillator, that he couldn't make up his mind. That's another reason Mike Getto was so good for him—he was organized and could orchestrate neat events. Plus he could get along with and schedule Jan Van Note and the Ray Girls, got them going around the state, bringing back some of the pizzazz and bounce that the 1968 campaign had.

"One of Ray's faults was that he liked to dabble too much in the campaign, and one of the benefits of that summer was that he was in no condition, healthwise, and was just trying to catch up in the office. I had heard horror stories from Clayton Ringgenberg about what was in his office—piles, stacks, of unanswered letters which he wanted to reply to and sign himself. He just didn't have time to make all those decisions."

MIKE GETTO "The governor did get out a lot; he wasn't reluctant to campaign. But one of their concerns was that he would try and direct the campaign too much. I remember sending Dutch Vermeer around the state a lot. He was in touch with a lot of different Republicans that the governor didn't have contact with. *How much of a presence was your opposition?* Well, if you hadn't reminded me of his name, I would have forgotten it. I don't remember seeing much of him. They had a debate, but I don't remember much about it. I just don't remember much conflict between the two. Maybe if Fulton had run a different, more aggressive campaign, we might have had more conflict."

JIM FLANSBURG "There were a couple things happening that year. The state budget forecasts were going straight to hell. That was no surprise to most people, because there's a loose connection between hog prices, which were way down, and state tax returns. And Ray is claiming he inherited the bankrupt system. He explained that Hughes built up these programs and departments and didn't plan for revenue; that was his escape. There was something to that, except that two years earlier he would have been crawling on his knees to get a huge tax rebate. In any case, in that fall of 1970 Ray did not have a clear grasp of the interrelationship of the Iowa economy and agriculture. And it was really remarkable that he didn't get beat, because he didn't take that seriously. Moreover, Fulton was coming with better treasury estimates outside than Ray could get inside."

MARVIN SELDEN "Fulton was out there telling people the state was in a lot worse shape than we said it was. As it turned out, the debts didn't show up until a little later. But, you know, there was never a governor who told me to make things look good. Ray especially was very forthright – he wanted to know how things really were, no politics."

BOB FULTON "He was tough to argue with sometimes, because he was doing some things I agreed with. He was changing the liquor commission around. I agreed with that. I agreed with him on the wiretap bill. I couldn't easily say that you should elect me because I'm nicer than Bob Ray, because I didn't even believe that.

"We had some debates, and I tried to get him mad. I have a tendency to be very combative. So after the first debate he wouldn't talk to me. That was the time I called him a Pontius Pilate. Most people thought Pontius Pilate was a bad man – really, he was just a guy who didn't accept his responsibility. Anyway, that burned him up, mainly, I think because the press was there and they laughed.

"The main problem with Bob's administration those first two years was that I knew that by not doing anything with taxes – either raising them or reducing spending – we were going to go broke. They knew that, Marv Selden knew that. I can't imagine that Marv wouldn't have gone and told him that, but once I started raising the issue, they couldn't change their stand."

MARVIN SELDEN "Bob Ray would be out campaigning and we'd get a call. He'd say, 'Bob Fulton just came out and said this or that, and I want to be reassured that your figures are right.' Bob Ray was real worrier. 'Now you're sure on this?' he'd ask. Even after you were sure, you had to be right."

DUTCH VERMEER "Bob Ray had a knack at campaigning, and the public just liked him. When he'd come out on stage they'd just applaud and applaud. It was really tough on whomever he was running against; that bothered them. But Bobby Fulton was a tough campaigner."

BILL JACKSON "I don't remember that first campaign being any more frantic than those that followed; I guess they were all a little frantic. But Bob Ray never treated any election or primary, whatever the circumstances, lightly. You put your best and fastest and hardest foot forward all the time."

BOB FULTON "I ran as if I was a continuation of the Hughes term, which wasn't the smartest thing in the world. Tom Higgins, my press secretary, could see it, because he was a little detached. Park Rinard couldn't see it, because from his perspective that was that best thing you could possibly be anyway."

MIKE GETTO "Because of his connections, we did a lot of radio advertising. And we kept playing that Marilyn Maye song all the time. We had that tape, and every time we went to a parade or anything like that, we played it. 'Let a Winner Lead the Way.' Along with the Ray Girls, that was the big hit at a lot of county fairs and parades."

FROSTY MITCHELL "There was another song I suggested using that campaign. Tammy Wynette had this great country song, really a crossover of pop and country, which would have been great for an incumbent: 'Stand by Your Man.' What more could you want in Iowa than a crossover pop/country song for a guy who has been a popular governor, and all the radios are singing 'Stand by Your Man'? It would have been a great campaign slogan. I not only pitched it to Bob Ray and lost, then I tried to sell it to Jack Miller."

TOM THOREN "I started out as just sort of a volunteer and pretty quickly became an assistant to Mike Getto. He would be taking off to go on the road somewhere and he'd say, 'We need to call all the Ray chairmen in the state, and I've only reached fifteen of them, so start calling them.

"There's a vast difference between those campaigns and those today. We recorded contributions not because we had to but so that we could get them thank-yous and hit them up again. But it wasn't mandatory. It was pre-mass mailing. We would do a mailing of five hundred and that was our direct mail effort.

"On a one-to-ten scale, that campaign was probably a five in terms of organization."

TOM WHITNEY "Bob Fulton made the decision late in the campaign that he didn't want to go into debt. We really wanted to borrow some money to do some television advertising, and we went to Bob and said, 'Look, we can win this thing, but we've got to borrow some money.' Bob said, 'No, if I have to choose between being in debt and being governor, I'd rather not be in debt.' It was a personal choice.

"Bob Fulton could have been an incredibly good governor. And if he had been able to get his message across, over the television, in those last seven to ten days of the campaign, who knows that would have happened, because he was cooking and Ray was in trouble."

BOB FULTON "I was campaigning on the issue that the state was broke, and I finally convinced the press of that in the last two weeks of the campaign. That was my fault; I thought everybody understood me, but they just weren't listening. Finally George Anthan at the *Register* said to me, 'Bob, are you really saying accountingwise that we're not going to have any money in the treasury?' I said, 'Exactly.' Well, he went down and put Marv Selden on the spot, and though they couldn't document it, they did a good job reporting it, and that's really the only reason I came close.

"One night about two weeks before the election, I was having dinner with Anthan and [*Jim*] Flansburg, and I was raising hell with them. Flansburg said, 'Your problem is you assume we know as much about government as you do.' He said I should have done a background paper for them on the issue. I should have, but I didn't have the staff, only about three people for a statewide campaign. I think we spent $80,000 on that campaign."

BOB RAY "Fulton was painting a picture that we were in deep trouble, and while we did not get the revenues we anticipated, we were never in the dire condition he claimed. So there was truth to what he was saying, but there was no truth to the claim that we were covering up something or not being honest about our projections. I never told Marv to hide something; I always told him to give me any bad news quickly. I wanted to be the first to know."

CLARK RASMUSSEN "Bob Ray was very vulnerable in 1970, and we would have beat him if we'd had a little more money. We only lost by 35,000 votes, and we didn't really have the money to get our message across to the media. We also had a hard time getting Bob Fulton to campaign the way he should have. We had a chance to get Ray that year, we really did, but I guess we didn't realize it until it was too late."

BOB FULTON "I was surprised I came that close. When the last Iowa Poll came out, I was behind 48 to 32 percent. It would be a lot different campaign today. The press could have been more aggressive. There'd have been page one stories in the *Register* detailing my claims that the state was broke. They weren't doing anything immoral or anything, they were trying to win. And with the fiscal year ending in June and the election being in November, they didn't really have to release things. They'd have a harder time of that today."

GERRY RANKIN "The *Register* predicted that Bob Ray would win by 20 percent or something. He won by 2 percent. I could have sunk Ray, because the Democrats were in my office pleading with me to release the revenue estimates that I had. I just refused to do it, because it would have politicized the office of the Legislative Fiscal Bureau. But if I had released those revenue projections, Fulton would have been governor. Remember, Marv Selden was employed by the governor, and I think Marv played the political game. He would probably deny that all the way, of course."

BOB FULTON "On election eve I came to the conclusion I had lost way before he came to the conclusion he had won. I stayed in Waterloo, and I could tell by the way the Waterloo figures were coming in that I was close. But then I called down to Des Moines, and Bob just clobbered me in Des Moines and Iowa City."

BOB RAY "We got some things going, but it really was not a well-run or good campaign. It's funny how reporters like to remember that first reelection. They talk about how Bobby Fulton really did things well and gave me such a scare. That really wasn't the case.

"That was the year to throw out incumbents. Republicans lost governors in South Dakota, Nebraska, Minnesota, Wisconsin, Illinois, and

Oklahoma. Everybody in the Midwest went down except me. I was lucky to escape, especially since we just didn't have much of a campaign. I don't remember anything spectacular that Bobby Fulton did, or anything unusual.

"I felt extremely fortunate that I survived, but I don't think it had much to do with the campaign or me. They were just throwing out governors, especially Republican governors."

BOB BURLINGAME "The night of that election Robert and Rand Petersen and Frosty were making their rounds at the Hotel Savery, and I was up in the headquarters room. The phone rang and the voice said it was Bob Fulton's campaign manager. This was about 9:30, 9:45, and he said, 'Mr. Fulton would like to speak to Governor Ray and extend his congratulations.' I said, 'Well, the governor isn't here; he's out around the hotel. But I will undertake to locate him and have him return your call.'

"I got ahold of his press secretary, Bill Thompson, and told him Fulton's office had called to concede. Thompson reported back that Robert was not going to accept his concession; he wouldn't call him back. The phone rang again and it was the Waterloo headquarters. I was stalling the guy at the other end and finally he said, 'Goddamit, I don't want to talk to you. Fulton wants to talk to the governor.' Ray refused to talk. So Thompson rounded up Rand Petersen, who said he'd see what he could do. They finally got him to make the call, but it was not easy.

"Robert is not a good loser. He wants to win, and he's as capable as most people who come to that kind of job or stature are of playing hardball. He was extremely disgruntled with Murray, me, and others that he did not win against Fulton with a greater bang. He blamed the staff for his not winning by a bigger margin. He made his dislike, his dissatisfaction, clear not by breaking arms or anything but just by being aloof."

BOB RAY "About 10 P.M. they were predicting me the winner, but I only had something like a 10,000-vote margin. I don't remember what percentage of the precincts were in, but I said, 'I'm not going to make any statement, because I could still lose.' The networks predicted me a winner and wanted a statement, but I refused. I don't think I left my room at the Savery to accept the win until after midnight."

BOB TYSON "We were at the governor's mansion at two in the morning, and Bob was complaining that the margin wasn't big enough. I said, 'Stop and look. You're the only Republican governor left between Michigan and Colorado.'"

Ray carried the big cities and county seats and squeaked by Fulton by 34,000 votes, the closest election of his gubernatorial career. A third candidate, Robert Dilley, representing the American Independent party, grabbed over 18,000 votes. Fulton showed well in the rural counties but was hurt in the cities by his suggestion that taxes might need to be raised. A potential third term lay ahead for Ray—just two years off—and even as they packed up the voting booths in 1970, two prominent Republicans were already making noises about challenging the incumbent—Roger Jepsen and Attorney General Richard Turner.

BOB RAY "After that near defeat, I decided that if I were to run again I was going to be organized. I didn't want to find myself at 10 P.M. on election night refusing to go down and accept the victory. But I take the blame for not asserting myself and not preparing, not planning for the campaign. I promised myself that wasn't going to happen again."

ROGER JEPSEN "I know by personal witness and testimony, the staffs in your office and on your campaign—whether you're running for governor or lieutenant governor or president—the staffs are the ones that really get fired up. And it was hard to neutralize my staff in 1970. I'd been declared the winner by an overwhelming majority about ten minutes after the polls closed, and the governor was not a clear winner until I think ten the next morning. [*Jepsen clobbered Iowa City legislator Minnette Doderer by 85,000 votes.*] My staff saw that and got excited. Of course, they weren't party to the agreement that had been made that if I didn't challenge the governor in 1970, the Ray people would back off and help me in 1972."

IX:
THE SECOND
TERM,
1971-1972

Bob Ray claims the toughest year of his gubernatorial career was 1980, when he was forced to go back and cut close to $200 million from his budget to keep the state in the black. A continually worsening farm economy, drained by the dual despairs of the 1970s—high inflation and high interest—was destroying families, farms, and businesses, and the state's pocketbook was bearing the brunt of the disaster. Ironically, the other "toughest" year of Ray's fourteen-year governance was also due to problems on the farm. After his second election, in 1971, the governor was quickly forced to the drawing board to come up with a plan to pay the state's bills and save face.

All through the 1970 campaign Bob Fulton had predicted that the revenues Ray and comptroller Selden were anticipating would not be there. But Ray and Selden at first stood by the anticipated $1.25 million surplus they expected to be on hand by the end of the fiscal year, June 30, 1971. In October of the election year, however, Selden had lowered his estimate of the surplus to $782,000, and legislative fiscal director Gerry Rankin

"The State of the State" address, 1971. *Des Moines Register* photo. Reprinted with permission.

was quoted at the time as saying that "there won't be any balance." Still, candidate Ray repeated that the state was in the black.

On January 27, 1971, two weeks after he was sworn in for a second term (this time by Chief Justice of the Supreme Court C. Edwin Moore, whom Ray, as a young lawyer, had argued before), the governor announced a change in those revenue predictions. Marvin Selden now told him they'd be about $11 million short. Within two months the estimated deficit climbed to $25 million. Bob Fulton was angry: "This indicates that both Bob Ray and I knew the status of the treasury during the campaign last fall. The only difference between us is that I told the people prior to the election and Ray told them after the election. I think this is what makes people lose faith in the system, when you wait to tell the truth until after you've won the office." Bob Ray countered, "I was as truthful as I could be at campaign time. Our revenue projections had showed some drops, but it did not look like there would be a deficit." Fulton responded, "They deliberately misled the people on the status of the treasury."

Bob Ray blamed a sour national and state economy for the revenue slowdown. Revenues from state sales and income taxes were not what they had projected, as collections in the last quarter of 1970 were down. The state's population growth was slow; it was time to reapportion, and the state would lose a congressional seat. Less human labor was needed in agriculture, and this led to big declines in the rural population. Unemployment was at a thirteen-year high of 4.9 percent. Standing beneath a smiling picture of President Nixon, Rob Ray asked in his second inaugural that taxation, education, and transportation be the state's priorities. He urged the president to hasten federal revenue sharing. Soon after that message the governor's popularity fell to a career low of 41 percent. Among farmers, hard-hit by still-rising property taxes and declining incomes, it was 31 percent. State Democratic chairman Clif Larson spoke for the majority of Iowans when he claimed, "There is no way to solve the state's problems and not raise taxes."

BOB FULTON "Right after the election, the *Register* ran an editorial claiming the state of the treasury couldn't be as good as Ray said. I called up Gil Cranberg and asked that if it came out that there was a deficit over $5 million, would they publicly apologize to me for not listening during the campaign. They didn't, obviously."

MARVIN SELDEN "Predicting revenues was one of my biggest responsibilities. That's the nuts and bolts of the whole game. And I never had a governor tell me how to arrive at those figures, or what numbers to put in the slots. They would ask me how I arrived at my conclusions, but I always felt their questioning was not so much doubt but merely a need to know. It was going to be their name in the paper."

GERRY RANKIN "I knew before the election there was going to be a deficit. Early in 1971 I put out a news release predicting if the governor's budget was adopted, there would be a $25 million deficit. I got a phone call from Bob Ray. He said he wanted to see me down in his office. I went down to the lower office, figuring he'd be backed up by fourteen lieutenants and Selden, but he was in there by himself. He said, 'Gerry, how'd you come to that conclusion?' I had my files sent down and I went over it with him and he said, 'I think you're right.' On that basis he sent a revised message to the legislature. I think I gained a lot of Bob Ray's respect then."

MARVIN SELDEN "Francis Messerly of Waterloo and John Camp from Clinton County, budget chairmen in the senate and house, privately predicted we'd come up short, and they were right. We were all guessing a little bit. We thought the revenues would come back, but they didn't. I had to prepare a statement for the press for Bob Ray explaining the expected $17-million shortage. He was waiting for me by the circular stairs leading up to where they were waiting, and we visited about it briefly. He put his hand on my shoulder and he said, 'God, Marv, you ought to be a good enough accountant to make this work out.' That was a real challenge.

"I'm an accountant, not really a theorist, but I made some calls, got ahold of the head of the accounting department at the University of Michigan and also Al Augustine, Mr. Accountant for the Iowa Democrats, and worked out a new tax plan. Bob Ray was the happiest guy in the world when I showed it to him. And so was I. John Camp came in to look it over and said, 'I knew that son of a bitch would make it, but I didn't know how.' That was the highest compliment I was ever paid."

In order to balance the $500-million annual state budget, as required by law, Ray and Selden urged the legislature to freeze property taxes, increase state income and corporate taxes by 33 percent, and raise state cigarette taxes from ten to thirteen cents. He conducted extensive budget briefings with his department heads and encouraged the legislature to adopt his proposals quickly, including a complicated school aid plan that would shift a substantial part of local costs for education from the property tax to the income tax. He hoped to raise an additional $56 million in 1972.

BOB RAY "There had been a little dip in property taxes in the late 1960s, but it tapered off and then shot right back up, primarily because there had previously been no control over what the schools could spend. They got a bunch of money from the state, and the next year they expected the same and more, whether they needed it or not. At the same time, the farmers were giving me a real hard time because of the high property taxes. To complicate things further, the Supreme Court had just ruled that you had to provide reasonably equal amounts of money for each student, all the way from the very poor to the very rich school districts. We needed to come up with a way to address all those things at the same time, which resulted in the school aid formula.

"That was my worst session. Nobody blamed me for creating the problems, but they sure blamed me for not doing something about it. I couldn't just snap my fingers and say, 'Okay, don't pay property taxes.' The pressure was on. Everybody had talked about solving these problems for years, and nobody had yet come up with a reasonable plan. Marv Selden did a lot of work to put the plan together. It wasn't perfect, it didn't make everybody happy, but it solved the problem. But when I submitted it to the legislature there wasn't one vote for it, not a single one.

"None of the leaders in the legislature wanted to go with it, and everybody started working on their own plans. But they were not well thought, they had not done their homework and research, and in fairness to them, they didn't have the capabilities. They had no idea how much work and effort and expertise and man-hours went into that proposal. It doesn't sound that difficult today, but it was then. It was plowing new ground.

"Everybody thought they'd come up with a more simple plan; ours was too complex. They wanted to raise the sales tax by one cent and give it all to the schools. They were under fire too; they knew they had to do something.

"It was about that time I was learning that you have to let certain ideas run a course. You can't always force things, because if you make people angry by always demanding to have your way, your successes will be limited. Sooner or later, if you're right, they'll come around to your way of thinking. So I tried to be tolerant, and I remember saying many times, 'If there is a better answer, I want to know what it is. We want the best program. I've given you the best we can put together, but maybe there's something we missed.' That approach is somewhat disarming.

"After a long, bitter session they discovered that simply adding a tax would not sustain the program. They eventually accepted and adopted our plan. Over the years I was always tickled listening to legislators go out and talk about what a great solution to a very serious problem the formula was. You'd have thought anyone who eventually ended up voting for it had initiated it."

WYTHE WILLEY "The key to that plan is that it solved the problem and solved it for a decade. Number one, the school foundation plan put the money where the students are. It turned out to be a model for state-funded education around the country. It also got the state around later court cases in other states that said all children have a right of access to equal education. The plan helped eliminate rich school districts and poor school districts. And even though it took a tax increase, he never had to raise taxes again. When he solved the problem, he solved it for a long time. It was very important to his administration."

ANDY VARLEY "That was probably the toughest battle fought in my twelve years in the legislature. I was majority leader, and there were several plans being tossed around the legislature. Roger Jepsen had one and some followers, but I was very much on the Ray side."

DEL STROMER "I had put together a plan without a computer, without a calculator, primarily in a tractor cab, that guaranteed quite a little increase in state aid for a lot of school districts. He probably didn't tell you this, but when I introduced my plan, it got more votes than his, because I had a coalition of Republicans that, combined with the Democrats, could block just about anything. Well, Bob Ray called me down to his office. His right-hand man, Maurie Van Nostrand, was there, and they said, 'Stromer, how the hell do you make your plan work?' After some conference committees and haggling Ray ran with my plan, said it was his. That never bothered me, though, because the people in education knew who had developed the plan."

NORM JESSE "The legislature was struggling with the school aid plan long before they even heard of Bob Ray. From the first day I was there we struggled with it—what should be the proper course, whether it should be Stromer's plan or some other. That took place over years. It happened to take place during Ray's administration, but I wouldn't give him any credit for it whatsoever."

No matter its origin, Ray was able to get the school aid plan spelled out and enacted. Its strength was twofold. First, its passage slowed property tax increases which made the farmers happy. Second, it increased state support of public education, which made lots of people happy. Prior to this legislation, the schools were supported primarily by property tax revenues. The farmers agreed to the shift in income tax that accompanied the plan because it reflected their earnings, not their holdings. The bill also allowed for greater predictability in future revenue forecasting and enhanced long-range planning for the school districts. By the third year of its life, 80 percent of the cost of public schools in Iowa was paid by the state, and this guaranteed each school district, regardless of its local resources, the funds to finance the cost of instruction.

BOB RAY "It was really a gigantic step forward, and we became a leader in the country for school financing. But I think that was an example of something we did because we thought it was right, not because it necessarily had popular support. To many it just appeared we were raising taxes, but it was the best thing that could have been done." [*By 1986 state government was pumping $740 million into the public schools, the state's largest single expenditure, and changing times required revisions in the fifteen-year-old statute due to shifts in the population and declining property tax revenues.*]

JIM FLANSBURG "That same session, Ray's understanding of agriculture changed dramatically. He really learned the relationship of agriculture, farm prices, and the state treasury, learned that for the state to be successful, agriculture had to be successful. He also learned who the important people in agriculture were and plugged them into his kitchen cabinet, if not the formal Ray organization."

BAXTER FREESE "The problems that developed in agriculture were really out of his control, as they are today. The governor and legislature really can't control them. But they need to do everything within their limits to help agriculture.

"In the early years of his terms, it was obvious that he lacked an agricultural background, but he picked it up quite rapidly. Actually, we were better off without a farmer in the governor's seat, because a nonfarmer has a little more credibility with the consumer than a farmer does. It was more important to us to have somebody who was articulate and could communicate with the bureaucrats and the consumers for us.

"I worked quite closely with him in that second term trying to get property tax relief. In fact, there was a group of us that tried to help him. I guess all of us had selfish interests to a degree. Those of us in the cattle business were trying to get some tax relief, same for the corn and soybean and hog people. But we spent an equal amount of our time working on not only tax relief but with Del Van Horn at the Development Commission on promoting agricultural products. Ray was always willing to give us time for that."

JOHN SOORHOLTZ *By his own admission it took him a while to catch on to all the problems facing agriculture?* "Well, he was not alone in that respect. But he tried, probably beyond the call of duty, to gain a better insight. Farming goes in cycles, and he understood that there would be peaks and valleys and that you couldn't overreact. You need to bring forth programs and assistance that will be long-term rather than short-term, reactionary programs."

WYTHE WILLEY "After the 1970 election, the two guys on the governor's staff with agricultural ties, Dutch Vermeer and I, started working the commodity groups. We wanted to increase Bob Ray's popularity with them.

"There is an interesting relationship between the Ray governorship and the emerging strength of the commodity groups in Iowa. Prior to his terms, the Farm Bureau had been the number one agricultural group, always had been. But the Farm Bureau has a number of self-conflicting problems because it represents so many different people. Cattlemen, pork producers, turkey raisers, corn growers, soybean growers, dairymen— the Farm Bureau represents all of them, plus insurance companies, co-ops, and a tremendous number of nonfarm members. But in the mid-seventies there was a tremendous interest in the specific commodity groups, and they grew stronger.

"The Iowa Cattlemen's Association were big Bob Ray backers. They gave him free cowboy boots, and when he retired they threw a huge party down at the Amanas and said the greatest things about him. The Pork Producers were strong for him. The Iowa Corn Growers and the Soybean Association all accepted him, became very good allies. And he did a lot for them, things that were good for the state, too.

"Remember, this was that 'Des Moines lawyer,' and there was initially a lot of distrust. But as he spent some time with John Soorholtz of the Pork Producers, Baxter Freese of the cattlemen, and others, they warmed up to him. They had some battles, but he was pretty straightforward and frank with them, and they appreciated that. He got a chance to grow on them, and once he was on their good side they became very supportive. That was a good, sound core of support."

JIM FLANSBURG "The second thing Bob Ray learned in 1971 was also the result of the embarrassment of the deficit. He immediately forced better treasury estimates, better fiscal reporting in state government. And from there it seems to me the Ray governorship was basically one long list of successes."

With the budget balanced, 1972 got off to a much smoother beginning than the first three years of the Ray governorship. In his State of the State address that year Ray also firmly established his moderate approach to state government, outlining a twenty-five–point legislative agenda many assumed had been secretly written by a Democrat. His "priority issues" for that session of the Sixty-fourth General Assembly were to tighten control of information in the state's crime computers, legalize bingo, liberalize Iowa's abortion laws, grant a bonus reward to the state's Vietnam veterans, gain majority rights for eighteen-year-olds, authorize health maintenance organizations, provide better financing for the Iowa Civil Rights Commission, improve prison conditions, pass a collective bargaining law and no-fault insurance legislation, and organize a statewide voter registration drive. State Senator Jim Schaben listened to the speech and said afterwards, "He'd run as a Democrat if he thought he'd get elected."

Looking back, Ray gives a lot of credit to his staff for improving the public image of the governor's office. Dutch Vermeer was still his liaison upstairs in the legislature, but three new, young staffers – Wythe Willey, his new executive assistant, a cattleman, lawyer, and office politico; Dick Gilbert, who'd left the early staff and then returned as press secretary; and Bill Jackson, who did the governor's scheduling – had shaped the office into an efficient, better-oiled operation. "We were simply forcing Bob Ray to be Bob Ray," says Gilbert, a professed twenty-four-hour-a-day Ray cheerleader.

Ray was also beginning to ply his smooth manner on the national scene, conferring with Richard Nixon on many Washington, D.C., trips and leading a delegation of eight governors on a twelve-day trip to Japan to calm the Japanese leaders after Nixon reopened diplomatic ties with China. By mid-1972 the governor's approval rating had soared to close to 70 percent.

·

JERRY FITZGERALD "From then on he appeared to be strong, and once you appear to be strong, then you can start using your abilities, because just having the ability frankly isn't enough in politics."

X:
THE
TJERNAGEL
AFFAIR

L ike the plane crash in his first campaign, one event cemented the public's image of a "strong" Bob Ray in 1972, and once again it involved a plane wreck. This time, though, the candidate was not on board. The wreck involved an Iowa Air National Guard jet that demolished the farm home of Peter and Marie Tjernagel near Story City on December 9, 1968. Ironically, on March 5, 1968, another plane crash, this of a Wisconsin Air Guard F102 had taken the home of Emma McCarville of Cresco, and almost four years later there had been no settlement in either case. After many futile attempts by representatives and senators in Washington and Iowa's attorney general, Iowa's governor got involved in the federal-state squabbles, hoping to get the federal government to settle up with the two families. In an unprecedented but legal move on Friday, April 21, Ray grounded all federal aircraft and vehicles assigned to Iowa National Guard units until the federal government paid off the Tjernagels and the McCarvilles.

MARIE TJERNAGEL "It was in the evening, about 6:15, December 9, 1968. We heard this horrible, horrible noise. My daughter had just looked in the oven to see if dinner was ready. My one son was out in the barn finishing

Marie Tjernagel. *Des Moines Register* photo.
Reprinted with permission.

up chores, and the other son was helping his father, an invalid, into a wheelchair to come to dinner.

"She was just raising herself from the oven and everything just boomed. The telephone flew across the kitchen, all the windows caved in, and a big ball of fire rolled between me and her. It burned my hands, and my hair was scorched. There was fire all over and we had to go all through the house to the south door to get out. My son, who was outside, was thrown forty feet. All the windows in the car outside were blown out and it was on fire.

"While I was at the hospital, right after the crash, a nurse said that they'd already had a call from the Pentagon, asking about the condition of the family. To me that was fantastic; it hadn't even been a half hour. It was an Iowa plane with federally employed men in it. And that's what took so long, because the state of Iowa wanted to have the federal government pay, and the federal government wanted the state of Iowa to pay.

"My husband died fifty-two days after the crash. I thought they were related, but the doctor and the government wouldn't go along with that. I got very tired of fighting after a while."

JOHN BEAMER "I was the head of the tort division of the attorney general's office at that time, which defended the state in tort litigation. We investigated both the Tjernagel crash and the other case up in Cresco about the same time, involving a Wisconsin jet. That was the McCarvilles, where the lady ended up living in a chicken coop. Everybody was screaming that the Air Force should pay and I kept pushing it, trying to get something resolved.

"I thought it was the Air Force's responsibility to pay because it was a training mission to shoot down Russian aircraft. It had nothing to do with state business. I spent a long time myself on both cases, and Nick Lamberto at the *Register* kept writing stories about it, and eventually the governor's office got involved, in a big way."

MARIE TJERNAGEL "I had to make out a claim listing what we had in the house, listing everything, each pair of socks the kids had, shoes, everything. We had a lot of antique furniture, irreplaceable, and they kept telling me the government doesn't want to pay for sentiment, which really soured me. I wasn't trying to get sentiment out of it; I wanted value, that was all.

"Three years after the accident I had a nephew go to Washington to try and stir things up. He went to H. R. Gross's office and he didn't even know about it. He was my representative. Then I got letters from several congressmen, Harold Hughes was one of them, saying they had proposed legislation to help get us paid. They had made it into a bill. But even I knew that was at the bottom of their priorities.

"When President Nixon came to dedicate Lake Rathbun, Governor Ray spoke to him about the problem, and he said, 'Well, have them write to my press secretary, Ron Ziegler.' So I wrote a letter and mailed it on the twenty-ninth of February in 1972. I sent a copy also to the *Des Moines Register* and they ran it on the front page, March 1. A sociology class at Story City said, 'We're going to help that woman,' and they raised a house-to-house petition, got 15,000 signatures and sent a copy to the governor and to the president. That's when Governor Ray grounded the aircraft."

BOB RAY "It was a new issue to the public, and to me. It had gone on for years, and the military, especially the Air Force, had been leading these people to believe that they were going to take care of it. Two years later they then said they had to go to the state, so the attorney general got involved and [*they*] had come to their end.

"The lawyers couldn't get anything done, and finally they said that the parties should collect from the state of Iowa. That blew everybody's mind, because they were on a federal, or national, mission. The state didn't have any funds to indemnify the loss or damage."

DICK GILBERT "The idea of grounding the National Guard, taking dramatic action through the Guard to bring the feds back to a negotiating position, was Bob Ray's idea. It was not Dick Gilbert's idea or anyone else on the staff.

"We first talked about it on the back stairwell [*of the governor's office*]. He said, 'I'm the commander-in-chief and I can do it.' So we checked on the executive order, put the press conference together, and Dutch started negotiating with the National Guard, Wythe with the feds, who didn't like this at all.

"It was a classic Bob Ray move, a good example of doing the right thing the right way. Everybody woke up and said, 'Wow, a master stroke.' But the fact that it was able to work so well was that we finally had all our ducks in a row. The staff had really come together and the governor was totally confident in himself."

BOB RAY "As commander-in-chief, if I said so they could not move a vehicle. I decided that was the only thing to do. I could write letters, I could threaten to sue, but who knew how long that would take. Just before I grounded the Air National Guard, though, I thought I would pay the courtesy of calling the commander in Washington and advising him and the White House.

"I got a call from a general and he wanted me to think this over carefully and reconsider. He threatened that we were a strong National Guard and that it could have repercussions. I said, 'What you're saying is you're really threatening me, and you're going to take something away from us if I do this.' He said he didn't want it to sound like a threat, but that was the only way I could read it. Finally we got to the heart of the matter. He said, 'Governor, it's important to you, the state, to the National Guard, and this country that you see the big picture.' I said, 'Would you like to come out to the state of Iowa and tell an elderly woman living in a chicken coop exactly what that big picture is? You've destroyed all her property, her home, everything she's worked for, and you say you want me to see the big picture? How would you like to explain that to her? I'll bet you ten-to-one that while you owe her $70,000, you've already replaced the multimillion-dollar jet.' He didn't respond. 'If that had been a Russian jet that destroyed her property, we'd be at war. From her point of view, you are the enemy. So we grounded them.' And I don't think there was a person out of 220 million Americans that thought you could ground the National Guard, least of all me."

JOHN BEAMER "I don't think the feds cared; they just figured we were hurting ourselves. But it got national attention, was written up in *Time.* They were forced to deal with it.

"So we all flew to Washington. We met first at the office of the vice-president, Spiro Agnew, who was the liaison for all the governors, and then we went to the Pentagon, and the Air Force lawyers said, 'Well, there's a remedy against the state.' I said, 'We're not here to talk about legalities, we're here to get compensation.' They didn't resist, and I think they eventually paid around $200,000 to the Tjernagels and the McCarvilles."

BOB RAY "Joe May was the adjutant general at the time, and he and Wythe Willey went to Washington to negotiate. Wythe hadn't been on the staff that long, and I remember we got several calls from people wanting to know why I had sent my 'wife, Billie.' While Joe May couldn't publicly agree with me, I think he was on my side. He felt the people in Washington were responsible. They just couldn't ignore it."

JOHN BEAMER "I've still got a picture on the wall of us in the Pentagon—Wythe, General May, later head of the National Guard, Roger Gilbert. We're all sitting around the room. Spiro Agnew set it up. John Dean was involved.

"I sure appreciated the governor's stepping in, because our legal arguments weren't going anywhere. It seemed like I'd had the whole federal government on my back until Bob Ray came along and relieved that. It was a case I didn't think we'd ever got resolved, but he brought it to a head.

"Those are the kinds of cases that are rewarding, because there was so much doubt and anxiety and work involved. But it turned out well for the families. To be real honest, I didn't think those guys at the Pentagon would fold. But I think the dramatic action of the governor, coupled with the support he got nationally, brought it to a head. I don't know where he thought of the idea, maybe out in the garden, but it was a good one."

BOB RAY "There was a risk, of course. We had a lot of people in Iowa dependent on the National Guard for extra revenue, as a career, the things they advertise. They could have taken that away from us."

BILL JACKSON "It was one of those early things he did that got some action, and we got a lot of press. It showed him to be a firm, decisive leader. You've got to remember that he was following in office Harold Hughes, who was a very dynamic, forceful, deep-voiced, big guy. Bob Ray was obviously not so big, didn't have that rich, deep voice. So I think he was fighting that a little. Grounding the National Guard showed people he could be the type of leader I think most people wanted."

TOM THOREN "I was out campaigning for the governor in Winterset not long after that and was introduced to a farmer on the street corner. He said, 'Oh, I like Ray, you know. He does what he thinks is right. He clobbered the National Guard, and by God, you know, that's the same reason I liked Harold Hughes.' That just epitomized how we were trying to sell Ray, as being quiet but getting the job done, doing things that needed to be done, and that played right along with it."

JERRY MURSENER "The Tjernagel case really set the tempo—you know, 'Boy, if he's going to ground the National Guard for these people, then he'll do it for me.' That's really when he started to develop this rapport with the people. I always had the feeling that people out in the state, the people who called him Bob when we were out campaigning, that when they went to the polls they felt like they'd just voted for their friend Bob. Now, admittedly, most of the people in the state had never met him, but he had this way of conveying this confidence level, and I think the Tjernagel case really got that started."

The quick success of the grounding also had an effect on two challengers to Ray's throne. Another election was bearing down on the governor, and Paul Franzenburg was again going to challenge Ray. But the bigger challenge was being mounted within the governor's own party by his lieutenant governor, Roger Jepsen.

PAUL FRANZENBURG "I was about to make a campaign speech at a Rotary Club in Sioux City when I heard he had grounded the National Guard. It took all the zip out of my speech. It was a normal thing to do, but one had to wonder where the commander-in-chief had been all this time. It happened some years before, remember. But it received a lot of publicity, made him look firm and favoring the underdog. He was a master of that sort of thing, though, a good politician."

ROGER JEPSEN "Ray's campaign people were looking for ways to stop me, and the way to stop me was to change the governor's image. They did it with the grounding of those planes. It was a masterstroke, orchestrated perfectly. He became the governor who poked the nose of the president, stood up against the bureaucracy, and so forth. It was a masterpiece, and he had the machinery geared up. Overnight, every piece of Republican mail going out was about Ray."

DICK GILBERT "It definitely stole some thunder from Roger Jepsen. He and Bob Ray had been going around and around about the reorganization of the Department of Transportation, and Jepsen was going to release his proposal that same weekend that Ray grounded the National Guard. His plan got one paragraph under a twelve-point headline. Ray just knocked him right out of the park, really underscored the power of the sitting governor.

"Most importantly, it created an awareness that here was a governor that was tough, that could stand up for what he believed in, who cared about people that were powerless, and what better group to take on than the military bureaucracy? It was obvious that here was a wrong just crying to be righted."

BOB RAY "Most of the things you do in office aren't the kind of activity that gets big press, and if it does, people don't always understand what you've done, what you went through, or why you did it. This was something they could understand – grinding everything to a halt, which meant that one person became as big as the mighty, powerful military complex. I think they understood that, and I think they kind of cheered it.

"Boy, it made me realize that it's extremely important that the military always be directed by civilians. I would never have dreamed before that incident that the military in our country would intimidate people to the extent that we saw in that incident."

XI: JEPSEN I

Not since Art Donhowe, or perhaps Bill Scherle, had Bob Ray felt so angered by a fellow Republican. He and Roger Jepsen, a forty-three-year-old Davenport insurance man, had never gotten along, despite the fact that they shared the top of the statewide Republican bill for two elections. Their styles were diametrically opposed, and Ray didn't feel the two-term lieutenant governor had ever given him much support in the legislature. Ray's speechwriter and researcher Bob Burlingame pared their relationship to the bone: "There was nobody whose guts Robert Ray hated more than Roger Jepsen's." Like him or not, though, Jepsen was a proven vote-getter with good conservative support throughout the state and a powerful Republican opponent.

ART NEU "Roger entered the legislature the same year I did, in 1966, and was not a particularly distinguished legislator. He wasn't bad, just not very effective. Then he goes out and gets more votes in 1970 than Ray. And once he was elected lieutenant governor and took over the senate, he started running for governor right away. You could see the friction developing between Ray and him right away.

"I didn't see Bob Ray that much at the time I was in the senate, but in caucuses and in small conversations Roger would make clear his unhappiness with some phase of the executive branch and say the governor wasn't providing strong leadership, that kind of thing. It was pretty obvi-

Bob Ray and Roger Jepsen. *Des Moines Register* photo. Reprinted with permission.

ous the two weren't getting along. They were entirely different personalities, and Bob did not even attempt to disguise his dislike for Roger Jepsen. He felt him to be a menace to his personal career, which he tried to be. That was an unforgivable political sin to begin with, but as far as I could tell neither had the slightest empathy for each other emotionally, intellectually, or any way. I think Bob hated his guts. Roger was the number one enemy."

GERRY RANKIN "I'd been in meetings between Ray and Jepsen when I wished I'd been somewhere else. They'd be down in the governor's office, shouting at one another. It was not pleasant. Jepsen was always trying to position himself to come out with something rather dramatic and he could never quite make it. Ray always outmaneuvered him. I was close to Jepsen and I would describe him as a pure politician. Ray was honest-to-God interested in what was happening in Iowa."

MAX MILO MILLS "Roger came in thinking he had beaten the system, including Bob Ray, so he had a chip on his shoulder from the start. Plus he had a patently conspicuous aggrandizement on his own behalf and his political future. Everybody ahead of him was fair game, and he didn't make any secret of it.

"Simultaneously, I don't think he ever politically embarrassed Bob Ray, I don't think they ever had a public falling out. But I carry as a scar several situations where the governor needed something out of the legislature that he couldn't get because he was being cut off by Roger. We used to have parties and our favorite charade would be me and the governor, facing the crowd, with our arms around each other. Then we'd turn around and I'd be holding a knife and the question was, What were the names of these two people? Jepsen and Ray."

ART NEU "There are two kinds of lieutenant governors. There are the kind that are running full-time for governor, and there are the kind who like the legislative end of it and spend a lot of time mastering the legislation and the procedure and staying out in the legislature. I think Bob Fulton and I were the latter kind. Roger was the former.

"Early in the legislative sessions Roger would be active; he would even come to the caucuses sometimes. Then toward the middle and later, when we really got into the legislation and the controversy started, he was out a lot, an awful lot. But still, when he wanted to interject himself into an issue, he was terribly effective because he had a lot of support. I'd say the majority of the Republican caucus supported him when he ran against Ray. And a majority in the house as well. *Why?* I think because as a fellow legislator they viewed him as one of their own. The governor was felt to be too distant, overprotected by his staff. Legislators didn't feel like they had access to him. Roger had an uncanny ability to help them with their political problems; he was good that way. Ray recognized that. Roger had the time and was good at that stuff. The governor can't hold hands, didn't have the time. Philosophically, the older legislators were more comfortable with Roger, more conservative."

BOB RIGLER "Jepsen also had a lot of special-interest groups backing him. In those early days Bob Ray was never really popular with them. We always heard that David Stanley's father was fairly generous in Jepsen's campaigns, and that's why he wanted to reward his son David with the majority leader's job in 1968."

JIM WEST "In 1970, 1971, Ray had all sorts of difficulties with the legislature. That's why the lieutenant governor decided to test the waters. There were a lot of complaints from legislators – Republicans and Democrats – and there were a lot of lobbyists, a lot of Des Moines interests, that were really down on Ray, felt Ray was headed the wrong direction."

KEN JERNIGAN "The fact is that Bob Ray did not sit atop the Republican party despite the fact that he was governor. During his first couple terms he and Roger contended strongly for that leadership, and if there had been a contest between the two in 1970, the outcome of that contest is certainly problematic."

BOB RAY "Roger had a tendency to be sort of intimidating with the senators because he liked and used the power of the office and they were really more accountable to him than to me. They saw him every day and they didn't see me every day. The major problem was that Roger wanted to be governor."

MARVIN SELDEN "I would see Jepsen maybe once a month. I assume he was busy politicking, a pure unadulterated political beast. One night he called me at home, towards the last day of a session, and asked if he could see me first thing the next morning. He and Bill Harbor came in and closed the door and leaned over the desk to me and said, 'What do we have to pass to get this session over with? I don't want any of this long-range planning stuff.' Bob Ray would never have said that. He'd have said, 'You get out when you've passed this and this, and you're staying until then.'"

ROGER JEPSEN "The more successful the legislature was, the more we did, the stronger I became, the worse my relationship with Bob became. They [*the governor's office*] had their machetes out daily. We were heading towards a deficit, and I came out with a major tax reform plan, laid it out on the front page of the *Register*. Bob Ray came back and said I sounded like a Democrat."

ART NEU "The increased exposure of Roger didn't really help Roger any. He would take some positions that were really marginally thoughtful at best. During the student unrest he wanted to go in and crack heads, that sort of thing. At one time or another any politician might get annoyed with the media or a segment of it, but Roger would issue some ringing denunciations of them, claim the colleges were all socialists, the faculties were socialists. Universities and intellectuals really turned him off."

ROGER JEPSEN "Bob was not a very forceful guy when he first went in; he couldn't make decisions. As lieutenant governor 38 out of 50 senators were Republicans, most of them my classmates. The majority leader of the house, Bill Harbor, was my best friend. I think I ran a tight ship.

"Bob just kept not making decisions, and on a couple occasions I probably upstaged him or took off on him a little quickly. I was very romantic—still am—and was very willing to be second man and to serve. All I wanted him to do was simply open the door and let me in. I wanted to be part of the team. Of course, that never happened.

"I was ambitious and I drove hard and worked hard and was very intense and aggressive. It wasn't the easiest thing being governor with me, either, I suppose. I understand all that. But it was two-sided."

BOB RAY "Roger would probably say that he tried, and I certainly would say I tried, but it was not easy for us to work together. He had a different style than I. I can remember meeting after meeting where Roger would come in late and leave early, and during he'd always go make a telephone call. He had a habit of sitting at the end of the table and asking questions which led you to believe he already knew the answers. It was not what you would call a real compatible relationship.

"He had his eye on the governor's office from the very beginning. He asked for his own limousine and driver. He took every speaking engagement available."

ROGER JEPSEN "In 1970, very candidly, the only way that Bob Ray got reelected was because I did what I agreed to do, and that was work hard for the whole team, not challenge him for the nomination. And work hard I did, and the togetherness was fine, because all of the Bob Ray folks were happy. I had announced for lieutenant governor soon after I was first elected in 1968.

"The Ray folks had insisted I announce because they were worried that I was going to run against him in 1970. So I said okay, and six or seven months into my term I announced for reelection. It was really a team effort in 1970, and even with that team effort Bob barely made it."

BOB RAY "Roger used to brag about winning by a bigger margin than I did in 1970. That never bothered me particularly, if it made him feel good. The fact is that the key position outside of the president of the United States, the key political election, is the governor's race. If you've got the governor running and senators running, the governor's race is going to have more focus than the senatorial race. More people know their governor, and the people are interested in their governor. He represents them daily and they feel like they know him, want to know him. It's more exclusive than being a senator. So the money was put in the governor's race, the issues highlighted on the governor's race. I don't think Roger ever had to talk about an issue during his lieutenant governor's race. Mel Synhorst used to take great pride that he was the leading vote-getter in the state. Now, that's wonderful; his name was better known and he campaigned less.

"It always irritated me when Roger would lead people to believe that I would not make a decision. Every time he was given a chance to make decisions, he would back off. But he was gaining a reputation, which he wanted to, of being a strong leader, at the same time contrasting that with me, whom he tried to paint as not strong.

"It was never that I didn't like Roger, it's just that he made it very difficult. There was always the feeling that he was cutting me down without my presence, by innuendo and things of that nature. I remember the time I went to Wadena and came back and went into the hospital with a gallbladder attack. I was in the hospital and a reporter asked Roger what he thought about my going to Wadena. Roger's response was that he didn't know why I was going up to a place like that and affecting his future the way I did. He felt that since we were on the same ticket, if I lost, he'd go down too."

JACK MacNIDER "The feeling in 1969 was that Bob Ray was going to stick around for a couple terms and that Roger better cool his heels. So we were encouraging Roger to announce early for the lieutenant's race and stay the hell out of a 1970 primary."

ROGER JEPSEN "I'll never forget that meeting, up at Governor's Day [*at Clear Lake*], at 2:30 in the morning on MacNider's porch. Senator Jack Miller and a bunch of others were there. They told me that if I would just lay low, stay out of a 1970 primary with Bob, then I could have the governor's race in 1972. Well, they all must have gotten political amnesia."

JACK MacNIDER "We were trying to avoid an intraparty fight. There were five or six of us there. I'm sure the state chairman, John McDonald, was there. Now, we didn't assure him that Bob would get out in the future. All I told him was that if he would go along with our proposal, we would certainly back him in any future endeavors he might have. Not necessarily the governor's race, but for any other political office he might seek. We were trying to get him to cooperate."

BOB RAY "That same Governor's Day, people were coming up and telling me that Roger was touching base with people about running for governor and that they thought they had persuaded him not to. A lot of lobbyists were telling Roger he should run. They worked primarily with the legislature and were big supporters of his. I hate to lump them all together, but some lobbyists love to make a politician feel good. There might have been some that encouraged Roger for their own advantage. I think the signal was loud and clear: They couldn't expect any special favors from me."

ROGER JEPSEN "I just proceeded on that basis, thinking that everything would shake out. I've never talked with Bob about it, and I'm not sure he knew about his lieutenants' promise. But they gave me the impression that it was his desire and his promise.

"He had control of the party machinery from the topside, which I never paid any attention to. That was another dimension of the battle. I kind of wanted to just be around, be on the team, and I would have been happy if they had included me. I remember in those days, frankly, it hurt me to not be included in some things. Everybody would have been better off, including me, frankly and factually, had I been included. But that was not to be. All those years I felt there was a wall in front of that stairway to his office."

BOB RAY "Roger had talked to people about running in 1970, but he never talked to me. Later he told people he backed off so that I could run. In 1972 he felt it was his turn, but he didn't have any agreement with me. I don't know whom he talked to, but he decided to run against me without ever consulting me."

JOHN McDONALD "Had Roger not been quite as aggressive, sought more accommodation rather than confrontation, he might have had more luck. But Bob Ray, given that challenge, was darn well going to run. He really responded."

BOB RAY "I really wasn't sure that I would run for a third term. In those days, two terms was plenty, or at the most, three. And I credit Roger for keeping me in the governor's office. He really made up my mind for me. I didn't have to think about whether I was or wasn't running after that. That was a big turning point. Once Roger decided to challenge me, without ever coming and asking what my plans were, he made my plans for me. That's the kind of challenge I needed."

JOHN McDONALD "The state party didn't take any on-the-record action, but I was always an activist for Bob Ray, and I considered the state headquarters an extension of the governor's office. I'm sure there are people who would disagree with that philosophy, but that's the way I did it. However, at the same time I maintained the independence to run that office as I saw fit. The governor never told me what to do. As far as any official position of the party, there was none. The only official position of the party was that it was our job to preserve incumbencies. I'm sure there was no doubt in anyone's mind what the direction of the state chairman or the state headquarters was in that race. I never had any feeling other than that Bob would run for a third term."

Ray announced his plans to run for a third term in February 1972. If elected, he would be the first Republican elected three times since John Hammill of Hancock County, who was Iowa governor from 1925 to 1931. Jepsen had been out and running for several months, and Ray said of his lieutenant governor when he declared, "I never know the position of Roger on many issues. I've never been able to determine them." The Ray team was chaired once again by Rand Petersen but boasted a new campaign manager, Tom Stoner, a wealthy Des Moines businessman. Robb Kelley, president of the Employer's Mutual Insurance Company, was named state finance chair, and Robert Brenton, president of the Brenton Banks, was the campaign treasurer. They already had a hardworking foursome of young fieldworkers out around the state. Bob Liddy (son of Iowa agriculture secretary L. B. Liddy), Ed Redfern, Cal Crane, and Tom Thoren had been working for the governor's reelection since June 1971, trying to identify and bolster the governor's weak spots, pick out Jepsen's, and report back.

<u>DICK GILBERT</u> "The early Jepsen challenge really strengthened the Ray organization, plus we had the benefit of a massive Nixon machine going around the state. But when you're so close to the governor's office, you overestimate your own vulnerability, and we knew that any mistake could take us down. So we weren't taking anything for granted; we were running scared.

"The Ray organization, highly touted by the press in 1972, consisted, thanks to Tom Stoner and John Murray, of a handful of young guys running around the state. There was also an infusion of new blood on the staff in 1971 with the addition of Wythe, myself, and John Murray. We enjoyed working with each other and had a good time. I don't recall much intraoffice or internecine rivalry in that period, and we had kind of a can-do attitude. One of Stoner's little rubrics was that good luck follows hard work, and that was really true in 1971 and 1972. The whole effort was a good example of gubernatorial initiative backed by a solid staff, good press relations, and exquisite timing."

<u>TOM STONER</u> "John Murray was worried about Bob Ray. He realized the race of 1970 was too close, didn't feel it had been professionally managed, and that Bob Ray needed to do more in terms of developing a real strong base across the state. That sounds ridiculous to say today, but it didn't exist then.

"John asked me if I would be willing to help find an office for a small organization and take charge of it. Interestingly, about that same time I was approached by Roger Jepsen through a mutual friend, Chuck Maxwell. He asked if I would be interested in meeting Roger and Carroll Lane for breakfast at the Hotel Kirkwood. A thirty-minute breakfast turned into a two-and-a-half-hour meeting. The bottom line was whether I would run his lieutenant governor's fund-raising campaign. In the back of their minds, of course, was a run for the governor's seat, but they weren't disclosing that at the time.

"But I had some difficulty finding areas of agreement with Roger Jepsen's approach to government. About a week later I made the comment to Verne Lawyer that if I could ever do anything to help out Ray, I'd do it. The next day I got a phone call from John Murray, asking if I would be willing to meet with the governor, that he'd like me to be his campaign manager."

<u>JOHN MURRAY</u> "Tom was initially concerned that Ray would want to fiddle around with decisions in the campaign. He's a frustrating person to work with because he is a perfectionist, he wants to make a lot of the decisions. He doesn't want things to go wrong, and it's his damn campaign, let's face it.

"Tom was an incredible choice as campaign manager. He was a peer and he could stand up to Ray. He also was going to take Ray to the limit, force him to delegate power. Plus he knew how to manufacture the scenery which was so important in a Ray campaign."

BOB RAY "He agreed to help us and then took time off from his business, disappeared for a month or more, and came back with this big black book. He had mapped out the entire campaign.

"Once Tom had his plan and his three-ring notebook organized, we sat down and filled in the slots. We worked together to find the right people, and we'd go over and over the list. I preferred a person to manage my campaigns who had good common sense and a strong organizational background. I wanted someone in charge of research, scheduling, advertising, but I liked to be involved in all those areas.

"I found after my first election that of all the experts you could hire, most of them weren't as experienced as I was. I knew what I liked, and even if I might have been wrong, I wanted to be comfortable."

TOM STONER "Bob Ray had done everything – campaign manager, state chairman, he'd been candidate and governor, and he'd run it all. It was hard for him to let go of things. So I wanted to make sure that everything that was done in the campaign would be open, that nothing would be kept from me. I knew that Bob Ray felt that way – he'd lived his whole life that way – but I wanted it stated out in the open. We came to an agreement, and we went out and put together the best organization the state had ever seen."

STEVE ROBERTS "If I had to name two people who made Bob Ray, besides Bob Ray himself, they would be Roger Jepsen and Dick Gilbert. Jepsen provided the challenge he needed, and Gilbert helped shape his public image. And once he cranked that campaign up, there was no tomorrow."

DICK GILBERT "The one thing you don't do with Bob Ray is crowd him or push him. If you come to Bob Ray and are up-front and say, 'Gee, I'd like to do this. What do you think about it? Can you help me? Show me the way? What's your advice? and work with him, you're going to get along fine. But if you go in there, whether you're a legislator trying to get a bill through or a politician trying to get something for yourself or a mayor trying to get a road and say, 'You will do this,' or 'I want you to do this, and you're going to do it, Governor,' you were going to get some opposition. He was a very determined governor."

BOB RAY "I don't think any candidate ever welcomes a primary, yet you know it sometimes can strengthen you. Once Roger announced, people started really looking critically at me and him and who was doing what. I think some even decided that I was making decisions, and some began to look at what our relationship was like. I think the public thought we got elected together, as a team, and that he was carrying water for me. But it was pretty tough to carry water for someone you wanted to unseat. I decided I was going to run like never before."

BILLIE RAY "Bob didn't want to make up his mind whether to run or not that early, but when you've got somebody out there asking people, 'Would you be my county chairman?' or whatever, that puts some pressure on. Most political campaigners are pleased to be asked to do something, so they'll work for anybody. Bob really felt he had to get out there and ask for people's support."

RAND PETERSEN "It was very simple. Knowing that Roger Jepsen wanted the job was enough to keep him going. Just to keep him from getting the job."

DICK GILBERT "Roger was running around the state doing all sorts of things, spending nights in legislators' homes, kind of what Jimmy Carter would do years later. He was running hard. The best thing that ever happened to the Ray administration was the Jepsen challenge. It forced us to get back in touch with our base and to get organized early for the next campaign.

"It sharpened everybody up. If somebody made a request for a letter to be read at a fund-raiser, you knew darn well you better get it out fast or they would go to Roger Jepsen, who was just waiting out there. Or if they wanted an answer from our office, the idea that there was somebody out there challenging us quickly sharpened us up. As far as actually plotting and scheming to undercut Roger, I don't think we ever did that. Jepsen, in retrospect, and I swallow hard to say it, over the years did the office and Bob Ray a service in a reverse sort of way by challenging him. It made us stronger.

"One of the reasons Bob Ray managed to be a successful governor was because he had a fairly thin skin. Some people would say, 'Well, it would seem better if a chief executive had a thick skin.' I submit that the guys who get in trouble politically are the ones whose skin is too thick to be sensitive to the letters to the editor, public criticism, and all the other stuff. He was able to always respond to this stuff. He paid more attention to it."

JOHN MURRAY "From my vantage point, the challenge consumed a lot of

Ray's time and emotional energy. We'd be working on something unre-lated to the campaign and he'd say, 'Well, that throws a wet towel on Jepsen.' He really had a mind for the particular, whereas I was trying to be more general."

DICK GILBERT "We made an effort to make sure that what was written and said about him bolstered his confidence. In terms of our immediate effort, it was directed primarily at rebuilding Bob Ray's own confidence. When you have a guy like Roger Jepsen running around the state saying bad things about you, most people aren't paying any attention, but Bob Ray was, and it really bothered him. So we made it very clear to the staff and the people around him that we would use words like 'The governor is very firm on this,' or 'He's very strong on this.' "

TOM STONER "Walt Shotwell came up with the slogan of 'Governor for Governor,' which I think he may have gotten from a Rockefeller cam-paign, but that didn't make any difference. It had never been done in Iowa and it really spoke to the point.

"Even to those people who might have felt more philosophically aligned with Roger, there is a certain sense of loyalty about Iowans, who don't want their governor kind of muscled around and pushed around. The slogan spoke for the way we tried to position the governor in the cam-paign.

"Roger was the usurper, and that's the way we tried to position him, and sooner or later that worked. Also, the governor became a tougher guy. I think after the Wadena thing he was perceived as being just a little fuzzy on some things, and this really toughened his image."

TOM THOREN "The challenge also really tested our organization in the field. We had to pick the best workers, analyze who could get what done. The organization had been pretty soft, and on the surface you could see why Jepsen thought he had a chance."

JIM WEST "I helped Roger organize the state, to see if there were people out there to support him. We had a good organization back then; that's what helped him in 1978. But we ran out of money. The governor cut him off from funds. Ray has always been given credit for having a good or-ganization, but I've never been able to find it. He, particularly over the years, with all his appointees, had a ton of supporters out there, but they weren't really organizational types. He pretty much relied on the Republi-can party organization as far as people to get out and do the work. He would have people identified in every county, and as I say, he drew on that reservoir of appointees and he did that very skillfully. Even the Democrats gave him support."

ROGER FERRIS "Roger's numbers looked pretty good. He had a good following, and lots of people were grumbling about Ray, so it looked like a reasonable opportunity.

"We organized county by county, did our best to raise money. We did work outside of the state party organization because, generally speaking, though they were cooperative, many of them favored Bob Ray.

"In retrospect, I don't think things went very well for us. There was initial enthusiasm, but about that same time Bob Ray was turning things around. We encountered the phenomenon of people being willing to talk about dissatisfaction, but when faced with the actual process of having to take sides, things just didn't go the way they needed to."

ROGER JEPSEN "In the larger cities the party organization belonged to Bob Ray because of his work as chairman. In the rural areas there'd be more of a blend, I think, and a natural identification [*with me*] because I was a little more conservative.

"He really controlled the state party, though, and if there's a list of two or three or four differences between us, one of them is that in my entire political career in Iowa, I didn't really interfere or get involved with state party politics. I didn't want to get involved in those battles like he did."

BOB RAY "Roger felt that if he could raise enough money quickly, that I would back off. He always believed that a successful campaign required a goodly sum of money and that if you could raise it quickly enough, your opposition wouldn't try to buck it."

JIM WEST "Tom Stoner was able to dry up the financial support, and everybody started backing away all of a sudden. Up until early in 1972 we hadn't had much problem raising money, then you see it start to clamp down. Also, Ray had begun to do his job better, became a better governor. And with Gilbert promoting him in the press, he managed to turn it around."

BOB RAY "I don't recall specifically going to people saying, 'You better not contribute money to Roger.' But I know that was a factor, because at that time I think my stock had gone up and his had gone down. I was campaigning and beginning to relish it. I was into it. Some of the campaigns I really never got that feeling, but here was a challenge that made my blood run fast. That's just what would have happened if Hughes had run in

1982, that would have been the kind of challenge to get me off my duff. We might have had a real battle, but even that would have been different than with Roger. There was a question of loyalty involved."

DICK GILBERT "There are some guys that really deserve a lot of credit for Bob Ray being able to withstand that challenge. Stoner, [*Jack*] Pester, [*Marv*] Pomerantz, [*Robb*] Kelley. They went to people like the Young Presidents club and said, 'Let's get behind this guy.' When some of those substantial young businessmen from around the state said, 'Look, we're for Bob Ray,' it meant a lot, especially because it was a time when it was more popular for some of these conservative young businessmen to be for the guy that said all the right things, literally. That diverted some resources that might have otherwise gone to Roger. But it was more than just money; it was the peer pressure within this very influential area of the political community of young Republican businessmen."

ROGER FERRIS "We ran the campaign almost exactly one year. I don't know whether or not Bob Ray got to anybody, or whether his organization did, but it is a fact that certainly one of the problems that our campaign was plagued with was there was not very much money. Certainly not enough. I don't know exactly what made up Roger's mind to drop out, but I do know that the leadership people that we needed to attract were not attracted. Those people that we always knew would be for us were for us, and the people we knew would be against us were against us, and all those people in the middle were likely to be against Roger."

JACK MILLER "I had a hell of a problem out here [in Washington] because of that Ray-Jepsen squabble. The state chairman and others implored me to see what I could do about getting an appointment from Nixon that would satisfy either one of them.

"I unearthed a very attractive appointment for Bob Ray—which he subsequently turned down. I unearthed a reasonably good appointment for Roger Jepsen. His handicap was that he wasn't a lawyer, but it would have been a good spot for him, one that he could have gone back and run from. For all practical purposes, this appointment would have been the end of the road for Bob Ray, but he wouldn't have had to worry about anything from there on out. I told the troops in Iowa that I'd found this, but I didn't tell them what the job was, never told anybody. But I said, 'You've got to face the fact that while maybe you or I would grab this appointment, we're not Bob Ray.' "

ROGER FERRIS "The rumors were always going around that Bob Ray was going to get some Washington appointment, and we were always hoping."

DON JOHNSON "I know there were overtures made more than once, because I talked with President Nixon about them. Bob Ray was very well thought of, and he should have been; he was a vote-getter. But there were conservatives in the national party that thought he was too liberal, a great concern for some."

BOB RAY "[*Senator*] Jack Miller came to my office after Roger announced and asked, 'Bob, have you ever considered a job in Washington?' I said no. He said, 'You know, there are lots of really great jobs in D.C., and if you have any interest, with my contacts we could set you up with an awfully good job. If you're interested, let me know.' I wasn't, but I asked him why he was so concerned. He said since he was going to be on the same ticket in 1972 he felt an obligation to try and avoid a conflict between two leading Republicans. I said, 'Well, if you think one of us ought to get out of the governor's race, have you talked to Roger about a job in Washington?' He said, 'Well, it's not as easy to locate a job for a lieutenant governor.' I said, 'That's a great criterion, to decide that the person to get out of the race is the person you can get a job for easiest.' I said, 'Jack, you're our United States senator, and unless you got caught with your hand in the cookie jar or something vicious, I feel an obligation to support you. But you come in here, tell me you're interested in avoiding a conflict and it would be better if I, the sitting governor, got out and took a job somewhere else. How do you think I feel about that?' He said he was just trying to be helpful. You know what the job was? Customs court judge. And after Jack Miller lost his election in 1972 he took that job."

HALE GREENLEAF "In September 1971, in a survey we did for the Ray campaign of Republicans and Democrats, we found an approval rating of the governor at 62 percent and 24 percent disapproval. We also tested Ray–Paul Franzenburg and Jepsen–Franzenburg. Ray and Franzenburg divided 46 to 32. Jepsen and Franzenburg stood 26 to 42. Measuring Republicans only, we had Ray with 62 percent, Jepsen with 20 percent. Roger should have decided to get out then."

TOM STONER "Around May 1, 1972, with the primary election set for June, I got a phone call from Jepsen's campaign manager, Roger Ferris. He said he wanted to come over and talk.

"We met in my office at the Des Moines Building. It was a pretty neutral place. I remember him asking me – this was during the Watergate days – if the place was bugged. He presented me with a deal. The lieutenant governor would be willing to drop out of the race and preserve unity within the party if he could be assured of some place in the administration.

"I said that was a question I couldn't even comment on and told him I'd have to call the governor. But the governor was in Tokyo, so I got ahold of Wythe and we went over to the capitol building in the middle of the night and tried to find him by phone. First we tried to get him on a train and couldn't and finally got him at his hotel. We woke him up, I remember, and his response was very simple: No deals. I said, 'Okay, I'll transfer that message.' I called Ferris the next day, and two weeks later Jepsen dropped out."

ROGER FERRIS "We hoped to extricate ourselves from the campaign in the way that would cause least harm to everyone concerned—the party, Roger, Bob Ray, who was obviously going to be the nominee—and just in general begin the process of putting things back together as far as the party was concerned."

BOB RAY "Tom Stoner called and said that we had a contact that said Roger was considering not going through the primary. He wanted to know if we'd make some kind of concession for him. I said, 'If he wants to withdraw, that's fine, and we'd welcome it, but at this stage I would just as soon go through with it. Let's let the votes be counted.' He wanted a graceful way to bow out, but my attitude was, 'Fine, but I don't have any concession to make.' We'd gone this far, he'd put me to the test, we knew what the polls were saying, I thought it would do me some good to go ahead and have a primary battle."

ROGER JEPSEN "The chicken coop affair really helped him, plus the fact that the party really ground away, brought out the big guns. All those promises I was still expecting to surface never did. My numbers weren't very good, and I knew we were in for a bloodbath, a bloodbath that even if I'd won I was in a position where I may have won the battle and lost the war."

DICK GILBERT "Bob Ray and I were on our way to Pella—he was going to be in the Tulip Festival parade—and a call came in over the radio that he needed to get to a phone, so we stopped at my apartment. The phone rang and it was Jepsen calling to say he was getting out of the race. Right in my kitchen. I remember I was leaning on the ironing board."

DUTCH VERMEER "After the Tulip parade everybody came over to my house—Stoner, Dick Gilbert, lots of campaign people. There was a party here that night. Bob Ray had been kind of owly for some months, but he was sure happy that night."

BOB RAY "I was happy Roger withdrew, but at that moment I was really geared for that contest. It's like cutting off a football game in the third quarter when you're ahead. I wanted to complete the game. There was that excitement of being challenged and I wanted to win."

DICK GILBERT "It is very tough to challenge a sitting governor. You'd better have your act together. Like the old adage says, If you're going to hit the king, you'd better kill him."

DENNIS NAGEL "Bob Ray has a memory that goes on forever. I'm sure today he could give you a list of every major Republican in 1972 who supported Roger Jepsen."

XII: RAY VERSUS FRANZENBURG, 1972

TOM THOREN "After Roger dropped out, we were sitting there with a full-time campaign staff and no primary. We were geared up and it was a real letdown, so we all took a two-week vacation."

ED REDFERN "Still, we didn't want to get caught with our shorts down. Both Stoner and Bob Ray understood that we needed to know where our votes were and that the party organization had to keep active."

TOM STONER "The general election campaign was really a very boring affair by comparison. And the death of [*campaign worker*] Bob Liddy totally disheartened the campaign. It was one of the very saddest things that ever happened in my life. He was killed in a car accident after the primary and we—Bob Ray, Wythe, a couple others—had to go out and tell his dad. The campaign was never the same after that; it just took the heart out of us."

Paul Franzenburg beat out John Tapscott of Des Moines for the Democratic nomination in a June primary, but things looked bleak for Ray's second-time opponent. Ray's popularity ratings hovered between 65 and

Paul Franzenburg. *Des Moines Register* photo. Reprinted with permission.

70 percent. The mid-1972 polls showed the incumbent governor beating Franzenburg 54 to 27 percent.

Ray held off on any hard campaigning until the first week of October, with the general election just five weeks away, and ran on his record. Franzenburg claimed that Ray never really understood the condition of the state treasury and used unusual accounting methods to make it appear the state's books were in good condition. He criticized Ray for not speaking out on the "great moral issues," declaring that "we need a state leader who will use the prestige of his position to speak out against the hideous war in Vietnam that is bankrupting our economy and desolating our national spirit." Ray's counter was simple: "At no time have I ever seen a major party slip so far, so fast as the Democrats in Iowa have in the past two years."

TOM STONER "Franzenburg was a nice guy but was not a big threat to us. There were no major issues at stake."

BOB RAY "I think people often forget that we are not a Republican state, especially then, and I considered Paul a very strong candidate. Remember, if he had played that first contest wisely, he would have stayed on the highroad and not let me get to him, and he would be the incumbent. But this second time we really had a well greased organization. The campaign was geared up, we knew what we wanted to do. The second time around, Paul was not as crisp."

PAUL FRANZENBURG "I ran in 1972 because I was disturbed with what he was telling people. I also thought that the things that Bob Fulton had warned about in 1970 – the deficit of the state treasury – had come true and that aroused me to run. As former treasurer of the state, I knew I was right in reference to the taxes – I knew that you just don't have the money in the treasury until you have it. He had no business dealing with anticipated collections, so he absolutely misrepresented the truth in regard to the deficit. But that was not a very appealing pitch for voters. Yet, without meaning to sound too virtuous, I thought that the chief executive of the state ought to level with the people.

"The general election was a very bad campaign for me, a rotten campaign. I was running against an incumbent who was starting to get his feet on the ground."

ED CAMPBELL "Paul was a good candidate, but I think too many times people want the office so goddam bad they lose sight of the problems and the issues. Bob Ray hadn't rocked the boat, he had a good public image, he appeared to like the job. So why change?"

PAUL FRANZENBURG "He was a popular man, plus he had the resources of the governor's office at his beck and call. Being an incumbent helps unless you are just a particular damn fool, and he used those resources well — very well."

BOB RAY "There was one article, I think Flansburg might have written it, which compared the two campaigns on the same day. I had been to the office and then flown out for a noon meeting and then flown to a couple more afternoon stops and a dinner and then back home for a good night's rest in my own bed. Paul had started that same day in Dubuque and driven across the state to Sioux City. Didn't see anybody all day long. And he lost his speech and tried to get out of his last appearance. Quite a contrast. I always thought he was deserving of better than that.

"I also, as governor, could get an appearance anywhere, almost any time. I had standing invitations most places, and wherever there was an event, they liked to have the governor come. I felt a little sorry for Paul, but not sorry enough that I wanted him to win."

BOB FULTON "I always felt that Paul ran more on image than issues. You know, 'I'm for Iowa, Iowa is great, all together we're going to make Iowa great.' Now that might beat a guy that's got a bad image himself, but you're not going to beat a guy with an image like Bob Ray that way."

BO BELLER "Franzenburg came around and asked for my support. I was not impressed. All of his answers to our questions seemed processed; he just kind of spewed them out. When we'd ask Ray things, he'd give us an honest answer. We didn't always agree with him, but you knew he was being honest. Lots of my friends and colleagues were surprised that I liked him, in part, I guess, simply because he was Republican. But I always thought he was heads above his Democratic opposition, both in terms of honesty and intelligence. This coming from the president of the student body at the University of Iowa."

HAROLD HUGHES "I think Paul was as capable as Bob, and had he been elected he would have had the courage, the intelligence, and the capability of doing the job. But it's personality and style, it's a personal relationship that people feel, and it would have taken a real strong personality with a strong relationship with the people of Iowa to have challenged Bob Ray."

"Always remember, a Democrat is a guy who doesn't know all the answers, but is sure that if he raises enough of your taxes, he can find them," criticized Ray on his way to spending $100,000 in beating Franzenburg. It was a bloodless fight lasting less than three months from primary to general election, and it saw Ray introduce computerized mass mailings and phone solicitations to Iowa campaign fund-raising. "A Good Man Doing a Great Job" was Ray's slogan, and it helped trounce Franzenburg by 230,000 votes—at 58.6 percent, the highest percentage win of any Republican governor in state history. Ray was the state's top vote-getter and won all ninety-nine counties. His winning margin was bigger than Richard Nixon's. The day following the election, the governor and his staff went back to work. Carroll lawyer and eight-year state senator Art Neu was elected lieutenant governor, defeating Democrat Bill Gannon. His predecessor, Roger Jepsen, moved back to Davenport and back into the insurance business.

XIII: THE THIRD TERM, 1973-1974

"A fter that third election I felt good about the office," Ray says. "It was probably about then, for the first time, that I was beginning to feel like I was on top of the job. The awful session of 1971, Roger challenging me, all that was behind me." Bob Ray continued to follow his own best instincts in that third term, claiming he had gotten the state in order and that he intended to spend this term on the state's future. He had unmatched public approval ratings hovering in the mid-70s. Mid-term, they peaked at a career high of 82 percent. Only 5 percent disapproved of the way he was doing his job. Even the farmers were of good cheer, giving the Des Moines lawyer a 61 percent approval rating. Attitudes had changed since the days in 1971 when they had stormed into his office, pitchforks in hand.

His staff—led by Willey, Gilbert, Jackson, Vermeer, and Bill Smith— had congealed. (John Murray left the governor's office just before Ray's third election and was elected state senator from Ames. Over his six-year tenure, he and his former boss clashed as often as they agreed, in part, says Murray, because of the governor's high expectations of his former executive assistant.) In the legislature the governor found his relationship with the leadership much improved. Lieutenant Governor Art Neu worked with the governor's office much better than his predecessor had. Both houses were led by Republicans. Cliff Lamborn of Maquoketa was the senate's majority leader, and an old Ray ally, Andrew Varley, was elected Speaker of the House.

Nelson Rockefeller and Bob Ray. *Des Moines Register* photo. Reprinted with permission.

Ray's political strength was climbing at the same time. In a late-1973 profile, the governor was labeled "the key figure in all of Iowa politics." Ambitious Democrats and Republicans alike based their own future political agendas on Ray's moves. Speculation ran rampant that he would meet Harold Hughes in a race for Hughes's U.S. Senate seat in 1974. When Hughes opted to retire instead of run for a second term, Ray privately breathed a sigh of relief. He hadn't wanted to challenge Hughes. He was perfectly happy as governor and thought it ultimately a more powerful, elite job than senator. But had Hughes run, it might have been up to the "key figure in Iowa politics" to take on the incumbent. Ray would never have wanted anyone to say he'd backed down from a tough fight. In Washington, shortly after Ray's third inauguration, political pundits began to mention him as a potential vice-presidential, or even presidential, candidate.

His political fortunes were bolstered by a booming Iowa economy. The governor's budget called for a record high of $1.6 billion and Marvin Selden anticipated a surplus each year of that term of anywhere from $150 to $250 million. Economic improvements marked a major shift in the way the governor's office moved in his third term compared to the first two. Inflation was increasing farm incomes and making city-dwellers' paychecks fatter. The state's unemployment stood at 3 percent.

The governor was happy with his efforts to reorganize state agencies and make them more directly responsible to his office. His highest priority for that third term was to create a department of transportation, combining the Commission of Aeronautics, the Highway Commission, the Motor Vehicle divisions of the Department of Public Safety, the Transportation Regulation Division of the Iowa Commerce Commission, and the Iowa Reciprocity Board. His bill was not made law until the second session of that term and was fought hard by a coalition of trucking and road-construction lobbies. He also adopted a Democratic proposition to remove the sales tax from groceries and prescription drugs, a repeal estimated to cost the state $28.9 million a year. Not too surprisingly, conservative critics in the state legislature, notably Terry Branstad and Chuck Grassley, thought many of Ray's proposals more Democratic than Republican. This term also saw the governor promote, and the legislature pass, appropriations of $10.2 million for two state office buildings, the Henry A. Wallace Building and the Herbert Hoover State Office Building, both completed in 1978.

RALPH BROWN "Bob Ray did not view the legislature as the governor's equal. He is very much action oriented [*slaps his hands*], wanted to get things done [*slaps his hands*], and things did not happen like that in the legislature. It was a frustrating place. At the same time, Bob Ray was very, very successful with the legislature, and a lot of new, innovative programs were implemented during those first three terms. It really helped when Art Neu came in, because things were becoming a little more difficult between Ray and the legislature. It also helped that Andy Varley was leading the house. The three of them were a very good leadership team."

TOM THOREN "Art Neu had pledged to work closely with the governor, and he lived up to that pledge. We charted every bill in the governor's State of the State message and budget message. Every piece of legislation he considered his. We could tell you at any time what committee it was in, what subcommittee, who the members were. It rolled pretty smoothly, and really for the first time it became Bob Ray's legislature."

BOB RAY "I liked Andy Varley. As a leader he would decide what he could do, and then he'd talk to you, or you'd talk to him, and he'd smile and you'd know that that was as far as you were going to get with him. He would not get angry with me, or try to tell me I didn't know what I was talking about; he just decided what he could do, and that's what he was going to do. When he didn't work with us, he was very nice about it, but he was headstrong. Now, Cliff Lamborn in the senate had not been a big supporter of mine when I first ran for office, but he later became a good friend. Art Neu and he didn't agree with me on a lot of issues, but they were wonderful to work with.

"It surprised me how hard the legislature and the press jumped on the proposed DOT [*Department of Transportation*]. It took three years of pushing to get it passed, and the press kept writing about how it was the most important piece of my whole program. I honestly didn't see it that way. It wasn't intended to be. It was just a logical, right step to make. I wasn't going to back off, but it became a very prominent part of the program, mostly because of the emotion in the legislature and the press's attitude. That was a good example of a bill we really stuck with, even though it wasn't adopted quickly."

BILL HARBOR "After his first two terms Ray became one of the best governors in the state's history. *Even though he didn't represent your philosophical brand of Republicanism?* Right. The vast majority of the time, the decisions he made were made because they were the best things for the state of Iowa, partisan politics aside. He *learned* to be a good governor, and the things he encouraged, like the DOT, made the state more modern."

CHUCK GRASSLEY "One of the reasons legislators felt more inclined to oppose him in 1969 and 1970, even in 1971 and '72, was because his popularity was in the 50 to 60 percent approval range. By 1974 it was between 70 and 85. So it wasn't bad for a legislator to be lined up with the governor then."

DON AVENSON "The Democrats really passed his agenda in 1973 and 1974. We put up 44 votes for collective bargaining for public employees out of 45 Democrats in the house. He only needed seven of his own troops to pass it. Democrats provided the vast majority of votes for his programs. Same with the Department of Transportation; without us that wouldn't have passed. We worked closely with both the governor's office and the lieutenant governor, which helped in the next session, when the Democrats controlled both houses."

After the governor and the legislature came to grips with the increased money surplus, two major events dominated those two years: the energy crisis and Watergate. On the former, Ray proved to be a leader nationwide. Along with Maurie Van Nostrand, Sam Tuthill, and Energy Policy Council director Ed Stanek, Ray, according to the *Register*'s Jim Flansburg, "defined what Iowans needs were, looked into where Iowa's energy came from, set up a system of priorities in case of a shortage and established a pool to draw from when regular supplies gave out." Few governors, or President Nixon, did as much planning. On Watergate, Bob Ray stood by the president publicly through the end of 1973. After being misled in private by the struggling Nixon once too often, Ray began to distance himself early in 1974. It was an election year in Iowa, and he could foresee Nixon's problems affecting Republicans nationwide. As a member of the prestigious Republican Coordinating Committee, Ray, along with Barry Goldwater, Bob Dole, and others, conferred on ways to rebuild the party after Nixon's resignation. When Jerry Ford took over as president, Ray suggested he pick a governor for vice-president, sensing a more-than-usual need for a good liaison with the states. During Ford's deliberations, Ray was one of five considered for the job. Bob Ray liked Ford. He was much more his kind of guy than was Nixon. "He's the kind of guy you can trust your wallet with," he said, but later turned down a couple of opportunities to be in his cabinet.

<u>BOB RAY</u> *After that third election lots of people started suggesting you run for the Senate. Why didn't you?* "I didn't think I should, at first. Then I thought maybe I should. A lot of good people want to be a United States senator, but I looked at it and it just wasn't my cup of tea.

"By then I had some training as an administrator and as an executive, and I liked it. It's exciting, you could see things happen that make a difference. I watched the senators and I thought so often you've got to try and find a niche and you've got to keep doing things so people back home won't forget you. It's a slow, tedious process.

"There was temptation, though, and enough people tried to talk me into running that I couldn't dismiss it lightly. Some of my colleagues wanted to get elected governor just so they could build a record, get the name recognition, and run for the Senate. There are some benefits. You can carve out a life almost the way you want it. I've had some tell me that you can go home every night, put your feet up and watch television, read, do whatever you want, or go out every night and make the circuit. Nice retirement benefits and all that stuff, plus some excitement – you're where the power is. They wanted Bill Milliken up in Michigan to run for the Senate too. We used to commiserate on the phone a bit. We'd try to figure out the reasons why to run or not."

After six years on the job, Ray's management of the state appeared to be on smooth ice. The reorganization he had begun at the outset was well underway – he had a newly consolidated Department of Transportation, an Energy Policy Council, a growing Office for Planning and Programming, a revamped Department of General Services with centralized purchasing. The state's liquor control board had been reorganized, property taxes were under control, public-school financing was lined up, the state's antiquated judicial system was being reformed, and the treasury had a surplus. Despite the rumblings of conservatives in his own party, his third was the term Bob Ray got his feet on the ground. In his own oft-used sports vernacular, the governor had his eye on the ball.

XIV: RAY VERSUS SCHABEN, 1974

At the end of his statehouse press conference on the morning of February 27, 1974, Bob Ray asked if there were any further questions. Getting none, he began to pack up and head for the door, but paused. "You've been asking me for weeks now about my political plans and I've told you that when I make up my mind I'd tell you. So I want to tell you this morning that I'm going to run again and seek this office once more."

The previous day the state senate had passed the bill ordering the organization of the Department of Transportation. The same Republican legislature had recently passed the bill approving collective bargaining for public employees, had taken the 3 percent sales tax off groceries and prescriptions, and had shifted more of the tax burden from the property tax to the income tax. Unemployment in the state stood at 2.7 percent, and by June, Marvin Selden was predicting a surplus of over $200 million. It appeared that the governor was in good shape to be elected to the first four-year term in over 100 years. (The first three governors after Iowa gained statehood served four-year terms, but the state's constitution was rewritten in 1857, and the governor's term was reduced to two years. In 1968 the constitution was amended, and in 1972 the terms of the governor, the lieutenant governor, the attorney general, the secretary of state, the auditor, and the treasurer were expanded to four years.)

Three Democrats had announced for a June primary that would decide who would challenge Ray. William Gannon, a former state legislator and previous gubernatorial primary candidate, was favored over former state Democratic party chairman Clark Rasmussen and state senator Jim Schaben. Helped by the pouring of $70,000 into his primary effort (including $30,000 out of his own pocket), Schaben upset Gannon. Ray's press secretary, Dick Gilbert, set the tone of the campaign for Schaben soon after his

Jim Schaben. *Des Moines Register* photo. Reprinted with permission.

victory: "[He] is in the big leagues now, running against a three-term governor who won every county in his last election."

Schaben came out swinging, accusing Ray of cutting ribbons and issuing press releases instead of dealing with problems and claiming that Ray had staffed the burgeoning state bureaucracy with cronies. He dubbed Ray's terms the "imperial governorship." Prompted by trucking interests who poured money into his campaign, the three-term state senator from Dunlap claimed he would dismantle the just-approved Department of Transportation soon after he was elected.

Ray countered, accusing Schaben of having "the worst voting record in the Senate" and calling on Iowans to "contrast my five-and-a-half years of performance against his loose talk, flip flops and absenteeism." On a swing through Corning and Atlantic in September, Ray told a partisan audience, "In this campaign for the first four-year term in modern history, I believe the issue is clear: Which candidate can do the best job of leading Iowa from now until 1978?"

JOHN McDONALD "Once we got him established, the Democrats were battling tough, tough odds, once he really became 'The Governor.' By 1974 he had become a nightmare to the opposition."

TOM STONER "After the 1972 election I had told them not to invite me to the governor's mansion for parties, to take me off the list. 'I don't want to see you guys. I don't want to see you, governor,' I told them. I was tired and had lots to do other than politics. And it was great to be away from it.

"Then, late in 1973, the word got to me that Bob Ray wanted to see me. One day I arranged to meet with Dick Gilbert and him. He told us he was thinking about running again, but he would not run unless Dick continued as his press secretary and I came back to run the campaign. If either one of us wouldn't do it, he said he wasn't going to run. Of course, we were flattered; he said just the right thing and we accepted. Whether Gilbert put him up to it and Gilbert had gone through the charade first or not, to this day I don't know. But it was very shrewd on his part."

DICK GILBERT "He got us both in his downstairs office on a couch. He was sitting at the end of the table in his big chair, and he turned to us and laid out the political situation he was facing. Republicans across the country were in trouble because of Watergate; the statehouse looked like it was going to go Democratic. He said he'd already had three terms, 'I don't know if I want to do it anymore,' and then he told us the one condition under which he'd run was if Tom and I would stay with him. We walked out of there like we had a real mission—you know, our state is calling us, the governor of our state has asked us to do this thing, what a sacrifice we're making. Years later, we still wonder how many guys he did that same thing to."

BOB RAY "I did tell them [*Stoner and Gilbert*] that. I really gave that 1974 race a lot of consideration. I'd been there some time, I knew that every year thereafter it was going to take something away from my ability to earn, to go into a new career. But I think at that time I liked the job, was enjoying what I was doing, and I honestly thought I could still make a contribution. I always felt that if I were to seek the office again, I had to want do it and had to be convinced I could make a contribution. At that time I could really have gone either way. When Stoner said he would manage the campaign and when Dick Gilbert said he would stay, it made the difference. I'd gone through enough campaigns to know I didn't want to fight all that by myself."

BILLIE RAY "By this time it had become pretty much a way of life, and I was comfortable. I could take it or leave it. The first two reelection campaigns, I really wished Bob had wanted to get out just to get away from the pressure and difficulty of the job. But after six years I was more accustomed to that way of life, more comfortable with my role. Plus we were on the brink of getting Terrace Hill, and I still hoped I'd be able to finish that project off. I was somewhat afraid that if Bob didn't run, or if he lost, it might not get top priority."

TOM STONER "Our effort in that race was to get people to look at Bob Ray as a person, not as a representative of the Republican party, because we knew it was gong to be a disastrous year for Republicans because of Nixon. In 1972 we had built a strong organization. It was still in place, and that helped solidify our effort quickly.

"We focused on the leadership of Bob Ray. We didn't really feel that being the incumbent in 1974 was much of an asset. And his strength as a good administrator was a tough sell. We shot the commercials for the race at the governor's mansion. [*Walt*] Shotwell helped us on them. They were a very tight picture of Bob Ray talking, and his human nature, his sincerity, his integrity and forthrightness just poured out."

BOB RAY "Dick Nixon created clear problems for any Republican on the ticket that year. I decided I just had to do my thing, and I made appearances with the idea I wanted people to know me and that I wasn't just another Republican associated with what was happening in Washington.

"I felt like I was doing a pretty good job by this time, and Tom was a little concerned about how we were going to go to the people after that many years and have a vibrant, active campaign. Tom worried mostly about what else was there for the administration to do. How could I go out and tell them everything was bad after I'd been in power so long? What's left for you to propose? So we put together those long-as-your-arm door hangers so that people would know that there'd been a lot accomplished while I was governor.

"I had singled out two groups of people that I wanted to concentrate appearances before. One was young people, the other was the farm community. When we had good invitations from either of those groups I tried to take as many as I could. That was different from any of the other campaigns. I made an extra effort to get on the campuses and talk to as many people as I could about what I was doing, because I knew there would be an attempt to blame all Republicans for Nixon. I wanted to not be against or down on Nixon, I just wanted to keep the doors open. We disapproved of Nixon and Ted Agnew as much as the Democrats, and we wanted to make sure that was clear. Poor guys like Wiley Mayne, who really believed in our system of justice and believed that everybody should have their day in court, hung on to make sure Dick Nixon got fair treatment and was sabotaged. He waited too long.

"[*Congressman*] Bill Scherle came into my office during that campaign, and I was pleased because I thought I'd worked hard to befriend him and always without success. He came and said, 'You know, there are only two of us who can get elected. It's up to us to take hold and run this party and survive and try and get somebody else elected with us.' But he went out and ran his own campaign. He wouldn't appear with his opponent, and the days were gone when you could refuse to do that. He should have been far more knowledgeable than [*Tom*] Harkin was, but he wouldn't debate him, wouldn't appear with him. And he lost."

DICK GILBERT "Republicans, by and large, did not fare well that year. We were in the field with a poll when Ford pardoned Nixon [*September 8, 1974*]. Stoner and I had an emergency meeting at the Holiday Inn South with this poll that showed Ray's popularity had gone right down the drain with that pardon. He bounced right back, but everybody was mad at Ford for pardoning Nixon. Had the election been held that day, it would have been all over for Ray."

TOM STONER "It was a very different race than 1972. That year, after the primary we ran as a party; it was an asset. By 1974 we had reconstructed the strategy and decided to run apart from the party. We thought we had to. We would purposely have the press meet him in a nonparty event, and then he would go to the party event after the press coverage had taken place. We did everything we could to focus on Bob Ray as a leader and a statesman, not as a partisan politician, not as a Republican, which ran against his grain."

BOB RAY "I was in the White House a number of times at the beginning of 1974, and each time I would come out the press would want to know all about Nixon – was he pale? was he nervous? did he look ill? – and I would say, 'No, to the contrary, he was extremely friendly and gave us more time than was allotted,' which was true. Usually the president gets up, says excuse me, and walks out of most meetings. But he wasn't doing that. The only thing that made me think he might be under a lot of strain was that he swore so much. I thought he was just trying to be one of the guys. But when the transcripts of his taping came out, I realized that's how he always talked.

"There were a couple times, though, that really caused me to lose faith in Nixon, prior to his resigning. I was chairman of the Midwest Governors' [Conference] in 1972 and we met up in North Dakota. Jim Exon from Nebraska was really angry at the administration and wanted to draft a big resolution spelling out what he saw wrong in the administration's views on the cattle industry. I convinced him that it would be better for me to talk to the administration rather than draft a resolution, which tends to just anger people.

"I came back to Des Moines and called [Nixon's aide] John Ehrlichman and told him to pick two or three of the midwestern governors to come with me to see the president so we could explain our side. Well, they were scared to death that we were trying to embarrass them. I tried to explain that I had saved them from embarrassment. They wanted me to just come see the president by myself. So I didn't go. They were really frightened of criticism.

"Another time was when the president had been getting a lot of flak, in 1973. He had been down in Miami talking to the newspaper editors, and we were having a governors' conference in Tennessee, and he came up to see us. He was asked at this meeting of Republican governors if there were any more time bombs that we could expect, or be prepared for. He leaned back in his chair and said, to the best of his knowledge, no. That made us as governors feel much better. Afterwards we had a press conference with the national press, and three of us told them that the president had told us there were no more time bombs. It was the next week that the eighteen-and-a-half-minute gap was made public. That just shot his credibility with us."

DICK GILBERT "Bob Ray was elected for one reason: hard work. But once he got in office, he built that Ray organization through association, and it was a high-quality organization. He had the ability to make everybody consider him a close friend. He could come into a town and draw a crowd easily, gather the most influential people around him.

"He also made every effort to make friends before he needed them. One of the reasons he was tough to beat was because he didn't polarize people. The unions couldn't hate him like they could Reagan or Jepsen, so it was hard to marshal opposition against him. Even the Democrats, when they'd attack him, they'd say he was a nice guy, he doesn't do anything, but he's a nice guy. But they couldn't say he was a bastard or a mean spirit or uncaring. Those who attacked him that way, with nasty asides, hurt themselves."

ROBB KELLEY "Bob Ray was a clean candidate if there ever was one. Prior to 1972 I'd been president of the Chamber of Commerce and was United Way chairman, but I'd not raised money for political enterprises. But I'll tell you, it was easy to raise money for Bob Ray. His reputation was infallible. There were some Democrats, some very prominent Democrats, who would give money to Bob Ray and for a while there you could take money from them without reporting it. So these Democrats said they didn't want to be listed, but they'd throw some money in – Joe Rosenfield, Bernie Mercer, and some others, good Democrats. I know Tom Stoner got some money from others."

BOB RAY *Did you actively pursue Democratic voters?* "I always felt that I represented all the people in the state, and I needed Democratic support as well. If I were the right guy to be leading the state, then I really needed their support, and I felt a lot of Democrats shared my basic philosophy. I think I had some strength in their party.

"There were three Democrats in the primary that year – Jim Schaben, Bill Gannon, and Clark Rasmussen. In the beginning everybody thought Gannon would be the nominee. It seemed like he was the strongest and he had run before, but Schaben came out of western Iowa, where they all stuck by their own. There was some fear on our part that he was so strong in the primary – and our surveying showed he had a lot of strength in the western part of the state – that maybe that would spread and grow and even appeal to Republicans who'd like to see a governor from their part of the state. And, of course, Schaben played up the auctioneer and farmer bit pretty well. We took him very seriously.

"I always thought he was a decent legislator, and we had gotten along well. He'd even said complimentary things about me. But in that campaign year his approach changed. He'd always been a pretty nice guy, but once he was out campaigning he just let the arrows fly. He felt he had to show himself as a big, tough guy, but I didn't think that sold very well.

"One thing that really gave Schaben a boost was the *Register*. We saw his primary win coming for the last couple weeks before the election, but the *Register* seemed more surprised. They really sensationalized his win. It was like a new star was born. It was big, big news, like no one ever expected him to win. He got a big ride out of that."

ED CAMPBELL "I don't know what happened to Schaben, though. It seemed like from the day after the primary it was all downhill. It just never went anywhere, and in part because so many so-called liberals took a walk and voted for Ray."

RAND PETERSEN "Schaben was a neighbor over here in western Iowa. I had known him a long time, and one day, before he announced he was running, he said, 'You know, I don't know, maybe I'm crazy, because I know if I run against "Uncle Bob," I can't beat him.' I told him that day that from my experience, if you're going to win your primary, don't spend your money on radio advertising. He took my advice, won, and afterward came back and said, 'Well, I don't suppose I'm going to get any more advice from you.' I said, 'I guess not.'

"I felt sorry for Jim, because he really convinced himself he was going to win. I saw him just a week before the election, and he still thought he was going to pull it off. But he just got clobbered."

LOWELL JUNKINS "As long as Bob Ray and the state had $200 million in the bank to take care of his political favors, there wasn't any candidate out there who could touch him. And every candidate since Bob Fulton tried to out-nice him. You just couldn't beat him that way."

DICK GILBERT "We did a lot of policy and position research and voting and issue research for that campaign. But we didn't do any research on the personal side of the candidates, didn't try and dig up dirt on guys. It just wasn't done. The only time that was brought up was in the 1974 campaign, though, and it was a great lesson for me in terms of how government could abuse itself if the people there don't exercise extreme discipline. Late one night we were in the downstairs office, talking about where in the hell Schaben was getting his money. We knew the trucking industry in the state was less than enthusiastic about Bob Ray's candidacy, and we also knew that Schaben was a real friend of the trucking industry. We had reason to believe they were dumping a lot of bread into his campaign, perhaps in violation of the law. We didn't know that for a certainty, I'm not accusing anyone of violating the law, but somebody had gotten ahold of his campaign disclosure statements and noticed a large chunk deposit. We wondered where in the hell he got $30,000 or $40,000 overnight. Did he borrow it from a bank? Did somebody give it to him? How could we find out? I remember thinking the banking superintendent could find out for us because he worked for us. It would have been easy for us to call him up and say, 'Hey, would you mind checking?' Then it hit me that's just the kind of power that got Watergate started. The real crime in Watergate was guys in office using the power of their office to perpetuate themselves. Even in state government, the abuse of power issue is always a potential."

BOB RAY "By 1974 I was more of a seasoned politician, and I liked other politicians who could stand on their own accomplishments and their own visions and their own ability to achieve. I thought Jim Schaben had something to contribute. During the years he'd been in the legislature I'd thought he'd patterned himself to be what I would call a good politician. People who are honest about what they believe don't play the game that they have to knock somebody because that's the popular thing to do to get some press. I really thought Schaben was going to be tough.

"But as the campaign progressed, he turned into what you expect politicians to turn into. He started shooting from the hip, swinging, hoping he would hit somebody. I was kind of disappointed in Jim, and it just got worse, not better. It wasn't a very pleasant campaign. It wasn't very lofty. He started dredging up stuff, like in that eleventh-hour debate. It was indicative of the kind of campaign he was running; he was like a loose cannon. It reminded me of Curly Hultman's eleventh-hour bomb against Harold Hughes back in 1964. [*In their last public debate, on the Friday before the Tuesday election, Schaben, speaking last, accused a state tax official of taking illegal gifts from a lobbyist and claimed Ray should have known. Ray spent the weekend trying to respond. He believed Schaben had bushwacked him. In the Hughes case, Curly Hultman's attempted eleventh-hour bomb did him about as much good. In a similarly timed debate, he disclosed that Hughes had a drunken-driving conviction in Florida. A recovering alcoholic, Hughes garnered public support over Hultman's disclosure, not disapproval. Hultman's plan backfired.*]

"Campaigns sometimes bring out the best in people, and sometimes the worst. That campaign brought out the worst of Jim Schaben. I liked him better as Senator Jim Schaben than candidate Jim Schaben."

TOM WHITNEY "The biggest problem with Democrats who ran for governor against Bob Ray is that none of them ever had enough money. They didn't have access to it, and the business community didn't support them. They got nominal support from organized labor, and more of that in congressional and senatorial races than in gubernatorial races. The most unfortunate part of the Schaben-Gannon race was that Gannon made the decision to save his money for the general election. Schaben decided to spend it in the primary. Schaben wins, Gannon loses. Schaben turns out to be a terrible candidate. Ray did everything right, Schaben did almost everything wrong. After Bobby Fulton lost, our candidates were pretty sad."

DAVID OMAN "There were four of us who were the young guys hired to do the fieldwork for the Ray campaign. John Spooner, Roger Stetson, Dick Woods, and I. We were the young gunners who went out into the state promoting Bob Ray."

PAT MILLER "Stoner and I were the only two carryovers from the 1972 campaign staff. Bev Campbell and Larry Pope did all the opposition research. The finance crew was pretty much the same – Robb Kelley, Jack Pester. The difference between the 1972 and 1974 campaign was that the 1974 campaign was much more competitive and better organized. Part of that was due to the fact we didn't have a primary opponent and no tragedy, like Bob Liddy's death. And Schaben was the type of candidate you wanted to just out-hurrah.

"I was assigned his hometown of Dunlap to check the phone banks on election day. I drove into town and there was this big Bob Ray billboard covered with black paint. I got mad and went around and put Bob Ray bumper strips on every car in sight. People got so motivated for Bob Ray that it was easy to put together an extensive organization for him.

"Since then I've been around the country, worked in campaigns all over, and I'm continually amazed, because I naively thought all politics were like Iowa politics – clean, up-front, no filtering of this and that. I worked in Kansas City, in a mayor's race, and they were buying votes – you give street money to certain people and they turn out the vote for you. It was a whole different ball game, one that does not exist in Iowa."

ROGER STETSON "I've been involved in a lot of campaigns since, but that was one of the best, especially watching Tom Stoner organize it, down to the smallest level, from his big black notebook. We had target precincts and targeted every type of interest group—'Cosmetologists for Ray' and 'Chiropractors for Ray.' We recognized the problem of being too identified with being a Republican in that campaign, so we tried to go beyond the regular Republican precinct workers, supplement them with special-interest groups and young people.

"One area we worked especially hard was Iowa State, which tends to be a more conservative campus than the University of Iowa. It was a campus with a very high level of voter turnout, and that year they voted for Bob Ray, John Culver, and Tom Harkin, in very big margins. [*In Story County, Ray had a 9,710 margin, Culver a 2,441 margin, and Harkin a 6,195 margin.*] It was those sort of results that guaranteed his win.

"Stoner was also very big on what he called 'Hoopla': Hoopla Often Overcomes People's Lazy Attitudes. One of the first campaign events was a parade in Modale, in Harrison County, near Schaben's hometown. Tom thought it would be a good idea if Bob Ray went to the event. We took seven carloads of people and filled Stoner's plane with 'Ray Girls' and flew them over there. We put bumper stickers on every car, we had signs in each store window in downtown Modale, and all the little kids were waving Bob Ray signs. It was amazing to see the look on Schaben's face as he came down the street, seeing all these red-and-yellow Bob Ray signs in his home county. It got him off on a low note.

"Something else that can't be underestimated in that campaign was Billie Ray. She was an integral part of everything we did. They had just returned from China as the campaign started, and I'd say no less than 100 coffees were planned with Billie, and the main topic of conversation was China. Nixon had just opened the door to China, so there was little information back about the country, and all of a sudden Iowa's first lady had been there. She and the governor were good together, but she was actually better on her own. She never talked about issues, never got into any controversies, always very pleasant, charming.

"The Ray Girls? Yes, we were still using them in 1974. In fact, John Spooner and I both married former Ray Girls. They were right for Bob Ray, though I'm not sure anybody else could have pulled it off. But campaign styles have changed a lot just since then. Negative campaigning in 1974 just didn't exist. Everything was positive, upbeat."

LARRY POPE "That was a misleading campaign for somebody to be involved in for the first time. It would give you a false sense of perspectives about state campaigns. For one reason, Bob Ray was very involved in the campaign, and key decisions were made away from state headquarters. Wythe Willey was actually making many of the decisions, but it was certainly a bifurcated function, with Stoner, Wythe, and Bob Ray making all the decisions. Don't underestimate the tremendous impact Wythe Willey had on all of Bob Ray's campaigns and on the way Bob Ray ran his office.

"I was involved in opposition research in that campaign. They wanted to know what Jim Schaben was like, what he was saying. Schaben had come up pretty quickly and they didn't know that much about him, and he had given out an aura of effectiveness. So I went out and interviewed people he had run against in the past. As the campaign progressed I was out trying to identify his strategy. It did sound a lot like what Donald Segretti did for Nixon, but they were very careful to instruct me to act in a very ethical manner. But they still had a very strong need for political intelligence. I did a report every two weeks—big, fat folders of information.

"Some people have a placid attitude towards opponents. Bob Ray was not that way; he would get mad. I remember going up to Sioux City for a debate with Schaben, and in a staff meeting beforehand there was lots of anxiety about what Schaben might say to make Bob Ray mad. Their concern was that Bob Ray not get mad in the debate, because he was so far ahead in the polls. Stoner and Willey just kept saying, 'Now goddamit, Bob, no matter what he says, don't get mad at him.'

"I picked up some good campaign rules from Bob Ray that year. One was any time you see a toilet, use it, because you don't know the next time you might see one. Another time Terry Branstad and I got trapped on a boat late at night. Somebody asked us if we'd like to go for a ride, and what I expected to be a ten-minute ride turned into two and a half hours. I went back and told Dave Oman and he said, 'Oh, that's one of the governor's rules: Never get on a boat, because you can't control it.'"

DRAKE MABRY "Bob Ray truly enjoyed the ceremonial part of being governor, too. The grand openings, the ribbon cuttings. Most governors detest that stuff. Hughes hated it. But Ray really loved that stuff. Maybe it got to him privately, but he never let on."

DEL VAN HORN "He called me in June of 1974 and asked what I was doing on the Fourth of July. He wanted me to do some traveling with him, so we flew all over the state, going to parades. He was a real campaigner. He took his Fourth of July and spent the entire day going to everybody else's celebration."

It was the most bare-knuckled campaign of Ray's career. He felt that his previous opponents, Fulton and Franzenburg, had understood state government and that their campaigns were based on honest disagreements over how state government should be run. He refused to lump Schaben in that same category and called Schaben's campaign literature "deceitful garbage." The Democrat, said Ray, was "shotgunning" for an issue. Schaben stood to the right of Ray on abortion and to his left on the issue of the rising consumer interest rates. He accused Ray of a "dirty rotten trick" when the governor declined to debate him on a Cedar Rapids television station, then waited until Schaben appeared and claimed his own right to appear under the fairness doctrine.

Schaben's accusations notwithstanding, even Democrats around the state weren't convinced he was the best candidate. Shortly after his primary win, 48 percent of the Democrats said they'd vote for Schaben for governor, but 36 percent said they'd vote for Ray. In October, at the Democrats' annual Jefferson-Jackson Day Dinner in Ames, 8.4 percent of the highly partisan crowd polled said they were voting for Ray. On election day, Ray proved his overwhelming popularity, garnering 58.5 percent of the vote and topping Schaben by 166,000 votes.

XV: THE FOURTH TERM, 1975-1978

In January 1975, days after his fourth inaugural, Bob Ray was invited on an ABC morning television program to talk about the condition of Iowa's economy. At a time of nationwide prosperity, based largely on double-digit inflation, Iowa's revenues were flourishing, unemployment was low, the farmers were readying for another record-breaking season. The state, and its four-term governor, who had now held the office longer than any of his thirty-seven predecessors, was at a peak.

That could not be said of the governor's own political party, especially back home. The sour taste Richard Nixon left in voters' mouths had a dramatic effect on Iowa's partisan lineup. Democrats Dick Clark and John Culver, the state's two U.S. senators, were recognized as two of the nation's most liberal. Six of the seven representatives from the Hawkeye State to the U.S. House were Democrats. The lone Republican was eight-term state legislator Chuck Grassley, elected to replace H. R. Gross in the Third District. Bill Scherle and Wiley Mayne, both elected in 1966, fell to Democrats Tom Harkin and Berkley Bedell.

For the first time under Bob Ray, Democrats also controlled both houses of the state legislature. The Republicans lost six seats and control of the senate—now led by Des Moines's George Kinley—and seventeen seats and control of the house—now led by Dale Cochran from Eagle Grove. They would retain those majorities through Ray's fourth term.

Des Moines Register, Tom Hooper photo. Reprinted with permission.

The executive council of state leaders still boasted a full slate of Republicans – Lieutenant Governor Art Neu, Secretary of State Melvin Synhorst, State Auditor Lloyd Smith, State Treasurer Maurice Baringer, Secretary of Agriculture Robert Lounsberry, and Attorney General Richard Turner – but for the first time since Harold Hughes's governorship, Democrats outnumbered Republicans under the golden dome.

That didn't appear to bother the highly partisan Ray. In the past he'd often complained about the backstabbing he suffered from fellow Republicans in the legislature, and he wasn't convinced that dealing with a deck full of Democrats was going to be all that different. The faces would change at the governor's weekly leadership luncheons, but he knew they still had to contend with his own huge personal popularity and past successes to get much accomplished.

This term was to be Bob Ray's "power term." He'd been on the job nine years and accomplished much of what he'd planned. As the term began, his approval rating stood at 81 percent. The average for governors around the nation was 49 percent. By 1977, 98 out of every 100 Iowans recognized his name. He joked about trying to figure out who the missing 2 percent were. In a nationwide Gallup poll, 17 percent recognized his name among ranking Republicans. By this time he'd filled almost all of the 1,800 appointments to boards and agencies in the state, and those appointees – Democrats, Republicans, and independents – owed him for their positions. In October 1976, a few months after Iowa celebrated the nation's bicentennial in a big fashion, a job coordinated from the governor's office, the Ray family moved into Terrace Hill, the former Hubbell Mansion on Grand Avenue, which was still undergoing renovation.

WYTHE WILLEY "The difference between Bob Ray and most politicians in the 1970s, especially those who survived Watergate, was that he developed an amount of credibility that astounded politicians and pollsters alike. They couldn't understand his enormous popularity. He worked so hard and won the support of people such that eventually people got to the point where they would say, 'Well, I don't know whether the drinking age should be raised from eighteen to nineteen, but if Governor Ray thinks it's the right thing to do, he must be right.' He eventually developed so much personal credibility that the actions he took received an initial favorable response. Hardly anybody else was able to do that during those Watergate years.

"But what he was recognized for around the country, especially by other governors, was his reorganization of state government. I was always told by the political advertising and public relations people that management, good management of state government, was a nonsexy issue, that it was nothing, you couldn't sell that in a campaign. Nobody was going to reelect Bob Ray because he was a 'good manager,' they'd tell me.

"That first four-year term we had an opportunity, since we didn't have to run for reelection right away, to sit down and talk about our goals, what we wanted to do in the next four years. And one of those goals was to do a better job managing tax money, managing our resources. You've got to recognize that running state government is not too much different, managementwise, than running any other operation with roughly 45,000 employees. All the management tools, theories, principles apply, and we were then able to sit down and think them through. It was kind of a luxury for a governor to be able to do that.

"Bob Ray was trained as a lawyer, not a manager. He had to learn on the job. We had people in management positions who were technically trained – the head of the Conservation Commission was a wildlife biologist, the head of Social Services was basically a social worker, the head of the revenue department was a person that worked with numbers. But they were responsible for managing as well, just like the governor was. So we instituted management training programs, courses about decision making, performance appraisal, delegation of authority, just like they teach at the Harvard Business School. We spent some money doing it, and that wasn't always a very popular expenditure. Legislators would come up and say, 'What the hell are you training somebody to be a manager for? You're supposed to hire people with that kind of capability.' But we, like most big organizations, realized you have to train people continually. All of this was new to state government.

"We also recruited and hired some really top management people, along with the reorganization and training. People like Mike Reagen as head of the Department of Social Services and Vic Preisser at the Department of Transportation, real management hotshots. We hired from out of state, recruited a lot of people from within state government, switched a lot of people around. Because of Ray's long tenure he was able to develop this modern management. If the office had kept changing hands during the 1970s, I don't think it would have progressed as it did."

<u>BOB RAY</u> "By this stage we could do things with a better perspective based on previous experiences. The trivia was out of the way. But it never gets easy, because you either had new problems developing or old ones recurring, and you had to deal with them all. Sometimes experience helps, but a lot of times you're in a whole new ball game.

"We used to weigh carefully whether we wanted something we proposed to be known as a new program. On one hand, it was nice to let people know that you were coming up with innovative, creative ideas. One the other hand, 'program' had such a bad connotation because it seemed everybody had a 'program' for everything. A little dab of money here, a little dab of money there. New programs aren't necessarily solutions.

Where did the revenue surplus in those years come from? "Good times. But there were bad times then, too. Granted, you had money, so you could do a lot more, but when you have more money and inflation starts to skyrocket, then everybody wants that money, and you can never give them enough. I don't know how you measure it, but it's almost more difficult than when you don't have enough. Then everybody knows that and quits demanding it, they start working together to figure out how to sustain themselves with no increases. It was possible to do more when we had money flowing in, but inflation was the primary factor for those excesses. We weren't out raising taxes to bring in that extra money. But when inflation got into double digits, we couldn't keep up with it. You just couldn't increase salaries, for example, equal to the inflationary rate.

Those surpluses sure looked good to the public, though. "Yes, but we knew the bubble would break. That's why we tried hard not to use that money for recurring expenses. That was the time I always thought we should build, because it would be cheaper using that inflationary money. If you spent the money on recurring costs, when the economy tapered off you'd have that built-in obligation every year. We knew that and I think we did a fairly good job planning for it."

ART NEU "There wasn't a big need to raise taxes during the period, because of the growth and inflation. What we were doing was essentially taking the state funds—mostly the income tax, and to a lesser extent sales tax, revenues—and sending it back to relieve property taxes. If there is a criticism to be made, it might be that we did so much of that that certain state programs suffered in the process. I worry sometimes about some of the state programs that maybe starved too much in order to relieve property taxes."

BOB RAY *Did it make a difference that you had to work now with a Democratic-controlled legislature?* "It was different, because you really didn't have the feeling that they were there to help your program. Thus it was not easy to try and sell a program. Any time you change from one party to the other in the legislature there is a strong feeling that 'We now need to be the leaders.' I think in almost every session someone wanted the [*legislative*] leadership to provide the budget. The Democrats, particularly when they took control, that's what they wanted. But they couldn't do it. It's grand talk and they worked at it, but it just wasn't going to happen. You really need the governor's budget – not that it can't be changed, they could certainly try and improve on it, but to try to put together a budget with 150 people is unrealistic."

DAVID OMAN "The best thing he had going for him in terms of his relationship with the legislature was that he had been there longer than most of them. By that time you could probably count on your fingers and toes the number of people who had been there longer than he had. By the late 1970s you could count them on your fingers alone. He had encouraged many of them to run, helped them to win election. So the legislators, by and large, had respect for his political acumen, his endurance, his tenure, his savvy and that was very helpful to him."

CAL HULTMAN "The governor came up with the budget and that became our benchmark. The legislature massaged it, played with it, and normally adopted 95 percent of it. That's how it worked while he was governor."

JERRY FITZGERALD "It was really easier being the minority. You didn't have to worry as much about the day-to-day stuff, the nitty-gritty work. You have to care to that stuff when you're the majority. Doesn't matter if the work is good or bad, you've got to do it. I didn't get much sleep those four years. Even if I was in bed six hours, I'd only sleep four, spend the other two worrying. Every Sunday night I'd go to George Kinley's house and we'd plot and plan for the upcoming week."

"I am the one who is elected by the people, not the directors or the commissioners. So I am the one who is ultimately responsible for what happens in state government." So said Bob Ray in 1975 as he continued to try to strengthen the authority of the governor's office by making more and more of those directors and commissioners directly responsible to him. He fought hard to wean that authority away from the legislature, did everything within his power to limit the directors and commissioners who had autonomy or who were appointed by their own boards. Prior to Ray's governorship the state had been largely controlled by a handful of independent commissioners who reported to the legislature or to no one. The governor up until Harold Hughes's terms was often a weak link in the chain of command. Both Hughes and Ray recognized the need to strengthen the governor's authority and slowly began wheedling and plotting to gain more and more direct control over the 130-plus agencies of state government.

MAURICE BARINGER "Early on in the 1960s, Iowa was starting to get a stronger executive branch. During the 1960s and 1970s the ability of the governor, granted by the legislature, to appoint department heads without having as many confirmed by the senate or having the governor appoint them rather than have them selected by a board or commission, grew. The chances of getting more-professional people are better if they are appointed by the executive rather than by boards and commissions. The older, in terms of service, legislators didn't want to give up the patronage they had under the old system of the 1950s, but newer, younger members coming in produced the desire to see government function more efficiently without the legislature having to become full-time and become involved in the administration process. And to do that they helped increase the authority of the governor's office. It makes for better accountability and responsibility. If you know that one person can fire you, it's a lot different than if you've got a board of six or eight."

DAVID OMAN "Both [Harold] Hughes and Bob Ray were able to convince the legislature to make some changes in the way that boards, agencies, and commissions were structured so that the governor could make the appointment of department heads, not the citizen members who sat on the boards. That made the department heads more accountable to the governor. Sometimes it took a couple years for the legislature to see the wisdom of particular changes.

"A lot of the boards used to be governed by three people who were totally independent of the governor's office. A lot of them served terms that outlasted the governors', and they could keep some daylight between themselves and the governors, not have to be part of the team. That, coupled with the consolidation of state agencies, really strengthened the governor's office. The Department of Transportation was created. The Department of Environmental Quality, since renamed, was created under Ray. Job Service was reorganized. They used to have three people run that agency. Now there's a director hired and fired by the governor. The streamlining and consolidation were the two biggest changes. Also, the size of the governor's staff grew during Bob Ray's tenure. When Governor Erbe was there he had just two assistants, a couple secretaries, and a clerk. When Harold Hughes left office he had five administrative assistants. By the time Governor Ray left office we had eight administrative assistants, and a total of about twenty people working directly in our office."

BOB RAY "The one thing that continued to strengthen state government was giving the power of appointment of the department heads to the governor. I took the position that it wasn't the structure that made the government work, it was the people, and it was my responsibility to provide the leadership to make those boards and commissions work. I knew that it was not good management to have the legislature deprive the governor [of] the power of appointment of the directors who run the agencies of government. They couldn't very well hold me responsible, as they should be able to, if I couldn't control those appointments. They liked to do that, but in fairness I don't think they were able to; there really was a demarcation. If I made the appointment, they never hesitated to hold me accountable. [But] it was very easy for me to say, 'Hey, I agree with you, but I can't hire and fire that guy' [if I haven't made the appointment].

"Most of the legislators thought the governor had far too much power anyway. There was a degree of jealousy involved. Yet they couldn't run their businesses back home the way they expected me to run government, without the ability to hire and fire. So I would encourage them to give me that authority and try and take advantage of it. Usually it took something going haywire before they would give me the power to appoint a director. The Commission on [the] Aging was a good example of that.

"Leo Oxberger was one of the first judicial appointments I made. I really struggled with that because I wanted so much to make that system work better. People were coming in and telling me I should be sure that my appointments weren't tainted with politics and didn't have the appearance I was just appointing my friends. Well, I woke up one night, trying to evaluate all that, and said to myself, 'I believe in the system, and for years I've been trying to encourage people to work in the political system. Now I shouldn't favor Leo because of that, but I certainly shouldn't reject him, either. I shouldn't reject him just because he'd been active in the Republican party and he was my friend.' So that made it very easy, and it was a good decision.

"One problem with the kind of system we have in Iowa is that the governor doesn't have a cabinet and he can't appoint all of the department heads. That doesn't mean that the ones I would appoint were necessarily any better than the ones the boards and commissions would appoint, but it means that you have a different rapport. But when you do the screening yourself, or someone does on your behalf, and you make the final decision, that person knows whom he or she works for. When the board makes the appointment, that person obviously has to work for that board, not always the governor.

"A couple examples. One was the ombudsman. I couldn't convince the legislature that we needed that one. It was a new concept. I'd seen it in Hawaii and I thought we ought to have one. I thought it would work to benefit of government as well as the constituents. If you had a complaint, say in Social Services, and you went there and talked to a caseworker and didn't get satisfaction, went to a supervisor and didn't get satisfaction, ended up with the commissioner and didn't get satisfaction, and you were still angry and convinced they were wrong, you could go to an outside party, the state ombudsman. I didn't want it because it would lighten the load in the governor's office, it was just better to have someone totally impartial investigating a complaint and looking for answers. If government were wrong, we wanted to correct it.

" 'The legislature said, 'that's our job.' But there was no way they could spend the time and do the follow-up; they didn't have the staff. So when I couldn't get it from the legislature I got federal funding for it. In two years we proved the value of it and finally persuaded the legislature to accept it. Then they wouldn't let me make the appointment. It took them about a year and a half to make their first appointment. There was a legislator who wanted the position, and they told me they couldn't vote against him, but they didn't think he was the right person for the job. That shows why it didn't make sense for them to make appointments.

"I also had a tough time early on with the Department of Public Instruction. I talked to the board and told them the persons who'd been superintendent had served well, but I had some reservations about a reappointment. I thought they ought to know that. The appointment required senate confirmation, and I told them I didn't think they could get that confirmation if I opposed it, so if that were the person they insisted on appointing, I wanted to talk about it further. Without consulting me again, they reappointed him.

"That proved to me they weren't listening, they weren't in tune. It didn't fly; they couldn't get him confirmed and eventually backed off. That's where I had to use my influence, because I thought they were wrong. And it was unfortunate, because I wasn't angry with the person they wanted appointed. I just felt we needed new leadership. I always thought that I shouldn't have to work that way; I shouldn't have had to do indirectly what I should have been able to do directly. But that's the way the system worked."

DAVID OMAN "On the average, the governor made 500 to 600 appointments a year, and there were just shy of 2,000 total. During his tenure he appointed every board and commission member at least once and some-times two and three times.

"Politics played precious little part in the day-to-day appointment proc-ess, the fraction that people assumed, which was good. The problem was not that we had to check out so-and-so's political credentials and make sure that he or she was a true-blue believer or something like that. The problem was we always had so many specific requirements to meet for each board membership. Some had to meet certain income levels, some had to be just below the poverty line. And we usually didn't have files full of those names just sitting around. You also had to mix in demographic considerations – gender, race, age, geography, and political persuasion. We spent most of that time hunting up the proper number of Democrats and independents that were required to be appointed, tracking down qualified people who were interested in serving to fill a certain niche.

"We never really told prospective appointees that if appointed they were expected to surrender their political allegiance or sacrifice in any way. All we asked was that if they ever found themselves in a situation where they were at odds with us, to at least do us the courtesy of talking to us first so that we didn't have to read about it in the morning newspa-per. People were pretty good about that."

BOB RAY *Is the governor's office more powerful due to the changes during those fourteen years?* "That's hard to answer, because a lot of power was taken away from the states when the Great Society programs were started. The idea was to go directly to the people, let them be on the boards and decide how to spend the money. Disaster after disaster struck when that happened. The Great Society programs often bypassed the states and went right to the cities. There were people in Congress who loved that, because they represented cities more than states. That, too, ended up badly, because when the programs were cut off, the cities ran to the states and said, 'What are you going to do?' But they didn't want to talk to us until the federal government cut their supply off.

"I think the governor's office became stronger – more powerful, if you want to use that term – but it really was a matter of perception. We really didn't demand much from our people; we tried to work with them. We didn't threaten to fire people if they didn't do things our way. I didn't make appointments on boards by getting firm commitments that they'd do this or that for me. I just tried to get people who would be rational and listen carefully, use good judgment, and would work with us. I think we had some success with that approach."

TOM HIGGINS "I think Ray found it easier working with a Democratic majority. He's really a centrist anyway and was pretty comfortable with Democratic logic."

GEORGE KINLEY "The bottom line on Ray is that he was a good caretaker. He did a good job for the state, didn't raise taxes, because he believed if you raised taxes the legislature would try and overspend the money anyway. But from 1975 to 1978, when we controlled the legislature, we left him with a $150 million surplus. When you have money like that, it's pretty easy to keep everybody in line."

DEL STROMER "He always worked hard to find a balance, the middle ground. He didn't shoot from the hip. You could rarely get a commitment on whether he was going to veto a bill. He also didn't let the press play with him. He would be evasive, aloof, just a little hard to get to. Branstad, if you mention the press, he's ready to meet them in three minutes. You know, I get criticized a lot because I talk about Branstad and I talk about Hughes and I talk about 'The Governor,' as if Ray was the only real governor. But that's the way I feel."

JIM WEST "Those four years we were the minority we stuck pretty close to him because he had the edge. If the governor said no to a Republican plan, we'd never win. Between the governor, the senate Democrats, and the house Republicans, the governor got pretty much what he wanted that term. He'd compromise at the very end of the session, but never until then. Honestly, he probably had as tough a time passing legislation through Republican legislatures as he did Democratic ones. The meetings were different, though. When the Republicans controlled, the meetings were in private, in the governor's office, instead of on the floor of the house or senate. Your battles were private rather than public."

NANCY SHIMANEK "He definitely controlled the agenda those years. He had four things going for him: one, he had good ideas; two was his political and personal persuasion; three, he obviously had the support of the people around the state; four, he had the experience to know how to get things done. Plus he'd turned his office into such an efficient operation that it had all the information, accessibility, and power in terms of bodies to turn out the necessary information."

DEL STROMER "When Jerry Fitzgerald became majority leader in 1975 he immediately began running for governor. The speaker, Dale Cochran, had entertained the idea he'd like to be governor, but he just didn't quite have enough smarts to put it together. So when Ray would attack the legislature during those years, it was more aimed at Fitzgerald. One time, the last week of June, the Shriners came into his office wearing clown suits and Bob Ray said, 'Oh, I thought the legislature adjourned already.' "

As well as being popular at home, Ray's successes had led him prominently into the national political scene. In 1975 he turned down an offer from President Ford to become secretary of the interior. That same year he was elected chairman of the National Governors' Association. In 1976 he was mentioned often as presidential timber and was considered as a running mate by Ford at the Republican convention in Kansas City. Throughout that term Ray was on the road—to Russia, China, Israel, New Guinea, and elsewhere internationally—and was invited to speak at every imaginable conference in virtually every state in the nation. He was comfortable with his job, had a strong staff with his full confidence back home, and he was out representing Iowa, and himself, at every available opportunity.

EARL USHER "By this time, people always recognized him, wherever we'd go. Everybody knew him, even in faraway airports at six in the morning. It got to a point where the troopers had traveled with the governor so much that we'd go downtown to pick something up, walk into a place, and people would start looking for the governor. They'd even started recognizing his troopers."

FROSTY MITCHELL "Harold Hughes held a press conference once and said, 'The people of Iowa elected me to run the state. They don't expect me to run out to Strawberry Point and plant a tree and then jump across the state and cut a ribbon at a new supermarket. So if you're writing the governor's office about those kinds of things, don't.' I thought that was pretty good. But Bob . . . Jesus, he loved that stuff. If he could ride in three parades a day, he'd try. But he was never as bad as the new governor; he's even more public. I don't think Terry has realized the campaign's over."

BOB TYSON "Nixon's staff looked on governors like the governor's staff looked on members of the board of supervisors—as if they didn't have much clout. Presidents generally bring in governors if they've got agricultural problems—you know, bring in four or five farm-state governors for the TV cameras, use them as a sounding board. But ordinarily they view them as kind of a nuisance."

GERALD FORD "That's not the way I viewed Bob Ray. We had a very good personal relationship. Within the Republican spectrum he and I were almost the same part of it. I wish I'd been able to convince him to join my cabinet, as either secretary of the interior or secretary of agriculture. But he felt he had an obligation to carry out his term as governor, that he'd been elected and ought to fulfill his term.

"On domestic programs, I certainly respected the advice and comments of middle-of-the-road, moderate governors like Bob Ray, and Bill Milliken of Michigan. And in the mid-1970s the states were in pretty good shape, so that we pushed very hard to expand the block-grant program, to give the states more money and more authority, in part because I felt that money was far better watched in the hands of governors like Ray and Milliken, for example, than some congressmen."

BOB RAY *President Ford says he offered you a couple jobs. Why didn't you take them?* "I ran for governor and that's what I intended to do. Constantly someone would think I wanted to be a judge or wanted to go into the cabinet. Little did I realize how difficult it was, when the president asks you to do something, to say no to him. And Jerry Ford was such a genuine, wonderful guy, that made it especially hard. He asked if I would take the job as secretary of interior. I finally told him I'd come to Washington and visit with him about it. I did, went into the Oval Office and told him I'd thought seriously about his offer and that I wouldn't if it hadn't been him asking. I told him I was flattered and honored, and that I'd love to work for him, but I just didn't think I should leave Iowa. He wanted me to take the Interior job and then eventually become secretary of agriculture.

"I'd known Jerry Ford a long time. I remember when he would come out in the 1960s and give a speech someplace. I was state chairman then, and I'd pick him up, drive him wherever he was going. He'd be all by himself, out grinding it out for the party, just carrying a little bag with his toothbrush in it. He had a full-time job in Washington, but he was willing to just pick up and go. He was always good-natured about it.

"When he was vice-president he worked well for the governors. He'd walk in, sit down, and listen to you. He never appeared to be fighting us, and he'd just try to figure out how to help. It was a pleasure to work with him. Much different from Nixon. You'd sit around the table with Nixon and questions would be raised about certain things and he'd point his finger at somebody, and say, 'Bob [*Haldeman*], you take care of that,' and 'John [*Ehrlichman*], you take care of that,' and he'd walk out. It didn't seem like anything ever happened. Jerry Ford, on the other hand, would sit down with me, almost like a brother, and try and help.

How did you get the job of chairman of the National Governors' Association? "Politics [*he laughs*]. When I first got elected I didn't want any of those offices. But I'd been the Midwestern Governors' chairman and the Republican Governors' chairman, and then I thought I'd like to be the national chairman. The job alternates between parties. Cal Rampton from Utah was the chairman before I, and several governors asked if I'd be interested. But Jim Holshouser of North Carolina wanted it then, too, so we had a little confrontation, a campaign. It's one of those things that once you get into it, you just don't say, 'Oh well, if he wants it, let him have it.' Anyway, I won.

"I was elected in 1975, at a summer session in New Orleans. We were trying not to have these fantastic, fun, pleasurable conventions, because most of the states were tightening up their spending. They'd always been pretty plush conferences, though. Probably the most plush I attended was one Ron and Nancy Reagan hosted in California. But in New Orleans it kind of reached a pinnacle. Ed Edwards was the governor, and they really put on a good show. It was later reported that that affair cost $10,000 per governor.

"But our big conference was in 1976, the bicentennial year. It was in Hershey, Pennsylvania. We paid a visit to Queen Elizabeth on her yacht in Philadelphia, then went over to Independence Hall and met Charlton Heston. The president was there too."

DWIGHT JENSEN "In a room full of governors, Bob Ray tended to stand out a bit. It's hard to describe in words, but he makes a very good appearance, and among his peers he was well known and well respected. One thing that turns other governors off is people who grandstand a lot, showboat. Most of the governors who were after things nationally, including George Wallace, Ronald Reagan, Nelson Rockefeller, would tend to come in and take over meetings to get media attention. Ray never did that. He was always well prepared.

"Guys like Cal Rampton, Dan Evans, Bill Milliken, Ray were the outstanding governors during the 1970s. They were the pacesetters who helped bring state government along."

DICK GILBERT "One time I was introduced to Frank Sargent, who was Republican governor of Massachusetts, as an aide to Bob Ray. He said, 'That Bob Ray, that's one SOB that's got his head screwed on straight.' Bob Ray had a reputation among his peers of being a guy that didn't come to governors' conferences to shoot off his mouth or get a lot of ink or raise hell, but when he got up to speak he was generally very persuasive, very cogent."

<u>KEITH DYSART</u> "The National Governors' Association is a club of fifty and if you're elected to chair it, it is because of the strength of your persuasive skills and preparation. At the governors' conferences all the governors and key aides would be there, along with the cream of the nation's media. There was always an atmosphere of competition. Here you had fifty men and women who were accustomed to being the center of attention, and while some members of the media were naturally attracted to the leaders of the megastates, others, of the stature of David Broder or Roy Apple, were attracted to talent. It's the fastest track imaginable other than running for the presidency.

"I and other staffers of the NGA agreed that Bob Ray was one of the three best governors of the 1970s. Bill Milliken and Dan Evans rounded out that shortlist. Bob was a real leader of that group, and he succeeded by his decency, because a lot of those guys knew they couldn't carry his briefcase when it came to decency and ethics. If he has a fault, it is that decency to an absurdity. And he led by quiet, individual persuasion, one on one. Bob Ray could flip most of the governors on their backs, one on one.

"Governor Reagan, by and large, was not willing to endure that type of competition. Naturally, he carried some clout because he represented a megastate, and he certainly got media attention, but he did not enjoy the respect amongst his peers that Bob Ray did."

With hard work and good luck comes, inevitably, some bad luck. In 1977, after almost a decade on the job, Ray was touched by some minor scandals. There may be a little quid-pro-quo appointment making, some looking the other way in party politics, but as a rule Iowa politics is as clean as the proverbial hound's tooth, and Bob Ray's "Jack Armstrong, All-American" image fit perfectly with that aura. But in 1977 several Ray associates got their names in the papers for something more than accepting awards from the Rotary Club. Beer and Liquor Control Department director Roland Gallagher was indicted for, and later found innocent of, accepting gifts and gratuities when he used a liquor salesman's membership to the Embassy Club in Des Moines. The adjutant general of the National Guard, General Joseph May, resigned his office after being found guilty of using military aircraft on several occasions to visit his fiancée in Florida. State comptroller Marvin Selden's name was found on credit-card slips discovered in a raid on a Polk County massage parlor. He left state government, after sixteen years as comptroller, in 1978. Labor commissioner Jerry Lee Addy was fired because of his connection with a case involving a stolen suit.

Though the phrase had not yet been used in a political sense, Ray's image had a Teflon coating of its own, and the minor indiscretions of a small number of his appointees didn't scratch it, or threaten his popularity.

Two conflicts involved Ray more personally in the last two years of his fourth term, though. One was the investigation of the National Guard initiated by a series of legislative queries and hearings during Ray's race against Jerry Fitzgerald for a fifth term in 1978. Then, in mid-1977 he was jumped by the press and the Democrats for accepting a trip to Taiwan, with the estimated $7,000 cost paid for by the Taiwanese government. Ray claimed he'd accepted the visit to "call attention to Iowa exports." A *Register* editorial claimed he should have paid his own way: "If a government official believes a trip abroad would be useful, the trip should be financed by the government or by the official out of his own pocket." Attorney General Richard Turner, rarely a Ray ally, wondered, "What state business is there in Taiwan?" but later cleared Ray of any wrongdoing, saying, "I don't see how the trip could influence any official action the governor could take." Ray claimed the *Register,* and reporter John Hyde, were out "to tear him to pieces." His former press secretary, Dick Gilbert, then director of corporate development for the Register and Tribune Company, opined that the governor was "a victim of his own success." New press secretary David Oman puts it differently: "He was on a roll, nobody had laid a glove on him, and this was the first example of something that might not have been right or proper and they jumped on his back."

BOB RAY "The worst experience I had with the press was after I returned from Taiwan. By that time I thought I had a pretty good track record. I always figured if I told the truth, that should be enough. If they wanted to make a couple phone calls, fine, but I was accustomed to telling the truth. But Flansburg was on my case about that trip. Even after checking with the State Department and not finding anything amiss with my actions, he still wrote there was a question about my breaking the rules of the Constitution.

"I always felt the press was pretty good to me, that most reporters were trying to be objective. The *Register* had never been particularly interested in my travels before, but when I got back from Taiwan, John Hyde called and wanted to talk to me right away. He came in and said, 'Tell me about your trip.' I told him it had been interesting, I had visited the Republic of China, and I thought maybe we could do more business with Taiwan. The first question he asked was 'who paid for it?' "

JOHN HYDE "The issue at hand was whether or not he'd broken state law, which at the time flatly prohibited anyone from accepting a gift of more than twenty-five dollars, a flat prohibition. And as I read it, and others, legislators included, read it, it was pretty cut and dried. Ray was quite upset about it. He thought it questioned his integrity. He was quite angry, the only time I ever saw him that angry. He called me up and wanted to know if I'd come back and talk to him. I went over, and he was still quite angry, visibly angry. I didn't even know he had a temper at that point. His argument was that there was no personal benefit in it for him; it was for the good of the state of Iowa."

BOB RAY "They had apparently decided that it was wrong that I allowed the Taiwan government to pay the expenses. But if you go to the Republic of China, you couldn't pay, you couldn't just call up a hotel and get reservations, you couldn't rent a car. This was about the time Mike Gartner had come on, and the *Register* was flexing its muscles, trying to test just how powerful they were. They wrote story after story about how I had perhaps violated the Constitution of the United States. I had checked with the State Department before I went and there had been no reason I shouldn't. They kept tearing at me and then took an Iowa Poll to find out if the people thought I should have gone or not and 63 percent said I should have. They never wrote another word." [*In January 1978, Taiwan bought $32.7 million worth of grain from Iowa, the single largest grain sale in Iowa history to date. Whether this was a direct result of Ray's visit is unclear.*]

It was a successful term for Ray, the biggest complaint being from fellow Republicans that on occasion he sounded more like a Democrat than one of them. He used the term to fine-tune his reorganization, sometimes using the legislature, sometimes his appointees at the agencies, sometimes both. He oversaw the rewriting of the criminal code, reorganized the Employment Security Commission, expanded property tax relief laws, revised open-meetings laws, and pushed several environmental bills, most publicly lobbying hard and heavily for the passage of a bottle bill calling for a deposit on returnable cans and bottles, which he signed in 1978. Though the state revenues continued to grow—including more and more federal monies and programs appropriated to the states under President Ford's block-grants push—and though the state's surplus ranged from $100 to $250 million, the boom economy began to wane by the end of this term. By 1977 Marvin Selden was predicting increased budgets and declining revenues. Ray was warned by business leaders around the state that the lack of industrial expansion and new industry start-ups cost Iowa 7,100 jobs in 1977 and was depriving the state government of needed revenues. As export prices dropped and grain surpluses rose, farm income declined. The governor's office was not unaware of the potential economic problems that loomed, especially because they were coupled with an uneasy national economy. In the opening paragraphs of his State of the State address in January 1978, Governor Ray noted that in 1977 "Grain prices dropped. Production costs went up. This has placed an unbearable squeeze on many farmers, particularly young ones. The ripple effect is now beginning to show up in cutbacks in the production of farm implements . . . that means jobs." In 1978, one Ray staffer remembers, "we adopted a 'hold the line' philosophy." "I never tried to take credit for the good things that happened economically," Ray says today, "just like I didn't want to take the blame when things weren't happening right, because there were so many things we didn't have any control over."

Terry Branstad, who was then a state legislator, remembers that "during that period, while the revenues kept rolling in at 25 percent above the previous year, we thought that's the way things were going to be forever. Land prices were always going to go up, revenue was always going to go up. We didn't know that it could go down. Now we've learned that's not true."

XVI:
THE BOTTLE BILL

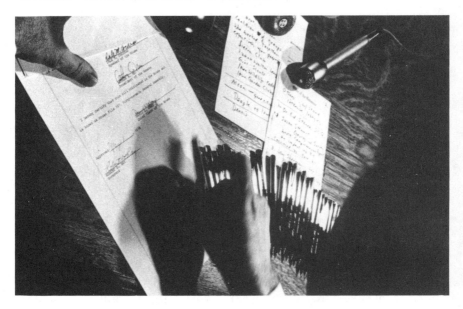

When Bob Ray left the governorship, hundreds of interviewers asked him to name the particular piece of legislation that made him most proud, the law created during his tenure that stood out as the best. In interview after interview the bottle bill, passed in the waning hours of the legislative session of 1978, during his fourth term, was the bill he mentioned first. He cited it because it had presented him with a real challenge.

In the grand scheme of public law, a bill requiring a nickel deposit on cans and bottles would hardly seem the highlight of a fourteen-year administration. But it was a perfect, if not *the* perfect, Bob Ray piece of legislation. It wasn't very sexy, though energy conservation was certainly a hot topic during the 1970s, but it had good, strong public support. A *Des Moines Register* Iowa Poll conducted in April 1977, showed 71 percent of the state's residents hoped it would become law. The bill did not raise any additional tax revenues, but that was not a priority in those days of treasury surpluses.

Signing the bottle bill. *Des Moines Register,* George Ceolla photo. Reprinted with permission.

A similar bill had been proposed in various forms over the years, and when Bob Ray included it as a priority in his 1977 State of the State Address, three states already had similar legislation – Washington, Oregon, and Michigan. "Energy can be saved, litter reduced, the environment improved and consumers benefited," claimed Ray in his January speech.

But the proposition was violently opposed, as it had been in other states, by a coalition of bottlers, beer and soft-drink distributors, and grocers, both in and outside of the state's borders, who launched an intensive advertising and lobbying effort to see that it did not become Iowa law. Opponents claimed it would destroy jobs, wouldn't clean up anything, would impose a tremendous inconvenience on consumers, and would increase the cost of beer and soft drinks.

Mary Fitzgerald, longtime lobbyist for the grocers, was an early but cautious opponent. "Bob Ray wanted that bill," she recalls. "Remember, he had a Democratically controlled legislature, and labor was against the bill. He had to pick up enough Republican votes to offset that, and the grocers were big contributors to a lot of Republicans. He did it masterfully. In fact that was an example of why he may be the best *politician* Iowa ever had."

According to Ray's press secretary at the time, David Oman, "It was an important bill because it touched people's lives. You can talk forever about how great the school foundation plan was, but there may be only five people in the state who really understood it. The bottle bill touched everybody, kind of like driver's licenses."

DENNIS NAGEL "The first time the bill was introduced in the Iowa legislature was in the early 1970s by state representative John Mendenhall, a conservative Republican from the far northeast corner of the state. It never went anywhere. He'd introduce it each year, it would be referred to the Energy Committee or some environment committee, and it would just sit. But as the seventies wore on, it gained more supporters.

"We got interested in it for a couple reasons. One was we were getting letters from citizens who were interested in it for environmental reasons. So we read up about the efforts in the two states that had litter control laws, Washington and Oregon. Oregon had the deposit approach, while Washington put a tax on manufacturers.

"Late in 1975, early 1976, we were putting together a list of possible ideas for the governor's annual program, and this concept of litter control worked its way onto the list, except it didn't have any specific form, because we knew there were two approaches. So we did some preliminary sorts of efforts to figure out which approach was better."

ED STANEK "We were at a National Governors' Conference in New Orleans, at a meeting of the Natural Resources Committee, and a vote was taken on whether or not the governors should go on the record for a mandatory national bottle bill. Governor Ray leaned over and said he thought that was something Iowa ought to pursue, and he became the only governor to vote for the national bill that didn't already have a similar law in his state.

"When we got back to Iowa he asked me to do an exhaustive study of the impact on all aspects of Iowa society. We looked at the employment aspects – we didn't have any glass factories in the state, so we wouldn't be putting bottlers out of work. There was also significant potential for reducing litter, which seemed to be working in Washington and Oregon. That was very visible, very public. It also made the system inherently more efficient and more cost effective. Instead of spending money for trash that ends up in a landfill, why not spend money for the contents of the container and then recycle the container?

"We looked at the effect on the economy and employment, on the environment, and put all the information into a package that was very defensible. He reviewed it and concluded it was good for the state."

DENNIS NAGEL "That report was completed in December of 1976, and about the same time Buz Brenton came into the office, without solicitation, as a citizen and environmentalist and recommended seeking passage of a similar bill. The thrust of our conversation with Buz was that the Oregon approach, the deposit law, seemed to be the most viable. The governor thanked Buz for coming in, and then we really sat down and studied the report. Early in 1977 we concluded that he ought to recommend it. We did not do a lot of beforehand contacting of groups that we knew would be concerned about the proposal. But the Republican leadership, who was in the minority for a second two years, came to us and said they wanted to be *for* something, not opposed to everything. That was another incentive to come up with some progressive proposals.

"I remember sitting in the house chamber during the governor's message, between Laverne Schroeder and Mary O'Halloran, who was chairman of the House Energy Committee and a very strong supporter of the bottle and can bill, when he proposed it. She couldn't believe it, but she jumped up and led the applause.

"His support of the bill made it legitimate, valid, put it in the spotlight.

Suddenly it went from a bill that nobody paid much attention to, to one that was discussed on the talk shows. Polls were taken on its support, and it drew support and opposition right away. Suddenly it was way up on everybody's list. We kind of caught its opponents off-guard.

"The beer distributors and soft-drink lobbyists were against it. Organized labor opposed it because it drew opposition from aluminum, steel, and glass producers. They saw fewer of their products being needed, so they opposed it. And, of course, the big Alcoa plant in Davenport and their big union were a presence. Retailers opposed it because they were going to have to take the dirty things back. All these people had economic interests, which is a great motivator. People see the light very quickly when it's their pocketbook in question. So they started working over the legislature pretty well, especially back home.

"On our side we had environmental groups, the Sierra Club, the Boy Scouts, the Farm Bureau, church groups – the do-gooders. And the initial response from the public was that they wanted it.

"It got out of the House Energy Committee in 1977 but we still had opposition from both sides. When it finally got to the floor of the house, the sponsors decided they couldn't afford to try to ram it through. The house passed a compromise version, and the bill was held over for Senate consideration in 1978."

BOB RAY "We pursued that bill methodically. I just thought that was one thing that we had in Iowa – our environment – that we ought to protect, preserve, and appreciate. It wasn't a brand new concept, but nobody in Iowa had really developed it."

ANDY VARLEY "It was one of those bills that had a high visibility, something that made an observable difference in the countryside. It's the kind of thing you can feel good about. It probably doesn't compare at all in the overall significance to the school aid formula, but it's something that the general public understood. You can drive across Iowa and see the difference."

JERRY FITZGERALD "It wasn't his idea, others had introduced it, there was nothing original about it. There just aren't that many original ideas in politics. But it is fair for him to take a lot of credit for it. Whether you agree with the method or not, the ditches are cleaner today, and that would not have happened without his support."

JOHN SCOTT "For the most part, if you were a politician at that time, you went out, especially in the rural areas, and said, 'Good God, we've got a bill that's going to clean up our roadsides and conserve precious metals and energy and perhaps save money all at the same time.' It was a bill that was attractive to people and readily understood."

LOWELL JUNKINS "Eighty percent of the people in the state wanted it. Once he proposed it, that bill was going to pass even if he dropped dead. Area colleges—a Harold Hughes initiative—didn't pass because 80 percent of the people wanted them; that was an example of a governor taking a leadership role, having vision."

MARY FITZGERALD "It did not deserve the publicity it got. The media liked it, in part because the governor was calling legislators in and telling them they were going to vote for this bill. That got the media interested. It makes a big difference when you've got the governor coming out and making an issue of a bill, making it one of his priorities for that year, especially with a governor as popular as Governor Ray was.

"We knew it was going to be tough to beat. I told my board after the State of the State address, 'Get ready. You might as well start building your little bins, because it's coming.' One of them, a very influential person, who'd made lots of contributions to the governor, said, 'I'll just go over and talk to him. Will you go with me?' I said, 'No, I won't. I've been there.' I said, 'You go and you're going to come out cut and bleeding.' He said, 'I don't think so.' 'Well, call me when you get out, about noon.' About quarter to twelve he called and said, 'Have you got any bandages and iodine?' To me it was not the most important issue that Governor Ray could have zeroed in on, but that was his prerogative."

JOHN SCOTT "I was the chairman of the senate committee that it was assigned to and its floor manager. It was perceived as the keystone of that session. As far as its importance is concerned, it certainly wasn't a revenue raiser, but I think it was perceived to be important because there was a great deal of popular backing for it."

DICK RAMSEY "I cosponsored the effort in the senate. Part of our strategy, with Senator Scott being a Democrat and I a Republican, was to round up support from both sides of the senate. But our strongest opposition came from *both* parties. Without the governor's leadership it would have been difficult to pass. I think it would have received attention and would have been worked on in the committees, but I doubt seriously whether we would have had the muscle to get the thing passed. The governor's office spent a lot of time on the bill, and they were taking some of the heat we were receiving. If they'd cave in, it would never have gotten through the legislature. But we had the assurance from downstairs that if we got it passed, he would sign it."

JOHN SCOTT "The governor's aides spent a great deal of time on the bill, an unusual amount of time, and did a good job. Remember, at that time energy conservation was a great concern, and there was a lot of discussion about the conservation ethic. If we get people to return their cans, maybe we can have the same effects in other areas. At that time, of course, the state was not suffering a lot of the problems that we are now. We did not have the deficit apprehensions that we have today. Everything looked nice and rosy."

DICK RAMSEY "As a rule, the governor's office wouldn't take on a group like the grocers. It's not smart to do that every day; you can't afford to. Interestingly, Alcoa eventually came around to our side. I think it's the exception for a Republican governor to strike out on a course that would pit him against, for example, an interest group that would normally be on his side, like the grocers. But I think he had a good sense of where the public would come down on the thing. He wasn't going to lose any public support over the bill.
"I met a number of times with Hy-Vee officials and with individual grocers in my area, and there was absolutely no support for it."

MARY FITZGERALD "The guys from Hy-Vee kept assuring me, 'Don't worry about Dick Ramsey. He'll come around to our side.' Finally I told Dwight Vredenburg [*chairman of Hy-Vee*], 'Dwight, honey, wake up.' Sometimes people in business don't always see the ramifications of what goes on at the statehouse.
"Bob Ray was very, very influential with many of the Republican legislators and very, very determined. There's one thing it takes to get a bill passed and that's votes, and there are several ways of getting them. The governor used his 'persuasion' by plain telling them you will vote for the bill. That was common knowledge. They were in there twisting arms."

RUSTY LAIRD "The beer wholesalers who I represented were totally opposed to it, and we formed a coalition with the soft-drink bottlers, the retail food dealers, some of the packaging people. And it was the one bill that the legislature just ran me over with. If it weren't for Bob Ray, it wouldn't have passed, though. He tipped the scales on that one."

BOB RAY "A lot of governors chose to stay away from similar bills, but once I proposed it I was wasn't going to let special-interest money defeat us. I think that's an example of where special-interest money was used for just plain power, more than any other time I can remember.

"The bottle and can distributors and manufacturers, the grocers, glass people spent millions of dollars trying to defeat that bill. They were, frankly, good people, but when it came down to their own special interest, the benefits of society were secondary. Some of the propaganda they put out was unbelievable.

"I thought it would have been a great opportunity for the industry – the distributors and the manufacturers – to step forward and say, 'Let's clean up.'"

MARY FITZGERALD "We were accused of being nonenvironmentalists and not being interested in the welfare of the state, that we weren't interested in keeping the state clean, which was not exactly fair. Our philosophy was that legislation, or any kind of government, when it's introduced, causes expenses of enforcement, and this bill was going to cost the grocers. We encouraged an education program instead of the bottle bill."

RUSTY LAIRD "Alcoa was with us at the start, but they bailed out, made a deal with the governor. Oregon had just passed the bottle law and put in a two-tier system. Their system said that if you've got a package that comes back and is refilled, like bottles, the deposit would be five cents. If you had a container that could not be refilled, like cans, the deposit would be ten cents. Well, it became an economic choice for Alcoa. They could see that if that two-tier system was adopted in Iowa, they would be at an economic disadvantage to the glassmakers. So they struck a deal with the governor to make damn sure there was only one deposit. In return, they agreed to drop their opposition."

DENNIS NAGEL "Bob Ray worked very closely with Alcoa because he was sensitive about their concerns; he didn't want to hurt an Iowa business. He was also concerned about the impact they could have because they affected all of the Scott County legislators, and there were a lot of votes there. So he talked with them on a repeated basis, trying to find out their concerns. In Oregon, when they passed the bill, there was a two-tier deposit system, a higher deposit for cans that were not reusable and a lower deposit for containers that any distributor could use, just put a different label on it. Well, aluminum cans don't work that way, because you've got to crush them. Alcoa thought that aluminum was being discriminated against. In December of 1977, early in 1978, they came to the governor, and said, 'We've looked at this thing again and we think you're right. We're going to back off, and though we can't be strongly and gung ho in favor, because the other aluminum companies still oppose it, we're not going to oppose it anymore.' That certainly eased our way upstairs with the legislature, because it took away some of the intensity from the opposition of the manufacturers and the AFL-CIO.'"

BOB RAY "The special interests claimed the bill would create a terribly high cost for the consumer and cried about how many jobs would be lost. I made an appearance in southern California when they were trying to pass a similar bill, and I had demonstrators, people who thought they'd lose their jobs. They screamed and hollered at me, claiming that the charitable organizations would be driven out of business because the Boy Scouts and people like that wouldn't make any money picking up bottles and cans. Just awful arguments. It was exciting for me that we overcame those special interests. We didn't have any money to speak of, to go on television and argue against them. And they were going right to the public, not limiting their arguments to the legislature. So we were forced to take them head on, outside of the rotunda.

"They talked about how dramatically the price would go up. It changed a little at first, because the bottlers saw an advantage. It gave them an opportunity to raise the price. Every time cigarette taxes would go up two cents, the price per package would go up a nickel, and they'd blame it on the tax increase. The bottlers did the same thing after the bottle bill was signed into law.

"Usually a governor's program includes that which he wants done, whether it is his number one priority, or whatever. So we always included things that didn't look as significant as well as those of extreme importance. If it were today, the bottle bill certainly wouldn't take priority over the farm crisis, but at that time I could spend time on it.'"

DENNIS NAGEL "He liked the bill because it was a case where he was responding to public interest and not beholden to any special interest. It was a classic case for his administration, because we were being opposed by a group that could be seen in selfish terms.

"There were some odd moments in our attempt to get it passed. One legislator didn't want to support it, and he was a key vote on the Energy Committee. I'd visit with him and I'd say 'Now look, we need this thing,' and gave him all the reasons. The farmers in his district wanted it; he knew that. But he couldn't support it, and we couldn't understand what the stumbling block was, because he basically agreed with the governor. We finally figured out what his problem was. He served in the National Guard, and the previous summer while driving in a truck there was an empty Coke bottle in the truck and one of the guys took a piss in it. That bothered him, that empty containers might have foreign things put in them. I tried to tell him that empty bottles have had things put in them for a long time and we've all survived. He finally came around and supported the bill, but it was a case where he wasn't being pressured by anybody; business interests hadn't gotten to him.

"Another legislator, an environmentalist, a strong Izaak Walton League member, was very opposed to the bill. We couldn't understand why, and Governor Ray said, 'Get the guy down here and let me talk to him. Maybe I can persuade him.' So we brought him down, and it was not an easy meeting. I could tell he didn't want to change his mind, and he never relaxed; he grabbed hard to his chair the whole time. Governor Ray said, 'Don't you think the people of your district want this bill? All the polls suggest they do.' Turns out this guy was getting a lot of mail from constituent grocers, putting a big squeeze on him. He was willing to bow to that pressure.

"Over in the senate there was legislator, a good friend of the governor's, who sat on the Energy Committee. We needed his vote to make sure there was no trouble. But other legislators told us he was unbending and that they needed our help to get him to vote yes, so we called him down, had a pleasant chat with him. He listened to everything we had to say, nodded his head, and then said, 'I'm sorry, I'm still not going to vote for it.' About six months later, after the bill had passed, we found that his campaign treasurer was the grocer in his hometown. Odd thing was he lost his next campaign.

"It's not like we were raising an additional $40 million for the state or reapportioning the school districts, but the bottle bill was definitely our largest accomplishment of that year. It also came in an election year, and it was a great bill to go out and campaign on."

In April 1978 the bottle bill, affixing a nickel deposit to all cans and bottles, passed in the senate by 36 to 11. The bill signing, on May 11, was the best-attended signing since Ray penned his name to the law permitting public employees to bargain collectively in 1974. So many legislators, lobbyists, and supporters wanted to have their picture taken with the governor that day they had to move the signing out of the governor's office and into the capitol rotunda. Smiling widely, he signed the bill at the foot of the rotunda's staircase with 200 people spread out behind him.

XVII: KANSAS CITY

The Republican National Convention in Kansas City fell in August 1976, smack in the middle of Bob Ray's fourth term. The featured battle of the convention was between President Gerald Ford and challenger Ronald Reagan, and Iowa's convention delegation turned out for the affair in full battle dress, its thirty-six members split right down the middle. As the convention got rolling, the delegates were split, eighteen for Gerald Ford and seventeen for Ronald Reagan, with State Representative Tom Tauke uncommitted.

One area of nonconfrontation among the Iowa delegates was the role of Bob Ray, who had been persuaded by Republican National Chairman Mary Louise Smith to chair the potentially divisive platform hearings. Ray was publicly identified as a supporter of Gerald Ford and was eyed warily by the Reagan faction of the platform committee. But during the two months prior to the convention and the week of hearings and drafting during the convention, Ray was able to put together a united, though admittedly conservative, platform. Despite including some items that ran contrary to Ford's, and Ray's, personal beliefs, like calling for a ban on abortions and reinstatement of prayer in public schools, Ray was credited with at least stabilizing the two warring factions.

There was also a contingent of Ray supporters who trekked down to Kansas City throughout the week to promote Bob Ray as a vice-presidential candidate. The group—led by Republican national committeeman John McDonald, Des Moines businessmen Marvin Pomerantz and Jack

President Gerald Ford campaigns in Des Moines, 1976. World Wide photo. Reprinted with permission.

Pester, and Des Moines lawyer David Belin—raised and spent over $19,000 on their promotion and found themselves head-to-head with similar groups promoting a dozen other candidates from various parts of the country. Secretary of Commerce Elliot Richardson, Secretary of the Treasury William Simon, Senators Howard Baker, Robert Dole, and Charles Percy, and Governors William Milliken of Michigan, Dan Evans of Washington, Missouri's Christopher "Kit" Bond, former Pennsylvania governor William Scranton, and the lone woman, Texan Anne Armstrong, were all being touted for the job.

Rumors are the lifeblood of conventions, and the red-and-yellow "Ray for VP" posters, pins, buttons, and brochures helped feed that hungry body all week long and certainly allowed the Iowa media folk some good speculation. When it came down to the final vote for the presidential nominee, the Iowa delegation went for Ford 19 to 17 after some particularly heavy lobbying from both sides, including one scene that placed Vice-President Nelson Rockefeller on his knees in front of Tom Tauke, begging him to support Gerald Ford. If Tauke voted for Reagan, as he threatened to, the delegation would have been split down the middle. His vote gave Ford a majority of Iowa's votes.

BOB RAY "I went to that convention as chairman of the platform committee. Mary Louise had called me and wanted me to take the job, and I said, 'Well, that's not what I want most in life to do.' But I went and talked to her. She wanted someone she thought could stand between the two groups—Reagan's and Ford's—and be fair. I decided that's where the battle was going to be fought if those two went down to the wire in a convention, which is what happened. So I decided I'd do it, because I didn't know that I'd ever run for office again anyway, and maybe I owed it to the party to make that contribution. I was really prepared for the worst. I didn't know what was going to happen. I thought that if I get torn apart, so be it; I'll give it my best shot."

MARY LOUISE SMITH "Generally speaking, the chairmanship of the platform and the permanent chairman of the convention go to members of Congress, one from the House, one from the Senate. But circumstances were such that we could change the pattern that year, and I wanted Bob Ray. And Gerald Ford was very high on Bob Ray.

"He didn't want to do it, but I think I talked him into it. He did a marvelous job. Interestingly enough, at the convention people had some very real doubts about his ability to keep that platform committee together. There were some controversial issues in 1976. Women's issues were in the forefront: the abortion thing, some others. I had no doubts about Bob at all, but people who did not know him as well, who had not seen him at governors' conferences or whatever, felt that he was not decisive enough, not strong enough.

"He gave them a lot of leeway at the first platform hearings in Kansas City, and people went out kind of shaking their heads, thinking, 'This is going to fall apart.' Of course, they came back the next day, and all of a sudden Bob Ray became the Bob Ray we all knew he could be, and in his firm and decisive kind of way, took charge, and it was an excellent platform committee."

BOB RAY "I think Mary Louise thought maybe I could keep peace and harmony, and she wouldn't have to worry with me there, because she trusted me. She never really gave me any instructions, didn't try to dictate or anything like that. She had her hands full with other things.

"I know Ron Reagan said Jerry Ford wasn't elected to that office, so it wasn't like he was taking on an incumbent that the people had selected. I saw that as rather artificial. I happened to think that Jerry Ford had carried water for the party for a long, long time. He wasn't the most colorful, charismatic individual that had ever run for office, but he was a good person and a breath of fresh air. He was such a delight to work with. I'd go into the Oval Office and sit on the couch and visit with him, and he'd pick up what you wanted right away, and then he went to work for you. Like other governors, I didn't think we could turn our backs on him. There wasn't any doubt where I was going to be in the campaign or at that convention.

"Reagan had lots of support in Iowa long before Jerry Ford had any. He had tested the waters before. There were a lot of ultraconservative ideologues in the Republican party in Iowa, and Reagan had a lot of popularity. I mean, how can you not like Ronald Reagan? I liked him, admired him for his abilities. I had no problem tolerating persons of varying attitudes and ideologies within the party, but Reagan – even after Jerry Ford was nominated – continued to cater to people who supported any candidates of their philosophy, be they Republicans or Democrats. That was a little troublesome. A lot of us thought we were pretty conservative in many ways – we'd been accused of that in the past – but we didn't think that everyone who had to have some government assistance was a moocher and a leech on society. Reagan could leave that impression.

"I selected some people to help on the preplatform. We had hearings that some say we should never have done. And when we got to the convention and I said we were going to open the platform hearings up to television, I was accused of defeating whomever the nominee would be. I thought, 'Why not let everybody see what the committee was talking about and discussing?' Also, some of these people would go in and be disrespectful of other people's rights. I knew that television would curb some of that. It worked out well, because most people wouldn't move from their seats, because they never knew when the cameras might be on them.

"On the first day in Kansas City, a Sunday, they wanted to throw out all of my appointees who'd done all the preplatform work. They were really armed for bear, mostly Reagan people. They were absolutely convinced that they weren't going to get fair treatment, that it was my job to cut them off at the pass and see that they didn't have a voice and that the platform be written to satisfy Jerry Ford."

DAVID BELIN "I worked as an unpaid special assistant, and that platform chairmanship was one of the toughest jobs I think anyone could ever do, and he handled it extraordinarily well. I went with him to Washington and various meetings of the platform committee, and the major challenge, of course, was to try to come out with a united platform. The party did, and it was to Bob Ray's credit."

JANET VAN NOTE "I was the first one in Kansas City. I was the administrative coordinator, so I went down and set up the offices, coordinated all the testimony in front of the full committee, had twenty to thirty pages working for me and about that many secretaries. We coordinated the subcommittees and got what they did in the mornings available by afternoon. We also coordinated picking up people at the airport, making sure they were in the right place at the right time and were on time to testify. I don't even know how we did it."

BOB RAY "We survived that first day, and by the time we ended, it had been a pleasant experience. There were some who were so uptight and determined that I was going to take advantage of them, and yet it ended up to be a pretty compatible group. When you think about it, that was the last time [*the party*] had that kind of controversy, too. There was a division, a breach, and mad politicians. We haven't really had that since. When I took the job I thought it could be the end of my political career. *Was getting Bob Ray's name out front a reason Mary Louise wanted you to do the job?* "I never thought of it that way. There were some nice people who went to Kansas City to campaign for me for vice-president, but I kind of shut that off. I was so busy; the platform committee took a lot of time. Secondly, when you get into a convention, the time just evaporates.

It really went fast. I think Mary Louise was looking for somebody she could count on."

DAVID BELIN "Obviously, Bob Ray was not willing to make the same kind of commitment that Jimmy Carter, a past governor, had made. And Jimmy Carter had, at least initially, from his own home state a group of individuals who were willing to go out and make that commitment as well. Now, if Bob Ray were to have started out to run for the presidency, he never could have gotten there. He just didn't have a big enough name to run against some of the national names. But if he had had what I called the vice-presidential strategy, he could have been vice-president in 1976. If he had run for vice-president, I think he would have been the vice-president, and once vice-president, he would have been favored to run for the presidency.

"I had been writing strategy papers for President Ford for some time, and in 1975 I became more convinced that there would be increasing pressure upon him to drop Nelson Rockefeller as his running mate. It was from an outcropping of that that I developed my vice-presidential strategy with regard to Bob Ray.

"I did not talk to anyone at that time, because I wanted to formulate in my own mind the best rationale. I was doing a series of monthly strategy papers for President Ford for various aspects of his campaign, and I put together in early 1976 the whole vice-presidential strategy once it became publicly known that Rockefeller was not going to be selected.

"Bob Ray was really in disbelief that he ever could be considered for such a position. He basically was a man who has a substantial amount of modesty for a political leader, and among other things he did not think that he had enough experience in foreign relations.

"My perspective was that in order for Ford to be elected, it would be helpful to have as a member of the ticket someone outside of Washington—someone who had had administrative experience, someone who had a very high degree of standing with the press, someone who had demonstrated an ability to win elections and to get votes from not just Republicans but from independents as well, and someone who could contribute in a major way to the running of a campaign. Remember, Ford had never run for statewide office before, much less national office.

"I tailor-made that strategy to the needs of the Ford campaign, and even if I hadn't been closely affiliated with Bob Ray, there was a natural attraction. The fact that they were both from the Midwest did not bother me, for the simple reason that I think there is less and less need for geographical diversity.

"As for his own concern about lack of foreign experience, what foreign experience did Richard Nixon have in 1952? What foreign experience did John Kennedy have in 1960? He had been a U.S. senator for only eight years. What foreign experience did Spiro Agnew have in 1968? As it became clear that Jimmy Carter was going to be the Democratic candidate, what foreign experience did Jimmy Carter have?

"I wanted Bob Ray to officially declare that he was running for vice-president early on, in January or February. I also did an electoral vote analysis to show where Bob Ray could help a ticket. Once it became clear that Carter was going to be the nominee, my position was that no one, not even Ford, would get anything from the South, so we had to write that off.

"In hindsight – but members of the kitchen cabinet said this concurrently – Bob Ray really had to get out front for this strategy to work. And he refused to do that."

DAVID OMAN "It was always viewed as a long shot, so no one ever allowed themselves to get their hopes up terribly high. But the feeling of the staff – Wythe, Dutch, and so on – and some of the kitchen cabinet supporters – Marv Pomerantz, John McDonald, Mary Louise – was that it was certainly viable and that he certainly had as much going for him as some of the rest of them.

"Once it was announced that Rockefeller would not be on the ticket, we began to try to posture him as the spokesman for the governors. That was the year he was the chairman of the National Governors' Conference, which afforded him more opportunities to travel to Washington to visit with people in the administration. Ford was a creature of Congress – he'd been there for twenty-five years – and a very good Republican, as was Bob Ray, and there was a lot of logic to combining someone who came from the Hill and someone who came from the statehouse.

"The Kansas City effort was launched without the governor's approval, but he was aware of it and he let it go forward. The fact that Kansas City was only 180 miles away was a plus, of course, and we wanted a lot of presence down there."

BOB RAY "I think we could have made a fairly good splash. We came out of that platform committee with a lot of friends, people that were expecting to be my enemies. I don't know that it would have made a bit of difference if there'd been some early campaigning going on, but I really had turned that off. But a lot of people close to the throne were willing to help me if I had just turned the faucet a bit."

JACK PESTER "We went down to Kansas City to try to drum up support.

We thought he was what was needed on the ticket. It was not a great year for Republicans, and he had done a good job of distancing himself from Nixon. And the Democrats were running a governor and balancing it with a guy from Washington. We thought we should try for the same balance."

JERRY PARKIN "What we were trying to do, basically, was get Bob Ray known outside of the Iowa delegation. We organized carloads of people to go down daily. I drove there in the morning and came back at night for three or four straight days. We'd leaflet the hotels, pass out buttons, and just buttonhole people as we could.

"The real ringleader of the effort was Marv Pomerantz. He was the pusher. They had just decided that with or without Bob Ray's approval, they were going to make the effort. Of course, there was a group from Texas promoting Anne Armstrong, there was a group promoting Bob Dole, and there were others who had people working on their behalf. It was a long shot, but we had nothing to lose. If nothing else, it brought the name Bob Ray to a lot more people's attention, and it probably had something to do with making him at last a semiserious contender for the job. He was on the lists of all the political insiders and news-media people."

MARVIN POMERANTZ "We sent mailgrams to all the delegations, but it was not something we spent six years on. For a period of a couple weeks we worked pretty hard promoting his candidacy.

"There's only one vote that counts in the selection of a vice-president, and that's the nominee's. But we talked to the various state chairmen, anyone who we thought would have some input to the president at that point or to people around the president. It's a pretty nebulous kind of thing. You're trying to get favorable press, you're trying to communicate through these various people, and you're hoping that the nominee understands your logic."

BOB TYSON "I was down in Kansas City on state business during the convention and Wythe Willey said he wanted to see me. I went over to his hotel, went to his room, and he had under his bed this stack of pictures of Bob Ray and Jerry Ford with their hands clutched, held high above their heads. He wanted to know what he should do with them. I said, 'Burn them.' He accused me of sounding like the governor. I said, 'Wythe, if the White House staff ever sees that, he hasn't got a chance of being on the ticket.' Marv Pomerantz and his people had printed them up. It was an old picture taken at some campaign rally in Des Moines."

BOB RAY "It made me feel good to think that I had people from Iowa who wanted to go to the convention to promote me. You have to appreciate that. But it was moving so fast at the time that I really didn't know who or what all was involved. I did end up with boxes of pictures of me and Jerry Ford that they planned to distribute, though."

WYTHE WILLEY "Bob Ray never gave anybody a signal saying, 'I want that.' He never had the fire in the belly. He never said, 'I'd really like to have that.' He was more laid back: 'If Jerry Ford comes to me and wants me as vice-president, okay. But I'm not going to launch a campaign.'

"In terms of things we [*the staff*] didn't do, I would have worked a lot harder to get Bob Ray that vice-presidential nod. And the first person I would have worked harder on was Bob Ray. We should have – and as a staff maybe we failed Ray – been more aggressive, both with Bob Ray and on the other side. I'll take some responsibility. I should have pushed him a lot harder, if that's what he really wanted. And maybe he should have said, 'I really don't want it,' and we'd have given up. But we – myself, Pomerantz, Belin, Pester, Mary Louise, John McDonald – if that's what we really wanted, we should have pushed him harder and not taken his 'We'll see how it goes' attitude, pushed him harder back in January and February of 1976, because I think it would have made a difference in the presidential race if Bob Ray had been on that ticket."

BOB RAY "I really felt strongly that wasn't the way, that lobbying wasn't going to help. It was a way to get exposure and maybe a way to get people to talk enough that the nominee might look at me, yet I didn't even know that I wanted to do it if I were asked. I also didn't really feel comfortable going about it in that fashion, because I felt strongly that the running mate had to be the choice of the nominee. We knew pretty much what the shortlist was. He didn't need people in the street telling him whom to go with."

DAVID OMAN "During the night when Ford and his people were making their decision, CBS set up a camera outside Bob and Billie's door, so I called them to warn them not to stumble out to pick up the paper or anything. Early in the morning, someone from the president's inner circle called and advised him that Bob Dole was the choice, which was a great disappointment to all of us. But if it were a disappointment to him, he masked it very well. I think it was almost a relief, frankly."

BILLIE RAY "He was supposed to get the call by eight o'clock that morning, so the press was parked outside of our hotel room. I thought, 'My gosh, don't let that phone ring. It would be terrible.' I remember thinking,

'If we can just get past eight o'clock, we'll be safe.' Well, the phone rang – scared me to death. It was somebody else. I guess I felt that real pressure, and it wasn't helped by the press outside the door, just ready to pounce on you. If he'd been selected, there'd have been no turning back. They'd be there outside your door until you won or lost. You know, it's wonderful to have somebody meet you at the car and take you someplace, but I'd give that up not to have the press everywhere all the time. I didn't want to get used to that."

JACK PESTER "We lobbied Ford pretty hard, but it was purely up to him. He was more comfortable with Bob Dole. He'd been in the Washington scene for, what, twenty-seven years by that time? He knew Bob Ray, probably had no objections to Bob Ray but was just more comfortable with Dole. Carter won because he wasn't perceived as one of the gang, and that's where we would have scored with Bob Ray. Remember, just one or two percentage points would have won the race for Ford. Now, I'm awfully fond of Bob Dole. He's a close friend, just like Bob Ray is. But I think Bob Dole was the wrong candidate."

DAVID BELIN "I'm personally convinced that if Bob Ray had taken the lead by the first of May, he would have been selected vice-president, for several reasons. There were a lot of people after the election, when asked why they voted and how, they said they were undecided but they voted on the basis of who was running for vice-president. Bob Dole came off terribly in the vice-presidential debate with Walter Mondale. He came off far too sarcastic, too this, too that, and I'm convinced that if Bob Ray had been in that debate and in that campaign, Ford would have won an awfully close election.

"The reason Bob Dole was selected was that Ford finally came out with a group of about five or six people, most of whom were vetoed by the Republican state chairmen in the South. Bob Dole was the only one on the list whom, for instance, the Republican state chair from Mississippi would go for. I don't think that group of five or six included Bob Ray.

"But I'm convinced that if Bob Ray had been Jerry Ford's running mate, Ford would have won, and if that had happened, Ronald Reagan would not be president today. Bob Ray would be president today."

JANET VAN NOTE "If Jerry Ford had chosen him, he'd have done it, never hesitated, and he would have been a fantastic running mate. But, you know, he had to be asked when he ran for governor the first time, pushed and pulled and told 'We need you,' and he finally said, 'Okay.' He wants to be needed."

MARVIN POMERANTZ "I've asked Gerald Ford subsequent to that election and he said, yes, he considered Bob Ray, but having once chosen Bob Dole he would never say that had been a mistake, though I think it was. I think it cost him the election. Of course, there were several things that hurt him.

"Bob Ray versus Walter Mondale would have been a very different debate, for example. I ran Gerald Ford's Iowa campaign in 1976, and he made a stop up in Ames the day that debate was held. The *Register* wanted an editorial-board interview with him while he was in the state, but we weren't giving any press interviews, no special treatment, so I had to develop a unique approach to handle that opportunity. At that point the *Register* hadn't endorsed anybody.

"Ford came out and got up in front of 10,000 people in Ames, went to an Iowa farm, and Bob Ray traveled with us. That was the day Ford got up and said it was really wonderful to be back in Ohio again. That hurt a little. But we had developed a way to handle the *Register's* request. I had made arrangements to get them on Air Force One, the whole editorial board, and they would fly with the president from Des Moines to Chicago. Tom Stoner and I accompanied them, they got their interview, and we landed at the Air National Guard terminal at O'Hare. They transported us across to a normal passenger terminal and we were going to catch the next plane back to Des Moines. Well, we walked into the United Airlines Red Carpet Room and the vice-presidential debate was on the tube.

"We had just come off Air Force One and we were feeling pretty good. We thought we'd earned some time with the paper and the editors. But here we stand watching Mondale and Dole, and Mondale was very articulate, had a nice demeanor, and Dole was really boring in, playing the heavy. Dave Kruidenier turned to me and said, 'That's it. That does it. There's no way I could endorse that ticket.' All the good work we'd done was dead after watching just thirty seconds of the debate. Now, if they'd gotten off the plane and seen Bob Ray in that debate, I think their attitude would have been different. They eventually endorsed Carter, though Ford carried the state by 28,000 votes."

GERALD FORD "There's no question Bob Ray would have been an excellent candidate, and if we had been elected, he would have been a first-class vice-president. In the process of making the final decision for vice-president, Bob was one of the final contenders. But we added up all the pluses and minuses and we selected Bob Dole, and I think Bob Dole's subsequent rise clearly indicates we made a good decision."

BOB RAY "When Jerry Ford's book came out, it said that I was cut early from that shortlist, Dan Evans and I, because we didn't have international experience. I thought that was nice of the *Register* to put that on the front page. Well, when Jerry Ford was here during the 1980 campaign, David Yepsen said to him, 'You know, most people think that the vice-presidential candidate did not help but hurt your campaign. Would you have been better off to have had Bob Ray on the ticket?' And Ford said, 'Yes, I think I would have been.' He was very complimentary. Boy, I'll tell you, I combed through that article the next day to see how they quoted him. Not one word. Nothing. I was there, I'd heard it. Yepsen wanted me to know that he had it in the article, but they cut it out.

"The last poll taken before the 1976 presidential election said that Carter and Ford ran even, but when you tested Carter and Mondale against Ford and Dole, Ford-Dole ran three percentage points behind. And toward the end of that campaign, for the first time I really felt like I'd have liked to be on the ticket. I saw what was happening, I saw what the issues were and how they were being handled, and I thought, 'I think I'm up to that.'"

"Do people really think I would have made a difference?" Ray wonders today. In 1976 he was one of the senior governors, their elected chairman. The Democratic nominee for president was a one-term governor from Georgia. Yet Bob Ray couldn't publicly—nor, I think, privately—see himself as a national figure. He's possessed of an odd mixture of ego and humility. "I don't know what the word is," ponders Mary Louise Smith. "I don't think it's modesty. It's not that Bob Ray isn't assertive. I think it's almost like it was imprudent of him to think he's that capable. I don't think he can define it either."

XVIII: THE GOVERNOR'S CONFIDANTS

Bob Ray's friends, his wife, and even his mother describe him as a loner. It's sometimes hard to imagine that the governor, surrounded by people day in and day out, dependent on public support, constantly tugged and torn by a wide variety of friends and influences, could really be much of a loner. But in Ray's case it is true.

On infrequent nights when no state campaign functions demanded him, he stayed home with Billie and the kids. While he was governor, they rarely mingled socially with friends, new or old. He admits he didn't know much about his neighbors on California Drive, where the family often went to "get away" on weekends.

He is not a "man's man" in the classic cigar-smoking, backroom sort of way, a strong but silent type. He kept his own counsel; there was never a feeling of cronyism in his decision making. He denies he ever had a "kitchen cabinet" of advisers and refuses to attach that moniker to the group of strong-willed, successful-in-their-own-right individuals he consulted. Meeting regularly but on no set schedule, there was a group that advised the governor, mostly on political issues. They met in a private room on the thirty-third floor of the Ruan Building, and their get-togethers were attended by Jack Pester, Marvin Pomerantz, Mary Louise Smith, Tom Stoner, John McDonald, David Belin, Wythe Willey, Dick Gilbert, and in the later years, David Oman.

Ray's concern about having a single publicly identified adviser (like Park Rinard was for Harold Hughes), or a group of them, derived from

Mary Louise Smith and Bob Ray. *Des Moines Register* photo. Reprinted with permission.

the fact that he never wanted people to get the impression that anyone was making up his mind for him. His decision-making process may have seemed slow to some, but no matter how long it took, the ultimate decision was always the governor's, good or bad.

DICK GILBERT "It wasn't a kitchen cabinet in the context that we sat around and made state policies. State policy was made in the governor's office by state employees. But these people were from various professions, disciplines, who would get together with the governor from time to time to just shoot the breeze about politics, what was happening nationally, to kind of stimulate the governor's thinking."

DENNIS NAGEL "They didn't meet weekly, they kind of met when people were available, but it sure seemed to me a more-regular-than-not basis. I don't think they talked issues very much at all, always politics. Issuewise, I was only brought into the thing a couple times, once on property taxes and once on the entire tax system, but I don't think they got into 'This is a good idea,' or 'This is the way you should do it.' He used them for a political sounding board. They were all great admirers of him, and I don't think it hurt for him to spend time listening to them talk about why he ought to become the president of the United States or something like that."

TOM STONER "We, this group of seven or eight people, met every so often with him for ten years, and never once did anything leak out of those meetings—nobody ever talked to the press about what was said. It was a great tribute to him that there was that kind of loyalty to him. It was a great sounding board for him. Nobody really used it for special requests."

MARY LOUISE SMITH "It was kind of a sharing experience, a sharing of observations about the general political scene. We might air our views on an issue or just visit, but I don't think we ever came together thinking we were going to tell Bob Ray what to do.

"One reason he disavows any official assembly is because he doesn't want to even imply to anyone that there were other people telling him or suggesting to him what he should do. As a matter of fact, we didn't."

MARVIN POMERANTZ "It was never formal in the sense that there was a locked-up group that he would refer everything to. That was simply not the case. But he wanted dialogue, he wanted to know what was going on in the state, what people were thinking, what their real concerns were, and this was one of the mechanisms he used in order to get grass-roots feedback."

DAVID BELIN "We talked about strategy, among other things, and the whole issue of whether Bob Ray was going to run in 1968, 1970, 1972, 1974, and then for a fifth term.

"The subject matter for discussion would not necessarily be determined for him, and as a matter of fact, in a substantial number of the sessions I was the person that chainlinked the agenda. We dealt with a wide range of things. If Bob Ray had a particular question that he wanted to get a sounding on, here was a way he could get a sounding board. Usually the meeting place would be the lower governor's office or occasionally we would meet in a private room at the Des Moines Club, just to get Bob out of the office."

BOB RAY "It really wasn't a kitchen cabinet; we didn't try and decide governmental issues. We'd maybe talk about them, but mostly we talked about political questions: Should I run or not? Are we going to have a senator or aren't we? Who's hurting? Is there anything we can do for the farmers that we are not doing? Sheer legislative issues and that kind of thing we didn't get into."

DICK GILBERT "That group of men and women could be in just about anybody's company they wanted, and I think Bob Ray recognized that, and he was proud they were his friends. These people that he looked to for counsel and support had track records of their own; they got to where they were before they were Bob Ray's friends. The whole secret of the Ray success over the years was he knew how to make friends where he needed them. So many times you see politicians get themselves very close and very tight, and it's only when they get in trouble that they reach out. Bob Ray built a network of friends on the strength of his personality and his integrity."

TOM STONER "One time he invited us to talk about the eighteen-year-old vote decision, which was the only time I thought he was looking for opinion from me. But he didn't follow my advice, and I think he was right. But he did listen to us. He likes to function like a judge, listen to opposing views, make a decision. That's how he works.

"That job is a lonely one, and every one of us were within ten degrees philosophically of him—Pester probably being the most conservative, Mary Louise the most liberal. But we were close enough for comfort, and he really felt that he could kind of banter with us. He loved to banter, and this gave him the opportunity to let his guard down a little."

JACK PESTER "Where we really started communicating well was when I walked in one time and told him there was going to be a terrible energy shortage and that they ought to start planning for it, because within six weeks there was going to be disaster. He was astonished, and he questioned and requestioned me. So he started having some people look at it, and I told him some things he could do, even though some of those things didn't advantage my business—in fact, probably disadvantaged me a little. Probably my whole relationship with Bob Ray cost me a lot of money, because there were some things we couldn't do—we never bid on any state business. I never had hard feelings over that. Those were some of the things you do if you're a citizen. That doesn't bother me, because the state has been very good to us."

MARVIN POMERANTZ "Nobody made his decisions for him no matter how close they were to him. He'd listen and get different viewpoints and consider as many different aspects of an issue that he could. But he made the decision. Nobody owned him, no one controlled him, and he did what he thought was right based on his principles and what was the best thing to do.

"He didn't rule by committee, but he was always interested in a tremendous amount of input. Even if he was firm in his conviction about an issue, he would take the time and make sure that he got the arguments from as many different perspectives as he could. He was hard to move, but if you had a compelling argument, a compelling reason, he wanted to hear you."

JACK PESTER "I never really lobbied him about people, appointments. I don't thing we could have if we'd wanted to."

BOB RAY "They never said you've got to do this or that, and they never really got involved with the daily issues. I never remember an issue that somebody was real vocal on, say being for or against pari-mutuel betting. I couldn't even tell you where they stood on most issues. We just didn't get into those things."

DAVID OMAN "He did not have a political godfather; nobody pulled his chain. That was not the case."

BOB RAY "What really was best for me was to get out among the people, though. I think far too often we spent too much time debating governmental issues, time that should have been spent out talking to the people. It was always enlightening, even though I'm sure there were times I came back not so encouraged."

BARNEY DONIELSON "Most of the people who say they were very close to Bob Ray are full of bullshit. I think there are some, but I've certainly never found them, from the time I was Polk county chair and he was state chair. He's an interesting person, in the sense that he didn't ever really share secrets with anyone. I just don't know of anybody who knew his personal thoughts on matters.

"I often thought that Rand Petersen might have been the closest, maybe Leo Oxberger. Bob Ray had tremendous loyalty to the people around him, although it wasn't always on the surface."

TOM STONER "Dick Gilbert could get Bob Ray to do things that nobody else could get him to do. Dick would call a press conference for ten in the morning, tell Bob Ray the press was on their way, and force him to make a decision. He didn't tell him what to do, just kind of encouraged him to decide.

"They were in tune politically, too, and Dick was the only person I know of that Bob Ray would be kind of vulnerable to. In terms of lifestyle and outlook, they're 180 degrees opposed, but Dick has a need to be around somebody whom he could clearly put up on a pedestal and really believe in."

JOHN REHMANN "All during the time that Bob was governor, Verne Lawyer is the guy who had his ear more than anybody. That doesn't mean that others aren't close to him, but I think if he was really looking for some help making a decision, he'd go to Verne."

BARNEY DONIELSON "Verne Lawyer is a very, very strong man, and he let Bob Ray get involved in politics. The average lawyer would have been out the door in about ten seconds if he hadn't worked as hard as Bob Ray. But Verne had a great deal of faith in him, and once he became governor I think Verne enjoyed his partner's success. After Bob was elected, Verne kept his name on his law firm's letterhead—you know, 'Robert D. Ray, on leave as Governor of Iowa.'

"Bob Ray is a very introspective guy, you know. We used to joke that maybe even Billie called him governor. He was never the kind who confided in other people. I think he did confide in Verne."

JANE MITCHELL "Verne kind of mothered Bob, and I think he genuinely enjoyed that, kind of a father figure. Verne's got a lot of common sense, he knows a lot of people, and I think the governor counted on him to give him some pretty straight advice, maybe tell him things others wouldn't."

VERNE LAWYER "He had the ability to make a lot of people believe that he was taking input and giving serious consideration to the input they were giving him. That's a faculty that serves a person in that position very well.

"I saw no evidence that a so-called kitchen cabinet existed, but I've heard guys claim they were a member of it. He listened to a lot of people and invited them to speak out, but I guarantee you he made up his own mind. I don't know of any single instance where anybody ever made up his mind for him. It's good politics to listen to others, and it's also how you pick up little morsels of information you might not otherwise."

JANET VAN NOTE "Verne would have loved to have Bob Ray come back and work with him. He says he would have paid him what he's making now just to have him come and sit at the front desk and smile at everyone. Verne liked to think that Bob was his boy, 'I made this happen' kind of thing. 'I pushed him along, took this cute kid and made him into a prince.' He was a lot of help."

VERNE LAWYER "Bob would talk to me, but he's a consensus kind of guy, so he was out talking to lots of people. I think maybe the biggest contribution I made was keeping the cash flow up and encouraging him in the early days. He really didn't need much advice from me, just friendship. He sometimes refers to me as being like an older brother, and even though I'm not that much older than he is, he always seemed more like a son to me. But I don't want you or anybody to get the idea that I was the mastermind or anything, because this guy is his own man. He knew what he was doing. He didn't have any mentors, which was one of his strengths. He wasn't overwhelmed by anybody, didn't try and mimic anybody."

JACK PESTER "I always had the impression that there were days Bob Ray wished he was out making money. I think he genuinely worried about what would happen to him after he left the security of the governor's office. I think he liked the things money did. But you know, we never did put him in any ventures. We could have, we discussed it, but I think he always felt there would be a conflict. He couldn't identify it, and to satisfy him it probably would have had to have been out of state, but we never did."

DAVID OMAN "Some of his peers were out there making money. They didn't have a whole lot of public accountability, and in the later years I think he was a little envious every time Verne settled a million-dollar case . . . and took his 30 percent, or whatever. It's not hard to do the math on that."

BOB RAY "I don't think there are many people, if given the chance, [*who*] wouldn't like to be governor. Whether they say it or not, whether they'd be willing to accept the responsibility or not, whether they'd really enjoy that life or not, there aren't many people who wouldn't like to be governor. At the same time, you really do make some sacrifices. I'd like to say I've been a successful businessman. I'd like to be a philanthropist, and if I had spent time earning money, I could do that.

"But I never got the feeling the people with whom I worked ever thought my job was easy. They weren't the kind of people that thought they could do my job better. They weren't the kind who'd say, 'You think that's tough, you ought to come over and run my business, find out how tough things really are.' "

JERRY MURSENER "Bob Ray wasn't exactly rich when he was a kid, didn't come from wealthy surroundings, and I think if you asked him tomorrow what the best job in the world was, he'd say governor. You get picked up every morning by a state trooper, live in a mansion, travel with kings and queens and presidents, fly all over the world. That life superseded a million-dollar bank account for Bob Ray."

If Bob Ray did have a single confidant, it was Billie Lee Hornberger, the skinny kid from church camp he'd met when they were both thirteen. College friends remember his constantly checking with his wife-to-be for confirmation: "Isn't that right, Billie Lee?" Like many politicians' spouses, she was the ultimate sounding board. "I always felt that if he asked me something, used me as a sounding board, he'd get a good, all-American reaction," she remembers.

VERNE LAWYER "How important was Billie Lee? I have always viewed them as one of the great love affairs I've been a firsthand observer to. She was 100 percent supportive as far as I could tell. Now, I didn't sleep with them, so I don't know what the hell they talked about before they fell asleep, but I never saw any evidence that Billie Lee was ever doing anything other than being supportive.

"She was always active in Bob's campaigns and with other state projects. The thing most people who are not involved in politics don't see is that the people of Iowa elect two people when they elect a governor – the man, and so far it's always been a man, and his wife. And the wife is expected by the people and the political apparatus to work full-time in the interest of the state, and she doesn't get paid a dime."

FROSTY MITCHELL "Billie can roll with the flow better than anybody. I can't imagine another woman I know who could have handled that job for that long. The remodeling of Terrace Hill was a full-time job, she oversaw the production of those cookbooks, and the campaign never ended. Plus she raised a great family, often by herself. She was the most underpaid, more-than-full-time employee the state of Iowa ever had. History will record that the absolute best bargain the state ever got was having Billie as the ambassador of goodwill not only in the state but at national conferences and around the world.

"By the time Bob left office, the voters of Iowa were voting for a team: Bob and Billie. And I really believe that when he ran in 1978, if she had told the media she didn't want him to run, people would have voted against him. I think she had that much influence. She turned into a kind of vice-presidential candidate, and when voters pulled the lever for Bob Ray, they were voting for the team. People voted for Bob and Billie."

TOM STONER "When I think of Billie, I first think of her as a campaigner. One time she was out campaigning and got let out of the plane in the middle of a cornfield. Somebody was supposed to meet her, but nobody was around. She said, in that high voice of hers, 'Well, let's just walk to town,' and set off. She was very determined."

BILL MILLIKEN "The wife of a governor is a very difficult role to fill. It's not easy to maintain one's identity. Wives, no matter how confident they are, get hurt when everybody in the room is trying to talk to the governor and ignoring her. It can be a demeaning role."

DAVID OMAN "I give Billie a lot of credit, for three reasons. First, because she was a very steady, omnipresent influence in the governor's life. She was always there; he could always count on her. She handled the responsibilities of first lady very well. I never had to wonder what his wife was doing – you know, 'Is she doing anything that doesn't fit with the image of the office?'

"Second, she was a great campaigner and superb asset politically. She would go with him and out on her own. Even in 1974 and 1978, when they had been in office for years and were heavily favored, she would go to the women's meetings, host teas or breakfasts or lunches day in and day out.

"Third, she has a good sense about people. Listening to the two of them talk in the car or the airplane on our way to an event, she had an innate sixth sense that was good for him. We would ask her opinion on television commercials and she was always able to focus right in on something.

"Often it was tough, tough duty, and we never heard her complain. She was concerned from time to time about the governor's intense schedule, but never in the sense that she felt she was being slighted or he wasn't paying enough attention to his family or her. She was always motivated out of concern for him and his health and well-being. She would pull us aside and say 'You're scheduling him too hard, he needs to slow down,' or 'He needs a break.' It was always motivated out of a concern for him."

BILLIE RAY "I grew up in the days when you went to high school, college, and then you got a job or got married. If you got married, you stayed home and took care of the kids. When Bob first ran for office I was busy as a housewife and mother. Generally women weren't as involved in politics in those days, and with three little ones I couldn't give a lot of myself to campaigns.

"I helped when I could, though. One time when Bob was state chairman, we hosted a reception at our house for Richard Nixon. It must have been in the early 1960s. Our kids were three, six, and nine. I didn't have any help to clean the house, so I cleaned the kitchen, dusted the bushes out front. It was a big deal. I had a caterer bring all the food, which was wonderful. I even cleaned out the refrigerator so there'd be room for the caterer's food. Well, Nixon came over, we had the little party, and as they were headed out the door, one of his aides came over to me and asked if we had a sandwich or two they could take along on the plane. Apparently they hadn't gotten anything to eat.

"Well, I had cleared out the kitchen, so the only things around were some three-day-old bread, some hard butter, and some Velveeta cheese, and the caterer made some sandwiches out of that. After they left I couldn't imagine what they must have thought when they saw these sandwiches.

"After Nixon was elected president we went to the White House several times. We'd stand in the receiving lines waiting to say hello to the president, and every year he'd say the same thing to Bob and me. He'd ask Bob how his leg was, because he knew he'd been in the plane crash, and about the third time we were there he thanked me for those cheese sandwiches. I just about fell through the floor.

"Up until election day in 1968 I don't think I ever once gave any thought to what it would be like if we won. My only thought was, 'My, when September comes, it'll be over.' I honestly never thought he'd win.

Then when he won, it wasn't like you're plucked out of one system and into another. He wasn't 'Governor' to me, he was still just Bob.

"When he first ran for governor I had no idea of the enormity of the job or the campaign. I figured it would be just a continuation of his job as state chair. I just never thought about it, didn't realize that running state-wide was a little different from running for Polk County attorney, didn't anticipate the tremendous amount of fund-raising and planning involved.

"For the first five years or so after he was governor I wasn't sure that I made much difference. Who cared about me? I wasn't told to do anything special, but after a while I realized that people do look at you a little differently, a little expectantly. If I went to a coffee with twenty-five women in a small town, it was like meeting with the whole town, because they talk to everybody and gave their impressions. That left an impact.

"All of a sudden the Republicans found themselves with a Republican governor, and they wanted to be treated to dinners and lunches at the governor's mansion. But there was no pattern for me to follow, no book; I just had to create one. I had no money, no budget, for lunches and the things they expected me to do. For one luncheon I got all my friends together and we made napkins. I was going over to our own house and borrowing our china and silver and crystal for the Republican women's lunches and things. In the old governor's mansion at 2900 Grand, when we moved in, there were old cheese jars for glasses. There were only enough matched place settings for fifteen or sixteen people, and sometimes we'd have dinners for fifty people.

"After running back and forth and borrowing things from home and my sister-in-law, I got the help of the Republican women and asked for each of the ninety-nine counties to raise enough money to help us buy a place setting of china for 100, about thirty-five dollars per county. Then I asked the Farm Bureau ladies to help me raise about $1,500 for silverware.

"Those first few years were especially hectic. I was asked to appear at luncheons and ribbon cuttings, and you're honorary chairman of about as many things as you can handle, whether it's the Easter Seals or International Year of the Child. Plus it seemed like I was always decorating the house for a party, getting the invitations out for the next one. I was making a lot of mistakes. Bob could see that I couldn't do it all, plus I was still doing the books for the radio station in Estherville we owned, taking care of the kids, all the family things. I was often up until three, four in the morning." [*Ray was majority partner in the Estherville radio station during most of his tenure, a business he got into with the encouragement and help of Frosty Mitchell in the 1960s.*]

BOB RAY "Did Billie tell you about the time we had all the security around the house? It was 1970. There'd been a lot of arsons, lots of threats, campus unrest, and we had some special Highway Patrol members guarding our place on Grand Avenue. One morning the help was there, the cook, the guards, the troopers were outside. Billie left the house to take the kids to school, and as she pulled out she passed a guy with a bag over his shoulder walking up the driveway. She didn't think much about it. Well, I had to walk across the hall from the bedroom to where my suits were hung, and as I crossed the hall I saw someone at the end of the hall, on the second floor. I thought, I wish the help would wait until I went to work.' It seemed a little early for anybody to be cleaning up. I got dressed and it wasn't until later that I asked somebody 'What are they doing up on the second floor?' This guy had walked in through all the security, past all the help, past Billie and me, with a bag thrown over his shoulder. Nobody stopped him or said anything to him. Turns out he thought the place was an apartment building and he was putting samples of deodorant by each door."

BILLIE RAY "When Bob was first elected, before we moved into 2900 Grand, Mo Baringer took me to see Bishop Dingman's home on Thirty-seventh Street. They were thinking of turning it into the governor's mansion. The Hubbells also wanted to sell Terrace Hill, but the state didn't want to pay the $50,000 they wanted for it. I thought we'd probably end up just living at home on California Drive until whatever change they were going to make was made.

"Years later I was taken over to look at Terrace Hill, and I could see the possibilities. But we lived at 2900 Grand for eight years, and it was almost like living in an apartment. We had a small bedroom – it didn't have room for a sofa or a television – and one little bathroom off it. We couldn't keep things in the medicine chest in the other bathroom, because when they'd have tours people would be looking in there to see what you've got."

CYNTHIA HENDERSON "Terrace Hill was given to the state in 1972, renovation began in 1974, and the Rays moved in in 1976. Billie's office started out in the tower room. It was a twelve-by-sixteen-foot room. When we moved in there it had an old table, a desk they'd gotten from state surplus somewhere, and one light bulb hanging in the middle of the room. The walls were kind of a gruesome tan, no carpeting on the floor, and one of the first mornings we were up there it snowed and we ended up with two inches of snow on our desks. As the renovation continued we got moved all over the place. After a while we realized how expensive it was to move the phones from room to room, so we just got a seventy-five-foot cord and pulled it around after us."

ROBB KELLEY "You have to give Billie a lot of credit. She was willing to live in that mess for several years, raise a family, live on the third floor of the monstrosity, raise money to do the work and save the building for posterity. She worked hard."

BILLIE RAY "I often wondered if people knew how hard I did work. I'd go to these banquets and I'd think, 'If they knew what I had done the last two hours before I came here, they wouldn't think my life was so grand.' That's what is different between the wife of an elected official versus a CEO's [*Chief Executive Officer's*] wife. Most often a CEO's wife is minimally involved in the affairs of the business. They aren't asked to speak just because their husband is president of the company."

BOB RAY "It was a hard way to raise a family. But I know in our case I thought the job and the scheduling were in a sense helpful to a happy marriage. Billie wasn't one that wanted to get involved in the politics; she didn't want to lead that life. But she was willing if that was what I wanted.

"I didn't press her to do anything like give speeches. She just grew into her job just as I did mine. The thing about it is that we didn't see each other as much as other families did, but we saw each other a lot, and in many ways much more. We always tried to go together to dinners and functions whenever we could.

"We had common interests. When she was working on Terrace Hill, I had an interest. I didn't want to do her job, I didn't want to be there all the time, I didn't want to hear about all of it, but when she wanted to talk about it or needed my help, I had an interest. She read the newspaper, she knew what they were saying about me, so we really had a shared interest. We have a lot in common, and we had so many opportunities to do so many things together. It was great."

BILLIE RAY "I think most people think that anyone in public life is really different. People probably assume I don't dust or do the wash or cook. But we're just like everybody else. Some people think I sat around in jewels and a sequined robe, like on the set of 'Dynasty' or something, and went to the club for lunch every day. People love to imagine you're something you're not."

BOB RAY "Billie is and was extremely important. It would have been a miserable career if I'd been out there doing my thing and she wouldn't have participated or wouldn't have wanted me to do it. I abhor the thought, can't imagine what that would be like. But I suppose it's probably good to think about that every once in a while, because I know I took a lot of that for granted.

"I don't think I was overly demanding. I never had to say to her, 'You have to go here or there with me.' We really never had a serious problem. I honestly don't know how it could have worked any better. We had a great rapport. If she needed me to go with her somewhere, or if I needed her, we worked our schedules out together. I don't know how I could have been more fortunate."

XIX: RAY VERSUS FITZGERALD, 1978

There was much speculation around the state—mostly among the media and fellow politicians, some with their eye on the governor's chair—about whether Bob Ray would run for a fifth term. It began the day after he was inaugurated for his fourth term in 1975. The governor would turn fifty in 1978—perhaps just out of his prime earning days, some close advisers counseled. If he was ever going to get out and make some money, now was the time, they warned. Besides, the state's treasury surplus was slimmer than it had been in the last half-dozen years, and the future of Iowa's economy was filled with uncertainties, promising unknown headaches for the state's elected chairman of the board. Being governor was going to be a different job in the 1980s.

Ray was torn himself, and he was pushed and pulled in a variety of ways by different groups. Some suggested he run for the Senate against Dick Clark, others that he hang up electoral politics and go back to a law career. Still others told him unabashedly that if he did run for another gubernatorial term, it should be with his eye on the presidency, or at least the vice-presidency, in 1980. But he still confessed no interest in the Club of 100 and the Washington scene. Sure, he'd like to make more than the annual $55,000 he was earning as governor, but money had never been his prime motivator. One big concern he had was that if he stepped down, a Democrat, or, maybe worse, Attorney General Richard Turner would fill his shoes. He didn't like either of those scenarios, so on February 23, 1978, flanked by state Republican chairman Steve Roberts, national Re-

Jerry Fitzgerald. *Des Moines Register,* Harry Baumert photo. Reprinted with permission.

publican committeeman John McDonald, and former national chairwoman Mary Louise Smith, Bob Ray announced he would try for an unprecedented fifth term.

One Ray friend suggests that the decision to run was motivated largely by indecision. The governor couldn't decide exactly what to do, and running seemed almost the easiest way out. In January that year, the polls showed him running ahead of the two announced Democrats, Tom Whitney and Jerry Fitzgerald, by margins of 62 to 14 and 62 to 12. And though he did not seem interested, a place on a national ticket in 1980 was not out of reach. One-term governor Jimmy Carter was currently midway through his presidency, and local and national logic had it that Ray was certainly as qualified, if not as driven, as the Georgian.

"The heavyweight champ of Iowa politics," as Jim Flansburg dubbed him in 1978, readied himself for the election by asking his longtime friend Marvin Pomerantz, a self-made millionaire and Republican party financier, to manage the campaign alongside Mary Louise Smith, who had recently returned from Washington, where she'd served as Republican national chairman during Gerald Ford's administration. They quickly hired the prestigious Washington, D.C., political consulting firm of Bailey, Deardourff and Associates, to handle their media, raised an unprecedented $600,000 for their statewide campaign, and persuaded Marilyn Maye to go back into the studio to update "Let a Winner Lead the Way."

The two Democrats vying to challenge Ray–"blips on the political radar screen" joked Flansburg–had been racing each other for several months before Ray announced. Polk County Supervisor Tom Whitney, who was thirty-three, had been in the race almost a year. The youngest-ever Democratic state chairman at twenty-four, elected the youngest-ever supervisor at twenty-nine, the brash hopeful was eager to become Iowa's youngest-ever governor. He charged Ray with a "breakdown of administrative responsibility" and set out to raise a lot of money from the state's Democratic power brokers. His hope was to raise the money quickly, tie up the few big givers, and stave off any primary competition. But it was widely accepted that house majority leader Jerry Fitzgerald, the thirty-seven-year-old three-term legislator, would be in the race. Labeled the "most adroit political organizer in the state," Fitzgerald quickly became the favored candidate to try and "out-nice-guy" Bob Ray. He announced in December 1977, claiming that Ray was stagnant. "After 10 years isn't it time we had a *new* governor?" he asked. He accused the four-term governor of being tired and worn out and of running a campaign emphasizing "balloons, ice cream, picnics and hoopla."

With a Democratic primary set for June, both candidates were prodded by state chairman Ed Campbell, who kept alive the Democrats' complaint

about Ray's "imperial governorship." But his harping went largely unheard. In March one statewide poll showed that 75 percent of Iowans had
never heard of Jerry Fitzgerald and 70 percent had never heard of Tom
Whitney.

In part because Ray had his own race under control, his hand was
evident in the concurrently run race for the Republican nomination for
the right to challenge Dick Clark for the U.S. Senate. One of the most
influential senators in Washington, Clark was up for his first reelection,
and the state GOP had approached a baker's dozen candidates to bear
their flag. As nominal head of the party, Bob Ray was consulted by many
potential candidates, and he tried to twist some arms on his own. Ironically, he continued to be the party's best weapon against Clark, running
ahead of him in all preelection polls. But with Ray not interested in the
Senate seat, Clark was confident. He'd walked across the state soliciting
votes in 1972 and came from behind to unseat two-term senator Jack
Miller. That confidence was not shaken when his opponent turned out to
be Republican outsider Roger Jepsen, who had come from out of nowhere
to beat Ray's favored candidate and friend Maurie Van Nostrand in a
primary walk.

DICK GILBERT "Sometimes we didn't appreciate the base the governor
had. We thought we knew how broad it was, but really didn't know for
certain. Well, I went over and lived in the Quad Cities late in 1977, and
that's when I realized how extraordinarily powerful he had become. It
wasn't a political base in the machine context, but a base of association
and followers and people. Just the crème de la crème within that community. The guy [Ray] could walk into any town in the state–he had Ray
chairmen in each of them–and people there considered him their friend. I
don't think anyone could have ever beaten him, because he was in the
state so deeply with the quality people. And not just Republicans, either."

BOB RAY "Nineteen seventy-eight would have been a perfect time to get
out. Things in the state were going well, and it would have been a good
time for me to start a new career. So there was some gamble to staying
another four years."

MARVIN POMERANTZ "There was consideration that he would not run,
but I encouraged him substantially. He wasn't completely sure he wanted
another term, and he was beginning to look at alternatives, and some
close advisers and friends were telling him that he was getting to an age

where he ought to be considering another career. From my perspective it looked like there was still potential for him in the national limelight."

DAVID BELIN "I was not in favor of his running in 1978, but I said he should not run unless he wanted to play a major national role in the Republican party and in the selection of a presidential and vice-presidential candidate in 1980. My position was that if you do run, you have a national stature, you're respected, capitalize on it and try and remove yourself from some of the day-to-day activities at the governor's office. Try and have a more major role in the direction of the country."

BOB RAY "The last couple times [*Michigan governor*] Bill Milliken and I talked, trying to figure out whether we should run again or not in 1978, we really couldn't think of many reasons to run. But we still did.

"We were in similar situations. Neither one of us had to have the job to live. Yet we liked what we were doing. I think both of us felt pleased that we were elected and reelected. Neither one of us thought the Senate was a place we wanted to go. After being governor, where you made decisions and things happened and you could see them happen, going and sitting in a legislative body like the Senate was not something that appealed to us. We talked back and forth, consulted with one another, and then separately decided to run again. It wasn't one of those things where we said, 'I'll run if you'll run.' "

GERRY RANKIN "A lot of people thought Ray should run for the Senate. I knew he never would. He could not have worked in a legislative body; he was an executive all the way. Plus he lived in a $3 million mansion, had a limousine waiting at his door, Iowa was his. All he had to do was say, 'I'm running for governor' and, bang, he was elected. If he'd gone into the Senate, he'd have been at the bottom of the ladder, a neophyte. But in Iowa he was king."

TOM STONER "He could have been elected to the Senate any one of three times, and I did everything to try and convince him to do that, because he would have made a great U.S. senator. But he liked being governor. He is so attached to the heartbeat of the state—and the heartbeat of the state ultimately became attached to him—that it was just a marriage for life."

WYTHE WILLEY "He didn't have ambitions of living in Washington or to be in the legislative process. Ray does not have that burning desire for power that some politicians do; it just wasn't in him. He was a better executive. If you follow the theory that real power is not exercised in our democracy, that you really govern at the consent of the people, Bob Ray was the right kind of man to assume the executive position the way our forefathers meant our democracy to be. Bob Ray did not want to be a king; he just wanted to be governor. Also, remember, there are always a lot of 'could haves' in politics."

BOB RAY "I often worried about people going into the Congress, I always said the air must be different there. It seemed to be difficult for them to remember who they were and whom they represented, because they become one in a select group that has a pretty high opinion of itself. I've seen people get elected and suddenly believe they were God's gift to the world, and all of a sudden they're telling people what's good for them instead of listening and evaluating and trying to produce for them. It's a fine line between being a leader and being dictatorial."

JERRY MURSENER "One time prior to the 1978 campaign he called me at the Republican campaign headquarters on a Saturday morning. He'd been putting down all the reasons for why or why not to run again. He was calling a bunch of people, pondering, and he says to me, 'Just tell me, will it be fun? If I go, will it be a fun campaign?' He was going back to the ambassadors of fun – guys like Gilbert or Oman or me – to see what we thought.

"When it really came down to it, especially on the political events, it wasn't going to be Marv Pomerantz up there in the plane with him, it was going to be Dave or me, or both. That was where it had to be fun. We had to have bands and balloon drops and fun things happening. Bob Ray cared more about a good balloon rise than any slick multimedia show."

PAT BAIN "I wasn't one of those who thought he should stay in any longer. He killed off ambitions in some very smart, talented men in Iowa, like Art Neu. Bob Ray would give you a thousand reasons why he didn't step down, but it was a mistake, a mistake that will take a long time to turn around."

WYTHE WILLEY "Tom Stoner once said that you can't grow little trees under a big oak. There were some of us around Ray who had no desire to get into public office. John Murray did, and it didn't work out in the long run. Some guys, by their style, literally spew out other candidates. Tom Harkin's people are always running for office. But Ray didn't believe in the political progeny theory."

JERRY MURSENER "If you stay around as long as Ray did, you tend to clog up the power avenues, so that guys like John Murray and Art Neu had no place further to go. Any ambitions they had to be governor were thwarted. *Bob Ray didn't encourage them?* No, he didn't. And he always waited until very late, after Valentine's Day, to announce what he was going to do, run or not. Some of the central committee members were concerned about that clogging up, because behind Murray and Neu there were others waiting for their chance–Brice Oakley for one. No little acorns were growing, and a result of that lack of growth is, who are the Republicans going to run for governor in 1990? 1994? Your legislative leadership is Del Stromer, Cal Hultman, who've been around a long time and probably don't have ambitions to be governor anymore. So who's sitting behind them? Are Leach and Tauke ever going to come back and run? Where are the young Republicans?"

GEORGE WITTGRAF "Lots of personal decisions about seeking high office were affected by the fact that Bob Ray stayed in office so long. Neu, Murray, Bill Huff (the former insurance commissioner), Tom Stoner–any number of people were affected by Ray's omnipresence. That's not a criticism of Bob Ray, but it's a reality that did affect the natural political growth of some people who were logical political heirs of Bob Ray. And while he was very successful, good for the state, good for the political party, it somewhat thwarted the development of political leadership in his mold. If he had moved on to the Senate in 1972 or 1974 or 1978, if he'd moved on to a cabinet position in the Nixon or Ford administrations, that would have allowed for more natural evolution of his political heirs."

MARY LOUISE SMITH "I have heard that in other states, too, that a long-term governor frequently impedes the development or bubbling of young leadership. It's hard to determine if Bob Ray's long-term stay impeded growth. I don't know.
    "I take part of the blame in not helping to establish more leaders that represented the philosophy of Republicanism that Bob Ray and I both shared. There were efforts to unite moderate Republicans, nurture them, but I think we probably could have been more of a catalyst for others."

LARRY POPE "Bob Ray always made his political decisions [*concerning who would succeed him*] based on what was right for Bob Ray. I don't think nurturing others [*for that job*] ever entered his mind. I'm not saying that was wrong, but it was characteristic. The Art Neu thing wouldn't even have entered his mind–you know, 'I've got to get out so Art Neu can move in.'"

ART NEU "I told him if he decided not to run, I'd like some lead notice, some time to get prepared. Whenever I'd hear a rumor that he wasn't going to run I'd go up and just say, 'Hey look, if you are going to step down, give me a little notice.' Then there were always the rumors that President Ford was going to appoint him to secretary of the interior or some damn thing. But I figured I didn't have much control over it, so I took a somewhat detached view. The press was really more interested in it than I was, gave them something to write about on a slow day.

"I always thought it a little clumsy for me to go down and ask him if he was planning on running for the Senate, or another term. I didn't want it to sound like I wanted him to get out. Now, if he hadn't run for that fifth term, I wouldn't have minded at all. But I knew he wouldn't run for the Senate; he would have been very unhappy in any legislative body."

BOB RAY "I thought seriously about not running that time, and I finally concluded that I liked what I was doing. I still thought I could make a contribution, and I thought I could get elected. I never really put myself up to the wire any sooner than I had to. I'd never set a timetable for announcing my decisions. The press used to think I should have a timetable, a day I was going to tell them what my decision was. I never thought I owed them that."

JERRY MURSENER "He announced so abruptly that no campaign materials had been put together. So [Walt] Shotwell, Oman, and I decided we needed something quick for folks to wear at a couple events already scheduled, so we printed up stickers that read 'The Best Governor We've Ever Had.' That quickly produced a consumer complaint [by Des Moines hairdresser Jerry Feick] against the Ray campaign for questionable advertising. That's just one reminder that the Ray machine didn't always run as smoothly as some believed. Later we settled on using 'A Good Man, Doing a Great Job,' which we'd used back in 1974."

BILLIE RAY "By that time I was pretty sure it would be the last one. I just didn't want him to go out losing. Plus it gave me time to finish my project at Terrace Hill. But I think we both knew it would be the last campaign."

JERRY MURSENER "I always thought Fitzgerald was the guy who would beat him. He had studied Bob Ray like a book. Back in 1972, 1973, we would sit around in bars and he would say, 'You've covered Ray a long time. Does he do this or that?' I mean, nobody that I know could have put more effort into trying to get the mannerisms of Bob Ray down more than Fitzgerald.

"But that was why it was so tough when he did run against him, because he simply couldn't out–Bob Ray, Bob Ray."

<u>TOM WHITNEY</u>   "I thought the greatest mistake was trying to out-nice-guy Bob Ray. How can you beat the nicest guy in the world by trying to out-nice him?"

<u>BOB RAY</u>   "I never really cared any time I ran who got nominated, because I psychologically just said, 'I'll take whoever runs.' Whitney would have lost in the general election for the same reason he lost in the primary: he defeated himself. But after the primary some of the Democratic party leaders started telling Fitzgerald how he had to start kicking me around, had to get tough, had to be more like Whitney. He took Whitney's campaign manager and I think Whitney even advised him some, and he started sounding just like Whitney.

"At the time I thought, 'Golly, Jerry, how will you ever know? If you lose, I'll always think it was because you changed your format. If you win, you probably did the right thing, but was it really you who won?' "

<u>WYTHE WILLEY</u>   "Fitzgerald is an interesting guy, and in a lot of ways he's a lot like Bob Ray. He's an extremely good political tactician, but he was never able to make that step from a keen political observer and tactician to candidate. If you got Fitzgerald in that legislative process and asked him what time it was, he'd tell you how to build a watch."

<u>JERRY FITZGERALD</u>   "I knew what the odds were; it was a long shot. I also knew that I couldn't stay in the legislature more than two more years at the most. I couldn't afford it financially. I also wanted to at least establish some statewide credibility."

<u>BOB RAY</u>   "I thought it was kind of amazing when Fitzgerald got nominated. He didn't spend a lot of money, didn't do a lot of campaigning. He'd gotten so you couldn't get any position out of him on anything. That's the reason why when leaders in the legislature run for office there's something that's lost in their leadership. I'd heard that he'd said he wanted to be a Bob Ray–type campaigner. *What's that exactly?* He wanted to run a positive campaign. He wanted to run on what he had to offer and compare that with what I had to offer. He just wanted to run a straightforward, honest campaign, which is what we always tried to do. He got nominated doing just that, not making many appearances, not spending much money, and I thought, 'This guy is going to be tough.'

"But as soon as he got through the primary, Ed Campbell, Tom Whitney, and others encouraged him to start attacking me. He attacked me in front of his Democratic friends at meetings. They liked it, and he began to feel comfortable doing it.

"He was quite capable of just debating the issues, but somebody obviously told him that wasn't going to make him a winner. I'll always think he would have fared better if he'd taken the highroad."

PAUL WILSON "Bob Ray had an unabashed love of the state, to the point of being almost corny to an outsider. It was an affection that the people and Bob Ray both had for the state, and you really had to know Iowa before you understood it. But I think it paid off, and it rippled down through the entire state. People were very proud to be living in Iowa. I think he communicated that, and that was the spirit of his campaign. It is the only campaign in my recollection in the last decade that was completely positive."

BOB RAY "It was a fun campaign because it wasn't a worrisome campaign. We didn't have to drag money out of people and hope for an issue and worry about what your people were saying and how to keep them going strong. It was put together pretty well. There wasn't the animosity that develops in so many campaigns. I enjoyed that campaign, more than others."

MARVIN POMERANTZ "It was the ultimate campaign."

WYTHE WILLEY "I'm going to suggest the three best campaigns ever run in this state. The best ever was that 1978 Ray gubernatorial campaign. We not only had Bob Ray and a very good, seasoned staff, but we had Marv Pomerantz, Mary Louise Smith, Dick Redman, and a good campaign administration. The second-best campaign was Ed Failor managing Dave Stanley against Harold Hughes for the Senate in 1968—damn near beat him. The third-best campaign is probably a tie between Grassley and Culver, and Harkin beating Jepsen. *Jepsen versus Clark?* That was a fluke."

BOB RAY "Tom Stoner and I had talked often about Marv. He's a rare commodity, and we were lucky to get him to help. He never makes you feel like he's doing something for you. He's always a person that will be there, will not argue or find reasons or try to evaluate why he can and can't. He just makes a decision he's going to do this or that and he does it. He never leaves you with the impression that you owe him something or he's done something special for you."

BOB TYSON "Bob Ray introduced Marv at a breakfast one morning a few years ago and said when Marv was a little boy his mother used to wash sacks—grain sacks—and Marv would put them in his little red wagon and take them around the neighborhood and sell them. He said Marv still has a little red wagon, only today we call it a Fleetwood."

MARVIN POMERANTZ "We raised almost $600,000, at that time the most that had ever been raised for a gubernatorial race, twice what he had raised in 1974."

JERRY FITZGERALD "We had no money. We spent $100,000 in the primary and $150,000 in the general. Can you imagine that in a statewide campaign? God, that's not enough for a congressional race. But I didn't have any choice. I had no money; that was never my strong point."

DAVID OMAN "The money was spent wisely, themes were developed, good people were hired. It was a first-class campaign. The advertising was top quality and the scheduling was good. There were very few dropped balls; we had a game plan and it just rolled along."

DAVID YEPSEN "He had another slogan that year, 'Progress with Stability,' which he used in front of college audiences or a women's group. But it was interchangeable, and he'd use 'Stability with Progress' if he were in front of the Farm Bureau."

PAUL WILSON "It was an enjoyable campaign because he had such an outstanding record. The sheer weight of it was a compelling reason for reelection, and, frankly, for that reason it was not the most difficult campaign. We worked hard, but on the other hand, there wasn't the fear that we might lose. We went to the barbecues and the county fairs and the parades and just had fun."

BILL CREWS "So many people wanted to see him, just mingle with him, that in September and October we had like forty barbecues in thirty different towns, fund-raisers. He loved that."

SUE MITSCHKE "He also really liked parades – for one reason, because he could see a lot of people and didn't really have to talk."

JERRY MURSENER "His success in that campaign and his tenure was this confidence factor. The ability to go into places and not be overimposing, to deal with things with a human touch. One time we did these things called Fun Mondays. He said they'd never work. We'd work with a local Republican party to get the streets closed, keep the stores open, we'd get bands, five-cent popcorn and dime hot dogs, and you could just come down and see the governor. No political speeches.

"The first one we ever did was LeMars on a hot July night, eighty degrees at eight o'clock. Oman, the trooper, the governor, me, we'd all sweat through our suits. All the way up there the governor kept saying to me, 'Jerry, this isn't going to work.' I kept assuring him. Plus it was too late by then; we were stuck in this little plane. We get there and there's a crowd of 2,000 just packing the streets. He gets up, does a little speech, and starts walking down the street. Out comes this old guy on a cane and says, 'I came down here tonight because I'm eighty-two and I've never met a governor.' And Bob Ray says, 'Well, I think it's about time you do. I'm Bob Ray.' Just so smooth. And that made the whole night for him. He's such a feel-good guy. He really liked those kinds of events."

BOB RAY "At that moment I didn't think there was a problem in the job that I would have felt uncomfortable handling. We really were at the place where any new problem that arose would have the same characteristics of problems we'd solved before. And once you've gone through a whole litany of different kinds of problems, and you live through them, you feel confident."

PAUL WILSON "In a lot of states the governor and the state were just consumed with survival. He had the opportunity to really focus on areas that were pretty far down on the list of priorities in some other states. And he had the opportunity to try and correct problems whose level in other states wouldn't even have been seen as a problem. I don't think Iowa could have ever had a better governor. He was responsible for a lot of the good feelings and the good times."

BOB RAY "One issue that came up was that I'd been in office too long. That was common. I think people like to see change, and I thought it might be a factor in that race, whether they liked me or not. But I didn't think that was a problem, and the votes bore it out.

"It's altogether different when you start running for a statewide office and people have never heard of you. Remember, I did it once, too. You have to grind it out, one by one. That's a different kind of campaign than when you're known by 98 percent of the population. They want you to come out, and you can go anywhere in the state either on a campaign appearance or official business and you feel like they want you. You don't have to force yourself on a group, pitch them."

GEORGE KINLEY "He was the best at presenting that image of Mr. Nice Guy and had the unique ability of being able to kind of avoid himself. He'd also appointed over 2,000 people to various boards and commissions by then, and you develop a certain following when you take care of people like that."

ED CAMPBELL "Even our people, the Democrats, got used to voting for him. I think 12 percent in that last election. It was awful for us."

Fitzgerald ran a low-key campaign, so low-key that many party leaders were convinced no one could hear him. His logic was that Bob Ray had won a few elections that way, maybe he could too. In October, two weeks before the election, Fitzgerald started blaming the governor for problems in thirteen state agencies, ranging from the Commission for the Blind, where he claimed there had been overexpenditures, to the Department of General Services, where he claimed $700,000 had been spent on a new vocational rehabilitation center without legislative approval. Ray's office claimed all of the "problems" Fitzgerald cited were being solved. But the biggest thorn in Ray's side during 1978 was the allegation that the National Guard was "plagued by illegal wiretapping and recruiting, inept administration and a decline in morale and strength." Ray had accepted the resignation of General Joseph May in late 1977 and appointed Junior Burkhead in January. Soon after the FBI, the Bureau of Criminal Investigation, and the state legislature were investigating claims that guardsmen were acting as bartenders and coatcheckers at the governor's mansion and that Junior Burkhead was running an inept administration. Ray dubbed the investigations a witch hunt, but Democrats claimed there were more severe problems than were being publicized.

JERRY FITZGERALD "The only thing that ultimately had any chance of catching hold was the National Guard issue. It was sort of symbolic of what you might say was mismanagement. The Guard was fighting each other, and all these factions inside were splitting up and leaking information. But Ray waited until after the election to fire Burkhead.

"Campaignwise, I thought there were more substantive issues, which I tried to talk about, but oftentimes the public is not interested in the nitty-gritty business of state government unless you could build up a bunch of it to support a larger picture. The only thing that was catching any attention in the press was the National Guard.

"We kept putting out programs on this and that, talking about things we were working on, but they never seemed to catch. Regardless of how unmeritorious the Guard situation may have been, it was a mess. Was it enough to throw a guy out of office? That was a long shot."

DAVID OMAN "Remember, you had a popular incumbent governor running for an unprecedented fifth term, and nobody had laid a glove on him. The press had not turned up anything, the opponent had not turned up anything, and then there's this miniscandal involving your National Guard adjutant general. Unfortunately, that fell on the heels of the problem with Joe May and his use of state-owned aircraft. So now you had two adjutant generals in trouble, and the press began to feel they had a story that was going to give him some real political problems, and they covered the legislative committee's hearing day after day, and, of course, the Democratic majority milked it for all it was worth. They scheduled them in October right before the election, and dragged the hearings out.

"They always tried to get him through the agencies, tried to link him tightly with them, as if he were running them on a day-to-day, hands-on basis."

BOB RAY "If you took each campaign and went back and looked, you'd find each candidate looking for an issue. They'll drum on one for a while and if it doesn't take, then they pick up another one. Good campaigns will start out with a pretty good strategy, emphasize one or two big issues and a few others, which gives you a reason to go out and talk.

"But you try and revolve your campaign around one or two major issues. Most campaigns, whether they think they know what those issues are or not, miss on an issue. So they struggle, trying to pick up on another one. I've long said that candidates don't make the issues anyway. All they can do is take what the people are thinking, develop them or exploit them. In Jerry's case, the only issue that he really got into was the Guard.

"There were some real problems, and the politics got in the way because I could not get into the situation like I normally would have. I could not afford, for instance, to call the adjutant general and say, you know, 'I want to know the truth, and if you don't tell me the truth, you're out.' How could I get tough when the GAO is investigating, the BCI, the FBI, and who knows who else. I had to let it run its course so that no one would accuse me of interfering or obstructing justice. And, of course, the legislators were up there having a heyday with their hearings. It probably prevented us from finding out about Burkhead sooner, because I couldn't ask him certain questions. That took a little fun out of the campaign.

"By any other state's standards, the National Guard problem was not a big deal. By Iowa's standards, it was a big deal. If the people out there had said, 'Wow, that governor must be covering up something or he must be promoting this kind of stuff at our expense,' then it would have been an issue. But they didn't think that, and Jerry kept pounding away at it, using all of his friends in the legislature. The legislators were involved in it for only one reason: politics. The Democrats were just looking for any reason they could use to fell me. It was their big issue."

Governor Ray won 58 percent of the vote, besting Jerry Fitzgerald by 146,000 votes. The day after the election Bob and Billie Ray flew to Austria, and the press in Iowa and around the country claimed that the five-term governor had drubbed Fitzgerald to position himself on the national scene. He refused to rule out a run for the presidency in 1980, but if he served out the term, he would have been in office more than twice as long as any of his predecessors.

Throughout the campaign, candidate Ray had put off questions concerning the future of the state's economy. "The key, we think, is to hold down spending," he said. Back in September 1978, Democrat Lowell Norland and Republican Jim West, the ranking members of the tax-writing House Ways and Means Committee, told the Iowa Taxpayers' Association that neither candidate was facing up to the economic woes on the state's horizon. They reported that "We'll have a campaign statewide that will be well-run, well-financed and well-publicized and that will never touch the major issues of the next General Assembly. There are complex economic problems facing us that take a long time to explain and a long time for the general public to understand."

After Junior Burkhead sent a guardsman to the governor's office posing as a reporter, Ray asked for his resignation as head of the National Guard on December 28, 1978, six weeks after the election.

XX:
JEPSEN II

I f the Ray-Fitzgerald race was a cakewalk, the battle for Dick Clark's Senate seat livened up backrooms and barrooms statewide. Roger Jepsen, who had been hibernating from politics since Bob Ray embarrassed him in 1972, woke up and caused some red faces himself. He announced for the Senate seat on March 9, 1978, the day before filing closed. He would face-off against Iowa Commerce Commissioner Maurie Van Nostrand, the approved candidate of Bob Ray and the state Republican party, in a primary three months later. Asked to comment on Jepsen's entrance into the race, Ray described his relationship with his former lieutenant governor as "strained." "Obviously I haven't encouraged him to run," the governor told reporters.

DAVID OMAN "We spent considerable time trying to encourage some good people to make that race. A lot of people, Governor Ray included, felt that Dick Clark was vulnerable. He talked to Marv Pomerantz, he talked to Cal Hultman, Mo Baringer, Jim Leach. Obviously he talked with Maurie Van Nostrand. He talked to Tom Stoner, but he just wasn't ready.

Dee Jepsen, Roger Jepsen, and Terry Branstad. *Des Moines Register* photo. Reprinted with permission.

In fact, I think he talked to Stoner first, but Tom waived it away, and for a while we were scrambling. Keep in mind that 1977 turned into 1978 and we still didn't have a candidate. Finally, in February, Maurie agreed to go. Then, right before the deadline, Jepsen jumped in."

JERRY MURSENER "When we were trying to find a candidate I asked Mary Louise Smith why she didn't run. She said, 'I'd love to run, but I don't want to serve.' I suggested she and Marv Pomerantz run as a team. Marv wants to be a senator, but you'd have a tough time selling Marv in Iowa. So I suggested to Mary Louise that she and Marv run as a team. She could serve six months, resign, and Ray could appoint Marv. She said she didn't think so."

TOM STONER "I went to Washington and met with Senator Bob Packwood and struggled with getting into the race. I met with a consultant who had done some polling. That was in mid-1977. It was the right time for me to do it, and Bob Ray and others were pushing me. It was fairly clear that I wouldn't have had a primary if I'd run, and Roger later told me he wouldn't have gotten in the race if I'd announced. In October I decided not to, for personal reasons. So then we tried to get Jim Leach to do it. Bob Ray met with him on Thanksgiving Day and tried to talk him into running. But he wasn't ready for it yet."

BOB RAY *How come it was so hard to find somebody to run for that seat?* "That's kind of the way politics are. You'll find six people out there running for a house seat in the Iowa legislature, and maybe four of them will be top-quality candidates. And none of them will get elected. Then you go into another district where it's a shoo-in, it's yours, it's going to be a Republican seat, and you can't get anyone to run. Sometimes nobody wants to run for the Senate, and I think partially it's because it doesn't have the same glamour as running for governor does. People seem to identify with the governor's position. They see him all the time. The senator's somewhere far off."

ROGER JEPSEN "When I first presented it to my wife, Dee, well, her experiences when I was in office before were not all that good. When I was lieutenant governor I thought Iowa wouldn't get started if I didn't get up every morning and get it going. I worked at that seven days a week. Had everything scheduled and organized, including my family, and it was a tough time for them. So my wife's recollections of politics, on a scale of one to ten, were about one.

"When I broached the subject of running for the Senate, we were in a new season of life. We had both come to Christ, had a personal relationship with Christ, her a lot longer than I. So we made our decisions in a different atmosphere, a different climate, and with a different set of values. We talked about it, prayed about it, and she said, 'No, we're not going to.' "

MARY LOUISE SMITH   "I remember the day Roger came into the headquarters on Ingersoll to tell me he was running. We'd heard he'd been making the rounds, looking for support. I told him not to run, and I called in Marv so that I'd have a witness. I just advised him not to run. I thought it was not only too late but that I did not think he was a viable candidate."

MARVIN POMERANTZ   "Mary Louise really got into it with him. We knew how Bob Ray felt, and we did everything possible to discourage Roger from running. We had a private meeting with Roger and Dee, and we really laid out how difficult it would be and how inept it would be and how counterproductive it could be, and he decided on his own that regardless of what anybody said at that point, he was going to run."

BOB RAY   "We hadn't talked to Roger, because I don't think anyone had any idea he was alive or what he was doing. He got in very, very late and it was strange in a way. In a primary in the Republican party there's a very strong conservative element. Roger appealed to that, but my gosh, Maurie Van Nostrand grew up with that element. But I think people identified Maurie with me."

ROGER JEPSEN   "They stepped up their search for a candidate when they heard I was getting into the race. They shifted into high gear. It was the same old story again; everybody at the top of the party discouraged me. The hierarchy of the party—Mary Louise Smith, the whole bit—they all said, not very pleasantly, 'You shouldn't run.'

"You know, I always did things the way the rules say the game is supposed to be played, and they always talked about the rules, but they never played by them. So I went according to the rules, and I started making the rounds. I knew how to do that, I knew who the players were. Mary Louise says to me, 'Well, if anybody's going to run, I'm going to run.' She says, 'I've looked at it, and it doesn't look like anybody can win.' She was very rude. But I went up and down the line, to Bob Ray and Mary Louise and the bag man, Pomerantz.

"I remember talking to Marv and Mary Louise at the same time, and they both punched me out. Marv Pomerantz said, 'Who do you think you are? You've got to have the blessing of the man, if you can get that.

Besides, Mary Louise is the one who can come closest to winning,' he said. I think there were a lot of people who thought about running, but nobody had the guts to run.

"But I was steeled for that; that was nothing new to me. The party had never helped me before. So then I announced, and the rest is history. They got Van Nostrand to run, and Mary Louise Smith intervened and got the national headquarters, the Republican National Committee – I don't care what anybody else says – got them to put money in against me in the primary. That did more to help me than anything that had been done so far."

DAVID OMAN "Roger came in to visit with Governor Ray and to tell him he was thinking about running. Governor Ray was very cordial, and it was probably a warmer meeting than both anticipated. He didn't discourage him. He didn't encourage him. He listened. He told him that he was not planning to endorse anybody publicly. He indicated he would support the nominated candidate, help whoever won the primary.

"The governor had high hopes for Maurie, thought he'd be a colorful candidate and a good senator. Keep in mind that energy issues were on the front burner nationally, and Maurie would have gone into the Senate as one of a handful of people who really knew what he was talking about on energy. But Roger was a free agent, he could do whatever he wanted.

"The governor asked Roger some obvious questions: Where is your money going to come from? Aren't you starting a little late? That sort of thing."

BOB RAY "When they came in to see me, Dee wanted me to know she was born again, and she certainly was impressive. She seemed very sincere. Roger indicated he was also born again and that their lives had changed, they were different. He said he kind of saw this as a calling.

"I really didn't think he would run. But I never told him he couldn't. That was totally up to him. When it came right down to it, he was going to run no matter what I said."

DAVID OMAN "Roger still had pretty good name recognition, people remembered who he was, and he had run statewide twice before. Also, the pendulum was moving towards more conservative times. Maurie ran a poor campaign, God love him. He just never pulled it together.

"Maurie wanted very much for the governor to embrace him, put his arm around him, endorse him. The governor's stance was that it was an open primary. He thought it was obvious to most people whom he preferred and felt that he really shouldn't inject himself to the point of trying to tell the average Iowa voter who he or she should pull the lever for, so he didn't do it. That hurt Maurie very much, personally.

"The governor accurately sensed that his active involvement probably would not change that many votes. It was a pretty clear choice between someone who was perceived as a moderate and someone who was riding the New Right wave. And Maurie had been closely identified with the governor, served in his administration. People knew that.

"He didn't endorse Maurie, he lost, and Maurie didn't like it. He popped off a few times afterwards. He was angry."

BOB RAY "I suppose if I were Maurie, I'd be angry too. If there's anything in politics that's really worthwhile, it's loyalty. Maurie was closely identified with me, and he wanted me to come out for him. That's why he got so angry with me. He considered it my campaign and that it was my responsibility to pull the chestnuts out of the fire for him. I could understand that; he'd helped me in my campaigns. He felt that I had encouraged him to get into the race, so I did some things for him, helped get him some people. But I had told him not to announce until he had his campaign structure lined up. By gosh, he couldn't wait, he wanted to run so badly. I'd seen that before, I'd seen it developing with him, and then he got really angry and started running against me. I could see our friendship dissolving because of it."

On June 6 Jepsen clobbered Van Nostrand at the polls, winning all but 6 of the state's 99 counties. He had outspent Bob Ray's candidate by three to one, primarily on expensive direct-mail appeals conducted by New Right fund-raiser Richard Viguerie and aimed at gut conservative issues like gun control, abortion, and the Panama Canal. With 25 percent of the vote in, Jepsen spotted "the trend," accepted the victory from behind a podium at the Hotel Fort Des Moines, and headed out the door for a celebration party at his home in Davenport. On his way out the door, he bumped into Mary Louise Smith, John McDonald, Marv Pomerantz, and Wythe Willey, coming to offer their hand in congratulations. Jepsen accepted with a smile.

The next day the Republican party boasted one of the more mixed-up slates in memory. Longtime adversaries Ray and Jepsen topped the list, joined by conservative legislator Terry Branstad, who had defeated Brice Oakley and Bill Hanson, both of whom were moderates. As a three-term legislator, Branstad had not exactly carried water for the governor, which he openly admitted.

<u>BOB RAY</u> *How did you handle yourself after that primary, with both Terry Branstad and Roger Jepsen on the ticket with you?* "I had really been out of the lieutenant governor's battle, and maybe I shouldn't have been. I was still operating under the belief that I should not get involved. I didn't think I could help. Although Brice Oakley may have been more closely identified with me, I saw more of Terry Branstad than I did of him.

"Terry was the campaigner of that lot. He would not let himself get drawn into the fire of the other candidates. He came and talked to me on occasion, told me what he was doing, and I never breached that confidence. Brice was out doing his own thing."

<u>TERRY BRANSTAD</u> "About once a month during the primary campaign I made an appointment with the governor to just report on what I was doing. I was the only one of the three candidates to do that. He always made time for me."

<u>JERRY MURSENER</u> "Right after the primary we had a little meeting— Terry, Roger, Ray, and their campaign people. The state party people put it together. We had it in Ray's office, and Steve Roberts and I, Wythe, Marv, Oman, Mary Louise, Jepsen, Dee, his son Jeff, Branstad, and whoever his manager was. We all sat around down there and nobody knew quite how to get started. Ray came in and shook hands with everybody, said, 'How are you doing?' and that did it. It was like a feeling-out period as they divided up their chips."

<u>BOB RAY</u> "There wasn't any question after that primary that Roger and Terry were better than the [*Democratic*] alternatives. I decided that I wasn't going to let the press spend the entire campaign driving wedges between and among the three of us. That's why we went over to our campaign headquarters, at Thirty-first and Ingersoll, the day after the primary and had a press conference. We went right up-front and told the press that we'd had our differences in the past, they'd reported them, and that they were behind us. We were three candidates on the same team, the same ticket, and we were going to support each other. And we weren't going to talk about that again. Frankly, it worked better than I thought. They really backed off."

<u>ED REDFERN</u> "I had worked for Maurie in the primary, even though we were supposed to stay out of it. But Jepsen had run against the governor before, and Maurie had always been a friend of the governor's, and I felt he deserved our help. Soon after the primary Jepsen came in and met with Bob Ray, and he related the meeting to us later.

"Roger had come in and said, 'Governor, if anybody says anything bad about you on my staff, they're going to be fired immediately.' The governor said, 'Roger, I really appreciate that.' He said, 'I don't think you'll have any trouble with anybody on my staff, either.' Roger asked, 'Well, what about Dave Oman and Ed Redfern?' The governor turned to me and asked, 'Ed, did you really tell [*Jepsen aide*] Wendell Harms you couldn't hold your nose and vote for Roger Jepsen?'"

DAVID OMAN   "After the primary, to his credit, Governor Ray did a lot of work for Roger Jepsen, and not many people give him credit for that. He made public appearances, put his arm around him, and indicated that he wanted this man elected to the United States Senate, that he wanted and expected Republicans to support the full ticket.

"One day, late in the campaign, David Yepsen came along on the plane and wrote about how the two were campaigning as a team. He made a reference to the fact that we had Teem pop on the plane. He thought that was real clever. It was coincidental."

JERRY MURSENER   "We went out and did a fly-around—sixty-four stops in four days, and probably twenty-five of those were Ray and Jepsen, and there was no flinching at all, no hesitancy on Ray's part.

"Every time we left an event, people thought we talked about the state budget all the way home. Not true. Dave [*Oman*] and I used to rate events—one to ten. After a few years of doing this, we had perfected the rating system. If we got to eat, it was one point automatically. If there was a public address system, we gave it another two points automatically. Well, we went to this one event that just fell apart. We get in the van and start driving to the next event. I asked Dave how we should rate it. Dave says, 'Well, a two. We all got to eat, didn't we?' Ray is sitting behind us in the back seat of one of the campaign vans and says, 'Well, I give it a minus fifteen.' When did he start rating events? we wondered. He claimed it was the worst event he'd been to in his whole life. So we argued from Manchester to Elkader about that, and about whether or not he could start rating events. There was always a laugh, a little humor, as we went back and forth across the state. There was never any concern about the outcome of that election. But I would say one thing: Unlike Jepsen, Ray always thought he could lose."

MARY ANN BROWN   "The people I dealt with around the state while I was working for the governor's campaign weren't for Bob Ray and against Roger Jepsen. They were all Republicans at that point, and the emphasis was on electing the ticket, not just Bob Ray. A lot of people thought that

Bob Ray was Jepsen's and Branstad's hope, so to speak. The bigger that Bob Ray could carry the state, the better for Roger and Terry."

WYTHE WILLEY "Ray is a very strong party man. The party to him was family. And contrary to a lot of successful politicians, he was very supportive of the party's candidates. He had a lot to do with Roger Jepsen getting elected in 1978. The key was that the paper made a big deal about how Bob Ray wasn't a big fan of Jepsen's. The *Register* set Jepsen up. They did it to Branstad, too. So the last week of the campaign Bob Ray puts his arm around Roger Jepsen and travels around the state with him. All these good Bob Ray people say, 'Well, if he's good enough for Ray, he's good enough for me.' Ray's influence on that campaign was immeasurable."

DAVID OMAN "He didn't have to do that; he didn't have to spend five minutes at his own campaign appearances encouraging Bob Ray faithfuls to vote for Roger."

BOB RAY "I will admit the press has reasons sometimes to be skeptical of politicians. They expect you to say certain things regardless of the truth. But I tried not to say things to the press that I didn't believe. Now, maybe you could tell how much I believed it by how much I would offer, or how silent I might be, but I told the press that Roger was catching Dick Clark. You could feel it, you could sense it. You couldn't prove it by a poll, but you went places and people were saying things differently.

"At the start of that campaign, people said, 'Well, it's too bad we didn't have a candidate for the Senate,' or 'Roger has absolutely no chance.' They totally wrote him off. But as we got close to election day and people began to talk about how Roger was going to do better than people thought, and you'd find people saying, 'We've got to stop spending in Congress,' et cetera. I really didn't know if Roger would catch Clark, but I could tell he was getting much closer.

"I think Roger caught that wave of conservativism. I also think the *Register* did a great deal to help him, backhandedly. They published article after article critical of him, for everything they could think of, and there's a time in a campaign when people get tired of reading political news, campaign news. All they read is the headlines. It got so that I wouldn't read them, and I had more interest than most. I think they drilled into people essentially that Roger was against Dick Clark and that Dick Clark was part of the problem in Washington, whether they meant to do that or not.

"By then Dick Clark was known as a big liberal and somewhat out of touch. I think once you get to Washington, unless you're Chuck Grassley, you can lose touch."

ROGER JEPSEN "Analytically, I think over all those years there was Bob Ray and myself at the top of the Republican heap in Iowa. When it got down to the final days, down to the belt buckle, the combination brought some pretty good victories. In a way, we were good for each other, even though he was stubborn, very stubborn, and I sure as heck was bull-headed. Our relationship was forged with the alloys of trauma, which made it very strong.

"As that campaign went on, I think I gained a lot of admiration from Bob. I don't think he thought I could win, but he never said so. But as we came down the home stretch there was no one in the campaign that was more supportive. He laid into Clark, when there were other Republicans in this state standing up for Clark."

XXI: THE FIFTH TERM, 1979-1982

If his fourth term was the peak of Bob Ray's governorship, the fifth was expected to witness his deification. But it got off to an inauspicious start. For the first time, the expenses of Ray's inaugural festivities were to be defrayed by a five-dollar donation from attendees, in part responding to critics who couldn't understand the necessity of any festivities the fifth time around. Unfortunately, a January blizzard kept many Ray friends and allies at home. The governor quickly held some fund-raisers to settle the debt, but it would not be the last scramble to cover a deficit Ray would face during this term. When the term began, however, conditions in Iowa seemed favorable. The state's unemployment stood at 3 percent (half the national average), exports topped $3 billion, retail sales and construction were up, and for the seventh year in a row revenue topped the comptroller's predictions. Requests for interviews poured in from the national press. In August 1980, 27 percent of Iowans polled by the *Des Moines Register* picked Bob Ray as their "dream weekend guest."

On the outside, it appeared this term would be the finest hour for the nation's senior governor. Ray, supported publicly by his oldest allies, was considered a potential national candidate, with his eye allegedly on a vice-presidential nod in 1980, perhaps even a favorite-son bid for the presidency. The other Republicans with visions of the White House – Ronald Reagan, George Bush, Howard Baker, John Connally, Phil Crane, John

Des Moines Register, Warren Taylor photo. Reprinted with permission.

Anderson – lobbied the governor for his support on their many trips through Iowa prior to the January 1980 caucus.

Ray traveled extensively, both nationally and around the world. He hosted Pope John Paul II in October 1979 at Living History Farms in Des Moines, a nationally publicized television event full of pomp and ceremony, along with a dollop of down-home Iowa sincerity. When the hostages were freed from Iran in early 1981, he hosted a welcome-home gala for Kathryn Koob, an Iowa native among the hostages. He organized a second blue-ribbon economy committee, headed by his 1978 campaign manager, Marvin Pomerantz. The committee hoped to trim and reorganize the state government Ray himself had molded to fit his own image over the prior decade. Finally, he took a leader's role worldwide in the resettlement of refugees fleeing Cambodia and Thailand.

During his fifth term, many longtime staffers left the governor's office, as did a handful of appointees. Executive assistant and political insider Wythe Willey moved over to work for the newly elected U.S. senator, Chuck Grassley. Susan Mickelson, who had been the governor's liaison with the state's biggest and most difficult agencies, moved back to Utah. Bill Jackson went back to manage WHO-TV. Legislative liaison Dennis Nagel enrolled in the University of Iowa's law school. Two staffers who had been with Ray since his first election also moved on. His original "graybeard," Dutch Vermeer, went home to Pella for good after a decade of advice, and Jan Van Note, who had first worked for Ray in his 1956 race for Polk County attorney, moved to Las Vegas to help manage the career of crooner Dondino. Governor-watchers speculated that these departures indicated Ray would not run for a sixth term. Others guessed that a new, young, energetic staff, many of whom had been in grade school when Ray was first elected, would reinvigorate the governor's office and spark Ray to run once more. Headed by new executive assistant David Oman, the new staffers were conservative and colorless, the epitome of good staffers, invisible but for their ardent support of their boss and the unifying flag pins worn daily on their lapels.

Comptroller Marvin Selden retired and was replaced by a young professional from the Delaware state government, former Iowan Ronald Mosher. Maurie Van Nostrand, frustrated by his losing senatorial bid, quit, and Ray named longtime Republican state legislator Andrew Varley to his post as Iowa Commerce Commission chairman. The president of the University of Iowa, Willard Boyd, left for the presidency of the Field Museum in Chicago. Secretary of State Melvin Synhorst resigned, and Ray filled his job with television host Mary Jane Odell. State Auditor Lloyd Smith died just before the fifth term began and was succeeded by Richard Johnson.

In his first budget address of the fifth term, in January 1979, Ray told the legislature that his budget anticipated a surplus of $111 million. Though he didn't address it, the governor's office was aware that for the previous few years the state had actually been spending more than it was taking in, making up the difference by spending the accumulated surplus built up by the double-digit inflation of the mid-1970s. After accommodating expected salary increases of $50 million, Ray and Selden anticipated that $60 to $70 million would be left over from their projected $1.6 billion budget for 1979. In his askings Ray proposed no general tax increase, except for slight increases on beer and liquor. The legislature turned that down. He also proposed a loan program, in conjunction with the Farmers Home Administration, to help young Iowans get started in farming. He also hoped this Republican legislature, the first he'd worked with since 1974, would create some incentives to attract industry to Iowa, including a phaseout of the sales tax on machinery and equipment, and a personal property tax.

The optimism expressed by the governor and his staff in 1979 knew no partisan bounds. In his inaugural address that year he said, "Last year, 1978, was a good year for Iowa. We moved out of a drought. Total personal income was at an all-time high. And today we find state revenue running briskly ahead of previous forecasts." Tom Urban, president of Pioneer Hi-Bred International and a leading Democrat, forecast that Iowans would be looking for ways to spend windfall tax revenues by the end of the 1980s. "We could see five- and six-dollar corn by the end of the decade," he optimistically predicted. State Comptroller Mosher, soon after taking the job, declared, "We do not predict a recession in Iowa." In response to the governor's optimism, the legislature's tax expert, Lowell Norland, weighed in for the Democrats in a much more optimistic tone than just a few months prior: "We're in good times, both in urban and rural areas. Even if we had a national recession, it's not going to be in Iowa what it is in other states—it never has been. We are in a very strong financial position and I think it's time we recognize it."

Even though the country was grappling with a decade-ending recession and skyrocketing unemployment and many Iowa farmers were beginning to voice concern about the high interest rates they carried coupled with dropping livestock and grain prices, Iowa's governor, legislature, economists, and a watchdog press all looked optimistically toward the 1980s.

BOB RAY *What kinds of things did you hope to accomplish in that fifth term?*
"I really don't remember in 1978 saying, 'You've got to elect me so that I can finish my big program.' There were always things pending that you

wanted to see finished, but I just remember thinking that by that time things were running pretty well. By this time I thought, 'My goodness, I ought to be able to run my office with less time than I gave it before,' because I wasn't having to experiment with everything."

DENNIS NAGEL "In 1978 Jerry Fitzgerald accused the governor of being in office too long, that he couldn't possibly keep his enthusiasm up for that long. So after we won the election I said, 'You know, he may have a valid point, I ought to watch the governor.' But he wasn't slipping at all; he just kept going at it, hard as ever."

BOB RAY "Having a relatively new staff was fun, because they were bright people, fresh and enthusiastic. We had as much fun then as at any time before. We never really had time to train anybody, though; they just had to be bright, quick people and pick up and do their job. It didn't take them long to learn some of the things that I insisted on and some of the ways which we did things."

BRICE OAKLEY "It was important that the governor have a good staff at that point in time because he was gone a lot, traveling. Having a new staff like he did then, it helped add some excitement to the job, helped him stay excited about the job."

DAVID YEPSEN "He'd been in that low-pressure cooker for a long time, and I thought he was getting kind of stale. Not in terms of bad management; he wasn't being co-opted or anything. It just seemed like he was flat, tired. There weren't many new ideas, no great policy initiatives coming from the office. They were getting the checks out and keeping government clean and efficient, but their excitement was at low ebb."

BOB RAY "After that fifth election I seriously didn't think I'd run again. I think mentally I felt like I would not, although, as before, I was going to let it kind of take care of itself. I didn't want to be committed either way. At the time, I remember saying it was going to be a fun four years, thinking this would probably be my last."

STEVE ROBERTS "Bob Ray really loosened up during that last term. He was much more outgoing and friendly, more relaxed. At Monsignor Tolan's annual bash in 1980, Bob Ray gave a little welcome and he joked that somebody had asked the monsignor if it was alright to have sex before mass and the monsignor had said, 'Yes, as long as you didn't block the center aisle.' Now, Bob Ray would not have made that joke ten years earlier."

BOB RAY "By that time it was getting to the place where, right and wrong, I felt my experience allowed me to confront some of the difficult economic stress that we were going to have. The high inflation and interest rates were stopping almost all growth. I felt pretty confident that I was good for what the state needed. Maybe that's a little self-serving, or maybe it was justification to have run in 1978.

"But you could always count on there being a crisis of some sort. We tried not to play them up, just tried to handle them rather than be sensational about them. I sometimes would think maybe we ought to do something a little splashier, a little more flashy. But I really preferred to manage government and create ideas and implement them rather than just be a public relations governor."

A public relations gimmick is what critics dubbed Ray's March 1979 announcement that he wanted to refund $50 million from the state coffers to the taxpayers. In a Saturday afternoon press conference, Ray claimed that Iowans had paid in more taxes than had been necessary, and he wanted to give back 10 percent of their 1979 tax bills, up to $250. The state would still be left with a surplus, he claimed. He argued that the rebate would "rev-up" local economies when those monies were spent at the local grocery and clothing stores.

The rebate plan was as big a surprise to Republican legislative leaders as it was to Democrats. Ray aides say the move was prompted by the governor's desire to reduce the inflation-swollen surplus before the legislature could figure out a way to spend it and also to put off a proposal being batted around the legislature to adopt 100 percent tax indexing. "He was frustrated because he had proposed a repeal of the sales tax on utilities, and he thought that was just a hell of an idea. Thirteen other states had done it or were getting ready to do it, and the Republican leadership wouldn't support him," remembers Ray legislative liaison Nagel. "I thought that was one of the greatest ideas since they put tomatoes in cans," adds Wythe Willey. "But nobody got excited about it. Ray laid it out and it died like an unfertilized egg. Had that happened, it would have narrowed the tax base, but he would have never suggested giving that $50 million back. [Dick] Gilbert and I thought it would be great, just like taking the tax off food and drugs. Tax relief of the purest nature."

Ten days after Ray proposed it, the rebate passed the house 90 to 5 and only seven senators voted against it. Giving money back to the people was a tough bill to vote against. "I think this is the most damaging political vote of this year. They [the Republicans] are digging our graves," said

Democratic representative Don Avenson, just after he voted *for* the rebate.

BOB RAY "Some people would say giving that $50 million back was my biggest mistake. I think that was one of the best things we did, certainly no mistake. The people didn't expect to get that money back; they weren't demanding it, and I knew there would come a time when we wished we had $50 million. But there wasn't any way we could have socked it away for a rainy day. It just wasn't going to happen. The legislature would have figured out a way to get their hands on it and created some new programs that would need funding for years down the road."

GEORGE KINLEY "One of the terrible mistakes Bob Ray made was when he sent the $50 million back. I was one of seven senators who voted against that. I thought they ought to keep the money, use it for one-time expenditures – buildings or whatever. They sent $50 million back, things turned sour, they started bonding, and it really cost the state a lot of money. Out of twenty-one Democratic senators, there were only four or five that voted against him, and we got a couple Republicans to vote along with us. It was hard to vote against giving $50 million back to the people. It's kind of like voting against motherhood and apple pie, and Bob Ray was kind of looked at as motherhood and apple pie. Sending the $50 million back was just another of those nice things Bob Ray was going to do for the state."

JIM WEST "He called me one night. I was chairman of the House Ways and Means Committee, and he said he wanted to give $50 million back. I thought it was a great idea, so we started charging with it. We were in the majority, and within a couple days we'd passed it in the house, and the senate had passed it. No problem."

GERRY RANKIN "That rebate was not right at all. I got $125 out of it and spent it on the way home. People went along with it only because it was so hard to vote against. They gritted their teeth and voted for it, because they didn't like it one bit. Ray didn't want to turn it over to the legislature because he thought they'd blow it. Ray's philosophy was that you can't trust the legislature."

LOWELL JUNKINS "I wish we'd just invested the $50 million somewhere. I got twelve dollars back, not even enough to take my wife out to dinner. But Bob Ray was hard to argue with."

DALE COCHRAN "I thought the Democratic leadership always had a reasonable relationship with the governor's office, and I ended up voting for the $50 million rebate. I really hadn't intended to, but I guess he wanted it enough that we weren't going to be able to stop it. When I think about that extra money I realize we were shortchanging a lot of research work at our universities, we weren't really looking towards the future like we should have. We should have had more foresight. But that's one of the problems with the human race."

PAUL FRANZENBURG "That rebate defies the rainy-day principle. He should have known that the political gains he obviously expected would be more than offset by the conditions that prevailed later. If you ask people today what they did with their rebate, few can answer. That was purely style over substance, the appearance of a very magnanimous gesture on the part of the governor.

"He has said since, when criticized, that it's just as well; the legislature would have just spent it. But that's a dodge, just the governor putting the blame on the legislature, because the governor draws up the budget. I've been in on that budgetary process, and I've presented my own as state treasurer. The governor reviews this very cautiously and comes up with his budget. Normally he will cut back on the askings of various departments, and then it's presented to the legislature. The legislature can, of course, do what it wants to object to something, but the governor always has the item veto. For Ray to say he had no control over that is to abdicate his responsibility as governor."

LOWELL NORLAND "I have to think everybody regrets the $50 million rebate. The public could have cared less about it; most thought it was silly. I never knew quite why he proposed it, but I would not pretend in any stretch of the imagination to know who Rob Ray really was, or what his private thoughts were. I never knew him to open up, and I never knew where his advice came from, where that idea came from. I think I know some places it didn't come from, but I don't know where it came from."

CAL HULTMAN "Some people probably still think that $50 million rebate was crazy. Thank God we did it, because if we'd put it into recurring expenses, we'd be looking at another $80 or $90 million a year today that we'd have to come up with. You know damn well that that extra revenue came from agriculture. That was about the last good year cattlemen had around here, and those revenues would not be there today.

"People complained about getting a check for $6 or $10, or whatever the hell it was. I felt there were only two things to do with that money: either build like hell or give it back. The University of Iowa could have gotten their little law school built and we wouldn't have had to bond for it, or the agronomy building at Iowa State and the teachers' building at UNI, those kinds of things."

NORM JESSE "It was grandstanding bullshit, purely political, and done at a time when the state had real capital needs. That money could have been spent on one-shot expenditures. His claim was that that money would have just been wasted on something, but there were a lot of proposals from various state departments on how to spend that money that would not have been recurring expenses."

WYTHE WILLEY "I can't be critical of anybody. The margin of safety built into the state budget is so slim. You're talking about a budget approaching $2 billion, with a surplus at the end of the fiscal year somewhere between $50 and $150 million. People today say, 'Well, you shouldn't have given that money back,' but if we hadn't, they would have spent the money. If I had to do it again, though, I would have strongly encouraged that we build a prison. Put $40 million into prison facilities."

DAVID OMAN "A one-time expenditure was discussed. Art Neu was heavily promoting putting the money into a new prison. In retrospect, that's exactly what I wish we would have done."

FLOYD MILLEN "If we hadn't rebated that money, though, we would have spent it. When the money's sitting in the till, every department's got their hands out for it. It was a surplus taken from the taxpayers and should have gone back to them. I supported that 100 percent. And when things got tight a year later, that $50 million would have been long gone anyway."

In 1980 the optimism over the state's economy that had marked 1979 didn't merely fade, it disappeared overnight. Across the Midwest, state economies had stalled, due in large part to the decline in tax revenues from agriculture. The deadly combination of 20 percent interest rates and 15 to 20 percent inflation knocked economic forecasting out of focus. Spending cuts were ordered, but high interest rates made any quick economic recovery difficult.

In Iowa, with its huge agricultural base, budget cuts dominated the news in 1980, and the governor scrambled to keep the budget balanced.

The projected $60 to 70 million surplus never accumulated, and the state's "float" was pared to nothing. Scapegoats were sought. "Grain embargo, federal budget policy vacillation, record inflation, uncertain monetary policy, OPEC policies, and deteriorating agricultural market conditions combined to decrease the reliability of any forecasts," claims comptroller Mosher today. Bob Ray placed a large portion of the blame on the Carter administration's handling of the Russian grain embargo. Many economists refuted the claimed effect of the embargo on Iowa, but taxes paid in by farmers nonetheless dropped by 16.7 percent in 1980.

The governor slashed his budget by $95 million in April and by $60 million in August, and then in December he ordered all state agencies to reduce spending by 1 percent to produce an additional $17 million cut. The *Register*'s Flansburg blamed the scramble on the state's leaders, arguing that they saw the decline in revenues coming but did little to prepare for it. The following years, 1981 and 1982, Ray fought cries from Democrats, and some Republicans, for general income and sales tax increases, preferring bare-bones budgets, increased fees, and small tax increases to keep the budget in balance . "Our hopes for recovery from the recession of 1980 were dashed by the recession of 1981," the governor recalls.

JIM WEST "I can remember a meeting we had at Clear Lake on Governor's Day in July 1980 about whether or not we should call the legislature back to deal with the deficit or have the governor just cut. There was 100 percent agreement that we wouldn't call the legislature back into session, because it was just prior to an election.

"Sales tax receipts were down, income tax receipts were down, yet we still had to fund state government, which hadn't been cut back very seriously. State government uses a variety of bookkeeping methods that began with Bob Ray to end up the year with a balanced budget. They could always hold up school aid payments, postpone big dollar payouts from the state's treasury, those kinds of things, to keep the balance up there. But those tricks wouldn't help in 1980.

"When Ray first took office there were some tough times, too. Marv Selden used to go over and make sure there was enough cash in the bank before he paid any bills, it was that tight. But that all changed in the mid-1970s, when those good agricultural years just stuffed the treasury."

LOWELL JUNKINS "Good times tend to make us all a bit lazy, and the legislature during the 1970s, Democrats and Republicans, tended to focus more on the problems of the day rather than the problems of tomorrow."

<u>LOWELL NORLAND</u> *Were those fiscal shortages attributable to the governor in any way?* "That's a good question, and it's got a lot of significance today. We were carrying a fair amount of surplus, $100 to $250 million, and it had been fairly stable for about four years, 1975 to 1979. Interestingly, we never thought about reducing taxes. I look back and I think we were very cocky in those years. As a state we thought things were going to go like that forever. *Democrats and Republicans?* I think so. It was part of that whole scenario that has brought us into such deep trouble today, because that carried over to individuals and their decisions relating to the agricultural economy, the decisions that we made in the 1970s. We're reaping the problems today. Of course, hindsight is really something. You wonder why we didn't do capital expenditures with the $50 million rebate, for example—one-time kind of things. Why didn't we build some of the university buildings that we've been bonding for ever since? Why didn't we complete our road network? Why didn't we put that money to some long-term capital use? At the time, there was not a hue and cry to do some of those kind of things. I have to think, looking back, that we were terribly shortsighted. Just awful. It would be interesting to know what Bob Ray thought, whether he thought it was shortsighted or not."

<u>BOB RAY</u> "Nineteen eighty was a tough year, and it got tougher because the economists, nobody, anticipated the recession was going to be deep and long-lasting. *Why couldn't anyone provide any better forecasts?* I just don't think anybody wanted to see it. It's like asking why the banker didn't see that farmland values were going to drop. It's just hard to believe. We'd had little downward dips in the economy before, but they'd usually level off and then go back up."

<u>DENNIS NAGEL</u> "For anybody to suggest that we saw that recession coming is ridiculous. I wish they'd been in our shoes. In March 1980 we felt we were in good shape, and by the first of April we were in serious trouble. It happened overnight."

<u>RON MOSHER</u> "That was a pretty tough time, a year of extremes. When I first took the job there was the $50 million rebate. There appeared to be more money than was needed. One year later we were struggling with reducing spending levels.

"The problems were brought on by a combination of things, but basically it was a souring of the farm economy at the same time the industrial part of the economy was souring. What had happened in earlier recessionary periods that caused people to view Iowa as recession-proof is that when there had been industrial downturns, farm prices were excellent, and vice versa.

"We had built an econometric model for the state. Basically, it described the interrelationships of the data needed to forecast what was going to happen. Data Resources, Incorporated, an economic forecasting firm, built it for us, and we used it in conjunction with Jerry Barnard, an economist from the University of Iowa. We tried to forecast the likely direction of the economy, and it's fair to say the results weren't satisfactory. The model never predicted as severe a drop in the economy as we actually experienced.

"We then decided maybe there were some judgmental factors that could be applied to the model's output. We formed an economic forecasting group made up of some pretty highly sophisticated economists and some people in private business that were responsible for long-range planning and met with them regularly. And I would say in spite of that we still did not succeed in accurately forecasting the degree to which the economy was dropping. *How come?* I don't know that anybody can tell you. I guess we were a microcosm of what was going on nationally. I honestly believe there was not one professional economist in America that correctly predicted the recession. The economies in the last few years just aren't like the economies before. Things are different, and the models that have been built to forecast are based on what existed before. The industrial base that used to exist no longer exists. It's now in Hong Kong and Taiwan and Australia and Mexico City, all over. And models cannot tell you when there is a structural change like that. All they can tell you is that if things tomorrow look the same way as they did today, here's what tomorrow will be like.

"One of the first times I brought a whole group of economists in to talk to Bob Ray, I was really concerned. I wanted to be sure that he wasn't hearing just one opinion, mine, that he understood the ramifications of what was going on, so we brought in a whole group. We sat with Bob Ray in his office and talked, and one of them, a very highly regarded economist from one of the biggest employers in the state of Iowa, explained their forecast, which predicted a robust recovery beginning in six months to a year. This was in 1980. It's obvious his forecast was grossly wrong. Everybody just simply missed the boat."

BOB RAY "The grain embargo had a much greater effect than it appeared it would at the moment. It was the wrong thing to do, and it sent a shock wave that we're still suffering from. And the worst thing was that Carter had really given his word that he would not do that. Jerry Ford quickly acknowledged his mistake when he tried it during his presidency, said it was wrong. Why Jimmy Carter couldn't see it, I don't know. I think he was so desperate to do something that showed strength, because the polls showed he was not a strong president, that he didn't take time to think. It was a quick decision, and nobody had a chance to do anything about it."

LARRY POPE "He made the decision very early on not to ask for an increase in taxes and instead cut back the budget. As the result, some social programs were going to have to be cut, and he took that personally. He was getting almost no sleep during that period. The hours were just extraordinary, and I never saw him in worse physical condition than during late 1980 and early 1981.

"When it got around to cutting social programs, he was asking for the names of people that were going to lose their benefits. We're talking about in-home service and stuff for the elderly, and the Democrats were running around claiming that all these people were going to lose benefits. Well, Bob Ray wanted to know that if Mary Johnson on the southeast side of Des Moines was going to lose some aid, how could she somehow get some replacement benefits.

"I don't think Bob Ray ever got enough credit from the conservatives in his own party for being such a fiscal conservative. He absolutely refused to raise sales and income taxes."

RON MOSHER "When you're going through a period where revenues are declining at a very rapid rate, it's hard to find places to squirrel money away. So I think it's safe to say we weren't misleading anybody. We did not pretend the situation was more severe than we thought it was so that we could somehow pocket the difference over in a corner and pull it out later, saying 'Aha, we found $10 million for you.' We really tried to be as open and honest as we could. There was nothing under the table."

BOB RAY "Talk about taking flak. Here the department heads were expecting an increase in budget and I'm cutting them way back. One of the good things to come from that year was that I saw people work together like I'd never seen before. Once the cuts were for sure, and once they got over the shock, once they started buckling down, they really worked well together – scrounged together, tried to do without, find new ways, better ways, to perform services."

WYTHE WILLEY "There was no way we could have anticipated the downturn in the economy. And the Iowa law that stipulates the governor can make across-the-board cuts was a godsend. A lot of agencies really had to tighten their belts, but I don't think it really caused much of a ripple in terms of state services. It could have been a crisis, but I think Ray and his administration handled it pretty well. And the problems we had in 1980 were not as severe as those we had in 1971, in terms of their impact on the Ray administration. I always said the only thing that was more popular than cutting the budget 1.6 percent was when he cut it 3.6 percent. The across-the-board budget cuts were very well handled, administratively and public-relationswise."

DON AVENSON "Everybody thought Iowa was recession-proof. This food-processing industry and this implement industry is recession-proof because the world is hungry. It's hard to go against the grain, and none of us tried; everybody was fooled. I think as a consequence legislators and chief executives are both trying to look a little further down the road today. But we could be fooled again."

WYTHE WILLEY "The state isn't all that different from the Iowa farmer who's managing his own little bailiwick real well, but outside forces just overwhelm him. I think that's pretty much what happened. The recession of the early 1970s did not affect us, because we had the grain sales. We barely felt it. So we didn't know how to deal with recessions."

LOWELL JUNKINS "I think Bob Ray lost, or maybe never developed, the ability to deal with an economy going the other way, down. His orientation was for working in better conditions. So he kept holding out, hoping things would get better, saying things would get better tomorrow. Instead they kept crashing, crashing, crashing. Quite honestly, I think he was worrying about his own future at the start of that fifth term and hoped things would just get better. He wasn't facing up to the fact that things weren't getting better."

BOB TYSON "When that economic crunch first surfaced, Bob Ray was out in Colorado and Denny Nagel was on the phone with him. Bob Ray just said, 'Tell Ron [*Mosher*] to cover it.' Dennis said, 'But there's no money there.' Bob Ray said, 'My God, Marv Selden could always find money.'

"Marv had told me one time that he used to pad the data-processing budget because nobody understood data processing. He was a very clever guy. Ron Mosher, on the other hand, is the straightest arrow you ever saw. Their styles were very, very different. But Marv wouldn't have been able to bail the state out in 1980; nobody could."

XXII:
THE REFUGEES

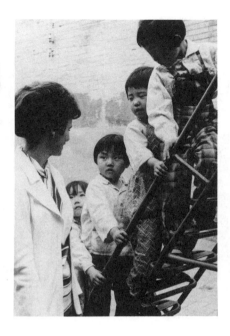

Six months after the United States withdrew from South Vietnam in April 1975, the first of an eventual 10,000 Indochinese refugees arrived at the Des Moines airport. When that plane touched down it marked one of the most gratifying – and, simultaneously, controversial – programs of Bob Ray's governorship.

By 1979 roughly 3,500 refugees, predominantly the Tai Dam from Cambodia, had come to call this farm state home, much to the chagrin of many Iowans, who believed jobs were scarce enough, welfare programs too stretched already, to accommodate these new citizens. The public's ire was raised even further when, on April, 29, 1979, a new influx of refugees began, these saved from the boats fleeing the shores of South Vietnam. Sparked by a "60 Minutes" piece on the boat people, Ray, along with Job Service director Colleen Shearer and Ray aide Ken Quinn, who was on loan from the State Department, embarked on a new resettlement quest, anticipating another 1,500 refugees that year.

In September 1979 a *Des Moines Register* Iowa Poll claimed that 51 percent of the state opposed any more resettlement in Iowa. There were already plenty of needy Iowans looking for work, people said, times were tougher, and the unemployed didn't need any competition. Despite the unpopularity of the resettlement, Iowa and Bob Ray became leaders in taking in refugees from Laos, Cambodia, Thailand, and Vietnam.

Des Moines Register photo. Reprinted with permission.

LARRY POPE "I think the finest thing he ever did as governor was the resettlement of the refugees. A lot of people didn't like it, but he didn't listen. He knew what was right and figured we'd learn to adjust, and we did. That elevated him to the level of statesman. It was a courageous thing to do."

BOB RAY "We first got involved with the boat people when President Carter offered to accept something like 60,000 refugees in 1978. This was before the boat people were front-page news. We looked at what we thought could be done in Iowa, realistically, so that we didn't overrun the citizens who were here, didn't create job problems. At that time Carter was standing up there saying we'd take these people, but he had no plans for them, who was going to pay for them or anything.

"I had asked Colleen Shearer to handle the refugee programs because we were primarily interested in making sure they had jobs. We decided that as long as we were taking x number, why take a few from Vietnam, a few from Cambodia, why a few from Laos. Why not take them from a specific area. That way they'd be compatible. That's how we got mostly Tai Dam.

"Colleen did the screening and reached that conclusion. Then Ken Quinn and I started talking about the boat people. We'd been reading in the papers and seeing on television how these people were being literally pushed out of Vietnam and then pirated by roving junks. I kept putting off resettling any more because I thought at that time we had a lot of things going on and there was a limit to how many we could handle. Then I saw Ed Bradley's documentary on the boat people, on a Sunday night, and I called Ken Quinn about 11 P.M. I asked him to meet me at the office, and we started planning that night."

KEN QUINN "We wrote a letter to every governor in the country, urging them to get involved in refugee resettlement, and got a couple responses, from Governor Milliken in Michigan and Brendan Byrne in New Jersey. The three of them ended up as part of the U.S. delegation to the United Nations conference on boat people in Geneva.

"Later that year, October 1979, we took a trip to China and then went to visit the refugee camps in Thailand. We ended up at this camp called Sa Kaew in the northern part of the country, where we saw this incredible spectacle—25,000 people, most of them barely alive."

BOB RAY "In one camp there was a big banner welcoming Billie and me because of what we had done for the Tai Dam. Then we visited another camp where 30,000 refugees had congregated in five days. People were dying around us, forty or fifty a day. It was shocking."

KEN QUINN "On the plane back from Thailand everybody was shaken. We'd seen people lying under these makeshift tents, dying from malnutrition, suffering from diarrhea, disease, many of them children, and the bodies were just carried in and out. It was the most awful thing any of us had seen. On the plane there was such a feeling of intensity.

"Governor Tom Judge from Montana kept saying he just wanted to resign and go back and try to help. Governor Dick Lamm of Colorado began writing a piece which would be published in the *Denver Post.* Governor Milliken was also writing, and Governor Ray began his speech for the convention of the Church of Christ in St. Louis.

"Usually when he was going to do a speech, somebody would give him a draft and then he would work on it, put the things in he wanted, but he usually would start with a core. This speech he wrote entirely by himself. It was a way to begin dealing with his own emotions. I remember that speech more than any other, for its emotion, and they raised $30,000 in the collection that night.

"Aid to the Cambodian refugees was a very controversial issue at that session, too, because there was some question about how involved the church should be, because of political issues. The governor gave this incredible speech about seeing people dying and reaching out. I remember one phrase particularly, maybe one of the best I heard him write: 'Jesus is saying to us tonight here in the Show Me State, "Don't tell me about your faith, show me.' [*"Don't tell me of your concerns for human rights, show me. Don't tell me of your concerns for the poor, the disenfranchised, the underprivileged, the unemployed, show me. Don't tell me of your concern for the rejected, the prisoner, the hungry, the thirsty, the homeless, show me. Don't tell me of your concerns for these people when you have a chance to save their lives, show me. Don't tell me how Christian you are, show me."*]

"Bill Simbro from the *Register* was along and wrote that it was more like a sermon than a political speech. To me that was the kind of thing Bob Ray did best, combining moral leadership with his governmental position. Rallying people, whether at a political convention or here in Iowa, to do things. He was a forceful moral leader."

BOB RAY "I decided before they came to Iowa I wanted them to have a sponsor, a place to live, and a job before they ever hit the ground in Iowa. That seemed logical to me. I didn't realize at that time that nobody else was approaching it that way. We started the Refugee Service Center not just for the ones we were willing to bring in through the program but also for the churches and civic groups who were also sponsors."

KEN QUINN "That trip led to Iowa SHARES [*Iowa Sends Help to Aid*

Refugees and End Starvation], which was really the result of three things. First was the governor's trip and the pictures that Bob Ray took that ran in the *Register* and the letters to the editor that followed. That prompted the *Register* to get involved, and I talked to Michael Gartner, who said that they were prepared to put their editorial pages at the disposal of an effort to raise money. That was extremely unusual. Then a group of religious leaders led by Rabbi Jay Goldburg came in to see the governor and offered to put an organization together to handle the resettlement."

MICHAEL GARTNER "I committed the paper in a way the paper had never committed before, running a big coupon on the editorial page. It was a hell of a cause, and we were literally saving lives, and it was a *Register* type of deal, a good social cause, and the *Register* waved the banner on good social causes. There were some people around the paper who thought it was an abuse of the editorial page, others that we were lining up too much with the governor. The newspaper hadn't raised money through its pages for anything since they got the school children of Iowa to buy an elephant for the Iowa State Fair in the 1920s. But it was my call, and in retrospect I'm proud of it.

"It was Ken's project, and he enlisted maybe a half-dozen of us. It fit Ken perfectly. You could tell it wasn't Ray's idea. Ray was never a man for the grand strategy, the global picture. Quinn was and is. But Ray was very receptive to a smart idea, and it made Ray look like a hero. But it was Ken who did all the work. He went around patting asses and kicking asses and smoothing the way. He was the worker, the cheerleader, the innovator, the creator. And the end result was that it saved lives. How many things can you say that you've done in your life that have saved lives? Not a whole lot."

BOB RAY "We decided that there were so many people wanting to do something that we ought to make sure they had that opportunity. So we didn't go out on a drive, we didn't try to appeal to them because we wanted them to give money. What we really did was open an avenue for contributions, and there was a great outpouring of Iowans' human kindness. Ken was instrumental in that, really put Iowa SHARES together and was the moving force behind that resettlement. [*SHARES eventually raised over $500,000, which bought food that was sent to Cambodia and Thailand.*] He was the kind of guy that any administrator would love to have around. He was always aggressive, always smart, and no matter what he wanted to do, he was never out doing it without knowing that it was compatible with what I wanted done. I never had to worry about him. He'd come back at me a dozen different ways to accomplish something he wanted. He was relentless. But he would never go out and do it unless I agreed. That's a gem.

"If I hadn't understood human nature as well as I did, the initial polls would have been very discouraging. Mostly that came from ignorance of the facts and some thoughtlessness. We got letters from people who said, 'After all, this is our country, not theirs.' Well, if our ancestors had taken that position, we wouldn't be here. It was shortsightedness. There were those who said, 'How can you give jobs to foreigners?' Well, they were taking entry-level jobs that were going wanting. I've had business people tell me that the refugees literally saved their business, because they could not hire people at competitive rates. I called one young man who had written me and complained that he hadn't been able to get a job and here I was giving jobs away to people who didn't even live here. I had someone count all the help-wanted ads in the *Sunday Register,* and I called him that afternoon. I said, 'Have you looked at the Sunday paper's want ads?' He said no. I told him how many there were and that maybe there was a job for him if he really wanted to work. We had a little discussion and finally I said, 'What I want you to do is, before the refugees ever get here, you go get yourself the best job you can, and then they won't get it.' He was complaining, before the refugees ever landed, that he couldn't get a job because of them.

"Believe me, it was not something done for political reasons. It brought out the greed and selfishness of too many people. And I felt sorry for those who were so selfish they couldn't see that we had any role to play in the saving of lives. A real benefit of that resettlement came to the people who sponsored the refugees. Many of them came to me and said it was the greatest thing in their lives. They had really done something for somebody and enriched their lives and their family's lives.

"When I left office I went by the Refugee Service Center to say good-bye, and they had a little presentation. One of them said, 'We are giving you this present because if it weren't for you we would not be alive.' That's gratifying. That made me think I had done at least something worthwhile during all those years."

XXIII: THE 1980 CAUCUSES

A minute fraction of the quarter billion people in the United States are qualified to be president. A small percentage of that fraction possesses the political savvy to be elected. Bob Ray was one of that small percentage. Many of the people he trusted for advice urged him to win big in 1978 and position himself as either a dark-horse or favorite-son presidential candidate in the 1980 election. Supporters in and outside of Iowa suggested that it would be even smarter to get tapped as a vice-presidential companion to one of the men seeking the nomination, campaign and win, then look toward a presidential run in 1984 or 1988.

Publicly, Ray claimed he'd been elected to serve a four-year term and wasn't interested in a national race for anything. Local skeptics wondered at the time if his actions might not indicate otherwise. In Gerald Ford's book about his presidency, *A Time To Heal,* he mentioned Ray as a potential vice-presidential candidate in 1976. "Although both [*Ray and Washington governor Dan Evans*] had done an excellent job running their states, neither had a national name. Nor did they project experience in international affairs." After his 1978 election it appeared Ray was out to eliminate that weakness. During the first two years of that term he traveled extensively, to Austria, Romania, Switzerland, China, Thailand, West Germany, and the Soviet Union. As noted in the previous chapter, Ray also added an experienced State Department veteran and former aide to Henry Kissinger, Ken Quinn, to his staff. The pair quickly intensified the state's involvement in the resettlement of Indochinese refugees, and Ray soon became an international spokesman for resettlement.

The first-in-the-nation Iowa caucuses required presidential aspirants of both parties to spend disproportionate amounts of time in the Hawkeye State in 1980. With a Democrat in the White House, most of those touring the main streets and rural roads of the state were Republicans, and all but one considered a visit to Bob Ray to be essential, in hopes that the five-term governor would throw his arm around them, endorse their candidacy, and provide them with a boost toward capturing the 115,000 Republican voters who would show up on caucus night.

Des Moines attorney David Belin and U.S. Senator Howard Baker. *Des Moines Register,* Warren Taylor photo. Reprinted with permission.

BOB RAY *What did you think about your chances as a presidential candidate?*
"I was amused by it mostly. The only time that I can remember really thinking about that was after Kansas City in 1976. There'd been quite a little publicity about my possibly being teamed with Jerry Ford, and during that general campaign I thought I could have helped that ticket. That's about the only time I seriously thought about it.

"But if I had really ever wanted to run for president, it would have been those last four years I was in office. I thought I was on top of my job, and I think I could have run and still done justice to the job. But you really have to get yourself psyched up to do some of the things that would have had to be done, and that's a big job. You have to develop a cadre of people who wanted you to do it, who would make the contacts, people who would help finance a race, a lot of financing and a lot of organizing, just to get up to the Iowa caucuses. Think about when Reagan started, back in the early 1970s, and he had a lot of charisma and a lot of money behind him, and an ideology, which gave him an army of people."

JANET VAN NOTE "Bill Brock called often. He was really encouraging the governor to run for president. He was head of the national Republican party at the time. Brock, Howard Baker, George Bush really thought the world of the governor. They really encouraged him to run for a fifth term."

BILLIE RAY "As my world expanded and I met the Fords and the Carters and the Nixons and the Reagans, I saw that a lot of people could do that job. Maybe not a lot, but a good number. And I think Bob would have done very well. But it takes a lot of desire. Reagan ran once and lost. Carter – that was his whole life, even when he was governor he was working towards that."

BOB RAY "I was unlikely to ever generate the kind of fighting spirit needed to run for president. But at the same time I was an unlikely candidate the first time I ran for governor. Internally that didn't bother me; I thought I could do it if I tried. But externally, others who perceived me as a candidate may have thought I didn't have the fire to run.

"It's the challenge, the excitement of the battle, that turns you on to politics. Just to run for governor, to run for reelection, you've got to get fired up. I think having been the state chairman, having watched a lot of campaigns, helped me a great deal. I knew what was realistic and what to look for to judge how well we were doing. I read a lot of polls and I helped draft a lot of survey questions. I had a pretty good feeling for reading the results accurately.

"If the conditions had ever been just right, I think I could have gotten myself psyched into wanting to run for the presidency. But I never did anything to cultivate that. I'd go out, and people around the country would want to talk to me about running. I was realistic enough to know that just because somebody has breakfast with you and suggests you run for president, that doesn't mean there's a ground swell out there. But I think we had enough contacts that we could have gotten something started. Then it would have depended on how much I was prepared to study federal and international issues. But it never really got to that place."

STEVE ROBERTS "Ray was not prepared to make the kind of sacrifice necessary. He was not prepared to give up operating Iowa or just let it drift. His first priority was always the state."

DICK GILBERT "If he had lusted after the presidency or vice-presidency, there's a chance he could have been there. But I don't think that's what he wanted to do. As Howard Baker said, you have to give up all shred of humility, and I don't think Bob Ray could have done that."

DAVID OMAN "In 1979 and 1980 those of us who worked for him still hoped something might break and he would end up on the ticket. But it was never really in the cards, because there were so many bona fide contenders, including Reagan and Bush and a half-dozen others."

BOB RAY "If I'd have run for president, I'd have had to do what Jimmy Carter did in 1976 and George Bush did in 1980. I would have had to make a commitment of two to four years and just gone out and chased it. Howard Baker was an example of how not to run for president."

DAVID OMAN "In 1979 and 1980 every one of the presidential contenders came to our office seeking the governor's support. He decided early on that Iowa was going to be open territory and that he wasn't going to cast his lot with anyone publicly.

"John Connally came in, and the governor was really impressed with him. He was such a macho guy, a man's man. John Anderson came in. They had never spent much time together. Anderson is pretty much an intellectual, and he would dominate any conversation. He would ask questions and answer them himself. Phil Crane came in, but there were a lot of philosophical differences between them. Bush, Baker, Dole. By September of 1979 they'd all been in to see the governor, some more than once.

"In September we went to Washington and had lunch with Reagan's campaign manager, John Sears. He made a real pitch for the governor to join the Reagan team, and with hindsight his pitch was absolutely correct. Reagan was going to be the nominee, and he laid out their strategy, laid out their calendar. The pitch was, 'We're on a roll. We're going to win. We'd love to have you with us.' It would have been a real coup to pick him up. None of the moderate governors, [*Illinois's Jim*] Thompson, [*Ohio's James*] Rhodes, [*Otis*] Bowen from Indiana, [*Michigan's William*] Milliken, [*Dick*] Thornburg from Pennsylvania, [*Delaware's Pete*] du Pont, none of them were endorsing Reagan. They were looking to get Ray on board so they could go after the rest. They wanted the governor to be the national chairman of Reagan's campaign.

"That same day, after lunch, we went over to the Hill to visit with Howard Baker. There was instantly a bond between the two of them; the chemistry was right. In the meeting with Sears it was just the three of us; at Baker's office it was Ray, myself, Baker, and his political guy, Jim Cannon. They talked about their families, their cameras, and when we left I know that Governor Ray felt very good about Howard Baker."

BOB RAY "John Sears talked to me about being the Reagan campaign's national chairman. I don't know what would have happened to that, especially after John left the campaign. But he had it figured—and I didn't really disagree with him at the time—that Reagan couldn't lose. It was his strategy that said Reagan wasn't going to campaign in Iowa, because he wanted a couple things. One, that Reagan not just get nominated but win the election, and secondly, not just to get elected but to be a good president. It was his strategy to stay out of Iowa, because he was the frontrunner and it would have just given these other guys a chance to shoot at him.

"He wanted me to get on board to tie the conservatives and the moderates together so that it looked like everybody was starting to support Ron Reagan. He wanted that ground swell to just lift the guy up so there wouldn't be any division in the party. He feared that division would be costly. He said he had Reagan's support in offering me that position, but John was sliced off the campaign early on, so I have no idea what they were thinking."

DAVID OMAN "Then in November Reagan came into the Des Moines airport and asked if Governor Ray would come out and meet with him on his plane. [*In order to meet Reagan on time they literally had to hustle Howard Baker out of Terrace Hill and to another gate at the airport.*] He did, but we were still trying to be helpful to all the campaigns. Bush had done an excellent job of organization in the state. Baker's campaign was floundering and we suggested people to him, ideas, we tried to be helpful. But they continued to execute with people from Colorado, Minnesota, and Texas who didn't know the state. I used to joke that the only precinct they organized was the one that surrounded the Rusty Scupper [*a former Des Moines bar and restaurant*]. By December it appeared that Baker was going to be embarrassed in Iowa and might not even survive, so they were begging us for help, and that's when Marv Pomerantz and Dick Redman were dispatched to try and help."

WYTHE WILLEY "Ray had some sensitivity, a good deal of sensitivity, in terms of his status as governor. He thought that when Ronald Reagan came to Iowa he ought to call on Bob Ray. That never happened. The time we went out to the Des Moines airport and Ray and I went out to Reagan's chartered jet and spent a few minutes talking, it was vintage Reagan. He told some little anecdotes, was very cordial and nice, but they never quite got together."

DAVID OMAN "The Reagan campaign in Iowa had the attitude that they had already won. That's how they dealt with people. They asked the governor to come out and meet at the airport, as if they were doing us some great favor by dropping in. Even Terry Branstad, who was a real Reagan supporter, had grievous problems with the Reagan campaign in 1980 and told them they weren't paying enough attention to the state. Meanwhile, George Bush was going around locking up votes right and left, and not just moderates but some conservatives. Eventually his way was proven right."

BOB RAY "I didn't see the candidates calling on me as flattery but as protocol. I knew all of them, except maybe Phil Crane. I got very pragmatic—they were looking for help wherever they could get it and Iowa's early caucuses were why I was so sought after. I think any one of them would have taken my support.
    "But I hadn't decided on one I wanted to support. Reagan, for instance. I had no idea what kind of candidate he was going to be. He had been coming into the state and talking to ultraconservative groups who were theoretically working for Democrats as well as Republicans."

WYTHE WILLEY "If we had a strategy, it was just to keep good contact with all the campaigns. Reagan had a tremendous reservoir of support left over from 1976, and Bush literally lived in the state for two years."

BOB RAY "George Bush and his people were the first to really woo me, but they respected my neutrality. They got upset when I ended up supporting Howard Baker, because they had laid off me in deference to my neutral position. I think they were bothered that I didn't consult them when I decided to support Baker, but Howard and I had a lot in common philosophically. We saw things eye to eye and he wanted my support in the worst way. But I decided that it would look bad if just before caucus time I came out for Howard, so I didn't. Then afterwards, when I did come out for him, it didn't do him any good. It didn't do me any good, either."

GEORGE BUSH "I would have liked to have had Bob Ray's support, but typically, he had made up his own mind and was very direct with me on that score."

WYTHE WILLEY "The only one he really had the opportunity to jump on the bandwagon with was Baker, who asked him to be his vice-presidential running mate early. He was going to change from tradition and offer a team early. That had never been done before. Reagan did it with Schweiker [*in 1976*], Mondale with Ferraro, but those were both last-minute preconvention efforts. Baker was willing to put Bob Ray on the ticket back in December of 1979. I frankly think that the difference probably would have been that Baker might be the vice-president now, instead of Bush. And given that, Ray might have joined the administration."

DAVID OMAN "It would have been a long shot. It would have been a historically unique thing to do, but in the great scheme of things, who would remember it? Only if it had worked. Had something like that been attempted, my hunch is that most of the other candidates would have abandoned the state. They'd have said, 'We will not contest Iowa. See you in New Hampshire.'"

WYTHE WILLEY "Baker said, 'I'm from Washington and I want to take the best Republican governor, somebody I'm comfortable with, somebody that's popular,' and he wanted Ray to get on early. Ray didn't go for that. He didn't give Baker an answer, and if you don't give an answer, the answer is no."

BOB RAY "I didn't think Baker's offer was the right thing to do. It just seemed like we were terrifically compatible, and I could have gotten excited about running with him if we had been nominated. I thought it was a sincere offer. I like to think he was looking at me not solely for political advantage. He wasn't going to offer the position to Jim Thompson when he needed Illinois and Bill Milliken when he wanted Michigan.

Regardless I thought it would look terribly gimmicky, like a show of desperation. And I didn't really think It would be that helpful.'"

WYTHE WILLEY "Meanwhile, John Sears put his eggs for Reagan in the Bob Ray basket. He kept thinking that he could come in and get Ray to deliver, therefore getting Reagan's core support plus Bob Ray's influence, and they could ace the election in Iowa. They made a number of calls to Ray, but they just couldn't sell him. And then Sears got fired right after Iowa's caucuses."

JOHN SEARS "I certainly would have been glad to have him if I could have gotten him in 1980, and I tried. But knowing him well, it was more realistic that he would remain neutral. And he did, certainly neutral enough as far as I was concerned. You don't really expect any more than public neutrality."

BOB RAY "It doesn't bother me that I didn't jump on somebody's band-wagon earlier, because I just didn't know which one would prove to be the best candidate. If I'd have thought, regardless of friendship, that one would surface as the right and best candidate, fine. Or if I'd had such a strong feeling for one, maybe we used to play marbles together or something. But I really couldn't do that.

"One time, after Howard dropped out, somebody from Reagan's camp came over and asked if then I was for Reagan and I said even though I was quite sure Reagan was going to be nominated and I would be totally in support of him, I wasn't going to make any big announcement until I felt the time was right. That didn't help me a lot. I wasn't looking for anything.

Didn't you want to see the Bob Ray kind of Republicanism, a more moderate Republicanism, continue? "At the national convention in 1980 one of the national news people came to me and asked the same question. He claimed we moderates seemed to be conceding without even raising a fuss. I told him, 'Look, everybody had an opportunity to enter the presidential race. They had strong methods by which they could bring their case to Republicans and people in general. Ronald Reagan won the nomination fairly and squarely, and no one can criticize him for what he's done to get himself where he is. It was a result of many people of the ultraconservative belief supporting him, and they are very prominent today. You're obviously going to have a stronger move of the party in that direction; that's just a fact of life.' "

JOHN SEARS "Bob was not always motivated by what might take him somewhere. He wasn't one to get ahead by tying his horse to someone else's bandwagon. And on his own he didn't necessarily want to be taken to Washington."

BOB RAY "I probably would have made a mistake anyway [*he laughs*]. If I'd jumped on a bandwagon that appeared to be to my advantage, I probably would have goofed it somehow. I always took the position that if I ever made a political decision, and I'm not talking here about selecting a candidate to back, but if I really did something that would just favor me, then the odds were I'd make a big mistake. With candidates, if I'd really wanted to pursue higher office, there wouldn't have been anything unnatural about looking for one to hitch my wagon to."

JOHN SEARS "One thing that always impressed people about Bob was that while he was a very good politician and had a good sense of the people and probably could have succeeded wherever he tried to be politically active, he wasn't the kind of person who only let his ambitions guide him. He was always anxious to be a level person wherever he was. Very often he would decide actively not to do something for all the right reasons."

KEITH DYSART "There's something tragically wrong with our system, though it's the best one invented yet, where the ingredients it takes to make a president and to win the primary marathon have absolutely nothing to do with the ingredients that we'd like to have sit in the chair. Bob Ray's got those ingredients. If he were from a megastate, he would have been president. If he had the driving, lusting ambition of Jimmy Carter, he would have been president. If he had a Hamilton Jordan who did nothing except plan and scheme and target and prod and provoke, and who was brilliant in that tiny, focused way, he would have been president. But he had a family priority and love of his state and its people, and he just didn't want it bad enough. There were higher priorities to him than personal aggrandizement. He is consumed with a quest for excellence."

Bob Ray eventually endorsed Howard Baker in the contest, but not until seventeen days after the Iowa caucuses, in which Baker had finished fourth, behind George Bush, Ronald Reagan, and John Anderson. *Washington Post* columnist David Broder awarded Ray the "Timex Award for Sense of the Strategic Moment" for the timing of his endorsement. Ray had claimed throughout the caucus season that he would remain neutral, and he did. He also claimed, as he had for years, that his endorsement wouldn't help anybody, that endorsement politics, especially in Iowa, where people didn't want to be told whom to vote for, wouldn't make a difference. He was probably right. He campaigned for Baker in New Hampshire, and the senator from Tennessee dropped out of the race a month later.

"The incident may point up why Ray isn't among the GOP candidates stumping the country. He usually plays politics the same way he governs, doing what he thinks is right and decent and only then looking at the political implications. It's a novel approach," opined the *Register*'s Flansburg in 1980.

Today, though, one Iowa congressman, a Republican, sees that decision to remain neutral as the biggest political mistake of Bob Ray's career: "He had four options. One and two, he could have come out early in 1979 for Baker or Bush, both moderates he liked. They'd have won the nomination and he'd have been vice-president. Three, he could have come out early for Reagan, who he knew looked like the winner, become his national chairman, and then been vice-president or in the cabinet. Four, he could simply sit out and host the event, stay completely above the fray. Instead, he jumps on the Baker campaign when it was too late to make a difference, assigns some of his people to help him [*Marvin Pomerantz and Dick Redman*], they can't do enough, and Ray comes out of it looking kind of foolish."

Howard Baker was not Ray's only endorsed candidate to fall in a primary in 1980. Breaking all of his own rules, several months after he'd come out for Baker, he told audiences around the state that his friend and former campaign manager and state party chairman Tom Stoner was his choice to run for the U.S. Senate over three-term congressman Chuck Grassley. Stoner spent over $700,000 out of his own pocket and lost the primary by 80,000 votes. So much for Bob Ray's testimonial support.

BOB RAY "I made that decision to support Tom feeling, like I did before, that I would not help the candidate. I wish now that I had helped Tom very early. Not that I'm unhappy with Chuck Grassley, but Tom was an old and good friend, and he'd helped me over the years. But I kept staying away from the question. The press would say, 'Well, wasn't he [*Stoner*] your campaign manager?' and I said yes, and they would say, 'Well, doesn't that mean that you support him?' and I said, 'Well, I certainly had great respect and admiration for him.' All of a sudden I was the center of attention because I wasn't taking a position one way or the other.

"I kept hearing a report on one radio station that I refused to support my campaign manager, and that was irritating. It was harming Tom, too, so finally at a news conference I said, 'Yes, I'm for Tom Stoner.' But it was too late to help him. Today, I'm sorry for what I did. I'm sorry about the timing, because if I were once going to violate that position, then I should have done it early enough to do some good. I think Tom understood, and Chuck Grassley too. [*When Grassley heard of Ray's endorsement in May 1980, his first response was, "That must mean Stoner's in trouble."*]

"Frankly, I came out for Tom, partially remembering my experience with Maurie [*Van Nostrand*]. I should have helped Maurie more. I probably made a mistake by not doing that. But I always took the position that I would do more harm to a candidate if I tried to come out and say I'm supporting this candidate or that."

TOM STONER "It wasn't until late April or even May, prior to a June primary, that he became more involved in my campaign. Looking back, one of the many things that should have been done was to really work closely with him. The winds were blowing in the conservative direction pretty hard, and there were a lot mistakes I made that he might have prevented. But he really stepped up to bat for me that last month. Whether it helped or hurt, I don't know. I think it would have been more important if he'd been more involved behind the scenes and with me as a person. Because unfortunately, or fortunately, people don't really learn how to run political campaigns, even though they've been campaign managers, until they've been a candidate. It's like sitting there with a stool and smelling salts, telling your guy to get in there and fight. I could hold the smelling salts for Bob Ray the candidate, but I couldn't be there for him when the debate started. Believe me, there's nothing like walking into that debate."

CHUCK GRASSLEY "If Bob Ray had been out there in January and February working hard for Stoner like he did the last couple months, boy, it would have been touch and go for me. I think I would have still won, because conservatives generally do have an upper hand in a two-person primary. His support may not have helped [in] getting the votes from the average voter, but if it enthuses your people to work harder for Tom Stoner than they might otherwise, that energy filters down to the voters.

"The average voter probably didn't know that Stoner had been Ray's campaign manager and that he had Ray's support. That's where Ray's participation earlier might have helped. Some of those average voters might have gotten out and voted for the governor's candidate."

PAT MILLER "Bob Ray's endorsement could have been utilized a little more effectively than that last-minute swing around the state. If we'd had some direct-mail pieces detailing why Bob Ray was supporting Stoner, that might have helped. But his endorsement never reached the 10 to 15 percent of the voters that we really could have used."

BOB RAY "I had people call me during Stoner's campaign and really jump on me for coming out for one candidate or another. I'd say to them, 'Mo Baringer's our state treasurer and he supports Chuck Grassley. Bob Lounsberry's the secretary of agriculture and he supports Chuck Grassley. Now, have you called them to be critical of them?' 'Well, no,' they'd say, 'but that's different.' Everybody who called or wrote me a letter complaining about that, I got back to them and asked them the same questions. Their answer was always the same: 'But you're the governor.' "

XXIV:
THE ECONOMY

The job of governor changed greatly during Bob Ray's tenure, and the biggest changes were in the administrative power that was centralized in his office and the budgets that office controlled. When Ray took office, the annual state budget was $350 million; when he left, it was just under $2 billion. When he took office, by his own admission, he was a Des Moines lawyer who had to work very hard to gain full understanding of the budget process and its complexities. His first two budgets were essentially written by state comptroller Marvin Selden, who had been at that job since 1961. By the end of his fourteen years, the budgets he presented to the legislature were Bob Ray's.

Between 1970 and 1983, state revenues, federal aid to the state, and

Debra Goldman photo. Reprinted with permission.

tax receipts all tripled. The state revenue base switched from a dependence on property taxes to a dependence on income taxes during the 1970s due to Ray's school aid formula and his continuing efforts to decrease property taxes. Inflation swelled the state's coffers. Perhaps the biggest economic shift was the increased federal monies sent to Iowa and the rest of the states through programs that began under Johnson and continued under Nixon, Ford, Carter, and Reagan. Between 1961 and 1973, 141 new federal agencies were created, many requiring offices and employees in Iowa. According to a study by the University of Iowa's Institute of Public Affairs, "State Government in Iowa," by Brian Carter, the federal government "seemed to be regulating and providing anything and everything. . . . This growth was in large part due to a growth in federal mandates. Iowa government had to create new agencies and offices in order to qualify for federal funds. In 1981 over $200 million (11 percent of the state budget) was spent to allocate these federal funds." Simultaneously, government employment in Iowa increased almost 19 percent during the 1970s, about the same rate as the increase in private employment but much faster than the population growth. (Between 1960 and 1980, Iowa's population grew by 3 percent, from 2.8 million to 2.9 million.) Today, nearly one out of five people in the nonfarm Iowa labor force works for one of the 3,000 units of government in the state.

How much effect does the government have on the ebb and flow of the state's economy? More specifically, how did Bob Ray manage the state's budget and its economic future when his hand was on the tiller? Many legislators and businessmen believe Bob Ray's legacy will be that he reigned well during good times. He struggled with lean years at the onset and the end of his fourteen years, and he ran the state government well during the economic boom times in-between. He won and developed friends in the business and agricultural communities. He was a cautious, pragmatic manager of the state, not a fiery, demanding leader. He worked with the Iowa Development Commission, admittedly more in the early part of his tenure, to encourage industrial growth and prodded the Office for Planning and Programming to pursue burgeoning federal grants. He organized two blue-ribbon committees on the economy headed by business leaders from around the state in an attempt to trim fat from the state's table of organization. The first, in 1969 was headed by G. La Monte Weissenburger. It made 593 recommendations with a potential net annual savings of $23.1 million and one-time savings of $9.6 million. Many of that committee's recommendations were adopted, and it was judged a huge success. The second, in 1979, was headed by Marvin Pomerantz. It made 386 recommendations with a potential net annual savings of $127.8 million and one-time savings of $37.3 million. Fewer of this committee's suggestions were adopted. In 1974 Ray oversaw the formation of "Iowa 2000," an idea originated by Ray and congressman John Culver. It was an extensive effort, chaired by University of Iowa President Willard Boyd, to look at the future of the state through the eyes of the people, not a blue-ribbon committee. Over 65,000 Iowans participated in town, regional, and statewide meetings that attempted to forecast what the state would be like in the year 2000.

MARVIN SELDEN "Two things really changed state government. One was Lyndon Johnson and his Great Society. They just threw money at us in the sixties. The other was when we raised every tax in the book for the school aid formula. We raised the income tax by 33 percent. In retrospect, we probably substantially underestimated what we'd get from that increase in income tax collections. Then the economy really took off, and there was kind of a double-barreled effect. Not only did we get the advantage of inflation but the increased revenues from the income tax boost.

"I'm sure if you went back and looked at the numbers that we said the school aid formula would produce, even if we hadn't had the inflation, we were probably one-third high. And that produced a lot of dollars and gave Ray a lot of money. Of course, we never had to raise taxes again, so it really carried us through a ten-year period. We built some buildings, we did exactly what we said we'd do with the school aid formula. Property taxes literally went down a couple of those years. So, yeah, I think we did exactly what we set out to do, and I think the extra money went for good causes."

DWIGHT JENSEN "During the Nixon years there was really more serious thought given to sorting out the proper roles for each level of government, whereas LBJ's decisions to turn programs over to the states had been more flavored by political pragmatism and restoring a proper balance. When Nixon proposed his New Federalism plans, it was a period where there were a handful of very strong governors throughout the country, including Bob Ray. Very able, forward-looking, imaginative leaders who naturally wanted more prerogatives for the states. It's not quite as simple as the old states' rights cry. There were some very, very good governors who were involved in the movement to try and bring the collective influence of governors together in Washington so that they could have a more effective presence and represent the interests of the states better. This dated from about 1973, when people like Dan Evans of Washington, Calvin Rampton of Utah, Bob Ray, Bill Milliken of Michigan fought hard for revenue sharing. They wanted extra dollars in their states, they wanted the prerogatives, they wanted the flexibility to use the money the states were getting as they saw fit. They wanted certain functions turned back to the states, and they were very active in seeking it.

"There was always a concern on the part of governors and legislators that if we start a federally funded program at some point, the people's appetite for it will be whetted, and the federal money will get cut off, and the states will have to pick up the tab. The concern on the other side, from Congress and federal administrators, was that if we give you this money, ultimately we want you to pick up some of the funding. So there was always some tension there.

"The growth of the governor's office was part of the evolution of things. Government was getting larger, the issues more complex. It took more people to follow them. People were asking and expecting more and more services, both from the legislative and executive branches."

DEL VAN HORN "We were getting things done in those first few years, but anybody could have, because of the state of the economy. If it was farming or running a business, you were progressing, things were moving, money was available. Those were the fun days for the Iowa Development Commission, and I think we did a lot of things that still mean a lot to Iowa's economy. *Did that sense of fun change as the 1970s continued?* Well, the governor got a lot busier and his support dropped off. He'd probably deny that, but it dropped off. I think he was spending time with other agencies, or he thought the IDC was in good hands."

TOM STONER "The 1970s were good times in Iowa, and how much of that is attributable to Bob Ray or any governor is kind of hard to delineate. But if you look back, had Roger Jepsen become governor, my sense is that the state would have polarized much more. I don't see him continuing with the reorganization of the state. We would have never seen the Department of Transportation, for example. If that part of the Republican party had taken over, I don't think the same track would have been provided. If Paul Franzenburg had been elected, I don't think he would have been able to garner the same public support for some projects that Bob Ray did. And Schaben was more or less a demagogue, a populist, and could never have moved the people of Iowa forward."

MAURICE BARINGER "One problem that developed during the period from 1975 through 1978, when we had a Republican governor and Democratic legislature, was that some of the spending practices created then have now come back to roost. That, coupled with the overly optimistic revenue projections for the late 1970s and early 1980s, made the state overly optimistic when we should have been overly pessimistic."

CHUCK GIFFORD "This whole economic mess we're in right now is not Republican or Democrat. It's a failure of our institutions and our basic system. It's a matter of fact that this thing's been coming for ten to fifteen years, maybe longer. Sure, I think there might have been things Bob Ray could have done about that, but let's be honest: Hindsight's 20/20 and foresight's a little dimmer. We could have been out ten or fifteen years ago when some other states were developing high-technology niches, but on the face of it I don't think you could have sold that in this state. I don't think you could have gotten the legislature to appropriate. I don't think you could have gotten business or labor to come together. I could sit here and criticize Bob Ray, for not restructuring the Iowa Development Commission and doing a better job of promoting and selling Iowa, really pounding the bricks to bring new industry to Iowa, but that wasn't just Bob Ray. You'd have to criticize everybody across the board. I didn't hear anybody running for governor on the Democratic side saying that either. There are other leaders in the state besides the governor, and nobody was calling for those things."

JACK PESTER "Some people say Bob Ray got out of office at the right time, considering the present state of our economy, but you certainly can't blame Bob Ray for any of that. I think now, if twelve years ago he would have known what he knows now, he probably would have advocated spending ten times as much on the Development Commission and writing specific tax laws to help industrialize Iowa. But that's hindsight."

ROBERT BUCKMASTER "After all, there is no one individual as governor who could have the ideas in every area. Ideas have to come from people who come talk to the governor, be they from universities, business, or so forth. Then he has to make the judgment about whether what they tell him makes sense. The ideas don't necessarily come from the elected official. He's really the conduit, he needs to be a good manager."

CAL HULTMAN "We've gone through back-to-back recessions and never recovered. But the things that have clobbered the state's economy were not Bob Ray's fault, or Terry Branstad's, or ours [the legislature's]. It was high interest rates and prior to that high inflation. You can't combat that;

Iowa is not an island. You're mixing in there with the real world and forty-nine other states and a federal government that's out of control."

DALE COCHRAN "Not to take anything away from Bob Ray, because he did a lot for the state and was a very popular governor, but I think he served at a time when a lot of people could have done a pretty decent job of governing. Compared to what a governor has to face today, it's a much tougher job."

GEORGE KINLEY "For a caretaker, he did a hell of a job. We're losing population, we're losing our tax base. Over that decade or so Bob Ray was in office he didn't do anything to make the state grow. We should have been working more when times were good on economic development. It's easy to second-guess somebody, but when I look back I don't see anything he did that provided any growth for Iowa. It was kind of a period where nothing went wrong, but nothing went ahead. He's perceived by the general public as a nice guy who did a hell of a job. Well, he is a nice guy. I just don't agree with the job he did. Had somebody else been able to do any better? I don't know. Nobody else could get elected."

FLOYD MILLEN "Why are we down in Iowa? It's related strictly to agriculture. With Harvester and John Deere based here, when the farm economy goes down, they suffer right along. I don't see how you can blame that on the governor."

JOHN SOORHOLTZ "A good share of our problems in agriculture today are attributable to factors outside the state: the cost of the dollar, high interest rates, inflation. I can't think of a time when Bob Ray overreacted to the problems. Even in the early days, when I disagreed with him on a number of occasions, he was very calm, the atmosphere was relaxed, and he was not challenging, didn't get hostile."

HAROLD HUGHES "I think history will look back and say that we should have taken more positive, constructive steps in our own fiscal arena here in Iowa, but more importantly than that, our voices should have been raised more on the national level, to try and influence national policy in relation to Iowa. One role of the governor which I consider to be a vastly important role and one most people never talk about is their contact and communication with the Congress and the president and the various agencies of the federal government. They have great effect on the development of the state, the future of the state, the industry of the state.

"You can get together in governors' conferences and pass resolutions until hell freezes over and you might as well throw the damn things in the wastebasket. Individual appeals need to be made, one on one. Bob had a string of Republican presidents, interrupted by only four years of Jimmy Carter, and I just don't think he raised his voice enough on national policy and national issues and their relationship to Iowa. I don't think the state did a very good job of representing agriculture and industry in Iowa in Washington. There is no congressional farm bloc anymore; it doesn't exist, it's fiction. One of the reasons I wanted to be governor again was to have a hell of a voice and an influence in Washington."

LOWELL JUNKINS "With his [Ray's] popularity rating, people in the state would have followed him quite a little ways, but it wasn't his style to do that. Before he left office, the unemployment trust fund was broke, the road fund was broke, and the general fund was broke. Did that contribute to his leaving office? I don't know. They were big problems."

DOUG GROSS "The job became very difficult for Bob Ray in the 1980s. The job was much less fun, because we entered a new economic era, one of contraction, not of growth. It was very, very difficult to get approval for spending programs through him, but it wasn't a heck of a lot of fun to cut budgets all the time, and that's what he had to do then. In addition to that, in those last days of his terms he seemed to be more interested in defending his past record than looking where we should be going in the future. It was good for him at that point to get out."

GIL CRANBERG "An issue through the years where he did not provide the leadership he could or should have was the general area of taxes. His general stance was to oppose general tax increases across the board. Instead, he would fool around with these sorts of bookkeeping measures, raise a little here, a little there, that ended up leaving his successor in the hole. He had enormous popularity, and he should have used that to talk straight to the voters and say, 'Well look, this is what we need. Taxation is the equitable way to get it. We have to do it.' But being against tax increases as a general principle is enormously politically popular.

"The thing that separates the truly great public officials and those who are very, very good but do not rise to the level of greatness is the extent to which they do tell people not what they want to hear but what they ought to hear. In the fiscal area Bob Ray did not rise to the level of greatness."

ART NEU "But if he had raised the sales tax in the good times, that money would have been quickly appropriated, and we'd be just as bad off today as we are. The money would have been used up and the tax base would be higher. There were several proposals over the years to set up a rainy-day fund. In those years we had a surplus, it was suggested we take some and stick it aside. But the legislature would have figured out a way to get their hands on it, if not this year, then the next. There were always plans on how to spend more money."

RON MOSHER "If you raised $100 million in new taxes, there would soon be $500 million in new programs on which to spend it. If you raise $1 billion in new taxes, there will be $5 billion in new program proposals. None of it solves the problems. When the sales tax was raised by a penny in 1983 we were at the low point of a recession. My recollection is that not much of that money was used to solve the budget problems. Nearly all of it was used for new things. If elected officials bite the bullet and raise taxes and risk being unpopular with the voters, they want to give them something in return. That gift in return is not just saying, 'Well, gee, we're not going to go broke this year.' It's a new road, it's a new building, a new program, a new anything. We [*Bob Ray's administration*] considered adding a tax in 1981, but it was an alternative not selected."

BOB RAY "I give them credit for the way they handled raising the sales tax after I left. Politically, they picked a time that people were ready to accept it and I don't know how you could raise any major tax, like the sales tax, with less of a problem than they had. But one thing came very true. I always said if you raise a tax like sales tax, and you don't absolutely have to have it, and if you raise more than you do have to have, it'll be spent the next day. And the very next day there were legislators talking about how they didn't have any money. They just can't hold money. They can't, and won't, put it away for a rainy day.

"It happened to me when I first started. The Hughes administration had raised all these different taxes, added the service tax. They had more money to spend, but when the department heads came to me during their budget hearings, they all wanted more money. They had just gotten big increases and I remember saying, 'Do me a favor. Go home tonight and think about it and do whatever you want tomorrow. But if you really can't operate without an increase, then you come back and tell me you can't.' Then my job was to help them find the money. A couple of them came back and said, 'Well, we think we can do without a budget increase.' Later in the year they'd come in and were just proud and pleased that they were able to do something they didn't think they could."

TERRY BRANSTAD "It doesn't do any good to go back and second-guess Bob Ray. I just know that during his fourteen years he had to make a lot of tough decisions, and I'm sure that in each of those cases he tried to do the very best he could. That's what I'm trying to do. It's easy to come back ten years later and say 'Well, you shouldn't have done this back in 1972,' but that's water over the dam."

RON MOSHER "Bob Ray had a tough relationship with business leaders in that last term. We really wanted to phase out the property tax on machinery and equipment, because a large number of business people had told us, and we had seen, they were simply relocating their plants in other states because they couldn't afford to pay the taxes in Iowa. We were convinced those taxes were an obstacle to Iowa development, but it was too late to get the legislature to pass it in 1980 or 1981."

GERALD THORNTON "That sales tax on machinery and equipment was a very punitive tax, and it contributed to the lack of manufacturing interest in the state. Historically in this state, we have had a farm-oriented legislature. Everything continues to be geared that way, although it's changing slightly. Without leadership in the governor's position, there's no way in hell that's ever going to change."

JACK PESTER "Bob is a lawyer, I'm a businessman. I tend to rely more, or understand more, about business. He tended to believe that you could solve problems through legislation and regulations. He'd never participated in business. He's participating today and he's terribly bright and I think you'll see him become more conservative because of his new job.

Isn't running the state, with 45,000 employees and a $2 billion budget like running a big business? "Yes, but it's not very well run. The Iowa government, and we [*Pester Marketing Company*] deal with thirteen, fourteen, fifteen, sixteen states, is probably the best-run state government I've seen, but it's still lousy.

He would probably suggest that you should have gotten off your butt, run for office and done a better job—for $50,000 a year. "Oh, I know it. And he's right. But that's part of the system—and the amount of money they'll pay a person to run it is part of the problem."

BILL FULTZ "Bob was suspicious of business people, and as a result I don't think he was a great friend of business. He never let himself get involved to great lengths with controversial, powerful people. He much preferred to get the support of the quiet powerhouses. As a result, he had a very bad relationship with Tom Urban at Pioneer and with John Ruan and Jerry Thornton at Meredith."

MICHAEL GARTNER "I always thought he could have used the governorship more effectively in working with the Merediths, Deeres, and Maytags to either keep companies here or to bring new companies in. But he always seemed almost aloof in that area. It wasn't a high priority for him."

ROBERT BRENTON "We are an agricultural state, and a governor can't have a lot of influence on agriculture, because the state just doesn't spend funds in that area. I went on a couple IDC trips in the early years, and on one to California Bob Ray was entertained by the guy who eventually built the Financial Center in Des Moines. That was a good example of the governor and the IDC going after business. So Bob Ray was good for business – as much as a governor can be."

BOB RAY "I always welcomed suggestions from the business community or anyone else. And the majority of them were wonderful to work with. They'd offer ideas, listen to explanations. Some of them didn't understand that you couldn't just snap your fingers and get things done, though. Working with a legislature of 150 different people is a different process, and not everybody understood that. Some, not many, didn't want to understand that.

"The people that made me angry were those that didn't come to us first and ask our side, look at the facts we were using. They wanted to play the power role. They could press an issue, get their name in the paper. The big-truck issue was that way. I didn't start out against big trucks. All I wanted was to know the justification for having a lot more trucks using our highways and what it would do for Iowans. [*Ray battled the trucking industry over allowing double-bottomed trucks to cross the state. The fuel shortage resulting from the mid-1970s energy crisis eventually led Ray to relent.*] Jerry Thornton carried the water for the truckers, and he didn't come and talk to us about what he had and how that might differ from our view. He just decided to run against us. The constitutional convention was another thing that made me angry. [*In 1980 Iowans for Tax Relief, headed by Dave Stanley, a one-time Muscatine legislator, and other groups were encouraging voters to vote for a constitutional convention. Their primary goal was to institute an amendment limiting tax rates. The convention failed at the polls.*] I went to their meeting and I don't think I could have said it any nicer, but I said, 'Take a hard look at what you have adopted, because it could well work against your best interests.' Jerry Thornton just insisted that I had no right to go to their meeting and say something contrary to their position. But he was wrong, and he could have really done harm to the business people. If there had been a constitutional convention, the business people couldn't have controlled it; the schoolteachers and labor unions would have controlled it, because they could turn people out."

<u>WYTHE WILLEY</u> "In 1984 Bob Burnett [*the president of Meredith*] went up to the statehouse and testified we ought to raise the sales tax by one cent. Jerry Thornton sat there quietly while his own boss said he wanted a raise in taxes. Jerry Thornton would take after Bob Ray about how taxes in this state were too high. Ray just gritted his teeth; that really chapped him. It was kind of a vindication of Ray when Thornton had to sit there and listen to his own boss say that raising the tax by a cent was okay. And that was after they'd already been raised by a penny in 1983."

<u>LOWELL NORLAND</u> "From the time I joined the house in 1972 we never raised taxes. The first major tax increase I voted on was the penny sales tax increase in 1983. In ten years with Bob Ray we never raised taxes."

<u>HUGH CLARK</u> "Everybody has encouraged new business to come to Iowa, but you've got to remember, Iowa is not a great industrial state; it's hard to attract big companies here. It's hard to change that image."

<u>ROBERT BRENTON</u> "I remember talking with one of our U.S. senators a number of years ago and saying, 'Hey, we have to do something about the development of Iowa. We are losing our people. None of my kids are staying here to work, they have to go elsewhere to find jobs. And this guy said, 'No, Iowa's a great place. We don't want the problems of the metropolitan areas.' That used to be a common attitude, a wrong one."

<u>JOHN FITZGIBBON</u> "We did things to encourage industrial growth. Maybe there were things we could have addressed more aggressively. A good example of a state in a less favorable position by far than Iowa that's done a great job is South Dakota. Their state government really helped pursue Citicorp aggressively, for example. They had more vision than most states. The boundary lines of the state mean zero anymore. No one could have outguessed the problems in Iowa, and I don't blame the governor's office, despite the fact he could provide real leadership. I think it was the legislature that lacked the real initiative. Same thing is true today."

<u>DALE COCHRAN</u> "We have really fallen behind in the research and promotion of our agricultural products. Iowa has been too modest, have not sold ourselves, were too conservative, and didn't move ahead trying to develop the state. The first problem is just selling Iowa to Iowans so they'll stay here. Once you've done that, you've got thousands and thousands of ambassadors. It's hard for the IDC to do that without ample appropriations, which we should have been supplying."

<u>BOB RAY</u> "I think you can promote agriculture. 'Fine Iowa Meats' is an example of people being industrious and working with the leadership of the state. We were able to do something, so the pork producers didn't just sit home and complain. They spent their own money, took their own time, and traveled around the country promoting meat. They couldn't have done that alone, but they could do it with the help of the state. But you know, times change. There were times in the late 1970s when the Democrats didn't want any part of those kinds of promotions. They had the attitude that business and industry were taking from the community, they weren't giving. For years I would try and make speeches about why we need good, valid business, and when I would try and recruit executives I would say, 'We don't want you just so we can tax you, we want you to provide jobs for our people. If you don't do that, you don't contribute very much.' I just love watching the Democrats today scrambling to try and put together a package to encourage industry.

"There wasn't any time that we weren't fighting to bring industry into Iowa. In 1975 we started losing industry because of the energy crunch. That's when the great exodus took place. First of all, they couldn't be assured they would have energy at all in the North. Secondly, they knew in the South they would, and thirdly, they knew they wouldn't need as much in the South, and fourth, they discovered that labor costs were less down south. That's when parts of the industrial Midwest and East started losing population.

"But we had some pretty good things going for us. People talked about reducing taxes. Well, we had a stable tax climate that I think business, industry, and executives appreciated. It's one thing to find you can get a little break here and there; it's another thing to look ahead and try and guess what's going to happen next year. We had a central location. Our transportation was not bad. Again, energy was a problem. We had a good work force, which was a primary advantage. We could boast, then and now, of that work force. Our education system is superior. Those are good, solid pluses. *Did they work as arguments for bringing industry into Iowa, though?* I think they did, until energy became such a big problem. We were in the running, we could compete. And that [*high energy cost*] was a big minus, because everything counted on it. It really became a fear of companies, because they had to have energy, one way or another. The worst part of it was that they'd also get what appeared to be great savings on labor in the South. We just couldn't compete.

"Today everybody talks about industrial development, more jobs, et cetera. I give the governor a lot of credit for promoting that. Even the *Register* has finally seen the advantage of doing that, too. Every time we'd lose a job under my administration the newspaper would write big headlines, but when we'd bring a new industry in, there'd be little mention. Plant closings got far more attention than plant openings.

"We proposed taking the tax off machinery and equipment as an incentive. But the Democrats fought that; they said big business ought to pay more. Now they're falling all over themselves trying to get it taken off. Since I've been gone they've raised taxes; you haven't seen them take taxes off except for new equipment and machinery and I applaud them for that. We took sales tax off food and drugs, we gave money back in order to keep government spending from going up, we tried to get the taxes taken off of utility payments, but neither the Democrats nor Republicans liked that idea, and I wanted to take taxes off machinery and equipment. But by the time we got to a point where we could take taxes off M & E [*machinery and equipment*], then our revenues had dropped. And no matter what you want to do, you can't always do it; you've got a budget to meet. There are good, logical reasons to take, say, the tax off M & E. But it's a lot harder to take a tax off than it is to put one on. And when you take it off you've got to have the money to replace it.

"I thought our first economy committee was tremendous and proved that they could work. But I think you have to be careful that every time you have a problem you don't try and solve it by assigning it to a committee. I thought both of ours saved us a potful of money. The Iowa 2000 committee was a little different in that it was really to get the people involved in thinking about what kind of state they wanted and what they were willing to do to create that kind of state. It was good. We had over 50,000 people participate in it. Unfortunately, it didn't go quite far enough. From my point of view, it was interesting when I read the reports, whether they came from groups who'd met in the basement of a church or school, or the big regional or state meetings. They all wanted to get government out of their lives, but every time there was a problem to solve they wanted government to solve it. I don't know if that's irreversible, but there's certainly a dichotomy there."

XXV: "I WON'T RUN"

The janitors were still sweeping up Veterans Auditorium after Bob Ray's fifth inauguration in January 1979, but speculation over whether he'd seek a sixth already filled the halls. If he did, and won, his eighteen years as chief of state would make him the longest-serving governor in modern history. Maryland's Albert Ritchie served fifteen consecutive years, for the record, while Nelson Rockefeller of New York was elected to four consecutive four-year terms but resigned two weeks shy of his fifteenth year in office. James Rhodes of Ohio served sixteen years, but not consecutively.

In interview after interview with local and national reporters, Ray put off questions about his political future, claiming it was too early to decide. By early 1981, with a November 1982 gubernatorial election within sight, Iowa reporters filled their pages and coffee breaks with a "Ray watch." Old staffers left him, energetic new ones joined on–was that an indication that he was dropping out or gearing up? He traveled more–was he building up his credentials or showing a lack of concern for state issues? He'd now served longer than any of his predecessors–had he stayed too long, or would the voters crown rather than elect Bob Ray? The *Register's* Yepsen and Flansburg teamed up for a story from Clear Lake's annual Governor's Day in mid-1981 that ran under the headline "Governor Robert Ray Is Running for Election." On Christmas Eve the *Register* was convinced that "Ray Will Run in 1982." Three weeks later, with the election ten months away, Flansburg wrote about the Condition of the State address under the headline, "Ray's Program Seen as Sign He'll Run for Office Again." On February 18, 1982, four days after Valentine's Day, Governor Ray gave the press and politicians what they wanted. Flanked by his family, he told a packed room at the capitol that he would not run for a sixth term.

Bob and Billie Ray announcing he would not seek a sixth term. *Des Moines Register,* David Finch photo. Reprinted with permission.

Republicans across the state and the nation, from Vice-President George Bush to Del Stromer, had pleaded with Ray to run again. They were convinced that the Republicans who hoped to replace him weren't up to the test. Friends claimed he wanted to get out and make some money. Others guessed Iowa's slumping economy made the future of the job look bleak. "It was a lot easier to be governor in the seventies than in the eighties," argued politicians of all stripes.

The question "Who will replace Ray?" had consumed the leftover 10 percent of political gossip for the previous four years. The front-runner in all books was one-term lieutenant governor Terry Branstad, a constant, seven-day-a-week campaigner. With or without the governor's nod, he was running. He misstepped only once, in mid-1981, when he confided to a reporter that his organization was so strong he could "even whip Ray." He quickly took that back, claiming that if the governor chose to run again, he'd be happy to serve another four years as his second. Remember, the last lieutenant governor to offer such a challenge never even made it to the paddock.

Some of Ray's own moderate Republican allies wished, not very quietly, that he'd made up his mind earlier, to allow Art Neu to raise some money and get into the race. Branstad, they felt, was too young and too conservative. But the by-now typical Valentine's Day decision by Ray left the field to Branstad, who was financed and positioned to launch. A baker's dozen other Republicans – including Steve Roberts, Tom Stoner, Iowa Commerce Commission chairman Andrew Varley, and Del Stromer – considered the run, but not for long.

The major Democratic challenge almost made up Ray's mind for him, almost kept him in office another four years. Iowa's second-most-popular politician, despite the fact that he hadn't won or run for election since 1968, came back to Iowa and mounted a short-lived campaign. Harold Hughes almost made the 1982 governor's race a battle of the superstars. National political columnists Jack Germond and Jules Witcover mirrored the sentiments of many Iowans: "Both men have reputations for conducting intelligent and clean campaigns and a dialogue between them could be elevating – itself, regrettably, somewhat of a rarity in politics these days." But Hughes bowed out of the race in January 1982 when it was discovered that by oversight he could not meet the race's residency requirements. Pragmatically, and perhaps politically, the former governor and senator had been away too long. The others who considered the nomination – Tom Harkin, Tom Miller, Jerry Fitzgerald, Roxanne Conlin, Ed Campbell, and George Kinley – proved to be too little, too late. Despite the fact that Ray had no handpicked successor waiting in the wings, his understudy wrapped up the part in a cakewalk against Conlin.

The governor maintained his popularity until the last—his approval rating near 80 percent in March 1982, even Democrats polled approved of his job performance two to one—and more than half the state's voters hoped he'd run for a sixth term. But in this test Bob Ray wasn't listening to the polls or the pols.

BOB RAY   "I think Billie thought it was time. Really, I thought about starting a new career, and if I stayed another four years it would have been even tougher to make that adjustment. Personally, there wasn't any advantage in staying. Of course, that was true four years earlier, too. Once in a while people would say, 'Well, don't you want to break the record, serve eighteen consecutive years and become the nation's longest-serving governor? I didn't run to break records; that would have been a terrible reason to stay.

"The bad economy was more of an incentive to run again, to try and live through that and handle it. But I'd really reached the place where even though, as always, I didn't sit down and think about will I or not, I knew I eventually had to make that decision. But I always put it off until I felt it was time to get serious about it. I really sensed before we made that announcement that I just didn't have the feeling I should run again. I was really flat."

VERNE LAWYER   "Billie Lee was a significant factor in his final decision not to run again. I really think she had a sense that maybe they were wearing out their welcome, that they should move on and let somebody else worry about the job."

DEL VAN HORN   "I remember talking to Billie, and she was saying how she'd hate to see what would happen if he ever lost. I told her it would never happen. She said, 'Well, maybe it's time we had a little time to ourselves.' That was my first hint that he was considering not running."

BILLIE RAY   "I didn't have any doubts that he would retire. It was the right time."

CYNTHIA HENDERSON   "When he was trying to decide what to do after his, as they call it, his kingship, I had several letter-writing campaigns going, to try and get him to stay, and I'd talk to Billie, and say, 'C'mon, just one more.' She said to me, 'Cynthia, four years ago you were saying, "Just four more years, then we'll let you go." ' I asked if four more would hurt.

She said, 'Yeah, I think it would.' She had very definite mixed emotions. But she came in the office there at Terrace Hill one day, and she had kind of this funny look on her face, and it was the next day that he was going to announce [*he wasn't running*]. She came in and said, 'Cynthia, Bob has decided not to run.' I about dissolved out of my chair, because I'd just heard from a pretty reliable source that he was going to run. She just sat down. I thought she was going to cry. She said it was tough, but she was definitely relieved."

BOB RAY "In many respects the governor's job is a lonely job. Most of the time you're with people, you're at events, you have a schedule that's full, and people wonder why anyone could call that lonely. But it does get lonely. You don't spend time with good friends, you don't go out for dinner, you don't go to movies, you don't do the things that you would do normally in life, cultivate friends.

"I didn't know my neighbors, I'd keep running into people and have to inquire where they lived. My time was pretty calculated for me. I'd have one hour and twelve minutes, or whatever, to wash my car at home, which was therapy for me, and I couldn't dawdle talking to some neighbor, even though I might have preferred to.

"When it came time to make decisions, I'd talk to people, get their input, and when everyone else had filed out of the room I'd try and balance it all and come to a conclusion. The next morning I'd tell them what I'd decided. That gets kind of lonely. There are certain things, no matter how much help you have, no matter how good your staff is, that you end up doing yourself. It was a much lonelier job than most people think.

"The only thing that would have gotten me to run again would have been if Harold Hughes had been able to run. The difference would have been the challenge."

BILLIE RAY "The party probably would have been insistent, too. It's a good thing he [*Hughes*] didn't run."

HAROLD HUGHES "I have really wondered what would have happened between he and I, and I don't have an answer. It would have probably been the most interesting race of the century in gubernatorial politics. It was a challenge, and I know he must have felt the same way."

BOB RAY "Some members of the press who'd been around a long time really thought that would be fun, Ray versus Hughes. Had I not run, I might have thought that it had the appearance that I wouldn't take on a big challenger, that I'd backed off. No politician wants to go out of office with people thinking that. *But if you'd run and beaten Hughes, you'd have still had the job.* Yeah, so either way I lose [*he laughs*]. If I lose to him, I'm a loser, and if I win, I've got to stay four more years."

ED CAMPBELL "Hughes was ready to go, and he wasn't worried about who his opponent would be. If you're going to worry about that, you might as well not get into it."

HAROLD HUGHES "I knew that my threatening to run wouldn't alter his decision one way or the other. He was never afraid of me, nor I of him. We would have each made our decisions independent of that, no matter what the hell the press thought.

"But I thought there was a danger in staying in the job too long. You build up too many barnacles, and they drag you down eventually. I thought Bob had done a pretty good job maintaining things, but the General Assembly was not undergirding the positions necessary to keep up with the changing highway needs, deteriorating bridge structures, diminishing levels of academic salaries, those sorts of things. There were an awful lot of issues out there worth campaigning on. Besides, I felt the party in the state needed to be brought together again."

DON AVENSON "I know Hughes was serious about it, because he talked to me about running for lieutenant governor on the same ticket. That would have been interesting, a challenge, but I decided that we were going to take control of the General Assembly and I'd have more power as Speaker.

"I seriously question now whether Harold Hughes could have beaten Bob Ray. Nineteen eighty-two would have been a time for a bright, aggressive, young Democrat to be thrown against Bob Ray and beat him. But Roxanne Conlin wouldn't have stood a chance against Bob Ray either. Hughes had no idea how big budgets were, no idea how extensive the area colleges were, even though he had created them. I mean he had no idea of what the state was involved in; he'd been away too long, been in Washington too long. I don't think he could have kept the bullshit up long enough to win."

DUTCH VERMEER "Bob Ray would have whomped Harold Hughes. In a real contest, out in the open, Hughes couldn't have given him much of a run, probably couldn't even have beaten Branstad."

DONALD KAUL "Hughes cut a much greater figure nationwide than Ray, though. His association with the antiwar movement and just his magnetism made him almost bigger than life. If he hadn't gone crazy with his religion, if he had just found agnosticism instead of Christ, found strength in that, he could have been president of the United States."

HAROLD HUGHES "We should have let Jerry [*Fitzgerald*] take that nomination [*in 1982*]. He would have beaten me and probably been the governor."

DAVID OMAN "Governor Ray is not the kind of person who had long-range plans for himself. He never sat down and charted a political future. The summer of 1981 came and went, and he honestly did not know whether he was going to run again. He was considering what was right for him, not what might be right for somebody else.

"He never spent a lot of time trying to position people or have somebody postured so that one, two, or four years downstream they would the apparent, logical candidate. He just did not do that. Whether that's right or wrong is for others to decide."

STEVE ROBERTS "In 1979 and 1980 I went around the state and visited with moderate Republicans, talking about what we would do if Ray did not run again. I had conversations with Art Neu, Jim Leach, Tom Tauke, and with Ray, and no commitments were ever made.

"Art Neu felt that if Ray was not going to run, he had to give somebody a signal by June of 1981. I told him he'd be lucky to hear anything by September of 1981. We spoke again in September and we both laughed. By the time he announced he wouldn't run, in February of 1982, Branstad had it pretty well locked up."

ART NEU "It was one of those things I could give or take. We sat down and I came to the conclusion that there just wasn't enough time. Terry had really worked hard to build an organization.

"I had gone to Ray once and told him that if he decided not to run in 1982, I'd like to know. I asked if he would give me some notice. He didn't.

"When he announced he wasn't running we got busy quick, took a poll, did some feelings for raising funds. I think we could have raised the money, but we didn't have a statewide organization. If he had gotten out in mid-1981, I could have made it a good race. If he had not run in 1978, I think I would have won; I could have beaten Fitzgerald. But this was 1982 and people forget fast. My name recognition was down, Terry's was up. People kept talking about who was going to succeed Bob Ray, and his name was talked about. He was lieutenant governor and he got around the state, built up an organization."

MARVIN POMERANTZ "Bob Ray was very close to Art Neu and had Art decided to continue as lieutenant governor, he would have had no trouble whatsoever in supporting him for the governorship in 1982. But also, the political winds were shifting. The conservative elements in the party were becoming more dominant. You can't be sure that Art Neu would have prevailed."

STEVE ROBERTS "I think he found Art Neu a fascinating, interesting guy, but he never picked a successor. That was his nature. He worked up until the last minute just like he was going to be governor forever."

RALPH BROWN "I spent some time with Art Neu in February of 1982, helping him decide whether or not he should run. I think it's fair to say that the thrust of the decision was that Art Neu was frankly unsure that he wanted to be governor."

GEORGE WITTGRAF "One of Art Neu's most attractive characteristics was his ability to see the forest for the trees. Political ambition was not an overriding factor in his activities and decisions. He did not become lieutenant governor in order to become governor; he wanted to lead the senate. Ultimately, when the decision was made in 1977, '78, not to seek reelection, [not] to hang in there to eventually become governor after Bob Ray, he simply decided from a personal standpoint. There were more important things than hanging around and waiting.

"Bob Ray never encouraged Art Neu to run for governor, nor did he ever do anything to make the possibility of Art running for governor any easier or any greater. Even in February of 1982, when Art Neu visited a few times with Bob Ray, he did not encourage him, but rather Bob Ray counseled him in a general sense just as he would have counseled anyone in a general sense about the possibility of being governor. *Do you fault Ray for that?* After spending fourteen years as governor and even longer in Republican party politics, Bob Ray had essentially decided that he was not going to be promoting other political figures. Had he pushed or helped Art, it would have been a completely different shift from what he was accustomed to doing."

RALPH BROWN "Sure, Bob Ray's staying in office that long did prevent other potential younger leaders from moving up. But was that a problem? I don't know. Had, for instance, Bob Ray chosen not to run in 1978, Art Neu would have run. I'm convinced he would have been elected governor. Terry Branstad would probably be neither lieutenant governor nor governor. Is that a problem? No, it's a result of Bob Ray's holding office for fourteen years. John Murray probably would have moved up, too, stayed in Iowa politics.

"There was clear stagnation in leadership, and we came out at the end of Bob Ray's years not having that many like-minded people in the party ready to move into higher offices. Art Neu is a perfect example of one who just gave up."

DAVID OMAN "We put a new staff together in the summer of 1981 with the assumption he would run. There was no hint or clue one way or the other. We wanted to get some sharp, bright, talented, aggressive people in there to reinvigorate the office so that if we were in a campaign in 1982, we'd be coming up with new, creative ideas. My feeling was that one of the reasons he struggled with the decision was because he felt a new burst of enthusiasm for the job because of the new people and the enthusiasm and energy of the staff. But by the end of the year the handwriting was on the wall. It was going to be too tough for him, if he ran again, to start a new career at the age of fifty-eight.

"It was a Wednesday, late in the afternoon, about 4:30, when he called us in to tell us he wasn't going to run. It was an emotional, touching moment for everybody."

GEORGE "PIC" WILSON "Just a day or two before that, two or three of us on the staff sat down with him and went over some of the things we would like to accomplish in the coming months. He left us with the distinct impression that he was going to go for it, run again."

RUSS CROSS "We tried to decipher from his scheduling whether he was going to run or not. But he never was the kind who would say, 'Now, we've got to go to this or that because it's a group I haven't seen in a while and I'm going to need their support.'"

JERRY PARKIN "In every election since 1970 there had been questions about whether Bob Ray would run again. When he made that decision in 1982 it startled a lot of people. His good friend Tom Stoner fully expected him to run again. Terry Branstad was blown away; he'd had no clue either way. I think that's the way Bob Ray made a lot of his decisions. He got advice, input, recommendations, and then made his decision, or he and Billie made the decision. Nobody made those decisions for him."

TOM STONER "By this time I was pretty much out of gas. I'd been in this game for the last ten years, had spent a lot of money, and was trying to get myself back into shape financially and physically. It had been an exhausting, emotionally exhausting, experience. But I guess in the back of my mind I thought maybe I'd run for governor sometime. But I hoped it wouldn't be any time soon. We were sure Bob Ray was going to run again.

"Jack Pester and I went over to Hawaii for a Young Presidents meeting early in February, and Bob Ray swore he would let us know what he was going to do. He never called. So when we came back I couldn't stand it. I called him at the governor's mansion. Billie answered the phone and she was very defensive. She is never defensive. Then he gets on the phone and he says, 'Well,' sounding all the time like a sixteen-year-old who'd just stolen a watermelon from a patch, 'I'm not running.'

"Billie was concerned because she was afraid my call might prompt him to change his mind. She wouldn't be sure until it really happened. She didn't have anything signed in blood."

BILL MILLIKEN "We probably talked as much during that period about our own political futures as any other time, and we talked constantly about whether or not we should run again. We'd laugh and kid about it, commiserate with each other. It was not an easy decision, but I think I may have decided a little sooner than he did. In 1978 I had the endorsement of every single daily newspaper in the state, with the exception of one. I'm sure if I had decided to run again, I would have won. But fourteen years was enough. Plus the state was in very bad shape economically.

"What Bob and I did is an opportunity afforded few people in this world, an extraordinary experience, so we never really complained about the job. Sure, you'd complain now and then, and feel abused, long for greater freedom. But the opportunity to make a difference, to struggle, struggle, struggle with a problem and every now and then have a breakthrough before your eyes and feel you'd made a contribution is a glorious feeling, glorious feeling."

DAVID BELIN *Did Bob Ray stay too long?* "I don't think so. I don't think it would have been too long if Bob Ray had stayed on another four years, as far as the state's concerned. I think it would have been too long as far as Bob Ray's concerned, because he had to do something to get some personal financial security. If he would have gone four more years, I think that he would have been too old to get the kind of job he got when he left."

JERRY MURSENER "Initially, he probably thought he'd stay for a couple terms. I remember one day in his first term bumping into Billie at the capitol, and she asked me if I thought he'd run again. He hadn't even finished his first term.

"I'm sure he didn't think he'd be there fourteen years. He probably just thought it would be nice to have that title forever and go back in with Verne and Jim Lawyer and pile up some money. I'm sure at one stage he thought both were possible—being governor and a successful lawyer."

BOB BURLINGAME "My answer is based not on theory but on looking around at what was available to replace him. So in the sense that he sort of ran downhill the longer he stayed in office, still at his very lowest point he was probably better than what we would have gotten as a replacement."

TOM URBAN "I think he began to run out of ideas in those last four or five years. He was leaning more on his survival capacity, ducking issues that might have been raised. He had learned how to finesse them, just hang on.

"The last few years of his term there was a lot of personal turmoil. I'm sure he was going through a whole series of considerations about running for higher office, trying to decide what he should do with his personal future. Many men, once hooked on public life, can never get unhooked, and he was able to, although I'm sure it was quite painful.

"If he now spends four or five years unhooked, it will give him a chance to find out who Bob Ray average citizen is again. It will give him a chance to step back and allow his natural philosophical bent to express itself without the pressures from day to day, and he will evolve one way or the other. His philosophy will find its natural position. And he'll probably end up being a stronger politician, more effective maybe, after four or five years out of office."

MARY FITZGERALD "He was extremely smart. He could see the handwriting on the wall. Nobody who has followed the economics of the state of Iowa could fail to see the picture as it was developing. The governor saw the picture. He'd served his time, served it well, and he said, 'Bye! Here you go, Terry.' "

XXVI: RAY AND THE LEGISLATURE

CLAYTON RINGGENBERG "The legislature was one thing that really got to him. It's not something you can control, and it's hard to deal with. It's a game, and you have to know the game real well. He knew it to some extent but was real reluctant to get trapped into anything."

CAL HULTMAN "I used to kid him he could make his decisions downstairs, but there were 150 folks upstairs waiting to tear them apart. Sometimes that's like driving a forty-horse hitch without any outriders."

BILL HARBOR *Did the relationship between the legislature and the governor's office change after Bob Ray took over?* "Yes, because Hughes was well received by the legislators. He had firm control of the legislature. When Ray came in we [*the legislature*] reassumed power. He had no real administrative experience and hadn't dealt with a legislature. It took him a while to grab hold of the reins. Although we cooperated pretty well, we were able to operate pretty autonomously for a couple years. I say that

Des Moines Register photo. Reprinted with permission.

with the knowledge that Ray never really understood the legislature in all of his fourteen years, and I'm not sure he wanted to. He wanted us to take his State of the State messages and run with them. A lot of times we'd go all the way around the block, try a lot of different things with his proposals, and end up doing them his way. He'd wonder why we couldn't have done that right off. But we had to look at all our options, deal with many different ideas, different interpretations."

BOB RAY "The most frustrating thing was when the legislature had not thought through a bill. They had not gone through the exercise we had gone through, they did not have nor had they listened to, the experts that we had, and just because they had one little idea I ought to completely wipe out my bill and accept theirs. Some were really good; they'd try and work with our proposal and try and make a change. And there were times when I didn't dare compromise or we wouldn't have had anything. There'd have been no way we could have gone the direction we wanted to go if I'd compromised. Part of that is the art, if I may call it that, of knowing when to compromise.

"It wasn't my style to yell and pound my fist. I gave a little thought to that early on, and I think that's kind of effective for a little while. It's also effective to stand at a podium and threaten 'This will never happen as long as I'm governor.' But you risk a lot if you're going to be in office more than a couple of years. And while I didn't know how long I was going to be there, I never seriously thought, 'Well, will I run again? Will I run twice?' That was part of my problem the first two years; I just didn't think about my future."

WYTHE WILLEY "It was perceived that Bob Ray did not understand the legislative process particularly well. That was an erroneous perception, because he was such a smart guy, he understood the process and he read people so well and knew how people interacted so well. He didn't come through the legislative process, and people didn't expect him to be a super guy with the legislature, whereas Governor Branstad has been a little burdened because he was in the house. People thought he [*Branstad*] would be able to work miracles because he'd been in the legislature.

"There are 150 legislators. They're each independent. They don't necessarily follow their caucus, they're hard to lead, they represent their own special interests, they represent their own district, and they're independently elected. Their allegiance is not to the governor. The best stick the governor has got to get those people to do things is his own popularity. The years that Ray was most popular–the last eight, nine years of his administration–he could get more accomplished."

DOUG GROSS "I've had legislators come to me and complain that Terry Branstad thinks about things in political terms all the time and they wished he'd be more like Bob Ray, who, they say, never thought in political terms, just tried to think what was right. What they don't recognize is the kind of approach Bob Ray took to things was politically the best approach to take.

"The bases he touched, his method of decision making, weighing, and talking to all sides, et cetera, that was a wise course to take, politically. You involved more people in the process, touched a lot of bases, made those people happy to be involved. They felt a part of the process. His nonpolitical approach was a very successful political approach."

DENNIS NAGEL "Remember, Governor Ray had been a reading clerk in the legislature in the 1950s, had followed it through the 1960s, helped legislators get elected to it, followed the issues as state chairman, and then worked with the legislature as governor. He saw it from a lot of different roles, and it would be hard to agree with anyone who said he didn't understand it."

BOB RAY "I used to think I was extremely impatient. We did the work and the research and put our program together. At first it was a little hard for me to understand why the legislature wouldn't just accept that. I learned that they had to start all over; that was their job. Not just to take blindly what the governor or anyone said. So they had to go through this ritual with committees, with hearings and studies, inquiries, and I had to learn to be tolerant of that. That was their function, and what we tried to do was offer any assistance, any help, that we could to help them better understand how we came to the conclusions we did.

"A lot of times they were sure they were going in another direction, and after a while they would come around to the conclusion that what we had suggested was the best way. Even then it wasn't unusual for legislators to have to change something in my proposals, just so that it wasn't exactly what I had submitted. But I understood that too. That was a maturing process for me, because no matter how right I thought something was, and for good reason, I had to convince 150, or at least half them, that I was right.

"I learned you had to have some patience, as well as knowing the facts, and be right. I really don't think I could have bulldozed my way through some of the issues any quicker. We got things done in a much more persuasive way. Del Stromer used to keep score of how we'd do each legislative session, and he could probably go back still and tell you how long it took to get a bill through the legislature. He used to say, 'You're way ahead of us. You proposed it here, and it was this many years before it was passed.' Maybe if I'd stood up and slammed the hammer down and threatened people, I'd [have] gotten things done faster. But I still don't believe that."

JOHN MURRAY "Ray never did have a close working relationship with legislators. People didn't understand him, and I think it was because he dealt with them like he did with me. I expected our relationship to have a little more personal contact to it, a little more ego massaging. But that didn't happen; that just wasn't the way he did business. It was the same with legislators."

BOB RAY "I couldn't play the game they play in the legislature, otherwise we'd never have any proposals adopted. I think that aggravated legislators, because often they wanted me to play the games they play upstairs. But I decided early I wouldn't do that. We couldn't tell one legislator one thing and another something else. We would simply say, 'This is the best we've come up with. If you've got something better, propose it and deliver some votes.' "

WYTHE WILLEY "Ray did not compromise much, and much of the legislature thought he was bullheaded. He liked to lay things out in a fairly precise manner and stick to it. He didn't go for a lot of give and take."

BOB RAY "Probably all of our legislative liaisons – Dutch Vermeer, Dennis Nagel, Doug Gross – were used in a similar fashion, even though their personalities and backgrounds and experience were different. They would help put together the program, and we used all of our aides to help us with the different agencies, commissions, and boards. The liaisons were expected to have a feel for all that was going on and what legislative matters we ought to consider and proposals we should make and how to implement and follow up.

"They really worked the floor of the legislature. They'd suggest if I should see this guy, or I'd ask if we should bring so-and-so down and talk to them. Basically, talking to my legislative liaisons was the same as talking to me. They were supposed to be more in tune to the legislature – who was doing what and who was supporting or not supporting us. Then we'd get together and try and decide my role. Should I call this one or that? Bring this other one down? Should I make a public pronouncement? What should I say to the press? That aide was my eyes and ears upstairs."

DENNIS NAGEL "We were not policymakers. We would see how far somebody would go, but we would not try to strike a bargain. He didn't need a deputy governor, he needed an aide. So the bargaining went on between the legislators and the governor.

"He was very effective at letting legislators know if there was any room to reach a bargain or whether, despite any number of votes they might have upstairs, he'd ever sign their bill. In 1979 or 1980 the legislature wanted to raise truck fees. Double-bottom trucks were a reality, but there was a question over their fees. Representative Laverne Schroeder was very supportive of the trucking business, and he proposed a bill that the DOT said would never cover the extra costs. I'm sure Laverne could have gotten that bill through the house, and probably the senate. Bob Ray simply told Laverne to forget it; the trucks were going to pay their way. That effectively stopped Laverne's proposal. It was something the governor recognized was absolutely right."

DOUG GROSS "Governor Ray was easy to work for in terms of being a lobbyist and also very difficult to work for at the same time. I'll try and explain. In terms of working with the legislators, he hated to compromise; that wasn't in his blood. We spent many late nights working up his State of the State message, and at that point he'd be convinced he had the best answers for the state of Iowa for the next couple years. He spent a lot of time mulling over the pros and cons of every decision. He was convinced he was right and was rarely willing to compromise.

"He was great at acting as the guy in the woodshed. I'd bring legislators down to visit with him, and particularly the Republicans knew what the governor wanted and why, and he was very good at enforcing his view. He was good at exploding at the appropriate time, getting very irate with them if he felt it was necessary.

"At the same time, he was very difficult to work for, because upstairs these guys, all 150 of them, live in compromise. If there is one place where it's obvious that the human race doesn't know one best answer to any human problem, it's in the legislature. But Bob Ray thought he already had the best answer in most situations."

BOB RAY *Would you compromise?* "I knew as a practical matter that you could get so rigid that you weren't effective, and you'd lose 98 percent of a good proposal if you were pigheaded. What I would not do, which I think infuriated some legislators, or at least aggravated them, was they'd come to me and start talking about compromise, and I'd refuse to talk with them. I learned quickly that it wasn't a matter of compromise. You like to be flexible enough that you don't always have to have it your way, but if a legislator came down and said, 'What will you take?' or 'Can you get along without this in this bill?' if I said yes, then that's where they'd start from. I couldn't do that. I wanted them to promote the whole proposal, not a piece of it."

<u>DOUG GROSS</u> "Another difficulty working with him was that he'd out-served almost all the legislators. Any time you thought you'd come up with a new idea, he had more than likely heard it twice before and knew if it would work or not."

<u>BOB RAY</u> "I never thought I could dicker, so to speak, with any one legis-lator, because that legislator wasn't speaking for the whole body. If a person would come to me and say, 'I've got 53 votes guaranteed if you take this section out,' then I might be able to say, 'That's not going to hurt the bill, run with it.' But no legislator could do that. So they all came down with their own little priorities and many times really abused conversa-tions they had with me. They'd go back upstairs, 'The governor says this,' or 'The governor won't do that.' It wasn't uncommon for someone to say, 'The governor says he'll veto this,' when the governor didn't say that at all. But it worked to their benefit, for their ammunition. I called one of them on it once, and he said, 'Well, I just didn't know how to get their attention.' But I couldn't accept that approach; it wasn't truthful.

"When it came down to voting, there were times when I would say, 'Well, I see that you can't get the votes for our proposal, and I'd be better off giving up a little if we can get it passed.' But I wasn't willing to barter until then.

"I learned very early that when a legislator comes into session, he or she is just overwhelmed with bills and work and everything else expected of them. If a proposal wasn't a simple matter, if it had never been intro-duced before, it had a long way to go, because you could not really expect them to adopt something just on blind faith.

"Sometimes we'd try extra hard to get them to understand a bill, try and get it through that session. If we didn't make it in one session, we'd try and keep it alive. Several times on the last day of the first session of the term, we would weigh carefully whether we wanted to force a vote. If we didn't think it could get through the second house, we would decide to not force the vote and lose it. Then we'd try again the next session.

You said in speeches more than once: "Always remember, a Democrat is a guy who doesn't know all the answers, but is sure that if he raises enough of your taxes, he can find one." "I still believe that's the basic difference in the parties. One problem I always had when a legislator would kick at me, or slap at me, in public, I would try not to indulge in personality squabbles, so I would say 'they' or 'it,' meaning the legislature. Then I'd catch the wrath of the good legislators who were supporting me.

"I always had problems talking about Democrats as a group, because I never believed they were all the same. There were always quite a few who agreed with me philosophically. But I still believe in that distinction. Democrats in general look for answers by spending more money. I thought that then and I think that now. That doesn't mean there aren't some Republicans who think that way too."

JERRY FITZGERALD "Bob Ray never understood the legislature, in part because when you're in the governor's chair, you don't want to get too involved with the give and take. It can get you in too much political trouble."

LOWELL JUNKINS "He'd have been happy if the legislature never met. The forefathers fouled up his life by having such a body. He'd get sick and couldn't eat from the time we arrived until we went home. The middle of May was probably his favorite time of the year; his Christmas present was when we adjourned."

DON AVENSON "The legislature can be a very progressive and effective branch of government with the right leadership. I don't think it deserves the rap Bob Ray gave it. He should have been above that kind of thing. I mean, to pick on the legislature is like picking on a retarded kid. Everybody expects you to pick on them. The governor didn't need to take cheap shots.

"All along I got the impression Bob Ray was trying to enhance the office of governor, make it look bigger and more powerful, by kicking the legislature."

LOWELL NORLAND "In one sense, Ray downgraded and belittled us, but in the other sense, I saw him sign stuff where there were major departures from what he had advocated. I was involved in the two greatest departures from anything he advocated—the 1976 and 1977 tax bills. I can't imagine any legislation which had such a major departure from anything he advocated, and what was eventually signed, than those two bills. So I had to think he respected our final product and felt that it was the best thing to do. Now, at the same time, he knew through Selden what we'd gone through to get that bill, and the reasons. I have to feel that he respected the process. I also think we did some very good work back then. Our goal was to beat his plan, and if we did, I think he recognized it and signed it. Maybe he wouldn't give us credit for it, but he signed it, and to me that was his stamp of approval.

"But I don't feel that way with the new governor. I feel pretty jumpy, and it downgrades the quality of work, because of the threat of vetoes. It's not the same kind of environment to work in. In that sense, speaking only for myself, I put in some very good years in a very good environment when Ray was here, to try and do good things, with a goal, basically, of beating the governor. And I think that's what it is all about."

BOB RAY "I always preferred to have a Republican legislature, but there were some advantages for us when we had a Democratically controlled house or senate. It was a lot easier to quarrel openly with the other party, who came at you from a direction other than a political one. When the Republicans disagreed with us, they weren't out to beat you, they were trying to make a name for themselves. The last thing a legislator wanted to be known as was a rubber stamp for the governor. It made them feel weak and inferior. I hated it when somebody was described that way, because I knew the person being accused was going to have to try and create an image contrary to that and it would make it difficult for us.

"The Democrats used to go bananas every time they'd see something that I would support that someone of their ranks had proposed somewhere along the line. I don't think you'll find any place where I would introduce [legislation] as mine exclusively if someone else had been promoting it. If it was an idea—the bottle bill, for example—that someone else had talked about and then I said I supported it, I always thought, 'Why aren't you thrilled?' Some were; they'd say, 'Well, finally the governor agrees with me.' But others would complain that it was their idea first. What difference did it make whose idea it was first? There weren't too many original ideas to start with."

MINNETTE DODERER "Essentially I agreed with Bob Ray. He sold half our programs. Just because he was sponsoring them as his own, should I believe that they were no good? No, I voted for them. Joann Orr, the senator from Grinnell, was the first one to suggest that we take the sales tax off food and drugs. It wasn't two months later that Bob Ray had it in his program, and he got credit for it. That's skill. Now, I don't know if I admire that particular skill, but I do stand in awe of his getting away with it. It also very effectively shuts up the opposition, because how can you complain?

"The Republicans would pick on him more than we did. They'd get angry because he was picking up Democratic programs and running with them. They didn't like it."

JERRY FITZGERALD "One thing Ray did very well was anticipate what was coming, what the cutting edge would be, and that tended to be on the Democratic side. He'd take an issue and do just enough to convince the progressives and the moderates in both parties to join him. Then the activists out on the wings of the issue would have to give him grudging support for trying. He was always moving ahead but rarely going out on point. That made it a lot easier for him to work with Democrats."

BOB RAY "A lot of ideas, like taking the sales tax off food and drugs, I would hear Democrats say, 'Hey, that's our idea.' I can remember saying, 'I think they did have the idea.' The difference is they never could tell you how to implement it. They threw the idea out and then let it just drop because they couldn't replace the money, and they couldn't tell you how they'd do it, they'd just say, 'Do it.' The difference was we figured out how it could be done, why it should be done, and then we did it. We had the resources to do that."

DOUG GROSS "He was especially effective during the late moments of a session, when nobody can agree on things, especially when we had Republican control and the leaders couldn't deliver. One night Larry Pope, then the majority leader of the senate, told us he couldn't get something done. Well, we knew he'd been playing both sides of the fence and wasn't being straight with us. Bob Ray blew up at him and it was very effective. Pope was duly chastened."

LARRY POPE "He was good on legislation; he studied the bills meticulously. I'll give him credit for that. And he had the process down, he understood how the process worked. But he didn't appreciate the personal relationships that go on in the legislature or how two legislative leaders might not be getting along and how that could impact. He would just say, 'Well, that's not right. If it's a good bill, they ought to be for it.' "

TERRY BRANSTAD "Like a lot of legislators, I kind of groused that we didn't get enough attention from the governor. But since I have been governor I've really got a much greater appreciation for the demands and responsibilities the governor has, and that the legislature is just one of many entities that the governor has to deal with. From the legislator's point of view, theirs is the only game in town."

ART NEU "He understood the legislature intellectually, but he never could appreciate the problems we had. He would sit down, develop a program, and he'd think, 'My, that's a good program.' Then it would go up to the legislature and it wouldn't always work. People would start to tear the program apart or nitpick it, and it used to drive him to distraction. He would say, 'Why are they doing this?' particularly when they were Republicans.

"I was down in his office one time explaining that I was having trouble getting twenty-six votes lined up. There were two Republicans I was trying to turn, without any luck. And I remember Bob Ray saying, 'I can't understand that. If you explain the issue properly, I can't see how our people, *our people,* could possibly not see the logic of our position.' I said, 'Well, obviously I can't do it. Let me bring them down and you explain it to them. I'd like to hear that.' He said fine, so we set up an appointment and I brought the two down. We're sitting in his office and he says, 'Well, so-and-so, I appreciate your coming down. I certainly know how busy you are,' and one of them interrupted him. His eyes got tight and his lips got real tight. He was obviously annoyed. You know, you just don't interrupt the governor.

"Well, the talk got over, and one of the legislators said, 'I really appreciate your having us down here. I know you're busy. You've taken the time to explain this, and I better understand your position, so I want to thank you. They left and Ray turned to me and said, 'See? I think I got at least one of them.' They both went upstairs and voted against him. I came back and congratulated him on the marvelous job he'd done and that I was going to keep sending people down for him to convince. He didn't think that was funny."

BOB RAY "I always felt I should have called legislators down to the lower office more. It was difficult. Some really felt neglected if they didn't get called down, some didn't want to get called down. That would change, depending on the bill, the mood, the period of time in the session. I can see things now that might have been helped if I'd used that lower office a little differently, but there are problems, too, with becoming too chummy with a legislator."

DICK GILBERT "The governor saw himself a lot like Matt Dillon, the sheriff on 'Gunsmoke.' There's the governor at the end of the dusty street, all by himself, and the legislature—this unruly, disorganized band that rides into town on an annual basis—at the other end."

TOM TAUKE "Because of his very strong popular support, he was able to succeed, for the most part, in getting the legislature to support his programs, in part because of the personal popularity and because his programs were very defensible, very moderate. He generally offered programs which commanded support from Republicans and Democrats alike, but I don't think he was successful because he had a strong personal relationship with the legislature."

JERRY MURSENER "I always suspected that Bob Ray had this little report card in his mind, and he kept giving legislators grades, everybody got grades. And he would assign little black checks next to your name, and woe the day you got too many checks on your report card, because life might all of a sudden not be as fun as it was before."

DEL VAN HORN "His ornery relationship with the legislature was more of a press deal with him. I think he understood the legislature pretty well, and he understood Democrats pretty well, and he played games with them, like all governors do. He had a lot of respect for the legislators on both sides of the aisle."

WYTHE WILLEY "One thing that people sometimes forget is that Bob Ray is such a good party man. And starting in 1966, when he literally single-handedly brought the Republican party back from oblivion, he had recruited a lot of the guys who were still in the legislature. He had a lot of personal old contacts with them, people who felt they owed him a little something. Plus he continued to be active in the recruitment and election process. One year he got the Republican state chairman over and he said, 'I hear you guys have thirty-some vacancies in the legislative races.' You know, 'What do you think your job is?' He was very tough. He said, 'We're not leaving here until we run down every one of those districts and find somebody to run.'

"He loved to go back down to the office and make recruitment calls. If the governor of Iowa calls you and says, 'I want you to run for the legislature,' it makes you more apt to consider it. Then if you get elected, and he called and asked you to run and he came out and helped you campaign, then when you go to the hill you're going to think twice about voting against him, because he's probably one reason you're there."

KEN JERNIGAN "The Iowa legislature is hamstrung in the same way that the U.S. Congress is today. You don't really go to congressmen to pass bills, you go to the staff. I believe now that the operative thing in Iowa politics is the shift away from a personal hand on things by the governor and the legislature to control by the staffs of [the] Office [for] Planning and Programming, the Legislative Fiscal Bureau, and the state comptroller. Money is power, and those three groups control the budgets much more than any governor or any legislator, and so it became a totally different ball game."

NORM JESSE "The fact is there is a legislature in Iowa. And I don't care how dumb you keep them in terms of information or how poor you keep them in terms of salary or how many limitations you place on the number of days that they can be in session or how much you make them hurt in the way of expenses, there still is going to be a legislature. And they'll do the best they can, and since you have to have one, it seems to me that the governor would be best advised to try and work with them. They do, after all, have ideas."

BOB RAY "The legislators truly felt we had knowledge that we wouldn't share with them. That just wasn't true. We based our actions on the facts we had, and we wanted them to know what we knew. Many legislators, though, felt they needed to do their own research to check on ours. They got their own fiscal director, which I applauded, because then they could check and double-check us."

CHUCK GRASSLEY "When I first went into the legislature, the senate was run by a majority leader named Buster Lyons. His whole game was just knocking governors, cutting governors, controlling things so much that governors couldn't get their way. That was the game, and there was some evidence of that when Bob Ray first took over. But the legislature changed dramatically while he was in office.

"I look back now at the years I was in the state legislature, and not only was it controlled by rural legislators, and I was one of them, but we also had a superior attitude. We really thought we knew how to run the state better than anybody from the city did. I used to think that the state would go to hell in a handbasket and that agriculture would lose out completely if the city people took over. But after a while, lots of rural legislators weren't voting the rural interests, and our public relations was hurt."

BILL HARBOR "The governor has sure grown more powerful during my stay in the house. That's maybe because we haven't had the strong leaders in the legislature that we had in the 1950s and early 1960s, the Buster Lyons. I think that's highly probable. But when you've been in there as long as I have, it's kind of fun to sit back and watch it all evolve, because everything they're doing today has been done, or tried, before."

KEN JERNIGAN "The real power shift went not from the legislature to the governor, the real shift went away from the legislature and more towards the bureaucrats. Up until the late '60s and early 1970s, the legislature had no fiscal bureau, no fiscal director. Once it got that, he took seriously that he should be the director and his staff grew and grew. The part-time legislators began to rely on that office more and more, rather than the comptroller's office. The deals were all cut between the staffs of the comptroller's office and the Legislative Fiscal Bureau, and by the time the legislature got ahold of things, enough small nuances had been set in motion, they were given just enough selective facts, that it was not possible to do other than they did. When I first started dealing with the comptroller's office, the budget took all of a couple pages. Now they run 120 or 130 pages for one department. No governor can possibly control all that. In reality, the comptrollers became more and more controlling."

SERGE GARRISON "The legislature improved immensely through the 1970s, though. When the annual sessions came into being and they beefed up their staff, they became what the founding fathers envisioned, an almost equal branch. But that one-person veto is still a force to be reckoned with. If the legislature would ever override a veto in Iowa, then I'd say they'd become equal, but they've never done that."

BOB RAY "For a while I thought we were headed for a full-time legislature. The Council of State Governments, the National Conference of State Legislatures, the Council of State Legislatures, they were all having seminars recommending it. Iowa's legislature always got high marks, except for the fact that it wasn't full-time. *Would you have been for a full-time legislature?* Of course not. I was a big supporter of annual sessions, and I've sometimes wondered why. We're much better off with people who have jobs like other people, drink coffee at the corner cafe, and know what the people are saying, thinking."

TERRY BRANSTAD "Bob Ray learned how to deal effectively with the legislators and how to recognize some of the various interplays that go on in the process without getting all wrapped up in it. My experience is a little different, in that I served in the legislature first, and in a sense that's an advantage, but it's also a disadvantage. It's an advantage in that I've been there, I have a personal, firsthand understanding of the legislative viewpoint. On the other hand, it's a disadvantage, because I've got people in the legislature that I served with that remember me as a legislator. It's been kind of tough to convince some of my former colleagues that I'm in a different role now as chief executive and I have to deal with them in a little different way."

DOUG GROSS "The difference between Bob Ray's and Governor Branstad's approach to the legislature is like night and day. With Branstad, I had to be the tough guy; he was the compromiser. We had a very good record that first session [*1983*] because the legislators were so used to the Bob Ray approach, the arms-length approach. What we did with Branstad was invite them to Terrace Hill. Many of them had never been there before. It was very effective and they loved it. But that wore off. The governor has to be respected as the governor, not as a legislator. Whether he's liked or not doesn't really make any difference, particularly with the legislature. If they spot you with your tail up, they'll chase you right through the fence. Bob Ray never got his tail up."

DENNIS NAGEL   "Bob Ray insisted his decisions were right and the legislature ought to go along. Some governors don't work that way. The governor we've got now wants to be loved by everybody and therefore will try to reach an agreement with anybody."

LOWELL JUNKINS   "I like Bob Ray, played tennis with him, enjoyed his company. He's a good guy, and that's the way he was perceived. But underneath all that was a very, very tough, mean, political guy. He did all of his getting even, all his whipping, where nobody ever saw it. Terry, on the other hand—and I like him personally; he's a decent guy, a family man—but politically I just don't sense he has his hands on the wheel all the time."

BOB RAY   "Terry's learning that there's a limit to how much you can demand and expect. There's a limit to how much you can bend over backwards and be nice and expect to get what you want. At first I was quite impatient. I thought I was right, my program was right, otherwise I wouldn't have recommended it. We knew what the answers were. It took me a while to realize that instead of being impatient and short we had to help the legislators, encourage them to get more facts. I think Terry understands that now."

XXVII: RAY AND THE STATE PARTY

Bob Ray is a loyal party politician, a Republican through and through. His relationship with the state Republican party was especially close—almost incestuous, said some—in large part due to the fact that he was often credited with resurrecting the fallen party after the 1964 Goldwater debacle.

The relationship between a standing governor and the state party of his persuasion differs from state to state. Generally the governor is recognized as the titular head of the party, consulted by the state chairman, sought out by prospective candidates seeking the party's nod, badgered by party officials seeking more authority. Bob Ray's relationship with party officials was all of that and more. Many think he would have loved nothing more than to call all the shots, hold both jobs, governor and state chairman. But time and other restrictions limited his hands-on involvement. Chapters could be written here detailing the intraparty squabbles between the governor and his aides and the state central committee, which ruled over the party. Over the twenty-two years Bob Ray played an active role in the party—from the time he was elected to the central committee in 1961 to the day he left the governor's office in 1983—he made many friends and a few enemies; he saw the party rebuilt at his direction and respond to his vision as governor, then slip from his grasp in the early 1980s. But the shenanigans, gossip, back-stabbing, and power-grabbing that occupy a lot of the time and energy of party politics are of limited interest to anyone but the players. Suffice it to say that from about 1968 to 1978 the state Republican party was Bob Ray's party, and everyone agreed.

John McDonald, Bob Ray, Steve Roberts, Marvin Pomerantz, and Wythe Willey. *Des Moines Register* photo. Reprinted with permission.

<u>WYTHE WILLEY</u> "Governors don't follow the theory that the party and the governor's office should be separate. I remember being at a Republican Governors' Conference and Bob Bennett, then governor of Kansas, said that the question of what the governor ought to do with the state party has the same answer as 'Where does a 400-pound gorilla sleep?' Anywhere he wants. The governor should have that same relationship with the state party—he does whatever he wants.

"Bob Ray, for the most part, exercised a great deal of finesse in that relationship, and I think it was a good, symbiotic relationship. The real keys were John McDonald, Margaret McDonald, Mary Louise Smith, and others who were team players."

<u>RALPH BROWN</u> "Bob Ray is responsible for the modern look of the party and the strengths of the party, the centrist role of the party. We have one of the best organizations in the country. Still. What he did in 1963 to 1966 is a Bob Ray legacy. I recently happened to see the manual that state headquarters put together in 1966 for legislative candidate training. It was exactly what they were doing in 1976 and are still doing in 1984.

"Our problem as a party in Iowa is that we also have one of the best Democratic organizations in the country to compete against. Bob Ray personally recruited many candidates who eventually became the leaders of the legislature in the 1970s. He was always good at bringing good people into the party, and there are a lot of people involved in Republican party politics in this state because of Ray's leadership both in the party and as governor."

<u>BOB RAY</u> "I never called up the state chairman, no matter who it was, and said you've got to hire this person or that person. I wasn't even that close to it. I always tried to help and be available whenever someone would ask me to help on somebody else's campaign—make appearances, help raise money, work with them. I had no desire for confrontation or to meddle in somebody else's campaign. So first and foremost, while I had a great desire to help the party, I thought I could stay pretty busy answering requests and then be primarily responsible for my own campaign. I always thought I did more good for the party if I ran well than if I devoted my time to things more extraneous and lost an election.

"I also never tried to tell the central committee what they could or could not do. I tried to be supportive. But one thing that happens with people on central committees is so frequently they get on and think they're moving up from the field of politics to then be in control, to make policy and to run government. All of a sudden they get removed from what their role really is—which is to elect Republicans—and they think they no longer have to do anything but travel, sit at the head table, and say a few words every once in a while. They forget that they are supposed to be responsible for winning elections in their district; that's their job. It's amazing how many of them go sour and forget what their job is. Instead, they go to meetings, sit around and complain, and eat steaks.

"When I was the state chairman, the central committee didn't always agree with me. But they always gave me enough rope. I don't think there was a failure, and if I would have failed, there would have been plenty who'd have said, 'I told you so.' The central committee's virtually sole purpose is to elect Republicans. It isn't to run government, it isn't to fail to support someone, it isn't to approve appointments. On the periphery, I think, there are all those things they can participate in, but they need to know what their role is in that participation.

"John McDonald always understood that. He didn't want to run government, he didn't want to tell me what to do, but he didn't hesitate to pass on his opinion or what he would hear or suggestions, and they were always welcome. I used to love to have people tell me what was going on, or how what we were doing was perceived, or if somebody thought we were doing something wrong. Of course, I wanted to know who it was, so I could evaluate whether it was coming from a valid source or not. John was really good about all of that."

DAVID OMAN "Some suggest the governor's office wasn't as political as we could have been. Critics felt we were far too political. When a new state chairman was being chosen, we would be involved and the right choice made. But in terms of the day-to-day functioning of the state Republican headquarters, our posture was hands off.

"It's easy in the abstract to say the governor's office should run the state party machine and seat all the people in the right races and all those things. But we had a lot of fires to put out on any given day. The luxury of time was simply not available. There would be days and weeks when we didn't talk about the political machine or the state party apparatus."

BOB TYSON "Bob had a lot of problems with central committee members in his own backyard, anti-Ray moderates—or independent moderates, as they liked to call themselves. Pat Bain, Ben Webster, John Merriman, and some others. Then in later years the conservatives got on the committee, and the combination gave him some real headaches.

"One time, a few years after they'd moved into Terrace Hill, Billie called and said they'd like to have a dinner with the people who had served on the central committee when Bob was state chair. They knew I could track them all down, and I did, except for one woman who had eloped with somebody else's husband and moved clear to Tennessee, which shows Republicans can have fun too. Never found her. Anyway, they all came and everybody had a ball, very congenial. As I was leaving, Bob pulled me aside and told me we should have invited the current members of the committee, to show them you could be in politics and still have a good time. They frustrated him considerably, and he frustrated them, I suppose, as well. Appointments were a big hang-up. The central committee wanted to pick all the appointments the governor made, or at least have final approval. That would have never worked, it would never get done, but they insisted on having a hand in anyway."

During Ray's governorship five men served as state chairman, a job he himself was elected to at age thirty-five. John McDonald, a Dallas Center lawyer and a big Ray booster, took the chair from Jack Warren in early 1969 and kept it until he resigned in 1976 to become a national committeeman. All sides agree that during McDonald's tenure the party was at its strongest and was most closely allied with the governor's office.

WYTHE WILLEY "It's hard to overemphasize the role that John McDonald played during the years he was chairman as an ally of Bob Ray's. John is an unassuming, quiet, but extremely competent guy in a group situation. He could get people to do things his way, and they didn't even know they were doing it. We always considered him a tremendous ally. I think it's really important that the party is strong, and the closer the governor and the senators are to it, the stronger it will be, the more influence it has on those elected officials.

"One of the problems with PACs [*Political Action Committees*] and individual giving from other parts of the country into Iowa, is that once a person gets elected, the party doesn't have the kind of relationship with an official that I think it should."

BOB RAY "John McDonald was without qualification a total friend. He understood politics, he understood the direction we were trying to go, he thought moderately. There wasn't any equivocation with John. He did what had to be done, and he always knew what the proper role of a state central committee was, which many don't. He was totally loyal to me.

"When he left, I didn't want to try to dictate to the central committee who should be the next chairman. I didn't particularly think that was my role. At the same time, I didn't want someone unfriendly."

JOHN McDONALD "I maintained my own independence to run that office as I saw fit. The governor never told me what to do. I hired my own executive directors, which wasn't always approved of by some of the governor's staff. Joe Gaylord, Ralph Brown, both of them were my people. It was my job to take care of the party and he always knew that things would be done with the best of our abilities."

In 1976 former Ray campaign manager and broadcast magnate Tom Stoner battled with central committee member Tom Tauke for the state chairmanship. Stoner won, and he kept the job for two years. He was followed by Des Moines lawyer Steve Roberts, who oversaw two big Republican wins in the state, the elections of Roger Jepsen and Chuck Grassley to the U.S. Senate. But the moderate Roberts was dubbed indecisive by critics (he resigned in 1979, only to be reelected) and his five-year tenure was marked by intraparty upheaval and the conservative surge that accompanied Ronald Reagan's 1980 election. He was dumped unceremoniously in 1981 by a cabal of anti-Ray moderates and conservatives. A longtime state pol and onetime Ray ally, Ben Webster, replaced Roberts. His election reflected a feeling among many observers that the governor had gotten his way for too long and meddled in party affairs too often.

TOM STONER "I was down in the Caribbean on vacation when I got a phone call. A guy came running down the hill and said the governor of Iowa was on the phone. I'm sure you won't believe this, but I really had no idea he was calling about the state chairmanship. He just said John McDonald had stepped down and they were looking around for someone who could get properly positioned to run for the office before John made a public announcement, so that the other forces wouldn't loosen his hold on the state party."

PAT BAIN "Tom was a lot different than John. He had been Bob's campaign manager twice and had run them like advertising amazons, lots of gimmicks, lots of fun. We had a lot of fun when Tom was state chair, but there were a lot of disagreements, too. The first one was when Tom Tauke, who was on the central committee, wanted the job as state chair."

BOB RAY "I was surprised that Tom wanted to do it, but I thought, 'What a wonderful choice.' Tom Tauke was already on the central committee, and he had had a lot of early successes in politics that I thought might well destroy him because he was very, very young. And when you're young and you have success and you're so aggressive and ambitious, it consumes you. Fortunately, that didn't happen, and I think he has really matured into an excellent congressman."

TOM TAUKE "We had three ballots in that election and I think the final vote was 7 to 5. The governor personally had a hand in that particular contest. He had what came to be known as the 'midnight meeting,' and it occurred the night before the central committee election, and he called the entire central committee up to his lower office and spelled out who his preference for the chair was. I guess he was persuasive enough to win, and I say now, thankfully."

STEVE ROBERTS "Bob Ray wanted Stoner to have the job, and I was the backup in case he couldn't get Stoner elected. Ultimately, it was my vote that elected Stoner. When he quit two years later, somewhat unexpectedly, they were looking around again for somebody acceptable, and I think I was, frankly, the best they could find."

WYTHE WILLEY *Did the central committee change when Stoner took over?* "Stoner was loyal to Bob Ray, but he has a very democratic management style. He did a good job with the central committee, but I don't think he gave as much of himself to it as others. With that democratic style, he tended to listen more to the central committee, and they might reach a conclusion for their own reasons. Then Tom would come over and say, 'Governor, on subject A we think this.' And Ray would say, 'I don't think that's a good idea.' Okay, so all of the work Stoner had gone through in the central committee to reach this conclusion was no good. Maybe we [*the governor's office*] should have been involved more in the central committee so that the 'right' conclusion came to the top.

"But if Stoner and Ray didn't agree, Ray would override him, and Stoner was put in the tough position of trying to get the governor to change his mind or go back and turn the central committee around. Stoner was popular, but now you can see our point about John McDonald.

He was much better than people gave him credit for. A lot of times it's the results that count, and not whether you get credit for doing it. Then when Steve Roberts moved in he had a completely different leadership style."

STEVE ROBERTS "I was a Bob Ray man, but of the second generation. I hadn't been with him in the 1960s, I wasn't in his inner circle of advisers. Both Stoner and McDonald were in his so-called Ruan Group [as the governor's kitchen cabinet was sometimes called because they would meet in the Ruan Building in Des Moines]. I was more of an outsider, although we worked well together. The fun thing about being state chair under Ray is that you had such a tremendous product to sell. You could take Bob Ray around over and over again to the same communities every few months and people would be fired up every time.

"As chairman, I believed that Ray was the titular head of the party and the governor's chair was the most important chair. But it was harder to keep control of the central committee. Stoner had the same kind of battles I had, lots of close votes. When I was eventually thrown out in 1981 it was by a broad combination of people – former Ray supporters, Branstad backers, and Art Neu people."

WYTHE WILLEY "Ray did not have a bad relationship with Ben Webster, but he was much more independent. Roberts never had the personal support from the committee that either McDonald or Stoner had. It's interesting – Jack Warren is an old truck driver, and his style was, 'Goddam it, you've got to get going' on this or that. John McDonald was a smooth lawyer, the most gentle, friendly guy in the world. Tom Stoner is a young, high-powered executive. They are all much different. When Steve came along he had some awfully big shoes to fill, and he tried to cover a lot of bases. He did a pretty good job in the electoral years, but he probably should have resigned right after the elections. But he hung on and got involved in the internecine warfare, and they just ganged up on him."

BEN WEBSTER "Some people said I was an enemy of Bob Ray's, but I don't perceive myself that way. Maybe we had some disagreements and fights, some public fights, but that didn't make me his enemy. I just wasn't going to be his errand boy. He was always talking about the team: you've got to be a team player, don't rock the boat, there's only one quarterback on the team, only one coach. He had a tendency to put things in football terms, which tended to irritate me, because that was not a particularly accurate analogy. I always thought it should be a two-way street."

PAT BAIN "The differences that Bob and I had were over turf, because both of us were from Des Moines. He felt that he should have called the shots on some decisions concerning Des Moines; I felt that I should have had some say.

"We had plenty of differences in our political careers, but I still have a lot of respect for him. He was an outstanding governor, and he represented my point of view on issues. But we differed a great deal on method and on people, it was primarily a matter of turf. We had no Republican governor when he was state chairman, and that put the state chairman in a very different role. He was the boss of the party. From the time he decided to run for governor, he wanted to select the state chair, including his successor."

BOB RAY "Pat Bain and Ben Webster were cohorts. They would bring people along their way. She had a different attitude towards her role in the party. There are certain people who are in politics to be somebody, not to do something. And that became her life. She believed, or professed to believe, that the central committee ran the party and the governor should not have a voice in it. The governor was to run government, and the central committee ran the party. I don't think in anybody's textbook of politics you divorce politics from an elected government position. But that ideology kept her in control. If she could sell that philosophy, she dominated a group of the central committee. John Merriman joined she and Ben in that philosophy."

JOHN MERRIMAN "Flansburg and Yepsen harp on this bit, when conflicts between Ray and the central committee would arise, that just like Harold Hughes, Bob Ray couldn't get along with the Polk County organization in their respective parties. That's a lot of bullshit. As time went on, the more he [Ray] wanted to be in charge, and at the same time more resistance developed to that."

STEVE ROBERTS "If you took the anti-Ray, or independent, moderates and the Ray moderates in the party and asked them twenty questions on issues of the day, you would find that they would agree 99 percent of the time. It wasn't philosophy, it was personality, it was who had the power."

BOB RAY "It's funny that Pat Bain was the one person on that central committee who was there because of me. I got her appointed back in 1963 to the seat I was leaving to become state chairman. Leo Oxberger wanted it too, and badly. There was no way in the world she would have gotten on there if it weren't for me. Even when I was still state chairman she was a problem for me. I have to give her the benefit of the doubt that she was a friend, but she saw her role differently. I always thought she saw her role differently because of her own ambitions."

In 1980, with conservatives in the party on the ascendancy, it became impossible for any one person to "control" the party, and Ray's grasp slipped. That year at the state convention the party voted to drop any reference to the ERA from the party platform, a direct slap at Ray and his backers, including Mary Louise Smith, a leading Republican supporter of the ERA nationwide. The same convention adopted a platform that urged that a constitutional convention be held to limit taxes and that suggested permanent indexing of the state's income taxes and the reimposition of the death penalty, as well as other planks Ray opposed. That convention, said a *Register* editorial writer, "bushwacked the most popular governor in Iowa history."

A couple more bushwackings stunned the party before Ray left office. First, Roberts was dumped and replaced by Ben Webster as state chair in 1981. Then, in early 1982, in a stroke of political high jinks the magnitude of which had not been witnessed in central committee politics since Leo Oxberger loaded the state convention to guarantee Bob Ray's defeat of Art Donhowe in 1961, a mixed bag of political operatives banded together to dump Pat Bain and John Merriman. Led by former Ray aide Ed Redfern (who was operating with the permission of his boss, John Ruan), Wythe Willey (the chief Iowa aide for Senator Chuck Grassley), Darrell Kearney and LeRoy Corey of the Iowa Conservative Union, and representatives from the Jepsen staff and others, the group, operating under the title of "Iowans in Support of President Reagan," set up an elaborate timetable of leaks, letters, and vote securing to unseat the anti-Ray pair at the upcoming party convention. To some observers it was an unauthorized move supported quietly by the governor's staff to get back at Bain and Merriman for years of headaches. "Bob Ray and Mary Louise [*Smith*] didn't believe I could do it," brags Redfern today, not too sheepishly. "Pat and John didn't know what hit them until it was too late." And what did Bob Ray think of all this? According to Redfern, "He just smiled."

JOHN MERRIMAN "Pat and I were defeated in 1982 by a combination of the right wing and a small group of ardent Bob Ray toadies. I don't think

Bob Ray would have allowed his people to get involved with the right wingers if he hadn't already announced he wasn't running for a sixth term. He wouldn't have wanted to jeopardize an election he'd be running himself. But when he dropped out, he effectively gave the signal to those people to 'Do whatever you want, I don't care,' because they clearly joined up to throw us out.

"Ironically, I was very optimistic about the race if Bob Ray had run for a sixth term. He's a smart man. I would never shortchange him on that, and he obviously had some problems with people like me on occasion. But for the most part that was a small deal. He had the natural desire to want to smooth things over and get along, to work together. Taking into account the big picture, it's kind of a shame we all didn't get along a little better. Maybe there'll be a next time."

XXVIII: RAY AND THE PRESS

FROSTY MITCHELL "One of Bob's aides once told me that if there were two people who wanted to see the governor at the same time and one was from the media, the other a legislator, Bob would sit down with the media first. He understood the importance of that. When the jury would go out at trials, Bob would kill time with Nick Lamberto and the rest of the reporters. He liked their curiosity, their inquisitiveness. In the 1960s his favorite people up at the capitol were Drake Mabry, Flansburg, [*George*] Lefty Mills. If I couldn't find him, I would always look in the pressroom. He was comfortable with those guys, and it paid off later when we were driving around to small-town newspapers and radio stations when he was first running for governor. Some guys are afraid of the microphone, afraid somebody will ask them a tough question. Not Bob, he was ready for it, he had the answers.

"He would have made a great Dan Rather type—if they could get him there on time."

JIM FLANSBURG "I think the Ray governorship recognized the needs of the reporters better than the Hughes governorship. But I don't think it had anything to do with the man's personal charm. Most of the people who covered Hughes would have charged hell with a bucket of water for

Governor Ray with press secretary David Oman. *Des Moines Register* photo. Reprinted with permission.

him. He was an interesting, fun man to cover. I don't know of anybody who ever thought Ray was particularly interesting or fun to cover.

"But after those first couple years in office, with Dick Gilbert on board, they did a good job of smoothing out the relationship between the governor's office and the press. Gilbert was the key to Ray's success as governor. And the reason I give him more importance in that than some was because, while he was in charge of dealing with the press, his responsibilities were extended far beyond that. He seemed to be in charge of keeping the governor in tune with the real people in Iowa, as opposed to the political hangers-on, the groupies, the political junkies."

CHRISTINE HANSEN "After Dick came back to the staff in early 1971 the office seemed to become more organized, there was better accessibility. We got quicker answers to questions, better background information, a more assertive attitude, more of a selling of the governor to the press, instead of just waiting for the press to come to them."

DICK GILBERT "One of the attitudes I had going in as press secretary was that while you have aides on the governor's staff who were liaisons to the other branches of government, I was the liaison to the press. I don't care what anybody says, the press in this country have an enormous influence on the outcome of events. Most of the time, thank God, they influence wisely and relatively unselfishly, except for the fact that they're very selfish about getting the stories for themselves. But the press operation of a politician as a government figure is just as essential as someone who was a liaison to the legislature, because the press is just as big a part of government.

"I came out of the newspaper business, and I never felt that I was manipulating the press. I felt that I served the governor and the public well by encouraging an open and free flow of information between the governor and the media. But the biggest reason I was successful as a press secretary was because I had a successful principal. It was easy to say good things about Bob Ray, and he did smart stuff. I never had to apologize for him; he didn't make many mistakes.

"It is important for the governor to have a good public image. If his approval ratings drop below 51 percent, it's difficult for a governor to function, in part because he is like the Wizard of Oz. All he can do is encourage people to do those things that they don't want to do but that are in their best interest or the best interest of the state. Look at the governor's office. It's got twenty-four-foot ceilings, there are thirteen kinds of marble in the wainscoting, the chairs are oversize, deliberately, so that when you walk in you know you are in the presence of the wizard.

"You walk in and say, 'Governor, we've got a hell of a problem with a highway in Dubuque,' and he'll say in a nice way, 'Well, what are you going to do about it?' You say, 'Well, we're going to do this and this and that.' He says, 'That's a good idea,' and off you go. You leave and you say, 'Well, the governor really helped us with our problem.' It's the same as pinning the medal on the lion and telling him he's now got courage. But that is only effective as long as the governor has a base of popular approval.

"So the function of the press secretary is an honorable one, helping the governor sustain the favor of public opinion or public approval. And you do that by open and honest communication. There's no magic to it. Everybody used to say Ray and Gilbert are public relations wizards and, you know, I loved it, of course, because I'm enough of a self-promoter, but I knew goddam well that wasn't the case. The truth is you just let him get the message out. I was an unashamed, unabashed, twenty-four-hour-a-day promoter of Bob Ray. I never let myself say anything privately to any member of the press that wasn't positive to Bob Ray. If I couldn't say how strong he was and how firm he was, how thoughtful he was, I didn't say anything. I didn't have to lie."

DAVID OMAN "Governor Ray has a lot of intuition, good skills, good judgment with regard to the press. Dick enhanced them. He made the resources available and saw to it that he was out and that the press had access to him. We produced a lot of speeches, lots of press releases, public service announcements, and kept the governor very busy.

"We used the press constructively. If there was an issue that the governor felt was important and he wanted to get out ahead of the curve, we considered the press just as we considered other elements of the decision making—the legislature, budget constraints, et cetera. And as you build a strategy to develop that issue, you consider how the press will cover it, what angles they'll be interested in, what local angles are important. If it's a state issue, how you can make it important at the local level. If it's a tax issue, you figure out what that means to the average citizen with his or her tax bill. You try to put things in people terms. You try to be respectful of the press and their deadlines, try to visit with some of the press people on background ahead of time.

"There were usually so many balls in the air at one time that we always wanted to avoid popping too many stories on the same news cycle or on the same day, because then you would just be competing against yourself for x number of column inches or x number of minutes of airtime on the news. We'd deliberately look at the week or ten days or two weeks coming up and pinpoint a day when maybe this would be announced, and tomorrow we'll do this and the next day that."

BILL JACKSON "He always felt that somebody in the press was giving him a hard time. He's the type who took it all very personally. If Flansburg said a negative thing about him, or his programs, or his staff, or his whatever, he took it personally."

DICK GILBERT "One night we were walking across the lawn at 2900 Grand, must have been in 1970 or 1971, and I said, 'Governor, how in the heck do you stand up to all this criticism?' He said, 'When I get criticized, I bristle.' He often talked about himself using euphemisms. 'I guess that's the human reaction, but,' he said, 'after I get beyond that, I recognize there has been a failure on my part and I have to do something about it.' He said, 'Failure can come in one of two ways. One, and it's just possible, is that the critic is right and that I should do something differently. Or two, it tells me that there has been a failure on my part to communicate adequately with a critic as to why it is I'm doing what I'm doing. If a critic only had more information, had a better understanding of all that's gone into this decision, perhaps he wouldn't be critical. In which case I have to double my efforts to communicate with people.' That explained why he would spend hours late at night calling people who had written a critical letter, explaining in great detail to individual citizens why he was doing what he was doing. It also tended to sharpen his own thinking."

BOB RAY "I don't know that I or anyone could ever figure out what the press expected. Occasionally they would think you could just do anything. On other occasions, if they didn't like something you did, they accused me of moving too rapidly. If you tried to do something not in accordance with their timetable, they'd go nuts.

"They didn't have to pass any legislation. All they had to do was write about it. They didn't have to get the votes, they didn't have to explain it, they didn't have to put it together. They could write an editorial and tell you what they think ought to be done, but I don't know any of them who ever put together a proposed bill, or had to do the research on one."

LARRY POPE "Bob Ray got incredibly good press, just unbelievable, and it used to agitate every other politician in the state of Iowa. Yet I never saw anybody get as mad at the press as Bob Ray. God, he would rant and rave against Flansburg, Yepsen, the *Register,* all of them, Gartner, all those people. I used to want to scream, 'Goddam, Governor, those people are in your hip pocket for God's sakes.' They used to skewer me, gut me, in the press, and Bob Ray would be screaming about some minor little thing."

BOB RAY "I never wanted to get to the place where I was immune to what the *Register* said about me, but sometimes I thought the way they reported was disgusting. But you couldn't get to a point where you dwelled on it, because it could make you ineffective. Sometimes it was hard not to do, though.

"You never knew whether you should try and correct things. Normally when something was way off base I or Dick Gilbert or Dave Oman would call and tell the reporter what we saw the facts to be. We didn't want a retraction or make any big thing out of it. We just wanted to let them know that we thought they were wrong. That worked most places except maybe at the *Register,* because they too often were defensive. Even if they were nice when they talked to you, you just had the feeling it wouldn't be too long before they'd get back at us.

"Flansburg was great with that kind of stuff. If you'd call his attention to the fact that you didn't agree, or that you'd like to have him know the real facts, then he'd take pride on Monday morning writing, 'Say, the governor was testy. There must be some truth to this or he wouldn't have called.' If you said nothing and then complained later, he'd say, 'Well, you didn't say anything at the time.' He loved to make sure that you couldn't win."

MICHAEL GARTNER "I always took it that he was the second closest reader of the paper, after me. He would pick out the smallest ribbing and stick it in his back pocket until the next time he saw you, even if it was three months later. He'd mention it, in a kind of offhand way, but he was just waiting for the opportunity to mention it."

GIL CRANBERG "I don't remember thinking of Bob Ray as a carper. I never had the feeling that he was nitpicking or anything like that. If he had a quarrel, it was an arguable point that he would make. In other words, there were some people who would come up or demand or beat us around the ears over something just really ridiculous. But we never had that experience with Bob."

DAVID YEPSEN "He always felt that the *Register* was his paper. He grew up with it, delivered it. He was a hometown boy, so we knew that he read everything in the paper and was very sensitive to his press."

DAVID OMAN "I always felt we had a good understanding with the paper, that if he truly felt there was a problem in terms of how they would put the spin on a story, we would let them know."

NORMAN SANDLER "The governor's office knew who the dominant player was, the *Register,* and always played to that. Not too surprising. But access was never a serious problem. It was physically impossible for the staff to go into a Reagan- or Nixon-like bunker mode. *Was covering Ray different from covering others, including Reagan?* Some court the media better than others. Some of them have personality and looks, the smooth style, and Ray is one of them. Now Roger Jepsen, on the other hand, looks good, from afar, as long as he's not talking. But Bob Ray answered questions in a nice, soft, soothing tone, which is what everybody wanted."

DAVID OMAN "The *Register* is the preeminent news source in the state, and if you decide to pursue a press strategy that works around the *Register* or that seeks to be at odds with the *Register,* you do that at great risk. Governor Ray never wanted to do that.

"If we were trying to get the governor out-front on an issue, maybe some upcoming legislation or an appointment, maybe we'd confide in Yepsen, hoping you'd see something in the *Sunday Register.*"

DAVID YEPSEN "They paid attention to the *Register.* Phone calls were returned, they went out of their way to make sure we were taken care of. They also understood how to use the media and the *Register.* When it came time to sell a program, the *Register* people—reporters, editors, whatever they thought they needed—were brought in early. Proper leaks were made, the proper timing was laid out. They understood that the morning paper liked something to happen at 10:30 at night and used that very effectively."

DAVID OMAN "Let me give you an example of the *Register*'s importance in the state. Say prior to the State of the State message somebody from the Sioux City paper would come in and asks the governor how he thought he'd done that past year and what did he expect for the upcoming year. It's all over in fifteen minutes. The *Register,* on the other hand, sends over three reporters, very well prepared, with a long list of questions on specific issues.

"Now, we've been fair to both papers, but the out-state papers would think that we had hand-delivered our program to the *Register.* They would gripe to Dick [*Gilbert*] and me constantly. But the *Register* would have come in and asked, 'What are you going to do about this specific issue? What are you going to propose? Why is it a priority? How do you think it will fare?' and have good follow-up questions. By the time they got through, they had a pretty good sense of where the governor stood on that issue."

JIM FLANSBURG "The *Register* rarely sends dummies to the hill. Somebody goes up there and studies state government, learns state government, and is capable of asking questions day in and day out that will embarrass the shit out of the governor, because there is no way that any one person, the governor included, can keep abreast of it all.

"So if I wanted access to the governor to ask him about how something is coming along on such and such, I got it because if I didn't get it, the press secretary and Bob Ray and his staff knew fucking well that I'd be at the next press conference and I'd put a vicious spin on that goddam question and embarrass the shit out of him."

DAVID OMAN "We always felt the *Register* had an interest in close campaigns, so they would point out some areas where we might be vulnerable and that would allow the opposition to score a few hits and perhaps tighten up the campaign and make better news."

MICHAEL GARTNER "Ray will tell you that his relationship with the *Register* was less than perfect. He once told me an interesting thing. He said, 'You know, I don't have a hometown newspaper.' He worried about that. He said, 'All these other politicians, everybody in the legislature, has a hometown paper, and I don't have one. I don't have a built-in editor like these other guys do.' I'd smile and tell him that was certainly one of the terrible hardships of his job and I felt terribly sorry for him, but that I didn't have a built-in governor, either, and I think that works out for the best."

LAUREN SOTH "They used to say that Bob Ray had the *Register* in his hip pocket. But you get that kind of comment any time partisan politics are involved. Some of my best friends in the Democratic party used to accuse us of that, that we never could say a bad word about Bob Ray and just go on and on, but I remember getting the same kinds of complaints when we supported Harold Hughes."

JIM FLANSBURG "Democrats used to yap at us that we 'made Bob Ray' and protected him, and they just never seemed to be able to take advantage of the issues we raised. I can remember getting frustrated as hell, because several times I'd sit down and write a bill of indictment against Ray, and the Democrats would read it and not pursue it. Ray would complain that I was doing their job for them, but there was another issue at stake. There were a lot of reporters out there who tended to get the idea that the man was perfect simply because the Democrats couldn't lay a blow on him. But that didn't mean no blows could be laid on him."

BILL THOMPSON "Flansburg was the one guy that would make me most uneasy, because you just never knew where he was coming from. He didn't necessarily do us wrong, but he was tough. When he first showed up, he was not one of the more likable members of the press corps."

BOB RAY "Flansburg is almost an enigma to me. I always thought that when Jim was out talking to people, at the scene of the action, he wrote very well, with good understanding. But I had problems with him when he'd sit up there at Eighth and Locust and write what he *thought* was happening, write his opinion. I never found it easy to deal with him. After a while I took the position that I was in public life, they're going to write what they want to write, and I'll try and correct it if it's too far off base, otherwise why get in a shouting match."

JIM FLANSBURG "I always had a pretty good idea of what would piss him off, and he'd sulk for months. He'd get over it, but I don't suppose he bitched at me more than five times."

DICK GILBERT "Flansburg had a lot to do with the 'Ray turnaround' in the early seventies. To understand that you have to realize that there was at that time a big turnover in the *Register*'s statehouse coverage. George Mills, who'd been there for years, had left and Flansburg had replaced him. George knew everything and everybody, and there wasn't any way that you were going to change him or his coverage. But Flansburg was the new guy, and he had a hunch that the real way to cover state government was to understand the governor's office in a way that had not been practiced before, while the rest of the statehouse press was covering the governor's office like it was another legislature. Flansburg was interested in Ray as a man and a personality. So we had a new governor, a new press secretary, and a new chief political writer slamming into each other. We generated a healthy respect for each other.

"Here's an example. When we put together the State of the State address in 1972 the speech got released in the morning, and all the afternoon papers got the story first. Flansburg was coordinating coverage for the *Register* and he was livid. He often got his way by bullying people, swearing, and he came into the governor's office pointing his finger at me in a rage. He said, 'Gilbert, you son of a bitch, that speech is going to be in the afternoon papers and all we're getting is a reaction story tomorrow morning.' He had wanted the *Register* to break the speech, and now he's saying he's going to burn our ass. I'm thinking 'Holy cow, I'm dead. My career is finished. He's going to fry Bob Ray.' True to Flansburg's word, he unleashed an army of reporters on the capitol. That's one thing the *Register* did; they could always outnumber you.

"In the meantime, the speech had gotten good reviews in the afternoon paper. When I picked the next morning's *Register* up I was surprised. Flansburg had tried to find somebody, anybody, to say something crappy about Bob Ray's speech, but he couldn't. 'Well,' I thought at the time, 'Flansburg may huff and puff and be a mean son of a bitch, but at his core he is fair and honest. He couldn't find what he wanted, but he reported what he found.' "

DONALD KAUL "Flansburg was as mean and tough a reporter as there was, but he was always easy on Ray. If George Anthan had stayed in Des Moines or if Drake Mabry had kept covering the statehouse, they would have nailed Ray a little more. They're the two toughest beat reporters the *Register* ever had. They'd burn sources and then come right back and use them again. Really tough guys.

"But whenever something went wrong in state government that was really Ray's responsibility, the blame always went to a subordinate, without much effort. In a sense it was the Reagan phenomenon in a milder way."

DRAKE MABRY "I knew Harold Hughes better than I knew Ray, and I used to get mad at Hughes, and Hughes used to get mad at me. I was never really mad at Ray, and I never really felt like I knew the guy. I don't think anybody was ever able to crack his facade. He played his thoughts and feelings more close to the vest than Hughes."

MICHAEL GARTNER "Bob Ray was a moderate Republican, and some- times he was even more to the left of moderate, and that's what the *Register*'s editorial page is. That's why John Culver always got along with the editorial page. Dick Clark, too, because we happened to believe that the same things were best for the people of Iowa."

DICK GILBERT "Any Democrat or anyone else that thinks the *Register* is intimidated by a public official doesn't know the *Register*. Bob Ray got a pretty good name through the *Register* over the long haul because he did a good job. He was a centrist, right-thinking governor, and it was easy most of the time for the paper, which is on balance a centrist paper, to be supportive of him. He rarely got in trouble with them over substantive issues, because he was pretty open with them and they had a lot of access."

GIL CRANBERG "We endorsed Ray all five times and frequently the endorsements were so backhanded they were more of a liability than a help. It is not an effort to drum up votes for a person. You're not just emphasizing all of the person's pluses and his opponent's negatives. You're simply explaining your position. Through the years Ray had quite a good record. We were in much more agreement with him than disagreement, so the question was, why kick him out? There was never a compelling reason to."

MICHAEL GARTNER "He also got great press from the national reporters. He was always accessible, and you'll find, whether in politics, business, or anything, the person who is accessible gets better press. Here in Des Moines Bob Houser and the Bankers Life people are always accessible to reporters. John Ruan never is. Guess who gets better coverage? I have told Ruan, 'If you were accessible, Christ, you'd be seen as a lovable teddy bear, just like Houser.' "

NORMAN SANDLER "Once Iowa caught on as a political state, reporters from Washington loved to go to Iowa. It's a great place to do campaign stories, great scene setters, the whole works. And every time they came through, they talked to Ray. They wouldn't get anything new from him, but he had a lot of insight, he was a nice guy, had a reputation as a very popular governor in a state that a lot of people respected, and he looked good on television."

JOHN HYDE "Look at what happened during Watergate. That was a dreadful time for Republicans, who found themselves on the record for or against whatever Richard Nixon was saying at the moment. Both Wiley Mayne and Bill Scherle lost elections in 1974 for reasons related to Watergate. It was a hard time for Republicans, a major party issue, and it didn't even graze Ray, didn't touch him.

"It wasn't an accident that he was able to avoid those pitfalls, it was a skill. But it was the same skill that made him difficult to report on. The standard joke among reporters was that you could go in and talk with him and he'd say something, you'd write it down in your notebook, and you'd look at it a couple hours later and it would have disappeared from the page. At the time it sounded like he was telling you something important, but he wasn't."

LAUREN SOTH "He was understanding and sympathetic to the role of the press, more than many politicians are. Although he didn't like everything we did, he was generally supportive of what the press was trying to do. On civil liberties, the First Amendment, he was outstanding. There's a philosophy of how the press works and what the freedom of the press means — it means freedom for being wrong as well as right."

MARY JANE ODELL "He had a good relationship with the media partly because he worked at it and partly because of chemistry. And partly because he is a very sincere man who loves Iowa. He didn't come across as having ambitions for higher office. It made him appear very trustworthy.

"You can't be in any high elective office without having an ego, but he also had a nice dollop of humility. He was someone that most Iowans could identify with. He was a great neighbor, the guy next door, my father, my son, whatever. Plus he's nice looking, a good-looking dude. He usually looked directly in your eyes, too, which was important."

DONALD KAUL "I like Ray personally. He had an edge to him personally that he did not have as a politician, as a public figure. He could zing you with a quip. Every time I'd see him he'd have something to say, and very often it was something I didn't have a good response to. He was quick, funny, and I admired that. *He says he held that humor in check for fear the media would distort his quips.* Well, he's right, but caution isn't a quality I particularly admire of him. If you're in the business of covering politicians, you want them to be less cautious. Jepsen was a terrific politician, from a columnist's point of view, because he was always out there falling on his face. Ray never fell on his face."

BOB RAY "I feel so strongly about our free press and the importance of it and the importance of it to government, yet I would often find myself talking about some of the things that I didn't approve of in the press. You know how coaches stand on the sidelines and yell at the officials? They do that mostly to encourage their players and not let the other side get an advantage. Sometimes I used to think that once in a while we really should scream at the press a little more to let them know what it's like to have people talking about them.

"I wish all reporters could be governor or president for a month, six months, a year. They think somehow it's a position where you can be perfect. I'll bet if you were as perfect in their way as they would like to have you, they'd find that it really didn't sound so good, really not what they thought.

"Reporters do not know what it is like to have your integrity questioned by the news media. When they take on your character, I don't know who could let that go by. Some people say they just let it run off their backs. I never wanted to. I wanted to make sure that I was always sensitive."

DENNIS NAGEL "You've got to remember that unless it was an article that appeared in the National Governors' Association newsletter proclaiming Bob Ray the most wonderful governor in this century, it was probably a negative story. It's amazing how sensitive you get about your name being mentioned in a negative way, even if it's in the last sentence of a story."

HAROLD HUGHES "The press became pretty uncritical of Bob. They sat back too easily, let him get away with a lot they would never have let me get away with. It's hard to criticize a good friend. Getting close in friendship is not healthy for the press or the officeholder. But we as governors do become manipulative, goddamned skilled at using the press. That's part of the business."

DENNIS NAGEL "One time a high school student came to interview him for the school newspaper. She came in and was scared to death. She couldn't get a word out. So here is the governor of Iowa trying to get this girl to say something. It was comical. I couldn't believe he was spending his time to do something like that. But it was typical. Here was another media request he was taking care of."

XXIX:
THE FINAL DAYS

In typical Bob Ray fashion, he didn't relax on the job until Branstad was elected and didn't cease "being governor" until the brutally cold January day his thirty-six-year-old successor was sworn in. The official log at Terrace Hill showed he checked in at 4:25 A.M. and back out at 8:03 A.M. on inaugural day. The transition after fourteen years to a new governor was relatively simple, aided immensely by the fact that Branstad was a Republican. Many key Ray staffers and appointees stayed on to help the new administration. Despite his protests to the contrary, Bob Ray was a tad envious of the new governor's easy transition. The fact that it was *his* people, Ray people, advising, counseling, initiating the new governor did not sit well with the staunch loyalist Ray.

It would take Governor Branstad the better part of his first four-year term to fully sign up his own team, and he kept many Ray appointees at some of the state's biggest agencies—Mike Reagen at the Department of Social Services; Banking Superintendent Tom Huston; Iowa Commerce Commission chairman Andy Varley; Insurance Commissioner, Bruce Foudree; Ed Stanek in the Office for Planning and Programming; John Beamer, chairman of the Public Employees Relations Board; Wayne Richey, executive director of the Board of Regents; Warren Dunham, chairman of the DOT; Ron Mosher as comptroller; Gerald Bair, director

Terry Branstad consults with Bob Ray. *Des Moines Register* photo. Reprinted with permission.

of the Department of Revenue; Larry Wilson, director of the Conservation Commission; and Robert Benton, director of the Department of Public Instruction. A few of these have since left, as have other longtime allies of the former governor—Colleen Shearer from Job Service, Jackie Day from the Board of Parole, Stan McCausland from General Services, Art Neu from the Board of Regents, and Bob Rigler from the Department of Transportation.

Many of the 82 percent of Iowa judges Ray appointed are still trying cases, as are seven out of nine of the state supreme court justices he named. Slowly, as the appointments to boards and commissions are renewed, the "Ray people" are being filtered out of state government.

BOB RAY "Maybe there's something wrong with me, but I had absolutely no problem leaving that office. It was a relief to be gone. I was just really looking forward to doing something else. And I think it showed a great deal, like at news conferences. I got to the place where I didn't want to answer questions about the future. Part of that was because I didn't want to be answering questions about what was going to happen next, after I was gone."

MARY JANE ODELL "After Terry was elected, the pressure was off and Bob Ray eased up a bit. Let's put it this way: Before the election it was like a flying phalanx coming into the executive council, or press conference, or whatever—the governor followed by a horde of aides. Everybody rose and said, 'Good morning, Governor,' and then when the meeting was over the phalanx sort of surrounded him and took him out. There wasn't much of a chance to just chat. That changed after the election."

LARRY POPE "I think Branstad as lieutenant governor wanted to get as close to Governor Ray as he could. But he was never part of the crowd, certainly not a Bob Ray man, no little flag pin."

STEVE ROBERTS "Terry Branstad's transition was a breeze. He kept many of Bob Ray's key people, and that's a big thing. If you've got a guy that is competent at running the Department of Revenue or the Department of Public Instruction, you don't have to worry about that for the time being. The condition of the economy wasn't that great, but the condition of the governor's office was good."

BOB RAY "Today the new governor comes in, has a four-year term, has the hearings all set for the budget process, has a staff in place, and even if he didn't show up that first day, the office would run smoothly for a while. He didn't have to worry about the notary publics, didn't have to worry about interviewing people, didn't have to worry about what appointments had to be made, or when. Remember, we had to thumb through the code just to see what positions we had to fill, and then we had to try to find out who was on the boards. Now they push a button and it all comes up on a screen.

"A lot of people felt that I was a little more part of the planning for the new governor than I was. I was willing to do anything, but my executive assistant, Dave Oman, was the liaison, and I think Terry accepted that as my participation. I think that helped the transition, but it sure didn't make it easy for me to get out of the office. I wasn't envious of Terry's easy transition. That was one thing I wanted to leave behind, an office that could run even if he weren't there. What I hadn't counted on was that that would happen before I left."

SUE MITSCHKE "David Oman was the real link between the two, but he was really working more for Branstad than Governor Ray in those last couple months."

DAVID OMAN "Governor Branstad approached me about three weeks after the election. I was looking at some other opportunities, and then he asked Ron Mosher, the comptroller, and Doug Gross, the legislative liaison, and me to stay. We talked about it one weekend and agreed to do it. But I knew that things would be different and that I wouldn't start out with the same rapport that I had built up over eight years working for Governor Ray. I wasn't really sure of what to expect.

"It wasn't easy on me. I was trying to shuttle back and forth between the two of them, still doing my work as his [*Ray's*] executive assistant and handling the ongoing daily chores, plus taking some responsibility for trying to wrap up the loose ends of the administration, and then work with the new governor on the budget, his legislative program, his inaugural message, his early appointments, his staffing, and I just felt torn apart. I literally had two schedules, a Ray schedule in one pocket and Branstad's in the other. I spent sixty days trying to work for both of them, and there were times I was scheduled to be with both at the same time.

"That was a very difficult time for me. It was hard for Governor Ray and it was hard for me, and we probably didn't spend enough time talking about it and defining what was going to happen. It created some difficult moments. Loyalty is very important to Bob Ray. We've talked about it subsequently, and I think he understands that I did what I felt I had to do."

JANE MITCHELL "The Branstad people were real wary of David. They weren't sure about trusting him, because he was a holdover from Bob Ray, and I think there was a certain amount of animosity. Bob Ray did not exactly welcome the transition with open arms, and I think David got caught in between. Bob Ray felt as though David had deserted him and gone to the enemy camp, so to speak, and of course the enemy camp thought, 'Well, he's a Bob Ray holdover and everything is going to be reported back to Bob Ray.' "

BOB RAY "One thing that was troublesome was that once I made the decision not to run, I wanted to help Republicans get elected, and then I wanted to take the last couple of months and just really clean things up, make it the best transition you could ever have. What really happened was that we had as good a transition as you could have, but the key staff members that Terry wanted to keep literally went to work for him. I took box after box after box of correspondence, an overwhelming amount, out of the office. Some states provide money for the governor going out and some staff. We were provided nothing. Fortunately, Susie [*Mitschke*] was there, but it took us six months to get it all cleaned up, correspondence done.

"I thought those last few days in office I'd have a great time saying good-bye to my friends, people I'd appointed, and what have you. As it was, we were still packing boxes up until that last night, just to get out in time."

DAVID OMAN "My sense is that he had a tough time giving the office up. He worked at the job right up until the last hour, still dictating mail, trying to organize the paperwork that he would take with him, and getting some of the files put together, getting mementos boxed up. He was there until well after midnight on inauguration day getting the office straightened up and his personal items out of there. Then he was in the next morning, finishing, putting the final touches on it.

"The morning of the inauguration was very sad, both for the aides and the secretaries, who were really struggling with their emotions. A lot of us broke down and cried, it was almost like there'd been a death in the family. People were going in and saying their good-byes, one by one, before going down to Vets for the swearing in. He was very stoic throughout. He thanked people and shook hands. He stayed in control, right up until the end."

CAROL DUNCAN "I left at noon and it was Governor Ray's office, went to the swearing in, came back, and it was Governor Branstad's office. It was a very emotional day. Remember, I'd been there all fourteen years. It was sad to see Governor Ray sit in his chair for the last time and know that when you came back he wasn't going to be there. And I think it was hard for him, too. He kind of dragged his feet, leaving things in the upstairs office, in the cabinets, until the last minute."

SUE MITSCHKE "After the inauguration we went to Garcia's and had lunch, just the family, really, and stopped later and had some ice cream. It was almost a relief. If you've ever lost anybody close to you, you know you're almost happy for the funeral to be over, because that's the finality of it. But there was a sense of loss, too, a void, an emptiness."

RANDI RAY WATSON "As he headed off for Washington after the inaugural, my mother kept asking him if he had any money, any credit cards. He hadn't carried those things for years. She used to say if she died, we'd all be in trouble. It was a big deal when he got a money clip."

BILLIE RAY "There was a sense of excitement about leaving, though. That first night back in our house on California Drive, it was neat not to have anybody else in the house the next morning. No help coming in, no troopers waiting, no rush to get down to the office.

"We had prepared ourselves. I had begun moving things back to the house the previous spring. We kept thinking we'd go through some sort of depression and tried to anticipate what it would be like. But the first morning after we left Terrace Hill it was so nice to get up and have breakfast in our own dining room and know that you didn't have the office downstairs."

BOB RAY "So many of my colleagues had told us about the terrible decompression they'd gone through. Even people who'd never been in office said that too. I honestly didn't think that would happen to me, but I didn't know. But I really never ever looked back. I never said, 'Wish I could make that decision again,' or, 'Gee, I'd like to be there today,' or 'I really miss walking into that old office.' Not one moment. But when I look back, that has kind of been the story of my life. I've enjoyed what I've done and welcomed the opportunity to do what I've done, but I can't remember any time when I said, 'Wow, I wish I could be back doing that again.' "

BILLIE RAY "All in all, I think we had a pretty good time . . ."

BOB RAY " . . . but let me tell you, public housing is just not like being in your own home. About three days before we left, we went over to our house on California Drive, boxes all over the place. We had to push boxes off the dining room table to eat. Your [*Billie's*] mother cooked for us, and we sat there and had a little dinner, and I thought it was like heaven. It's not that Terrace Hill wasn't nice, and it wasn't that sitting at that big table wasn't alright, but it certainly wasn't like being at home. We really had a feeling that we had come home."

XXX: THE FUTURE AND JEPSEN III

L ess than two weeks after leaving office in 1983 Bob Ray ended the "What will the governor do now?" smalltalk that had occupied cafes and newsrooms across the state for the previous year by taking over as chief executive officer of Life Investors Insurance Company in Cedar Rapids. The Dutch-owned insurance company was willing to pay top dollar (with an estimated total in excess of $300,000 annually in salary, perks, and stock) to attract Iowa's best-known name, luring the ex-governor outside Des Moines for the first time in almost thirty years.

He, with Billie's constant consultation, considered going back into law with a couple of old Des Moines friends, Art Davis or David Belin, and their big firms, but he'd been away from casebooks and courtrooms for long enough that he was afraid he'd end up a figurehead. He'd also looked at administrative offers from the American Red Cross, the Preferred Risk Insurance Company in West Des Moines (run by his friend Bernard Mercer), a Des Moines development group, and several others. If he had wanted to go to Washington in some capacity, as a judge, an ambassador, or an administrator, something suitable could have been found. But he opted for the challenge and the Iowa base of the Life Investors (where he eventually brought state comptroller Ron Mosher on as chief financial officer). He and Billie concurred that it would be easier being close to Des Moines, where they visit frequently and keep their California Drive home, but off the streets of their hometown, where they would be easier marks for comments and commitments.

Even though he seems challenged by and satisfied with the job he has, Bob Ray's name surfaces for virtually every top-level job that comes up in

Bob Ray and Frosty Mitchell. *Des Moines Register* photo. Reprinted with permission.

Iowa, as well as many national positions. The most intriguing and tempting to date was the presidency of his alma mater, Drake University. If the timing had been better, if Wilbur Miller had announced his plans to resign sooner, when Bob Ray was job hunting, that would have been tough to turn down. Going back to Drake and the neighborhood where he grew up would have been a coup for Ray, and he remains one of the university's biggest public boosters and most noted graduates, and he sits on the board of trustees. But Ray is nothing if not loyal, and he'd been on the job at Life Investors less than two years, so the Drake job came and went.

He has been mentioned as a candidate for the U.S. Senate (most prominently when it was revealed prior to the 1984 elections that Roger Jepsen had spent some time in a Des Moines massage parlor in the 1970s, a mistake he acknowledged and apologized for), the presidency of Iowa State University, a federal judgeship, and for positions as a U.S. trade representative, the secretary of agriculture, and the secretary of transportation. One job he did accept was a three-month stint as special assistant to UN chief delegate Jeanne Kirkpatrick late in 1984. A presidential appointment, Ray was promoted for the job by his friend and aspiring presidential candidate Vice-President George Bush. His experience has also been tapped as a testimonial-letter writer by various Iowa Republicans running for office, as an adviser to a group seeking a horse track in Cedar Rapids, as an arbitrator between two Cedar Rapids hospitals and as head of a sister-state committee with Yucatán, Japan, and Iowa. In mid-1986 Ray and Frosty Mitchell headed a group of investors who bought WMT Radio in Cedar Rapids. He is international chairman of the Friendship Force, headed a State Department select panel on refugees, and in early 1987 was offered the job as director of AID, the Agency for International Development, by Secretary of State George Shultz. He is on the board of directors of Maytag, Iowa Electric, and Drake University. He has also continued a full schedule of ground breaking, grand marshalling, award presenting, and ice cream judging. If you didn't know better, you'd think he was running for something.

Have we seen the last of candidate Ray? "I participated in my own last campaign in 1978. But if I ever wanted to run again, I could get revved up and excited. I get asked frequently if I will, mostly out of kindness. Frankly, I think that's just a friendly gesture. People say, 'We miss you,' or 'Sure wish you were governor.' They're just trying to be kind." Those close to him admit that it is sometimes hard for him to keep quiet on issues around the state, but for the time being, especially as long as a fellow-Republican occupies the statehouse's lower office, he tries to maintain his position as a quiet elder statesman.

BOB RAY "I watched a little of a recent governors' conference. Those were wonderful experiences. As a matter of fact, I can remember going to one in Florida before I was elected governor and thinking, 'Wow, wouldn't this be something, to have the opportunity to associate with these people, represent your state.' We went out to one in Lake Tahoe soon after, and I thought the same thing, even before I was a candidate. Then I got elected, went to an awful lot of governors' conferences, chaired them. They were great experiences, but I looked at that one today and I thought, 'Wow, I'm glad I'm not there.'

Ever wish you were still up there, at the statehouse? "I was over at the capitol a couple weeks ago, up in the rotunda. It was pretty hard to get very far without stopping to talk to somebody, shake a hand. But every session you have different problems. They have problems up there now because so many people want to be governor. They're afraid of alienating people. But that probably wouldn't make any difference if I were there or not. You'd probably have the same situation."

CYNTHIA HENDERSON "Billie comes to all the Terrace Hill Authority meetings, and we laugh and kid about what's going on these days. She always comes in, greets the old staff. The first time she came to a meeting was funny. When people come to meetings they usually come in through the basement door, sign in, and she did that just like everybody else. I said, 'You didn't have to do that.' 'Why not?' she said, 'I'm going to do like the rest of them.' Of course, the security guards were just paralyzed. She just parked on the street and walked up the drive and through the basement.

"She thought she would really miss it, have a funny feeling when she drove by Terrace Hill. But she said one day soon after they left office she drove by and just smiled all the way."

BILLIE RAY "There's an external pressure that's there even if you don't think it's there. I could see a lot of relief in Bob after he left office. He didn't know the insurance business, but as he learned it he wasn't being written up in the press for his not learning fast enough or something. He could do it at his own pace.

"I really don't miss the job, though. We're not traveling on twenty-four-hour-a-day business; we have more time to ourselves. I enjoyed going all the places I went with Bob and being at the various functions and meeting all the people we did, but it got to be so constant that you just wished for a day off or a night off. Now I can get up in the morning and not have to be anywhere until two in the afternoon.

"One thing that surprises me is that people are still very thoughtful, very kind. They still give us a lot of respect. Bob is looked at as someone to consult with or to be involved with. To a lot of people he's still governor as far as their respect goes."

BOB RAY "People think, 'Gee, how do you adjust, not having a driver and all that?' The only thing I miss is my parking space. It was nice to have a trooper drive you, but I like to drive. I could have bought Number One [*the governor's limousine*] and hired a driver if I wanted. We could have a cook, an aide."

BILLIE RAY "He had good offers from law firms, but he'd have really had to reschool himself. He wanted to try something new. So he had a choice of doing something in government, but he really didn't want that unless it was something he just couldn't pass up. One thing that might have tempted him was being ambassador to Japan, though it was not offered. But we agreed that that would be a great honor, but in three months after you've gotten used to Tokyo, you find yourself in a foreign country away from all your friends and relatives.

"So he decided he'd really like to be a CEO. He had several opportunities, and we didn't think we'd move out of Des Moines. We decided, why not Cedar Rapids? We'd never lived more than five miles from our home in Des Moines anyway."

BOB RAY "We'd made up our minds that we didn't want to leave Iowa, but we never said we wouldn't. If something had been just perfect, we would have considered it. We didn't know of anything in Washington, even though we'd been asked if there was anything there we might like. Being an ambassador had some appeal if it had been to Japan. But that wasn't open, and it would have been necessary to get in line somewhere else."

VERNE LAWYER "You have to keep in mind that when he first ran for governor the assumption was he would get elected the first time, run again, get elected the second time, and then come back and practice law. That was sort of the game plan. Then the world changed, and there always seemed like there was something else to be done.

"But I had told him that if he ever left the office and wanted to come back and practice law, the office, the desk, everything would be there. And it was. We didn't even clean it out until after he went with Life Investors.

"If Bob Ray had devoted the same energy and the same drive and devotion to the law practice as he devoted to the governorship, he would be a million-dollar-a-year lawyer and be nationally known."

BOB RAY "I think the law firms saw me as kind of an arbitrator. At first they thought I might bring in some business, but whether I did or not, I would be able to negotiate when other methods didn't work. They'd be able to bring clients in and I'd try and resolve disputes. Plus I would have contacts with people in and out of government. That was kind of intriguing, and I also had three or four corporate offers, so my big decision was, do I want to try and use whatever administrative skills or talents I might have had or developed as a CEO or do I want to practice law?

"At first I thought that practicing law and sitting on boards would give me a lot more freedom, and I didn't want to be tied down. Since I'd been out of college I'd never had to work under somebody, except, of course, the three million Iowans I had to answer to, but I was still the boss. The more I thought about it, the less freedom I thought I'd have. Nobody was going to pay me that kind of money without me working for it, even though I'd have some flexibility of time. Then about the time I got my teeth into an issue or a case, I'd have to pack my bags and fly off to a board meeting somewhere. So that didn't sound like I'd be all that free. Maybe I'd have a better life as a CEO. Once I made that decision, it wasn't very difficult to decide on Life Investors. It was a growth company in a kind of exciting business, for the moment. For twenty-two years before I came in, Life Investors hadn't had an opening. The timing was just right.

"Ironically, I had met the Dutch people before, on a trip Billie and I took to Holland. Tom Collins, chairman of the board here in Cedar Rapids, had written me previously asking if I would be interested in one of several positions, but he was really thinking about this job. I hadn't even answered his letter. Well, I'd dictated it, but it was part of the backlog of stuff that didn't get done during my transition."

DICK GILBERT "I'm not sure Bob Ray would be happy in politics again. I think he'll always be interested, just like Joe Montana will probably stay interested in football all his life. But whether he'd come out of retirement to pass the football again after retirement, I doubt it."

FROSTY MITCHELL "I've always had a feeling that prize fighters and politicians shouldn't come out of retirement. They should just quit and stay out. Had Bob stayed right in there, I think he was unbeatable. But once you take that step back, some of the legend changes."

KEN QUINN "It's an enormous sacrifice to come back into the public sector in terms of money, but Bob Ray has a lot of loyalty to the country, and if some great challenge came along, he'd think about it. If Howard Baker or George Bush was president in 1989 and asked him to be secretary of state, he'd think about it."

HAROLD HUGHES "I could even live with Bob Ray as president, because I think he's smarter than Reagan. He knows better what the directions would be, and I think he's more sensitive to the needs of the people. I don't think Reagan has that capacity.

"The problem that Bob Ray will have is that everybody in the fucking state will want to make a whore of him now. How do you avoid this, guys like me and him. On the whole, people are unconscionable, and they'll use you if they can. Everybody in the world wants a piece of your act.

"I stayed out of the state to avoid this shit, and when I came back they descended on me. I must still get twenty to thirty requests a week, and I haven't run in a political race in sixteen years. I've gotten pretty good at saying no to people."

BOB RAY "I don't dislike being an ex-governor, but I agree with Harold. Sometimes people expect you to come out and speak to them, at your expense and on your time, just like it used to be when you were a public servant. I don't really complain about that – well, I might under my breath, but it's really complimentary. What they don't understand, and you don't try and explain it to them, is that you've got to make a living.

"Hughes limits his appearances by asking for an honorarium. But what really bothers me is people write and say, 'We would be able to pay an honorarium if requested.' Or one wrote, 'Will pay a $500 honorarium, but you'll probably want to give that to the United Nations Association.' And I think, 'That's not someone else's business.' If I want to give it to a charity, I'll give it to charity of my choice.

"If I could accept very many, I'd have requests by the hundreds. But you have to get good at saying no. It's the same problem I had when I was in office. There are so many events I'd like to accept, because you feel some empathy for the poor program chairman, or maybe it's a friend who's helped you in the past or somebody who works for my company or at some school where you have a particular interest."

BILLIE RAY "I think that's why there was no decompression after he left office. There's the same mail and requests coming in. If you left office and nobody ever said anything to you, I think you might feel a little lost."

BOB RAY *What happens if they stop calling?* "I don't know. I have mixed emotions about that. It's nice to be wanted, and every once in a while I think, whether I want to go or not, if I quit going, pretty soon I'll get in a place where I never have the chance, and I don't know if I want to get in that position. At the same time, when I say yes today and then two weeks from now I'll be in a hurry, won't have anything prepared, no one to do any research for me, and I start thinking about what am I going to say, I get mad at myself. I get in the car, travel someplace, and I think, 'Why am I doing this?' Or 'Where is this place, anyway?'

"One guy helped me a little bit. He does a time management course and I'd taken it before. He wanted to come and talk to me about doing one for the company. I told him I'd like to, but that I really didn't have the time. I told him that I was having a problem because I was still taking outside invitations and I'd like to stop, but I feel obligated to some people. He said, 'Look, you were in office fourteen years. You gave them all of your time for almost no money. You don't owe them anything.' And every once in a while, when I get thinking about how I ought to do something for somebody, I think of that.

"The UN opportunity was different, I really wanted to accept that. I was told the vice-president wanted to visit with me on one of his trips to the state. We visited, he offered the job, and I honestly had little idea what the job was. But I found it fascinating. It gave me a perspective that not everybody sees, reminds you that our country is just a spot on the globe. There are a lot of other countries, and people, out there."

BILL CREWS "The FBI called me to check on Mary Ann Brown, who was going to work for George Bush in the vice-president's office. It was a new guy who called, and in the next breath he told me he was checking up on another guy, Robert Ray, who was going to the UN, and did I know anything about him. I sent the governor a note and said I was really beginning to feel for the future of the country if they needed to do a security check on Bob Ray."

FROSTY MITCHELL "They hired Bob to run the company, not sell insurance. But I'll bet once he got to the UN he was selling it there. I can hear it now. 'Yeah, I sold a policy over in Africa. Got a group deal for a tribe over there.'"

GEORGE BUSH "Given his demonstrated interest in world affairs and given his breadth and vision, he was a natural for the UN appointment – one of the most prestigious a president can make. And from all reports he did a first-class job in New York advocating our foreign policy objectives and making friends from foreign lands in the process."

GEORGE WITTGRAF "There is no question but George Bush has made a very concerted effort to continue to promote Bob Ray's involvement in government. He was impressed with Bob Ray as a person, with Bob Ray's abilities and success as governor. The two most substantial things he's done are including the Rays in the trip to the Philippines for President Marcos's inauguration and then single-handedly promoting Bob Ray for the UN.

"Endorsement politics don't mean a great deal in any state, and may mean less in Iowa than in some other states, as has been proven in the past. But still, everybody would like to have Bob Ray in their corner in any future political contest, whether it involves the presidency, the Senate, the governorship, whatever. But I don't think that his involvement, particularly if it's principally an endorsement, makes very much difference. Whether you're running for senator, governor, or president, you've got to go out and organize across the ninety-nine counties, and you've got to do that with or without Bob Ray being in your corner."

GEORGE BUSH "Clearly, anyone running in Iowa would welcome Bob Ray's support. No question about that."

STEVE ROBERTS "There is a big difference between the styles of Bob Ray and Terry Branstad, almost night and day. I was on the stage in 1983 at the Lincoln Day dinner, and Bob Ray and Terry Branstad were both up there too. Branstad's trooper left him and started covering Bob Ray. That left Branstad alone on the podium, and he just jumped down and started talking to some people. Bob Ray never stayed late at anything. He came late and left early, and you were always left wanting more. Branstad's the last one there, helping pick up. He'll come to events he doesn't even need to. That's a matter of style, but it also shows how Ray created that certain mystique."

DON AVENSON "I've had some interesting conversations with Bob Ray since he left office. We had the centennial of the capitol in 1984, and it was one of the most interesting days I've spent there. All of the former governors were there. I'm sitting on the platform with all of them, and Hughes gave a speech that didn't make much sense, didn't have much content, but which brought tears to people's eyes. Terry Branstad gave his speech pitching the World Trade Center. Then Bob Ray gave a speech, his standard Bob Ray speech, and crushed between those two guys, Hughes and Ray, Branstad looked like a little kid.

"Then Governor Robert Blue gave a speech, and he went on and on and on. Halfway through, Ray leans over to me and says, 'Just think, Avenson, it could have been ten years of him instead of ten with me.' He and

Hughes are back there cracking jokes. It was one of the funniest moments I've ever spent with those people. They were laughing about each other."

JANET VAN NOTE "Bob would love to just relax. He's silly, he's funny, he's got a good sense of humor. I see him wishing someday he could just say 'Who cares?' Just be able to say, 'Why does everybody care what I do? What gives me this little pedestal and makes everybody expect things out of me?' "

In one of the more confounding political endorsements in recent Iowa history, Bob Ray served as honorary chairman of Roger Jepsen's 1984 reelection campaign for the U.S. Senate. Jepsen's six-year tenure had not been marked by distinction, and politicians across the state, Republican and Democratic, were surprised by Ray's involvement with the Jepsen campaign in a hotly contested battle with Congressman Tom Harkin. In June, Ray made some watered-down testimonial television commercials to support "his candidate," but come November, Ray's presence was not felt. When Jepsen desperately could have used the prominence of some last-minute statewide public hand holding by Bob Ray, much as he'd done to help Roger get elected in 1978, the former governor was at the United Nations in New York City, far from Iowa's voting booths.

DEL VAN HORN "How in the world Bob Ray let himself not only endorse him but be his honorary chairman I'll never figure out. Sometime I'll ask Bob Ray that, because he compromised himself there, one of the few times I've ever seen him compromise himself. From day one, even before Jepsen started to threaten running against him back in 1972, Bob Ray did not think Jepsen was trustworthy. He didn't like his style."

ART NEU "I was on the phone to him soon after he'd come out as Roger's honorary chairman, and I started to needle him about it, told him he had a short memory, and he cut me off. He said, 'I don't care. He's better than the alternative. That's the ultimate argument.' "

STEVE ROBERTS "Nobody would have ever believed that Bob Ray would help Jepsen walk across the street and, my gosh, here he is in his inner circle of advisers."

HAROLD HUGHES "If I were in Bob Ray's position with Roger Jepsen, I would probably do the same thing but do as little of it as possible."

DON JOHNSON "It didn't take much discussion to decide that the place Bob Ray could do the best job was to be chairman of the strategy committee, in the top of the so-called kitchen cabinet. And when Roger had that PR problem in the middle of the campaign, Bob was the first from Iowa to call."

ROBB KELLEY "When Jepsen got in trouble [*mid-year 1984 a radio report linked Jepsen to a Des Moines massage parlor*], people were really upset. Jepsen wanted to know what he should do, and some of us flew up to Waterloo to consult him. There was a rumor that Jepsen might resign, and people were trying to get Bob Ray to run for the Senate, or maybe Congressman Jim Leach. Bob Ray was there, Roger and Dee, Joan Lipsky, about seven or eight people altogether. They gave Jepsen some suggestions on how to handle himself, and Bob Ray talked to Jepsen pretty well, in a clear manner. He didn't try to be abrasive, he just simply said, 'Now, here's the way you should proceed from here on,' which was good advice.

"The funny thing was, here we were working for Jepsen, and in the past he'd been the villain. You have to hand it to Governor Ray for what he did in that situation. He'd had some phone calls from people wanting him to run. Yet he kept his cool, figured things would pass, and he'd have looked like a damn fool if he made a move or let anybody make a move for him. He knew; he'd been in politics a long time."

MARVIN SELDEN "It was a little hard for me to see how Bob Ray could endorse Jepsen. They tell me that Ray was one of those that flew up to advise Jepsen after the massage parlor story broke. Maybe that's how you build party loyalty, but I would have thought Bob Ray would have just let the son of a bitch get what was coming to him."

ART NEU "There's a measure of hypocrisy there that you just can't get away from as a politician. I remember going in and campaigning in some legislative districts where there was an incumbent Republican legislator running and wondering how they found their way back home every week from Des Moines. But you'd put your arm around them anyway and say, 'Herman here is a great man, he's represented you well. I like Herman, send him back,' even though he'd opposed us on major issues 50 percent of the time."

STEVE ROBERTS "I don't think you'll find any Jepsen person or conservative or anyone that will not say Bob Ray did his fair share. He could have just said, 'Hey, I'm in private business now, I'm done.' "

ROGER JEPSEN "I consider Bob Ray one of my most valued friends. I'm not going to say he's the best friend I have, but he's among them. He was very supportive and helpful in my last campaign. He was a true soldier who got right down, side by side, and supported me. He had nothing to gain by that, in 1984. The race in 1978 was the start in the change of our relationship, and one of the reasons was that we didn't have any staff to get between us."

BOB RAY "Roger initially asked if I would chair his committee. I didn't feel I could do that. I said I would be supportive and do what I could and so ended up being honorary chairman. I wasn't responsible for the campaign but available and free to help him. I wrote some letters and gave him a little advice on several occasions.

"I felt strongly that the choices were pretty clear, and this was a far better choice than Harkin. A lot of people in that campaign took the position that they didn't like either one of the candidates and they weren't going to vote for either one. It was a campaign where a lot of people said they were going to support the lesser of two evils. Regardless of the reasons, I didn't want to see the Republicans lose that seat, and I thought Roger would give us better representation for what I thought was good for Iowans and the country. I don't want you to think that you should vote for somebody just because of a party label, but I thought if the Senate was going to keep Republican control, if the president, whom I don't always agree with either, was going to get anything done, he was going to need the support that Roger would give him and that Tom would not.

"I think Roger convinced himself that it was God's will that he lost, that it was meant to be. But even during the campaign he left the impression with lots of people that his mind wasn't really concentrating. Fortunately for Roger, he could rationalize the reasons for losing in 1984 – the economy, the farm situation, and the *Register,* which I think he frankly does have a reasonable complaint against. But take all that together and it still doesn't compensate for some of the things Roger did over the six years."

XXXI:
THE LEGACY

<u>JOHN McDONALD</u> "He's a phenomenon in this state. There's no telling how long he could have been governor. That'll die down eventually, but I think he could easily have been elected two more times."

<u>GIL CRANBERG</u> "Why was he so successful? He did well because his appeal was beyond just Republicans. Independents, Democrats, all flocked to him, in part because of his middle-of-the-road, moderately progressive positions. The conservative Republicans didn't have any place else to go, so they had to vote for him. And part of his success was his personality. There was nothing abrasive about him; he was in sync with the mood, the outlook, the values of the people. Every now and then somebody like that comes along, but not often."

Des Moines Register photo. Reprinted with permission.

STEVE ROBERTS "Bob Ray was the kind of guy that *should* have been treated like the imperial governor, he was that good. The United States sometimes longs for a king, despite the fact we revolted against one from England. We want our leaders to be human like the rest of us, but we also like for them to have that charisma, that aura of nobility. Bob Ray made you proud to be an Iowan, proud to be part of the process. They were exciting times in Iowa, a great time to live here. I think the same kind of atmosphere prevailed under Harold Hughes. We had twenty years where we just had giants for governors."

HAROLD HUGHES "The governor's office can be used as a tool of great change and great good if the person in the office has got the sensitivity and ability to do that. Bob had that, he had a good heart. You can have a good heart, but if you don't have the skills, it won't make any difference. You have to have the combination."

DAVID YEPSEN *How much of Ray's 'Good government is good politics' adage is just rhetoric?* "I think that's probably true in Iowa. Outside of Chicago, there's kind of a midwestern civic pride in the ethics of their governors and leaders. You know, the ice-cream governor, the vanilla governor. That squeaky clean image of Iowa politicians existed before Bob Ray, but he capitalized on that, strengthened it. That doesn't mean they're not political; they just don't operate out in the open. People around Iowa won't tolerate hints of scandal, or even stuff that's legal but morally wrong. Ray insisted on good, solid, stable, clean government."

JERRY MURSENER "If Bob Ray entered politics today, I'm not sure he could get elected. Politics have evolved quite a bit since 1968, and the Ray Girls and red-and-yellow convertibles and those kinds of things might not work for him. He had this nice easygoing, nice-guy image, promoted extensively by Dick Redman, Walt Shotwell, and his rah-rah, hoopla-filled campaigns. They fit Ray's image, and people were looking for that back then. Now people are pretty cynical about politics and politicians, and I'm not sure that a Ray campaign with all that hoopla could work. Stoner tried it in 1980 and it just didn't work. Dick Redman gave it a little run when he ran for Congress in 1984 and it didn't work. Ray was there at the right time."

MELVIN SYNHORST "I don't see that as a period of any radical change, although I think there was a trend towards greater concentration of power in the office of the chief executive. I think Bob Ray had a very successful career. He was good for Iowa, and I think the record establishes that he was a man of great integrity. Government expanded tremendously during that period. We went from hand bookkeeping into computerization."

<u>DICK GILBERT</u>   "We've all been so preoccupied with power in state government that we forget to identify where the responsibility is. The responsibility, and the willingness to assume it, is what really drives state government. The legislature today is damn near powerless because they don't seem to be able to shoulder responsibility collectively. The governor doesn't seem to have a lot of power now because he has not been able to articulate his direction, his plan. The bureaucracy has more of what you call power because no one is willing to assume the responsibility.

"Ray was considered a powerful governor because he was willing to take the responsibility to make things happen. That's one of the reasons his staff had to work so hard, because he'd say, 'I will do this. I will make that happen.' All the way from details about citizens' complaints up to restructuring government. You don't get power by just waving your hands around; you get power by giving it away and delegating responsibility to various people, and that's how Ray ruled. Hughes did the same thing. Today there is no one person with that kind of power. There are factions of some small, strong bodies in the bureaucracy, but no leader.

"Bob Ray staunchly, to the point of stubbornly and vigorously, defended the role of the executive in state government. He protected that office, and he could get away with it because he was seen as an honest guy. He defined new parameters of the job, and now you have to be a pretty big person to do the job because of those parameters. He also defined the places he didn't want the legislature or the judiciary to go. Relations between the legislature, the judicial branch, and the governor's office under Branstad are much easier. Bob Ray kept a very strong tension going between the three houses, and he understood how the system works. Sometimes it would have been easier to give in, but he was very jealous and guarded the authority of the executive."

<u>HAROLD HUGHES</u>   "One thing Bob did that was very wise was to never just put things down because the other party came up with an idea. He carried them out, completed them, and used them as building blocks. He was constructive. He could see the road I was trying to travel and not only continued it, he expanded on it, added to it, and came up with new ideas, new thoughts. That's what good government is all about."

<u>ART NEU</u>   "Structurally, the office is still a weak executive, except for some changes like the four-year term. But I think it was the sheer force of

Ray's personality, and that of Hughes, that made the office that of a pretty strong chief executive. They proved you could make a strong office if you handle it right."

TOM STONER "Ray made the governor's office an activist place. The legislature would prefer to initiate the bills and simply allow the governor to decide which ones he would sign. They don't want the governor to be motivating programs over their heads. But the Department of Transportation, for example, was 100 percent a Bob Ray deal, and it rattled the rafters of a lot of conservatives in the legislature."

JIM FLANSBURG "He was a damn decent governor, did a damn decent job, but he just continued a trend. I know goddam well if Bobby Fulton had been in there, the same thing would have happened. I think if Franzenburg had been in there, the same thing would have happened. A lot of change in government is evolutionary, not due to the people who were there at the time. Nothing in government happens at the whim of one man."

BOB FULTON "When people thirty years from now look at what happened during the Hughes and Ray administrations, they'll just see a continuation of the same modernization. So for us Democrats to get mad at Bob Ray, guess who we'd have to get mad at?

"Leo Hoegh was the first governor to bring the message that we had to modernize state government. The legislature never forgave him for that. Then Loveless continued that by some of his appointments. He brought very, very good people to boards and commissions, who remained very loyal to him. Harold did it with his strength of personality. Bob Ray continued, using his administrative skills. But by the time Bob got there the governorship was quite strengthened. He furthered that, but the structure was already in place. Hughes had reorganized the Department of Social Services and the Department of Revenue, and the directors of both were appointed by the governor. The liquor commission was reorganized. We also passed several amendments to the state constitution which were adopted in 1968 – the item veto, annual sessions, reducing the legislature to 150 members. The four-year term was voted on but delayed until 1972."

FLOYD MILLEN "Hughes really started the changes when he set up the Office [for] Planning and Programming. That's the first time the governor ever had a staff of paid people doing work for him. When Hughes set it up we [*the legislature*] fought it, and we thought Ray would abolish it. Instead, it's gotten bigger, and the answer was always that we had to have it because of all the federal programs we had to administer. It has become a very powerful arm of the governor's office. Hughes made it and Ray enhanced it."

MELVIN SYNHORST "When I first went into government [*in 1949*] they rented a couple buildings downtown, had the State Capitol Building and the State Historical Building and an old converted warehouse called the Harvester Building. That was all there was of the capitol complex. Now they've built all those huge buildings and filled them to the gills and overflowing, and they're still renting all over the place. I've never quite understood why it was necessary, all those places filled with people gathering statistics and facts and figures. Part of that mushrooming was generated by the federal government, because they had all these funding programs, and the state got kind of blackmailed into doing certain things to qualify for the money. And instead of abandoning them after federal funding ran out, they just continued. I don't think these are all useless appendages, but I think they could be cut way back."

MINNETTE DODERER "A winner, that's what you have to call Bob Ray, as a politician. Because he never, ever let anything go by that would have hurt him in the long run. He never did. A slight, messages that said something about him that he didn't like, mentions in the paper that he didn't like. He never hired anyone or even appointed anyone without saying, 'If you disagree with me, all I ask is that you come to me first, before you go to the press.' His bases were always carefully attended to. As a consequence, I think we put up for too long with some inadequate administrators, because people were not willing to speak out about incompetency."

ED CAMPBELL "Ray had one unique quality throughout the course of his terms. He knew how to politically intimidate people, including the *Register*. A lot of people didn't realize that he had a real killer instinct, which I think he found he had in him when he was state party chair. A very hard, tough, vindictive guy. Very thin-skinned.

"He was not the kind of nice guy the press made him out to be. He could play hardball, protected his flanks, and if you fucked with him, that was it. I worked in the governor's office under Hughes, and let me tell you something. Ray used to brag about all those long hours he spent in the office. If he was spending seven days, twenty-four hours a day, at the job, he didn't know how to run it. All that going back to the office late at night, working over pizza and ice cream—that was great public relations, but that was all."

CLARK RASMUSSEN "Invariably he'd come in from a trip and take the press over to his office at ten o'clock at night and work until midnight or two o'clock. Good politics. Maybe he had a lot of work to do, I don't know. But it was damn good politics."

GEORGE KINLEY "He had the power of intimidation—if you said anything critical of him, you knew he'd be on the phone to you, asking you why you were criticizing him. That made you think twice before you said anything about him. Maybe that was sharp of him, I don't know. It wasn't a physical intimidation, but it was just enough to make you think twice. For most people that was enough. You've got to admire him for that."

MINNETTE DODERER "Bob Ray changed our form of government, and he did it for too long. He had it so good with the *Des Moines Register,* for too long. And he was so good that whenever they even hinted or threatened him, he'd get his staff down there or get himself down there and talk things out. I don't think they realized how much they were controlled by him. They certainly won't admit that, and I don't blame them. They essentially agreed with him is what it amounted to.

"We limped along for fourteen long years saying, 'The best thing we can do for Iowa is not raise taxes,' and 'The best thing we can do for Iowa is make do with what we have.' I remember Bob Ray saying exactly that many times. But whenever there was a new responsibility that he wanted to take on, I'd look around and there it would be.

"Look at the Office [*for*] Planning and Programming, which is directly under him, and how it grew. I've got to hand it to him, he was very skillful."

BOB FULTON "The only thing I really fault him for was keeping the job so long. Staying in that job for fourteen years shows a certain character weakness. Not a bad one, but a serious one. If you stay in office that long, what happens to you personally becomes more important than what happens to the structure. There's just no way around it. You stay in office that many years and you begin to start accommodating to perpetuate yourself. And despite the fact he had such huge popularity, he didn't seem to take many risks, again to perpetuate himself."

DONALD KAUL "I wrote a column for at least twelve years of his governorship, and I seldom was able to write about Bob Ray, and I loved to write about politicians. But he would hardly ever present you with a target. He'd be around the corner, give you a shoulder, and he'd leave. And occasionally he'd reappear, basically on the right side of an issue – capital punishment, which he was against, for example. He just never got very far out on a limb. He truly refined the politics of caution to an art. I suppose that's alright, but I regret that he didn't do more in a substantive way."

KEN JERNIGAN "No matter what you might say about Franklin Roosevelt, he at least knew what he wanted to do and set about doing it and got it done. And people loved him – or hated him. How many people do you know who hate Bob Ray? If somebody doesn't hate you, you've got problems if you want to be a leader. Start with every leader you ever heard of – Jesus Christ, Napoleon, Martin Luther King, Franklin Roosevelt. You can find people who detested them with violent passion. You don't find anybody who hates Bob Ray."

JERRY THORNTON "We seem to have a nature of people in Iowa who run for office who feel the most important thing is to get along with people instead of being constructive, taking risks. Bob Ray did an adequate job of running the state. He never did anything until he had an absolute consensus on an issue. That's quite evident and not a criticism. But he stayed in office as long as he did because he was not a leader. Some would argue that he was a leader because he did what the people wanted him to do. But it's like Thomas Jefferson said, 'When the people find out they can get something from government for nothing, you lose your government.' "

JERRY FITZGERALD "In his last term he was anesthetized. He was so torn between what he was going to do personally that he kind of disregarded the future of the state, though not consciously. You only have so many hours in the day, and when you're so torn between all these different things it's tough to concentrate. He had Republican candidates coming in looking for advice, he's got people encouraging him to run for higher office. It's hard to sit down and formulate long-range plans for the state under those kinds of conditions.

"The danger of staying in office that long is not that you change your positions or compromise what you believe in. The danger is that you decide not to expend the energy to make the difference even though you keep your original principles."

NORM JESSE "I don't view him harshly, not personally. I don't think he was a terrible governor. I just think he had the opportunity to be a hell of a lot better. He could have risked more, because of his popularity. I think that's one of the responsibilities of a politician. The state suffered because of that and because of the longevity of his term. He also insisted on no tax increases, which really hurt the state. Things that the state really needed to spend money on were not done."

TOM WHITNEY "If success is the measure of a good governor, then certainly Bob Ray was a great governor, because he had unprecedented success in terms of reelection. In terms of indelible marks upon the state, offering up to the community as a whole standards that are larger than sort of self-seeking goals, requiring us to reach out, to be better than we really are, to be more than we are, I don't think so.

"Grounding the National Guard, while it might be a headline in the *Register* and it might get him reelected, hardly represents any great moral crisis or any great confrontation of thought or any real insight into equalities that we should be seeking. I don't want to be overly critical, because the quality of life in Iowa was good. Ray fit the times. He's extremely likable. But I think in a general way the state did not, at a time when we had a very decent economy, achieve some of the things that could have been achieved."

LOWELL JUNKINS "You've got to have some vision, you've got to gamble a little bit. Bob Ray was not a gambler. You've got to make some investments even when they're risky, otherwise you'll never reap the dividends. He played things too close to his vest to do much of that."

ED CAMPBELL "I always faulted him for not getting his ass out on the line, not providing the kind of leadership that could have helped the state turn the corner in his last term, economically. He kept saying, 'We're alright. We're in good shape.' But the fact was we were in bad shape."

LOWELL JUNKINS "He tested the winds a lot. Threw the grass up and waited to see where it landed. He'd let the legislature sit around and play around with issues, watched it, and if it looked good, he'd jump on. He didn't often get into unsafe waters."

GEORGE KINLEY "He had tremendous qualities too. He was kind of 'Iowa.' But internally, when you'd have lunch with him, he was very thin-skinned, couldn't stand any criticism. In fact, the year he was going out as governor we had a disagreement on a particular piece of legislation, and he'd already announced he wasn't going to run. I did a television interview for WOI. It was kind of a rah-rah Bob Ray show, and I just called it as I saw it, criticized him on a couple things. Ray called me the next day—remember he's only got a few more months as governor—and he couldn't understand why I was taking him on in a program like that. He was very thin-skinned. But in his job as governor I think that may have stood him well, made him kind of an intimidator."

TOM HIGGINS "In general, though we clashed on more than one occasion, I have a very positive and warm impression of Ray. He is a very solid, steady guy with decent instincts who captured the mood of Iowa. In some ways I think his popularity was that he filled the cherished self-image that Iowans have of themselves. A modest and decent guy who also presided over a tremendous economic expansion."

BOB RAY "Times changed considerably. When I was first elected, nobody was talking about the environment; it was unheard of. Nobody was talking about the state government being involved in rail transportation. Nobody talked about energy. Look how many people we've got working in those areas today. It's a whole new ball game.

"There are several reasons state government got bigger. One is inflation, which provided for more spending. Two, the federal government was forcing state government to become bigger. Program after program was devised in Washington, D.C., and you had to participate; you really didn't have any choice. Consequently, the state's payroll increased, expenditures increased. Even though most of the money coming in was federal money, it took more state money to help administer. We'd hire people we didn't think we needed—the way you get your federal funds was to live up to their requirements. I'm not saying it was all bad. I think there were improvements to be made in the environment. I never quarreled with the need for OSHA, despite some of their silly rules and regulations. Job Service was a federal program totally on our payroll. I used to get really irritated when the federal government would talk about how the federal government hadn't grown, but look at how the states had grown. Well, they required it. That really changed the complexion of things.

"Go back and look at where all those additions came from, all those employees and the space it took to house them. Most of them were federal and educational. If your business grows, everybody thinks that's wonderful. Every time a new plant opening was announced, the first thing cited was how many employees that company would hire and how many more they'd have in another year. More employees meant they were doing their job better. With government it is just the opposite. You tried to tell people how much better you were doing by how fewer people you had employed. There were things that we were doing that really needed to be done, and it took more employees.

"We had a stable economy in this state for most of my years. We never shied away from innovation – take railroads or health services or family practice or the tuition grant program. We were willing to accept those challenges and find ways to make them work. The worst years were the first couple, because of the Vietnam War and the campus unrest, which were tragic. We had our economic ups and downs, but for the most part they were good years. I look back at those years with satisfaction. When you ask, 'What did I achieve?' I don't know. I'm never satisfied. Anything you can measure I wish we'd done more of it, or sooner, or to a greater extent. I guess I am just not one that is totally satisfied with anything. Yet I'm not one that dwells on things we didn't do perfectly or totally."

DICK GILBERT "I think his legacy will be just fourteen years of really decent government and kind of a commonsense approach to government, punctuated from time to time by really standing up against the popular notion of what should be done. For example, he took a lot of flack in order to shift more of the burden of education from property taxes over to income taxes. He vetoed the wiretap bill in the face of conservative opposition. His terrific restraint in the use of gubernatorial power during the campus unrest is a legacy. Obviously the thing that will impact the state longer than anything is his judicial appointments: eight out of nine supreme court justices and 90 percent of the district court judges."

GEORGE "PIC" WILSON "He established a good, broad agenda for the state and made sure it was followed. The educational system improved, transportation improved, health and human services were improved, the quality of life improved under Governor Ray. Towards the end he was maligned for not increasing taxes and not keeping things at the same growth rate as previous years. Frankly, I think the decision not to increase taxes was a good policy decision.

"He let government pretty much do its own thing. One of the first things he told me was, 'Let the experts do their jobs. Don't Mickey Mouse or fool around with them, just let them do their jobs.' They respected that and he got their loyalty as a result."

DON AVENSON "The reorganization of the DEQ [*Department of Environmental Quality*] and the bottle bill put real speed behind the environmental effort in this state. We've got a topnotch effort and Iowans accept this. We passed the superfund bill last year with fifteen minutes worth of debate. It took Congress four years and they're still fighting it. We passed it quickly partly because Bob Ray raised the expectations of Iowans about themselves, said, 'We're going to be proud of this state. We're going to show pride through how we govern it.' "

TOM STONER "I talked with an editor of a Maryland newspaper recently and he said, 'We have a choice here in Maryland every time we elect a governor. He will either be honest and incompetent or dishonest and competent.' He said the two previous governors were quite competent but essentially dishonest, and both ended up in the federal penitentiary. 'Our current governor,' he said, 'is a very honest man, but he's just totally incompetent.'

"In Iowa we don't seem to have to make that choice, or we certainly didn't have to when Bob Ray was around. He was terribly competent and absolutely honest. There were times when I, with my campaign manager's hat on, urged Bob Ray to say something, make some kind of promise, and he simply said, 'I can't do that because I can't fulfill it.' "

DAVID YEPSEN "He really shaped the public's perception of what a governor ought to be, what he ought to look like, how they ought to conduct themselves. He always acted like he knew that he was in control. He wasn't a great stump speaker like Hughes or [*John*] Culver, but when he walked in a room he filled it with the stereotype of what people expected their governor to be. If you ask Iowans today to define governor, they'd define Bob Ray." [*In the early months of Terry Branstad's governorship, he was introduced at one function this way: "Let's welcome the former three-term state legislator and lieutenant governor from Lake Mills, Governor Bob Ray."*]

VIC PREISSER "There is a whole generation of kids in Iowa who grew up thinking Governor Ray was one word. They grew up asking who's the governoray of this state or that."

ART NEU "I knew Branstad, Jepsen, Tauke, and Grassley when they were in the legislature, and though it's unfair, it's hard to talk about them as governor or senator or congressman. When I first met Bob Ray he was the state chairman. I never saw him up close in the setting of a legislature. If anybody has a frailty, any warts at all, you're going to learn about them in the legislature. And when you know people that well, it's tough to put them on a pedestal. I may respect them, but I keep thinking back to their days as legislators. That's unfair but true. But I always think of Bob Ray as 'the governor.' "

BILL MILLIKEN "He was what you might call a governor's governor. Other governors looked at him and respected him because he was intelligent and honest, open and solid. He wasn't on stage all the time. He didn't try to pretend he was something he wasn't. He was perceived to be a good administrator who understood the function of government and was able to use it. He was thoughtful in his approach, and when he spoke you had the feeling he had done his homework. Those are qualities admired by both the electorate and other officeholders. And I am convinced that one of the reasons that both Bob and I did pretty well in our states is because we were perceived, and I think honestly so, as trying to do what we thought was right."

NICHOLA SCHISSEL "His legacy will be his dedication to effective government and his real desire to help people, which are not always the same. More than just 'I want to see good government,' but 'I want to see good government that helps people.' Good government can be in a textbook, but unless you're willing to bend a little and make arrangements and get out and really help those people, then what good are you?'"

DRAKE MABRY "He's smarter than most politicians. Intellectually, he has a better grasp on how government worked. Probably the biggest thing he did was learn how to make the bureaucracy do things that he wanted them to do. I think Hughes would tell you today that he never quite learned how to get the bureaucracy to do what he wanted it to do. Now, if he'd stuck around another eight years . . ."

BOB BURLINGAME "From 1966 to the early 1980s an awful lot happened to the American mood, and Robert, more than most skillful politicians, is sensitive to mood. He was very much aware of the changing times in the basic sweep of American white middle-class sentiment. Of course, he was in a way the symbol par excellence of the U.S. white middle class – clean, neat, industrious, sharp, and so on. He's not unresilient to change, but I think part of his charm, part of his hold on the Iowa public, is his stability. The fact that he has, across this period of time, been more consistent than the majority of persons in public life was part of his success."

RALPH McCARTNEY "He is a self-starter, he didn't have to have anybody prompt him to act. He went to work in the morning and worked all day long and most of the evening, six days a week. *What motivates a guy like that?* Bob Ray is a complex man. He has ambition, which is healthy. He's got intelligence and courage and was motivated by his liking of government and by the power. I disagreed with him a lot of times, but I never questioned his motivation. He was not an office filler; he held that chair and he did what he thought was right. And he is an astute politician. Don't ever, ever forget that. He has the charisma, the personality, the brainpower, the will, the strength to be a good politician, and I say that kindly."

THURMAN GASKILL   "From a farmer's point of view, Bob Ray encouraged me to be proud of my profession. He came to my home and to my little community, which I don't think had ever hosted a governor before, and I'd introduce him as the man who had made me proud of my profession. He'd do that by telling us how proud we should be as Iowans because of the food production capacity of the state. Very simple, but I don't think others had stopped to think about that, promote it."

BOB RAY   "I have long been pleased with the changing attitude toward our state. I remember so vividly growing up, and even when I was first elected, people honestly apologizing for coming from Iowa. 'This is the hicks,' they'd say. There's nothing wrong with bib overalls. We have what the world wants, and if that isn't something to boast about, I don't know what would be. We've got the soil to produce food, which everybody envies. We've got people who have strong moral values. I think much of that is because of their roots in the soil. Sometimes people think that rushing up and down the street makes for progressiveness. That's not true; in fact, that's a waste of time.

"I think people are optimistic about this state, notwithstanding the poor economy and all the naysayers and doomsdayers. I'm optimistic. I think you'll see the day when agriculture flourishes again. It might not be in the same mode as before, but agriculture is the industry that needs to restabilize this state's economy. There's no reason for us not to have microprocessor plants, computers, and chips, and everything. But we have to be realistic. Every other state is gunning for the same thing. Our universities are just as capable as any other place. We have some drawbacks, like weather. I don't happen to subscribe to the notion that you can't hold on to the family farm. I'm still convinced the family farm is the reason that we do so well agriculturally. It's that individual, that entrepreneur, who knows how to produce from that natural resource that makes our agricultural system so good.

"I can go back to those days when I was on the central committee and was the state chairman, and I really had goals for the party. And we achieved a lot. We came from nowhere to succeed. I had hoped we would build Iowa into a strong Republican state, because I believed in the basic principles of the party. Now, that sounds like a cliché. Certainly all the good people in the state are not in the Republican party, but fundamentally the Republican party believes in the basic premises on which you build a democracy: freedoms and the free enterprise system, individual opportunity. I was really enthusiastic about making the party a modern party, one that wanted to improve conditions, not just thwart drives to make changes.

"I became governor and believed in our state to the extent that I thought not only should we talk about it being the greatest state, we ought to be sure it is the greatest state. To me we had the natural resources that we ought to take great pride in and we ought to protect and preserve and deal with gently. Agriculture was not something to apologize for, but to be proud of and promote. We believe in strong human rights in Iowa, and I thought that was something we needed to get everybody to understand, not that we can ever eliminate all prejudices, but we had to try and we had to promote this state as a state of tolerance. I've always been keen on a good educational system, and they still talk about how our people are well educated. Those things didn't just happen. I don't take credit for them. It was the system and what we did to develop that system.

"Eighteen years ago I didn't know what I wanted to accomplish. I'm a great believer in setting goals. If you don't have goals, you don't know whether you're achieving things. But at the same time I have not applied that to myself personally, as far as my career goes. As far as mistakes go, it seems like I ought to be able to tell you what my biggest mistake was. Some would say when I ran for office. I really don't know. I have to keep a lot of things in context. There are things I should have done differently, more aggressively. I know there are a lot of things we could have done for a lot more show, and sometimes that creates a better atmosphere, but I don't think that was a mistake.

"Successes? I think people thought government was well run. I believe they had some pride in our state and what we were doing. I think they were reasonably comfortable with my leadership, my style. I don't think you'd find many who thought we were dishonest. Did *I* do a good job? Yes."

BOB TYSON "Like Jerry Ford and Dwight Eisenhower, he was the right man at the right time. He led in a quiet and peaceful way. People had the impression that if some problem came up, Bob Ray would solve it. He will always be 'The Governor.' "

FROSTY MITCHELL "Bob Ray's tombstone will probably read 'Bob Ray, Governor, Nice Guy,' and probably nothing would make him happier."

XXXII: EPILOGUE

BILL THOMPSON "He's a smart guy. He had good feelings about the decision that he ultimately arrived at, no matter how long it took him. He had a good feel for people. I think he had a good sense, and a deep feeling, for Iowa. He had plenty of chances to leave and he didn't. He was not an efficient worker, he didn't appear to be efficient with his time, but who's to say what he was doing with that time that made him such a good governor. He took his time and didn't make bad decisions. But his greatest strength was his sense of humor and his ability to charm the media. And to be totally open and honest."

MARY LOUISE SMITH "A lot of people are touched by Bob Ray, and let me tell you why. He has a capacity for making people feel personally involved, and the best example is when you watched him campaign. I saw it happen over and over. He'd enter a crowded room at a reception or political event and end up talking to somebody one on one. He talked to them as if there were nobody else in the room. Often in a crowd like that you want to get on to the next person or you think, 'This isn't very important.' Not Bob Ray. He will talk to you as if you are the only person he's

Des Moines Register photo. Reprinted with permission.

interested in and yours is the only problem. It's a phenomenal skill, or quality. It's done out of a real sincere concern for people and a kind of personalized approach, and he did it with literally thousands of people across the state."

VIC PREISSER "He is good, capital G-O-O-D! And he is truly a Christian man. If somebody had told me he was out in the pond in front of the Grimes Building walking on water, I wouldn't even look over my shoulder to verify it. I would have just said, 'Yeah, he probably is.' "

REV. JOSEPH GRUBBS "I traveled with the governor quite a bit, and nothing I saw dispelled his public image, with one exception. When I was still his minister, before I joined his staff, we went to Israel and one day broke away from the tour group, just the four of us, he and Billie and my ex-wife and I. We jumped in a cab and went over to the Garden of Gethsemane. We walked in and he was so relaxed – there was no press around, no one who knew who he was. We knelt and prayed together. After we finished we got back in the cab and were riding back to the Jerusalem Hilton, and he was still very relaxed. When we walked through the revolving door of the hotel a television crew was waiting for him. Something had happened back in Iowa and they were waiting for his response. Immediately he stood about two inches taller, his shoulders went back and he was 'The Governor' again."

LARRY POPE "Jim Flansburg was absolutely right about Bob Ray. He used to say that he drove Democrats and Republicans alike crazy because they were always trying to figure out what Bob Ray was going to do next. But they would always try to figure it out from a political context, and they were wrong over and over again, because Bob Ray always made his decisions based on what was right. That's not to say he couldn't be political, but when it came to being the governor and making decisions as governor, he always took the position that if you do the right thing, you ultimately won't get in trouble. That gave him a sense of not only integrity but consistency. It's much easier to make decisions in government if you make them on the basis of what is right, not on what might be the best move politically."

WYTHE WILLEY "The best part of the job was the personal satisfaction of being part of something that was somewhat special, being part of a team that was able to accomplish a lot and work for a guy that had real high standards and very high goals. That sounds kind of Boy Scouty coming from a guy like me, but it was true."

<u>DICK GILBERT</u> "Bob Ray is a hell of a lot smarter than a lot of people give him credit for. They thought he was all public relations and charisma, but he is one smart guy. He's not what you would call a great intellect, and he makes no bones about that. He has tremendous retention and great intellectual integrity and stamina. He would stay on an issue like a dog on a bone while other guys feel along the wayside.

"He also has the ability to make you feel as if you are his best and closest personal friend, and perhaps at that moment you are. But it is a characteristic of many great leaders that you feel a real sense of personal service to the guy. One of the ways he motivated the immediate staff was not so much the fear of being chewed out or necessarily handing out high praise, because praise was very sparingly handed out, but by a sense that you didn't want to let him down. You did not want to incur his disappointment, not necessarily his wrath, because if you let him down you would no longer be in his grace. And the reward of working with Bob Ray was to be around him and to be within his grace. If you didn't perform well, you weren't in that light, and suddenly the fun of the job was all gone; it just became drudgery, and that's when you would see an aide or someone in government leave.

"One time, early in his second term, we were still at the office about three in the morning because the Farm Bureau was hounding us about the productivity formula. He was in his sport coat, his feet up on that big desk in his upstairs office, and this big old clock was ticking back and forth. I was twenty-nine, about as qualified to be advising the governor of the state as I would be to fly a 747, and very conscious about it. I said, 'Governor, you know the Farm Bureau feels very strongly about their position. They're a very powerful lobby and could cause a lot of problems for us down the road.' He turned his chair around and said, 'Richard, I know they've got a lot of influence, but I'm the governor of 2.9 million people, and I'm here to represent everyone's interest the best I can.' Now remember, this was an unguarded moment, at three in the morning, and he was talking to one of his personal staff, not some reporter. It was spoken with real conviction, and I thought, 'You know, this guy has really got his head screwed on right. That's the way the system is supposed to work."

What's left to say about Iowa's most popular politician? His staff and supporters have had their say, as well as a handful of critics. Over twenty years of political life Bob Ray accumulated many more friends than enemies, a testimonial to his firm but always moderating approach. I've left out page after page of anecdotes from staffers and appointees explaining why they loved or, though rarely, hated working for the man whom most still address as governor. Virtually everyone I sat and reminisced with expounded on the very private nature of Iowa's most public official and found it unlikely that he would ever reveal his innermost thoughts on events that shaped his tenure. To a large degree, they were right.

Like most people who sit for a seemingly never-ending parade of interviewers over a public career, Bob Ray has reduced his own career to a kind of clippings file in his mind. Ask about the grounding of the National Guard in 1972 or the resettlement of the boat people in 1979 and his memory spits out anecdotes phrased identically to the way they were five, ten, or fifteen years ago. That is understandable, considering the experiences and dealings he's had. Few of us possess the capability or desire to tell the same story over and over a different way each time. But based on the insights and experiences of his friends and critics, I think we were able to explore and, with the advantage of hindsight, examine some of those memories.

When attempting to sum up their boss and the reasons for his success, staffers and appointees alike stressed the same half-dozen attributes: his deliberate—many called it slow—decision-making process, which frustrated many but disappointed few; his incredible elephantlike memory, which sparked many to wonder if perhaps Bob Ray ought not to become the GOP's mascot; his hot and always effective temper, which some said he used with calculation to insure the perfection he demanded; the long hours that he put into the job, outlasting younger men and women, and always, always appearing fresh as a daisy, despite only two hours of sleep; and last but certainly not least, that desire for perfection that pervaded everything he did, that demanded that every letter that left the governor's office be *perfect,* that every curtain in his lower office hang straight so that he wouldn't be distracted in a meeting, and that every spider web be cleaned from his poolside rose bushes so that he could best enjoy his guests. Picky, perhaps, but from that demand for perfection he wrought order and consistency. Private he may be, but if you understand the ground rules that shaped his life, he is an open book.

Just as he was driven by that desire for perfection, there seemed always to be room for a game of Ping-Pong or a roadside stop for an ice-cream cone. The former he dominated and the latter was an addiction, not just a photo opportunity. "He knows the location of every Dairy Queen in the state," quips Frosty Mitchell. "It's like he's got radar." And maybe it stands as a symbol of how good life has been to Bob Ray, but those days of waiting in long lines as a boy at Reed's Ice Cream for nickel ice-cream bars are long gone. His Cedar Rapids condo boasts a refrigerator that churns out his favorite—is it peppermint this month? or maybe double-dutch chocolate?—at the push of a button.

Despite that "Nice Guy" epithet that Frosty Mitchell suggested should be inscribed on his tombstone, what really made for Bob Ray's success? In his fourth inaugural address, in 1975, he stressed that "government's goal is to motivate, not maintain; to regulate, not control." With that operating thesis and his hardworking, clean-living, gee-whiz attitudes firmly in place alongside his steadfastly held belief that good government is good politics, it would be hard to create from scratch an individual who could have done a better job of running the state during that time. A Democratic legislator wrote in 1982, as Ray prepared to leave office, that the governor "spanned the eras of Agnew to Falwell. . . . His appeal has been consistently to the better angels of our natures. . . . It is a hard act to follow." The dean of political journalists, the *Washington Post*'s David Broder, added soon after, "Bob Ray gave politics a good name. . . . In a time of overweening ambition, when so many of [*his*] colleagues viewed the possession of one public office as a springboard to another office [*Ray*] stayed at his work. . . . In a time when many view politicians with deep suspicion, the integrity, ability and durability of [*Ray is*] a powerful rebuttal to cynicism."

A *Des Moines Register* editorial of February 21, 1982, declared: "Lucky breaks, political and economic, contributed to the longevity of his administration, but if Ray was lucky to hit the scene when he did . . . Iowa was even luckier. . . . His leadership was not exciting. He sounded no trumpet calls to battle for pulse-pounding causes. He often chose to tiptoe along a cautious middle path, rather than charge some redoubt of privilege or tradition. But if this was a weakness, it was also a sage tactic that kept his administration alive to fight again another day. And win."

And in his final State of the State message, on January 11, 1983, Bob Ray summarized his career: "For 14 years, then, we have minimized the dangers and maximized the opportunities. Every year has been different. The compelling issues in one period have gone unmentioned a few years later. It was a former president of France who once said, 'To govern is to choose.' Our purpose, then, has been to choose wisely. We have anticipated issues early, identified courses of action, stuck by our guns and rallied Iowans to march with us in the direction of progress. . . . When I assumed this office in 1969 I said, 'Each successive Iowa governor has made his contribution . . . to the realization of mankind's quest towards a more perfect society, where illness and cruelty and bitterness and war will be no more. It is a quest which has no end, but which makes us a little better tomorrow than we are today.' I have sought to make my contribution as best I could."

INTERVIEWEES

DON AVENSON, a Democrat from Oelwein, was first elected to the Iowa House of Representatives in 1972 and has been the Speaker of the House since 1983.

PAT BAIN was the matriarch of the Polk County Republicans during Bob Ray's governorship. She replaced Ray on the Republican state central committee in 1963 and served on it until 1982.

BILL BALL, a former Black Hawk County Attorney, was Bob Ray's first executive assistant, serving for six months in 1969, through the first legislative session. He is now senior partner in the Waterloo law firm of Ball Kirk Holm and Nardini.

MAURICE BARINGER has been the director of the state's Advisory Investment Board for the Iowa Public Employees Retirement System since 1983. Prior to that he spent eight years—from 1961 to 1969—in the Iowa House and from 1969 to 1982 was the state treasurer.

JOHN BEAMER, a former assistant Iowa attorney general and chairman of the Public Employment Relations Board, is an attorney in the U.S. attorney's office in Des Moines.

BOB BECK, from Centerville, lost the Republican party's nomination for governor to Bill Murray in 1966 and to Bob Ray in 1968. The former publisher of the *Iowegian* in Centerville, he later served on the Iowa Development Commission.

DAVID BELIN was an adviser to Governors Norman Erbe and Bob Ray, and to President Gerald Ford. He served on the Warren Commission, which investigated the assassination of John F. Kennedy, and was executive director of the Rockefeller Commission, which investigated the CIA. He is the senior partner in the Des Moines law firm of Belin Harris Helmick Heartney and Tesdell.

ROBERT "BO" BELLER was the student body president at the University of Iowa for 1969–70. He now owns an executive employment firm in Minneapolis.

GERALD BOGAN was Bob Beck's campaign manager in the 1968 Republican gubernatorial primary and later served as the executive secretary of Iowans Right to Work. He passed away in August 1986.

TERRY BRANSTAD was for six years a Republican state representative from Lake Mills. He was elected lieutenant governor of Iowa in 1978 and governor in 1982 and 1986.

C. ROBERT BRENTON was the treasurer of Bob Ray's first three gubernatorial campaigns and is president of Brenton Banks, Inc.

JUNIUS "BUZ" BRENTON is president of the Brenton National Bank in Des Moines.

GEORGE BROWN was first a reporter, then a lobbyist for the state Republican party from 1966 to 1968. He is currently a lobbyist for the Iowa State Education Association.

MARY ANN BROWN, a former speechwriter for Vice-President George Bush, was a field staffer in Bob Ray's 1978 campaign.

RALPH BROWN was the secretary of the Iowa Senate from 1973 to 1975 and then the executive director of the state Republican party from 1976 to 1977. He is now a lawyer with McDonald Brown and Kimple in Dallas Center. He was cochair of George Bush's Iowa presidential campaign in 1980.

ROBERT BUCKMASTER, a Waterloo environmentalist and lawyer, served on the Republican state central committee in the 1950s. He was elected mayor of Waterloo at thirty-four. He is the president and founder of Black Hawk Broadcasting. He headed the Water Quality Commission under Governor Hughes and was chairman of the Department of Environmental Quality and the Iowa Natural Heritage Foundation under Governor Ray.

BOB BURLINGAME was a Des Moines radio journalist prior to becoming a frequent speechwriter and researcher for Bob Ray.

GEORGE BUSH, the vice-president, was the Republican party's national chairman from 1973 to 1974 and a presidential contender in 1980.

JIM CALLISON served on the Des Moines city council and as Polk County Republican chairman in the 1960s and was on the Iowa Development Commission for eight years. He is president of the Callison Oil Company.

ED CAMPBELL was an aide first to Governor and then to Senator Harold Hughes and Senator John Culver. He was the Democratic state party chairman from 1977 to 1982 and ran for governor in the 1982 primary. He is now a lobbyist, political consultant, and real estate salesman.

HUGH CLARK was president of Iowa's AFL-CIO for fourteen years, from 1966 to 1979.

DALE COCHRAN, a Democrat from Eagle Grove, was elected to the Iowa House of Representatives in 1964. He was the minority floor leader from 1971 to 1975, Speaker of the House from 1975 to 1979, and minority leader in 1981–82. In 1986 he was elected Iowa's secretary of agriculture.

KENT CRAFTS was president of the Drake University Republicans and president of the Drake student body in 1967. He quit both those positions to work full-time as a scheduler in Ray's first gubernatorial campaign. He is now a hospital administrator in Buffalo, New York.

GIL CRANBERG was the editorial page editor for the *Des Moines Register* from 1975 to 1982.

BILL CREWS supported Bob Ray as a Young Republican at the age of sixteen in 1968. He went on to become the campaign coordinator of Ray's fifth race. In 1981 he joined the governor's staff and later worked as a lawyer with the Iowa Department of Water, Air and Waste Management.

JUDGE ANTHONY CRITELLI worked on Bob Ray's first two campaigns, in 1956 and 1958. A Drake Law School graduate, he followed Ray as reading clerk at the Iowa House. He became a Democrat in the 1960s and was appointed a Polk County district court judge in 1974.

JIM CROSBY was an executive with the Des Moines Shopper Network. He passed away in 1987.

RUSSELL CROSS worked for Ames state legislator Reid Crawford, for the state Republican party in 1978, and for state auditor Dick Johnson before joining Bob Ray's staff as a scheduler in 1981.

A. ARTHUR DAVIS is the senior partner in the Des Moines law firm of Davis Hockenberg Wine Brown and Koehn and chairman of the state Democratic party from 1985 to 1986.

JACQUELINE DAY was the office manager for the state Republican party headquarters when Bob Ray was the state chairman. She worked as a confidential secretary for Governors Norman Erbe and Bob Ray and was appointed to the Board of Parole in 1978, where she served until 1985. She was a leading force behind the establishment of the Vietnam Veterans Memorial in Iowa.

MINNETTE DODERER, a Democrat from Iowa City, was first elected to the Iowa House in 1964 and served there until 1969 and then in the Iowa Senate from 1969 to 1978. In 1981 she was reelected to the Iowa House, where she still serves.

ALLEN L. "BARNEY" DONIELSON was the Polk County Republican chairman in the 1960s and was the U.S. attorney for the Southern District of Iowa, appointed by Richard Nixon, from 1969 to 1976. Ray appointed him to the Iowa Court of Appeals in November 1976.

CAROL DUNCAN started as a secretary for Governor Ray in 1968, worked for him throughout his fourteen years, and continues in the same job for Governor Branstad.

KEITH DYSART was legal counsel for the National Governors' Association from 1972 to 1976. He is currently practicing law in Hawaii.

ROGER FERRIS worked for the David Stanley U.S. Senate campaigns in 1968 and 1970 and was Roger Jepsen's campaign manager in his 1971–72 run at the governor's office. He is now a lawyer with the Des Moines firm of Nyemaster Goode McLaughlin Emery and O'Brien.

JERRY FITZGERALD, a Democrat from Fort Dodge, was elected to the Iowa House in 1972. He was majority leader from 1975 to 1979. He was the 1978 Democratic candidate for governor and ran in the primary for governor in 1982 and for Congress from the Fifth District in 1984.

MARY FITZGERALD worked for the Iowa Retail Food Dealers Association for forty years and was their lobbyist from 1953 to 1983.

JOHN FITZGIBBON was president of the Iowa–Des Moines Bank (now Norwest) from 1969 to 1982.

JAMES FLANSBURG became chief political reporter for the *Des Moines Register* in 1971. He is now the editorial page editor of the newspaper.

GERALD FORD was president of the United States from 1974 to 1977.

PAUL FRANZENBURG was the Iowa state treasurer from 1965 to 1969 and the Democratic nominee for governor in 1968 and 1972. He was appointed a commissioner with the Iowa Commerce Commission in 1983 by Terry Branstad.

BAXTER FREESE is a past president of the Iowa Cattlemen's Association. Ray appointed him to the Iowa Conservation Commission in 1981.

ROBERT FULTON was a state representative from Waterloo before he was elected lieutenant governor in 1964. He served from 1965 to 1969 and became governor on January 2, 1969, for fourteen days when Harold Hughes left office to join the U.S. Senate. He was the Democratic nominee for governor in 1970. He currently practices law in Waterloo.

WILLIAM FULTZ is the president of the Des Moines advertising firm of CMF & Z. He was a media/advertising adviser to the state Republican party and several Bob Ray campaigns. He was also a member of the Iowa Arts Council for seven years.

SERGE GARRISON was the director of the Legislative Service Bureau from 1967 to 1983.

MICHAEL GARTNER, former Page One editor at the *Wall Street Journal,* was named executive editor of the *Des Moines Register* in 1974, editor in 1976, and president of the company in 1978. He is currently editor of the *Louisville Courier-Journal* and chairman of Midwest Newspapers, Inc.

THURMAN GASKILL, from Corwith, was appointed to the agriculture promotion board of the Iowa Development Commission in 1972 and was appointed an IDC commissioner in 1981.

JOSEPH GAYLORD worked for the Republican state central committee from 1967 to 1974, was the executive director from 1972 to 1974, and is now the executive director of the Republican National Congressional Committee in Washington, D.C.

MIKE GETTO, from Kansas City, Missouri, worked in the presidential primary campaign of Nelson Rockefeller in 1964 and was Bob Ray's campaign manager in 1970.

NOVELENE RAY GIBBONS lives in Omaha, Nebraska. She is Bob Ray's older sister.

CHUCK GIFFORD is president of Iowa's United Auto Workers and a Democratic national committeeman from Iowa.

RICHARD GILBERT first joined Bob Ray's staff in 1969 as an assistant press secretary. He left to publish a newspaper in Eagle Grove and rejoined Ray's staff as press secretary in 1972. From 1975 to 1986 he worked for the Des Moines Register and Tribune Company. He is currently publisher of the *Pioneer Press* in Wilmette, Illinois.

CHARLES GRASSLEY, a Republican, served in the Iowa House from 1959 to 1975 and the U.S. House of Representatives from 1975 to 1981 and was elected to the U.S. Senate in 1980 and 1986.

HALE GREENLEAF runs Central Surveys in Shenandoah, Iowa.

DOUG GROSS was the campaign manager and chief legislative assistant for Congressman Tom Tauke before joining the Energy Policy Council. He signed on as Bob Ray's legislative liaison in 1981 and held the same job in 1983 for governor Branstad before going to work for the Board of Regents. He is now Governor Branstad's executive assistant.

REV. JOSEPH GRUBBS is a minister in Raleigh, North Carolina, and serves on the national board of the Friendship Force. He was Bob Ray's minister in Des Moines before serving as an administrative assistant for Ray from 1979 to 1982.

DOROTHY HALL was Bob Ray's ninth-grade English teacher at Callanan Junior High.

JUDGE RAY HANRAHAN, a Democrat, beat Bob Ray in the Polk County Attorney's race in 1956. After being nominated three times, Ray appointed him a Polk County district court judge in 1976.

CHRISTINE HANSEN was a statehouse reporter for the *Dubuque Herald* and the *Des Moines Register,* an FBI agent, Senator Roger Jepsen's first press secretary, and a lawyer for the Department of Housing and Urban Development before Bob Ray appointed her to the Iowa Commerce Commission in 1981.

WILLIAM HARBOR was first elected to the Iowa House in 1954 and has served ten terms there, including two as Speaker. He also served one term as a state senator, from 1957 to 1961.

CYNTHIA HENDERSON worked as an assistant to first lady Billie Ray and was named the administrator of Terrace Hill in 1983.

TOM HIGGINS was press secretary for Bob Fulton in his 1970 gubernatorial race and a member of the Iowa House from Davenport from 1972 to 1977.

CORRINNE HUBBELL lives in Des Moines and is a relative-by-marriage of Frederick Marion Hubbell, who lived in Terrace Hill, now the governor's residence.

HAROLD HUGHES was the governor of Iowa from 1963 to 1969 and a U.S. senator from 1969 to 1975. He is currently the chief administrator of the Hughes Center, a substance-abuse treatment facility in Des Moines.

CALVIN HULTMAN was an administrative assistant to Congressman Bill Scherle for six years. He was elected to the Iowa Senate in 1972 and served as majority leader from 1979 to 1983 and minority leader from 1975 to 1978 and from 1983 to the present.

JOHN HYDE is a Washington-based reporter for the *Des Moines Register.*

BILL JACKSON left WHO-TV in Des Moines to join Bob Ray's staff in the spring of 1970 and left in 1979. He is currently the director of cultural affairs for the Iowa State Historical Department.

DWIGHT JENSEN was a reporter for the *Des Moines Register* before becoming Governor Hughes's executive assistant. He later worked as Senator Hughes's press secretary before becoming director of public relations for the National Governors' Association in the early 1970s.

ROGER JEPSEN was a Republican state senator from 1967 to 1969 and lieutenant governor from 1969 to 1973. He served one term in the U.S. Senate, from 1979 to 1985.

KEN JERNIGAN was the director of the Iowa Commission for the Blind for twenty-five years and now works with the National Federation for the Blind in Baltimore.

NORMAN JESSE was a Democratic member of the Iowa House from Des Moines from 1969 to 1981. He is a lawyer with the Polk County Attorney's office.

DON JOHNSON was a national committeeman for the American Legion from 1964 to 1965 and director of the Veterans Administration under Richard Nixon from 1969 to 1975. He ran in the Republican primary for governor in 1968 and later served as assistant secretary of commerce and as an aide to Senator Roger Jepsen.

LOWELL JUNKINS was first elected to the Iowa Senate in 1972 and served as the minority leader from 1979 to 1983 and majority leader from 1983 to 1985. He was the Democratic nominee for governor in 1986.

DONALD KAUL was a *Des Moines Register* reporter and columnist for twenty years. He lives in Washington, D.C., and writes a syndicated column carried by over thirty newspapers around the country.

ROBB KELLEY is president of the Employers Mutual Casualty Company in Des Moines and was Governor Ray's campaign finance chairman in 1972 and 1974.

GEORGE KINLEY, a Democrat, served one term in the Iowa House before he was elected to the Iowa Senate in 1970. He was majority leader of the senate from 1975 to 1979.

RUSSELL "RUSTY" LAIRD is a lobbyist for the beer distributors, soft-drink bottlers, and others.

CLIFF LAMBORN was a five-term Republican legislator from Maquoketa and senate minority leader in 1975–76.

JAMES LAWYER was a law partner of Bob Ray's for fourteen years and is now senior partner in the Des Moines firm of Lawyer Lawyer Dutton and Drake.

MARGE LAWYER was a high school classmate of Bob Ray's and is James Lawyer's wife.

VERNE LAWYER began his Des Moines legal practice in 1949 and hired Bob Ray in 1954. A former treasurer and chairman of the National Trial Lawyers' Association, he continues to practice in Des Moines.

JIM LEACH, a Republican from Davenport, was first elected to the U.S. House of Representatives in 1976, and he has served six terms.

L. B. LIDDY was Iowa secretary of agriculture from 1963 to 1966 and from 1969 to 1972.

GARY LILLY was a high school classmate of Ray's, used to own Gary Lilly's Volkswagen in West Des Moines, and now lives in Arizona.

JOAN LIPSKY was a Republican member of the Iowa House of Representatives from Cedar Rapids from 1967 to 1979 and is now practicing law in Cedar Rapids. She ran for lieutenant governor in 1986 and lost.

JOHN LLOYD worked in Bob Ray's first primary campaign when he was a freshman at Drake University. He was a passenger in Ray's plane when it crashed in 1968. A lawyer, he later worked for Verne Lawyer and is now working for the Reynoldson law firm in Osceola.

ROBERT LOUNSBERRY was appointed deputy secretary of agriculture in 1969 and elected secretary of agriculture in 1972, 1974, 1978, and 1982.

DRAKE MABRY covered the statehouse for the *Des Moines Register* in the 1960s and was managing editor of the *Des Moines Tribune* in the 1970s.

JUDGE RALPH McCARTNEY was a Republican member of the Iowa House of Representatives from 1967 to 1971 and the Iowa Senate from 1973 to 1975. Bob Ray appointed him to the Board of Regents, and he is currently a district court judge in Charles City.

JOHN McDONALD, a Dallas Center lawyer, became the Republican state chairman in September 1969, a position he held through 1976, when he was elected Republican national committeeman. He was appointed to the Board of Regents in 1981.

JACK MacNIDER, president of MacNider Cement in Mason City, is a longtime Iowa Republican financier.

MARILYN MAYE, a Des Moines native and Broadway musical star, lives in Kansas City and continues to perform nationwide. She recently recorded an album of Harry Truman's favorite songs for the Truman Library.

WILEY MAYNE was a four-term Republican congressman from Sioux City, first elected in 1966.

BERNARD MERCER is a Democrat, lawyer, fund-raiser, and chairman of Preferred Risk Insurance Company in West Des Moines.

JOHN MERRIMAN worked on Bob Ray's campaign in 1968 and served on the Republican state central committee from 1978 to 1982.

FLOYD MILLEN, a Republican from Farmington, served nine terms in the Iowa House of Representatives and was Speaker of the House from 1979 to 1980. He is now a lobbyist for Blue Cross and Blue Shield of Iowa.

JACK MILLER, a former Republican member of the Iowa House and Senate from Sioux City, was a U.S. senator from 1961 to 1973. He is now a judge with the U.S. Circuit Court of Appeals.

PAT MILLER was the office manager of Bob Ray's campaigns in 1972 and 1974. She went to work for John Murray in the Iowa Senate, worked on Billie Ray's staff, and is now a producer for the political consulting firm of Bailey-Deardourff in McLean, Virginia.

WILLIAM MILLIKEN was the Republican governor of Michigan from 1969 to 1983.

MAX MILO MILLS ran in the Republican primary for lieutenant governor against Roger Jepsen in 1968 and lost. A former state senator from Marshalltown, he served on Ray's first campaign and transition staff. He later worked with HEW/HUD in Kansas City and with the Iowa Development Commission.

FORREST "FROSTY" MITCHELL first met Bob Ray when the future governor was March of Dimes state chairman and Frosty was a Des Moines disc jockey in the 1950s. The pair later teamed up in the broadcast booth, calling the University of Iowa football games on the radio from 1961 to 1967. He managed Ray's first campaign for governor and was later appointed to the Iowa Development Commission and the Judicial Nominating Commission. In 1985 he sold several of his Iowa radio stations, and in 1986, with Bob Ray and a group of investors, he bought WMT Radio in Cedar Rapids.

JANE MITCHELL worked as a secretary for Verne Lawyer and then, for seven years, for Governor Ray. She is now an administrative assistant for the director of the Iowa Development Commission.

SUE MITSCHKE was Governor Ray's confidential secretary from 1979 to 1983 and is now the confidential secretary for Gary Kirke at Kirke–Van Orsdel, Inc., in Des Moines.

RON MOSHER was named state comptroller in February 1979. A native Iowan, he had been budget director in Delaware under Governor Pierre du Pont. He stayed on as state comptroller under Governor Branstad and then went to work with Bob Ray at Life Investors in April 1983, where he is senior vice-president and chief financial officer.

JOHN MURRAY, William Murray's son, worked on Nelson Rockefeller's presidential campaign in 1968 and joined Ray's staff as executive assistant in 1970, serving until 1972, when he was elected to the state senate, where he served six years. He now teaches law at Texas Tech in Lubbock.

WILLIAM MURRAY, of Ames, was the Republican nominee for governor in 1958 and 1966. He is currently the Chairman of the Board of Living History Farms in Des Moines.

JERRY MURSENER is a former statehouse reporter for UPI and communications director and executive director of the state Republican party from 1975 to 1979.

DENNIS NAGEL joined Bob Ray's staff as legislative liaison in 1973 and worked for the governor until 1981. He is now a lawyer with the Belin law firm in Des Moines.

ART NEU was first elected to the Iowa Senate in 1966 and was elected lieutenant governor in 1972 and 1974.

LOWELL NORLAND was a seven-term state representative from Kensett. A Democrat, he served as majority leader of the house from 1983 to 1986.

BRICE OAKLEY worked as an assistant attorney general, was elected to two terms in the Iowa House in 1972 and 1974, ran for the Republican nomination for lieutenant governor in 1978, joined Ray's staff in 1979, and worked as his legal counsel until 1983.

MARY JANE ODELL hosted public affairs radio and television programs in Des Moines and Chicago for twenty-five years. She was appointed secretary of state by Ray in 1980 when Melvin Synhorst resigned and won election to the post in 1982, only the second woman to be elected secretary of state in Iowa.

RICHARD OLSON was the mayor of Des Moines from 1977 to 1982 and heads the Richard Olson Agency for the Principal Group.

DAVID OMAN, a former Waterloo television reporter, worked on the 1974 Ray campaign and joined the governor's staff later that year as assistant press secretary. He was named press secretary in 1975 and executive assistant in 1981. He continued on as Governor Branstad's executive assistant until 1984. He is now a vice-president of Heritage Communications and cochair of the Iowa Republican Party.

JUDGE LEO OXBERGER was the Polk County Republican chairman from 1958 to 1962, was appointed a district court judge in 1969 and a judge of the Iowa Appeals Court in 1976, where he is now chief judge.

JERRY PARKIN was the vice-president of the student body at Iowa State University in 1970, was the Ray campaign's youth coordinator in 1972, and went on to work at the Office for Planning and Programming and for Congressman Fred Schwengel. He is now manager of government affairs for Iowa Power.

JACK PESTER, a Republican party financier, is president of the Pester Marketing Company.

H. RAND PETERSEN, a longtime member of the Republican state central committee, was the chairman of all five Ray campaigns for governor. He is the president of the Shelby County Bank in Henderson.

KEITH PETERSON worked on David Stanley's 1968 senatorial campaign, then joined Ray's staff as an administrative assistant in 1969.

MARVIN POMERANTZ founded the Great Plains Bag Corporation and later worked for both Continental Can and International Harvester. He was the Iowa chairman for Gerald Ford's 1976 presidential campaign and comanager of Bob Ray's 1978 campaign. He is the president of the Mid-America Group in Des Moines.

LARRY POPE, a Republican, worked on the Ray campaign in 1974, was elected to the Iowa House in 1978, and became majority leader in 1980. He ran unsuccessfully for lieutenant governor in 1982. He is a law professor at Drake University.

VIC PREISSER was named director of the new Department of Transportation in 1974 and served three years there. He later served as director of the Department of Social Services for a year and a half. After leaving state government, he went to work for Iowa Beef Processors in Sioux City.

KEN QUINN worked on Bob Ray's staff from 1978 to 1982. On leave from the State Department, he had previously worked as a translator in Vietnam for Secretary of State Henry Kissinger. A former Dubuque resident, he is currently with the State Department in Washington, D.C.

RICHARD RAMSEY is a former Republican state senator from Osceola. He later worked as an administrative assistant in Governor Branstad's office and was the executive director of the Criminal and Juvenile Justice Planning Agency.

GERRY RANKIN was the legislative fiscal director for sixteen years, from 1966 to 1982. He is now an accountant with Gardiner and Company in Des Moines.

HARRY RASDAL managed the first half of Bob Ray's first campaign in 1968. He is an optometrist in Spencer.

CLARK RASMUSSEN was the state Democratic party chairman in 1966 and worked for Senator Harold Hughes. He managed Bob Fulton's 1970 gubernatorial campaign, ran in the Democratic primary for governor in 1974, and was elected Polk County clerk of court in 1975, a job he held until 1986, when he was elected a Polk County supervisor.

BILLIE LEE (HORNBERGER) RAY married Bob Ray in 1951, raised three daughters, and was first lady of Iowa from 1969 to 1983.

MILDRED RAY is Bob Ray's mother.

MICHAEL REAGEN was a county Human Services director in Syracuse, New York, before Ray appointed him head of the Department of Social Services in 1978, a position he held until 1986.

ED REDFERN was field staffer for the Ray campaign in 1971 and 1972 and worked for the Republican state central committee before joining the governor's staff in 1977. He now works as an administrative assistant for Senator Chuck Grassley.

DICK REDMAN first went to work for the Republican state central committee in 1959 and served as organization director, finance director, executive director, and fund-raising consultant through 1968. He then worked as a private campaign fund-raiser and consultant and ran for Congress in 1984. He is currently marketing director for the Mid-America Group in West Des Moines.

JOHN KEITH REHMANN is a longtime national Republican fund-raiser from Des Moines. He worked for Maurice Stans and raised $4 million for the Committee to Re-Elect the President (CREEP) in the early 1970s.

ROBERT RIGLER, a New Hampton banker, was a Republican state senator for four terms before Governor Ray appointed him to the State Highway Commission in 1971. He later became chairman of the Iowa Department of Transportation.

CLAYTON RINGGENBERG was a legislative researcher in 1955, the first full-time employee the legislature ever hired. He worked as executive assistant to Governor Ray in 1969 and 1970. He is the director of the Public Affairs Institute at the University of Iowa, a position he has held since 1965.

STEVE ROBERTS was the Republican state chairman from 1977 to 1981. He is a lawyer with Davis Hockenberg Wine Brown and Koehn in Des Moines.

NORMAN SANDLER works for United Press International. He covered the Iowa statehouse from 1975 to 1980 and now covers the White House.

WILLIAM SCHERLE was a Republican member of the Iowa House from 1961 to 1967 and a congressman from 1967 to 1975.

NICHOLA SCHISSEL was on Bob Ray's staff from 1979 to 1983, overseeing appointments. She is now with the Iowa Lottery Commission.

JACK SCHROEDER, a Republican state legislator from Davenport, was first elected to the Iowa House in 1950 and served two terms in the house and four in the senate. He ran in the Republican gubernatorial primary against Norman Erbe in 1960.

FRED SCHWENGEL, a Republican, served in Congress from 1955 to 1965 and from 1967 to 1973. He is now president of the National Capitol Historical Society in Washington, D.C.

JOHN SCOTT was a Democratic state senator from Pocahontas from 1977 to 1981. He now works in the attorney general's office.

JOHN SEARS was an adviser to Presidents Nixon, Ford, and Reagan. He is now a Washington-based political consultant.

MARVIN SELDEN was the state comptroller from 1961 to 1978.

COLLEEN SHEARER was director of the Iowa Department of Job Service under Bob Ray and headed up the Iowa Refugee Service Center and refugee resettlement programs. She now works in the Office of Legislative Management at the state capitol in Minnesota.

REV. BILL SHERMAN is pastor of St. Michael's Church in Grand Forks, North Dakota.

NANCY SHIMANEK was a three-term state representative before joining Ray's staff in 1981. She served as assistant to Chief Justice of the Iowa Supreme Court W. Ward Reynoldson, before being named to the Iowa Utilities Board.

MARY LOUISE SMITH was first elected Republican national committeewoman in 1964 and served as chairman of the Republican National Committee from 1974 to 1977 under President Gerald Ford. She was comanager of Bob Ray's 1978 campaign.

JOHN SOORHOLTZ is past president of the Iowa Pork Producers and the National Pork Producers. He was the first chairman of the Iowa Family Farm Development Authority and was elected to the state senate in 1983 and reelected in 1984.

LAUREN SOTH, a Pulitzer Prize–winning editorial writer, was editorial page editor of the *Des Moines Register* from 1953 to 1975.

EDWARD STANEK worked at the Department of Environmental Quality and with Ray and the National Governors' Association's Natural Resource Committee before becoming director of the Iowa Energy Policy Council. Ray later appointed him director of the Office for Planning and Programming, a job he held until 1984, when he became director of the Iowa Lottery Commission.

DAVID STANLEY, a former Republican state representative and senator from Muscatine, founded Iowans for Tax Relief. He ran unsuccessfully for the U.S. Senate in 1968 and 1974.

ROGER STETSON worked on Bob Ray's 1974 campaign. He is now a lawyer in Des Moines with the Belin firm.

TOM STONER was Bob Ray's campaign manager in 1972 and 1974, served as state chairman of the Republican party from 1975 to 1977, and ran for the Republican nomination for the U.S. Senate in 1980. He is the president of Stoner Broadcasting Company and lives in Annapolis, Maryland.

DEL STROMER, a Republican, was first elected to the Iowa House in 1966. He was Speaker of the House in 1981 and 1982 and has been minority leader since 1983.

MELVIN SYNHORST was first elected secretary of state in 1948 and went on to win thirteen consecutive elections. He held that position under nine governors until he resigned in 1980.

TOM TAUKE, a former member of the Republican state central committee from Dubuque, was elected to the Iowa House in 1974 and 1976 and the U.S. House in 1978, 1980, 1982, 1984, and 1986.

BILL THOMPSON was Bob Ray's first press secretary, from 1969 to 1971. Prior to joining Ray's staff, he was a journalism professor at Central College in Pella, and he now publishes a bird-watcher's magazine in Marietta, Ohio.

TOM THOREN worked as a field staffer in Bob Ray's 1970 and 1972 campaigns and later for the Iowa Senate and is a political consultant.

GERALD F. THORNTON is a vice-president of the Meredith Corporation in Des Moines.

MARIE TJERNAGEL lives in Ames and works at Iowa State University.

JIM and JOANN TYLER, college classmates of Bob and Billie Ray, live in Newton, where Jim has a law practice.

BOB TYSON worked for Central Surveys in Shenandoah before joining the staff of the state Republican party. He served as the party's executive director from 1964 to 1966 and then went to work as an aide for Congressman Fred Schwengel. He worked for Bob Ray at the Office of Economic Opportunity and as director of the Office for Planning and Programming from 1972 to 1981. In 1981 he was named director of the Energy Policy Council, where he served until his death in June 1985.

THOMAS URBAN, a Democrat, was mayor of Des Moines from 1968 to 1972 and is now chief operating officer of Pioneer Hi-Bred International.

EARL USHER is an Iowa state trooper who worked with the governor's office from 1970 to 1983. He now administers security for the state capitol complex.

DEL VAN HORN is a Greene County farmer and businessman. He worked under Ray as the agriculture director of the Iowa Development Commission before being named IDC director in 1974. In 1980 he was appointed to the Department of Transportation.

MAURICE VAN NOSTRAND served in the Iowa House from 1963 to 1971, worked at the Office for Planning and Programming in 1971, and was appointed chairman of the Iowa Commerce Commission. He was reappointed in 1977 and resigned in 1979. He ran unsuccessfully for the Republican nomination for the U.S. Senate in 1978.

JANET VAN NOTE worked for Bob Ray's Polk County Attorney's race in 1956 and was an original Bob Ray Girl. She joined the governor's staff in 1969 and worked as a confidential secretary until 1980. She now lives in Las Vegas.

ANDREW VARLEY, a Republican, was elected to the Iowa House in 1966, was elected Speaker of the House in 1972, and was named chairman of the Iowa Commerce Commission in 1979, where he still serves.

ELMER "DUTCH" VERMEER was a five-term Republican legislator from Pella and co-chaired Bob Ray's first two gubernatorial campaigns. He worked as the governor's legislative liaison from 1969 to 1980.

RANDI RAY WATSON, Bob and Billie Ray's oldest daughter, is a graduate of the Drake University Law School.

BEN WEBSTER was Polk County Republican chairman from 1969 to 1974 and was a longtime legal counsel for the Republican state central committee. He served as Republican state chairman from 1981 to 1982. He is a lawyer with Gamble Riepe Webster Davis and Green in Des Moines.

JIM WEST was a Republican member of the Iowa House from 1973 to 1981 and then joined the staff of Senator Roger Jepsen.

TOM WHITNEY was state Democratic party chairman from 1973 to 1977, a gubernatorial primary candidate in 1978, and Polk County supervisor from 1969 to 1984. He is currently a lawyer in Des Moines.

WYTHE WILLEY, a cattleman and lawyer from Manchester, worked for the Office for Planning and Programming before joining Bob Ray's staff in 1971. He was named executive assistant to the governor in 1972, a position he held until 1981. He now oversees Senator Chuck Grassley's Iowa office.

GEORGE "PIC" WILSON worked for the Legislative Fiscal Bureau and the Department of Transportation before joining the governor's staff in 1981.

PAUL WILSON was a producer for the political consulting firm of Bailey-Deardourff and worked on Bob Ray's 1978 campaign.

GEORGE WITTGRAF worked on Ray's first campaign and was appointed state youth coordinator in 1970. In 1971 he worked on Art Neu's campaign for lieutenant governor and then worked for Neu from 1973 to 1977. He is now a lawyer in Cherokee.

DAVID YEPSEN was a campaign staffer for Paul Franzenburg's 1972 gubernatorial race and has been the *Des Moines Register*'s chief political writer since 1982.

DON ZARLEY was a law school classmate of Bob Ray's and is now senior partner of Zarley McKee Thomte Voorhees and Sease in Des Moines.

Interviewed but not quoted:

Willard "Sandy" Boyd

Harry Braafhart

John Culver

Art Donhowe

Roy Edwards

Norman Erbe

George Flagg

Rolland Gallagher

Carole Harder

E. A. "Ernie" Hayes

David Hinton

Harlan "Bud" Hockenberg

Eva Hornberger

Dr. H. Richard Hornberger

Richard Johnson

Dr. John Kelley

Karen Slinker Kelly

Jon Kneen

Clif Larson

Irene Laverty

Mrs. Paul Lefton

John McCarroll

Stan McCausland

Joseph May

Les Menke

Susan Mickelson

Dan Miller

George Milligan

C. Edwin Moore

Barbara Oakley

Forbes "Ozzie" Olberg

Donald Payton

June Peterson

W. Ward Reynoldson

Hubert Schultz

Herb Selby

Michael Sellers

David Shaff

Samuel Solomon

Ken Sullivan

John Taylor

John Tone

Matt Wanning

Harrison "Skip" Weber

Linda Weeks

W. C. Wellman

Charles Wittenmeyer

INDEX

Citations for interviewees are in boldface.

Abbott, Gene, 64, 65
Abortion law, 106, 150, 177, 179, 219
Abrahamson, M. L., 34
Academy of Trial Lawyers, 17
Addy, Jerry Lee, 165
AFL-CIO, 175
Agnew, Spiro, 56, 110, 142, 182, 347
Akers, C. B., 34
Alcoa (Aluminum Company of America), 171, 173, 174, 175
Alpha Kappa Psi (business fraternity), 10
Alpha Tau Omega (social fraternity), 11
American Bankers Association, 29
American Independent party, 98
American Legion, 59, 60
American Red Cross, 318
American Republic Insurance Company, 22
Anderson, John, 224–25, 244, 249
Anderson, Merrill, 83
Andrews, John, 23
Anthan, George, 95, 308
Apple, Roy, 164
Armstrong, Anne, 178, 183
Augustine, Al, 101
Avenson, Don, 228–29, **236, 270, 282, 325–26, 338–39**

Babcock, Bill, 29
Bailey, Deardourff, and Associates, 202
Bailey, F. Lee, 17
Bain, Pat, **33, 205,** 292, **294–95, 297,** 298
Bair, Gerald, 312–13
Baker, Howard, 178, 224, 243, 244, 245, 246, 247, 248, 249, 250, 322
Ball, Bill, 79
Bandstra, Bert, 45
Bankers, in Republican party, 27–29
Bankers Life Insurance Company, 309
Baringer, Maurice ("Mo"), 77, **81,** 152, **156,** 198, 215, 252, **256–57**
Barnard, Jerry, 234

Beamer, John, **108, 110–11,** 312
Beck, Charlotte (Mrs. Robert), 61–62
Beck, Robert, 44, 48, 50, 55, 58, 59, 60, **61, 62, 63,** 66, 69, 70, 71, 72
Bedell, Berkley, 15
Belin, David, 44, **51,** 178, **180, 181–82,** 184, 188, **190, 204, 274,** 318
Beller, Robert ("Bo"), 85, **132**
Belli, Melvin, 17
Bennett, Bob, 291
Benson, Fred, 35
Benton, Robert, 313
Birth control, 87. *See also* Abortion law
Blue, Robert, 325
Bogan, Gerald, **61**
Bond, Christopher ("Kit"), 178
Bottle bill, 166–76, 283, 338
Bowen, Otis, 245
Boyd, Willard ("Sandy"), 85, 225, 255
Boy Scouts of America, 171, 175
Bozell Jacobs (advertising agency), 61
Bradley, Bruce, 43, 49
Bradley, Ed, 238
Branstad, Terry, 78, 135, 149, 160, 161, 167, 219, 220, 222, 246, 257, **260–61,** 267, 270, 271, 272, 273, 275, 277, **284, 288,** 289, 296, 312, 313, 314, 315, 325, 331, 339
Brenton, C. Robert, **56–57,** 120, **262, 263**
Brenton, Harold, 29, 30, 32
Brenton, Junius ("Buz"), 170
Brenton Banks, 120
Bright, Johnny, 10
Brock, Bill, 243
Broder, David, 164, 249, 347
Brown, George, **41,** 42, **45–46,** 49, **60**
Brown, Mary Ann, **221–22,** 324
Brown, Ralph, **135–36, 272–73, 291,** 294
Buckmaster, Robert, **257**
Buck Night fund-raising, 32, 41

Burgeson, Floyd, 22
Burkhead, Junior, 212, 213, 214
Burlingame, Bob, **41, 57,** 76, 77, **86–87,** 92, **97, 275, 340**
Burnett, Bob, 263
Burrows, John, 39
Bush, George, 224, 243, 244, 245, 246, **247,** 249, 250, 267, 319, 323, **324, 325**
Byrne, Brendan, 238

Callahan Junior High School, 3, 5
Cambodia, refugees from, 225, 237–41
Campbell, Bev, 147
Campbell, Ed, **131–32, 145,** 202–3, 208, **212,** 267, **270, 333, 336**
Cannon, Jim, 245
Capital punishment, 87, 298, 335
Capitol complex, 333
Carter, Brian, 254
Carter, Jimmy, 123, 181, 182, 183, 185, 186, 187, 202, 232, 238, 244, 249, 254, 259
Cattlemen's Association, 105
Centerville, 59–60
Central National Bank, 29, 32
Central Surveys, 35, 61, 127
Chamber of Commerce, 144
China, 106, 148, 161, 238
Chinn, Gary, 11, 29
Church of Christ, 239
Citicorp, 263
Civil liberties, 310
Clark, Dick, 151, 201, 209, 215, 222–23, 308
Clark, Hugh, **263**
Cochran, Dale, 151, 160, **230, 258, 263**
Collective bargaining, for public employees, 106, 137, 139, 176
Collins, Tom, 322
Columbus Junction, 60
Conlin, Roxanne, 267
Connally, John, 224, 244
Connie and Lou's Skyliner, 20
Conservative Union, 298
Constitutional convention, call for, 298
Corey, LeRoy, 298
Corn Growers Association, 105
Cottage Grove market, 4
Council Bluffs Nonpareil, 49
Council of State Governments, 288
Council of State Legislatures, 298
Couppee, Al, 29
Crafts, Kent, **55, 56, 57, 59, 61–62, 63,** 64, 67, **71**
Cranberg, Gil, 100, **259, 304, 309, 329**
Crane, Cal, 120
Crane, Phil, 224, 244, 246
Cresco, Air National Guard airplane crash (1968), 107

Crews, Bill, **210, 324**
Crime records, computerized, 106
Criminal code, 166
Critelli, Anthony, **19, 20,** 22
Crosby, Jim, 31, **32**
Cross, Russell, **273**
Culver, John, 45, 148, 151, 209, 255, 308, 339

Data Resources Inc., 234
Davis, A. Arthur, 318
Day, Jacqueline, **21,** 41, **58,** 79, 313
Dean, John, 110
Death penalty. *See* Capital punishment
Deere and Company, 258
Depression, the Great, 4
Des Moines, 3, 7–8, 60, 72, 76
Des Moines Club, 190
Des Moines Register, 11–12, 53, 60, 61, 66, 69, 71, 72–75, 84, 85, 86, 95, 96, 100, 108, 109, 117, 137, 145, 165–66, 168, 186, 187, 222, 224, 232, 237, 239–40, 250, 264, 266, 298, 303–9, 328, 333, 334, 336, 347
Des Moines Savings and Loan Association, 31
Des Moines Tribune. See Des Moines Register
Dilley, Robert
Dingman, Bishop Maurice, 198
Doderer, Minnette, 98, **283, 333, 334**
Dole, Robert, 69, 137, 178, 183, 185, 186, 187, 244
Donhowe, Art, 27–32, 58, 114, 298
Donielson, Allen L. ("Barney"), **35–36, 192**
Drake Park, 3
Drake Relays, 9
Drake University, 3, 3–13, 57, 63, 92, 319
Duncan, Carol **315–16**
Dunham, Warren, 312
Dunlap, 147
DuPont, Pierre ("Pete"), 245
Dysart, Keith, **164, 249**

Eagles (service fraternity), 23
Economic recession (1980–82), 231–36
Education, aid to, 102–4, 169, 171, 254, 255, 338
Edwards, Ed, 163
Ehrlichman, John, 143, 162
Eighteen-year-olds, voting rights, 106, 190
Eisenhower, Dwight, 21, 342
Elizabeth II (queen of England), 162
Employer's Mutual Insurance Company, 120
Equal Rights Amendment (ERA), 298
Erbe, Norman, 34, 45, 79, 80, 156
Estherville radio station, 197
Evans, Cooper, 41

Evans, Dan, 161, 164, 178, 187, 242, 255
Evashevski, Forrest, 46
Exon, Jim, 143

Failor, Ed, 209
Falwell, Jerry, 347
Farm Bureau, 29, 55, 83, 105, 171, 197, 345
Faul, George, 22
Federation of Republican Women, 40, 88
Feick, Jerry, 207
Ferraro, Geraldine, 247
Ferris, Roger, **125, 126,** 127, **128**
Financial Center, Des Moines, 262
Finkbine Golf Course, 12
First Christian Church, Des Moines, 6
Fitzgerald, Jerry, **106, 155,** 160–61, 165, **171,** 202, 203, 207, **208,** 209, 210, **212–13,** 214, 215, 267, 271, **282, 283–84, 335**
Fitzgerald, Mary, 169, **172, 173, 174, 275**
Fitzgibbon, John, **263**
Flansburg, James, **70, 93,** 95, **104, 105–6,** 132, 137, 165, 202, 232, 250, 266, 297, **300–301,** 303, 304, **306–7,** 308, **332,** 344
Flatt, Joe, 91
Fleming Building, Des Moines, 16
Foods and prescription drugs, sales tax, 139, 283, 284
Ford, Gerald, 44, 137, 142, 161, **162,** 163, 167, 177–85, **186,** 187, 202, 206, 207, 242, 243, 254, 342
Forst, Bill, 84
Forstener, George, 57
Fort Bliss, Tex., 8
Fort Riley, Kans., 8
Fort Snelling, Minn., 8
Foudree, Bruce, 312
Franzenburg, Paul, 70, 71, **72–73,** 74, **112,** 127, 130, **131, 132,** 133, 149, **230,** 256, 332
Freese, Baxter, **104–5**
Friendship Force, 319
Fulton, Robert, 70, **71–72, 81,** 82, 89, **90,** 91, **93–94, 95, 96,** 97–98, **100,** 115, **132,** 145, 147, 149, **332, 334**
Fultz, William, **261**
Fun Mondays election campaigning, 210–11

Gallagher, Roland, 164
Gannon, William, 89, 133, 139, 144, 147
Garfield, Theodore G., 76
Garrison, Serge, **288**
Gartner, Michael, 166, **240, 261–62,** 303, **304, 306, 308, 309**
Gaskill, Thurman, **341**

Gayler, Ben, 35
Gaylord, Joseph, 294
Germond, Jack, 267
Getto, Mike, 91, **92, 93–94,** 95
Gibbons, Novelene Ray (sister), **4–5,** 7, 9, **53**
GI Bill of Rights, 8–9
Gifford, Chuck, **257**
Gilbert, Richard, 79, 80, 85, 106, **109, 112, 121, 122, 123, 124,** 125, **126, 128, 129,** 134, 139, **140–41,** 142, 144, **145–46, 163–64,** 165, 188, **189, 190,** 192, **203,** 205, 228, **244, 285, 301–2, 303,** 304, 305, **307–8,** 308–9, **322, 331, 338, 345**
Gilbert, Roger, 110
Glanton, Luther, 17
Goldburg, Jay, 240
Goldwater, Barry, 36–39, 137, 290
Goodwin, Bob, 30, 58
Grain embargo, Russian, 232, 234–35
Grant Elementary School, 3
Grassley, Charles, **43,** 135, 137, 151, 209, 223, 225, 250, **251–52, 287,** 294, 298, 339
Great Society programs, 159, 255
Greenleaf, Hale, **127**
Greigg, Stan, 45
Gross, Doug, **259, 278,** 279, **280, 281, 284, 288–89,** 314
Gross, H. R., 39, 45, 77, 108, 151
Grubbs, Joseph, **344**
Gun control, 219

Haldeman, Bob, 162
Hall, Dorothy, **5**
Hall, Howard, 57
Hammill, John, 120
Hanrahan, Ray, **21**
Hansen, Christine, **301**
Hanson, Bill, 219
Harbor, William, 83, 116, 117, **136–37, 276–77, 287**
Harkin, Tom, 142, 148, 151, 205, 209, 267, 326, 328
Harmon, Buck, 84
Harms, Wendell, 221
Hawkins, Lex, 39, 45
Health maintenance organizations, 106
Henderson, Cynthia, **198, 268–69, 320**
Henry, Colonel, 55
Heston, Charleton, 163
Hickenlooper, Bourke, 36
Higgens, Tom, 94, **159–60, 337**
Hoegh, Leo, 45, 83, 332
Holshouser, Jim, 161
Hoover (Herbert) State Office Building, 135
Hotel Savery, Des Moines, 55, 67, 77, 92

Houser, Bob, 309
Hubbell, Corrinne, **50,** 62, 198
Hubbell, Crawford, 50, 62, 198
Hubbell mansion. *See* Terrace Hill
Huff, Bill, 206
Hughes, Harold, 34, 39, 42, 44, 52, 54, 55, 62, 70, 72–75, 77, 80, **81–82,** 84, 89, 91, 94, 108–9, 111, 125–26, **132–33,** 146, 149, 152, 156, 160, 161, 172, 188, 209, **258–59,** 260, 267, **269, 270, 271,** 276, 297, 300, 306, 308, **311, 323,** 325–326, **327, 330, 331,** 332, 333, 339, 340
Hultman, Calvin, **155,** 206, 215, **230– 31, 257–58, 276**
Hultman, Evan ("Curly"), 34, 39, 45, 56, 146
Humphrey, Hubert, 69
Huston, Tom, 312
Hyde, John, 165, **166, 309**
Hy-Vee Foods, 173

Iles, Charles, 22
Indexing, state income tax, 298
International Harvester Corporation, 258
Iowa, state of,
　Banking Superintendent, 312
　Board of Parole, 313
　Board of Regents, 312, 313
　Civil Rights Commission, 106
　Commerce Commission, 225, 267, 312
　Commission for the Blind, 212
　Commission on Aging, 157
　Comptroller, 286–87, 312
　Conservation Commission, 153, 313
　Department of Beer and Liquor Control, 93, 164, 332
　Department of Environmental Quality, 338
　Department of General Services, 138, 212, 313
　Department of Public Instruction, 158, 313
　Department of Revenue, 84, 153, 313, 332
　Department of Social Services, 84, 153, 312, 332
　Department of Transportation, 112, 135– 40, 153, 256–57, 312–13, 322
　Development Commission, 83, 87, 104– 5, 254, 256, 262
　Energy Policy Council, vii, 137–38
　General Assembly, annual sessions, 332
　General Assembly: Legislative Fiscal Bureau, 96, 286–87; Legislative Service Bureau, 21
　Insurance Commission, 312
　Job Service, 237, 313, 337
　National Guard, 85, 107–13, 164–65, 175, 212–14, 346

Public Employees Relations Board, 312
Refugee Service Center, 239, 241
Supreme Court, 22
Iowa associations. *See* second word in title, e.g., Cattlemen's Association; Farm Bureau
Iowa Des Moines Bank, 7
Iowa Electric Light and Power Company, 319
Iowans for Tax Relief, 262
Iowans in Support of President Reagan, 298
Iowa Poll, 71, 85, 96, 166, 168, 224, 237
Iowa SHARES, 239–40
Iowa State University, 148, 319
Iowa 2000, 255, 265
Iran hostages, 225
Israel, 161, 344
Izaak Walton League, 176

Jackson, Bill, **94,** 106, **111,** 134, 225, **303**
Japan, U.S. relations with, 106
Jaycees (Junior Chamber of Commerce), 24–25
Jensen, Dwight, 79, **163, 255–56**
Jepsen, Dee, 216, 217, 218, 220, 327
Jepsen, Jeff, 221
Jepsen, Roger, 75, 76, 83, 86, 89, **98,** 103, **112,** 114–16, **117–19,** 120–24, **125,** 126–27, **128,** 129, 130, 133, 134, 144, 203, **209, 216–18,** 219– 22, **223,** 256, 294, 298, 305, 310, 326–27, **328,** 339
Jernigan, Ken, **116, 286, 287–88, 335**
Jesse, Norman, **103, 231, 287, 335– 36**
John Paul II, 225
Johnson, Don, 48, 50, 55, 59, **60–61,** 62– 63, 66, 69–72, **127**
Johnson, Lyndon, 36, 38–39, 72, 254–55
Johnson, Richard, 225
Jordan, Hamilton, 249
Judge, Tom, 239
Junkins, Lowell, **145, 172, 229–30, 232, 236, 259, 282, 289, 336**

Kaul, Donald, **87, 270–71, 308, 310, 334–35**
Kearney, Darrell, 298
Kelley, John, 65
Kelley, Robb, 120, 126, **144,** 147, **199, 327**
Kennedy, John, 182
Kennedy, Robert, 72
Kieffer, Gene, 20
King, Martin Luther, 72
Kinley, George, 151, 155, **160, 211–12, 229, 258,** 267, **334, 336–37**
KIOA-Radio, 24

Kirkpatrick, Jeanne, 319
Kissinger, Henry, 242
Knudson, John, 55
Koob, Kathryn, 225
Kruidenier, Dave, 186
Kyl, John, 77

Laird, Russell ("Rusty"), **173, 174**
Lake Rathbun, 109
Lamberto, Nick, 108, 300
Lamborn, Cliff, 134, 136
Lamm, Richard, 239
Lane, Carroll, 34, 121
Laos, refugees from, 237–41
Larson, Clif, 100
Lawyer, James, 15, **16,** 17, **18,** 19, 20,
    35, 275
Lawyer, Marge, 16, 27
Lawyer, Verne, 15, **16, 17–18,** 19–22,
    27, 35–36, **48–49,** 74, 121, 192,
    193, 194–95, 268, 275, **321**
Leach, Jim, 206, 215, 216, 271, 327
Lefton, Paul, 55
Liddy, Bob, 120, 130, 147
Liddy, L. B., 34, **50,** 77, 120, 130
Life Investors Insurance Company, 318,
    321–22
Lilly, Gary, **5,** 55
Lincoln Club, 29, 61
Lincoln High School, 24
Linge, Jack, 64
Lipsky, Joan, **43,** 327
Living History Farms, 225
Lloyd, John, 64, **65**
Lodge, Henry Cabot, 38
Lomas, Anna, 50
Lounsberry, Robert, 152, 252
Loveless, Herschel, 332
Lynner, Darwin, 32
Lyons, Buster, 287

Mabry, Drake, **18, 149,** 300, **308, 340**
McCartney, Ralph, **43,** 49, **340–41**
McCarville, Emma, 107, 110
McCausland, Stan, 313
McDonald, John, 40, **50,** 119, **120,
    140,** 177, 182, 184, 188, 202, 219,
    291, 292, 293, **294,** 295–96, **329**
McDonald, Margaret, 291
MacNider, Jack, **118, 119**
MacVicar Freeway, 3
Manufacturers Association, 29
March of Dimes, 23–24, 32
Marcos, Ferdinand, 325
Martin, Verne, 31, 35
Mason City Gazette, 65
Maxwell, Chuck, 121
May, Joseph, 110, 164, 212–13
Maye, Marilyn, 68, **69,** 94, 202
Mayne, Wiley, 77, 142, 151, 309

Maytag Corporation, 319
Mendenhall, John, 169
Mercer, Bernard, 144, 318
Meredith Corporation, 263
Merriman, John, **59,** 292, **297, 298–99**
Messerly, Francis, 101
Mickelson, Susan, 225
Midwest Governors' Association, 143, 163
Millen, Floyd, **231, 258, 332–33**
Miller, Elmer, 31
Miller, Jack, xi, 77, 94, 119, **126,** 127,
    203
Miller, Pat, **147, 252**
Miller, Tom, 267
Miller, Wilbur, 319
Milliken, William, xi, 138, 162, 163, 164,
    178, **195,** 204, 238, 239, 245, 247,
    255, **274, 339–40**
Mills, George ("Lefty"), 11, 37–38, 52, 300,
    307
Mills, Max Milo, 76, 77, **79, 115**
Mitchell, Forrest ("Frosty"), **18, 24, 46–
    47, 61, 63–64, 65–66,** 67, **68,
    69, 70, 71, 72, 73–74,** 77, **94,** 97,
    161, 195, 197, **300,** 319, **322,
    324, 342,** 347
Mitchell, Jane, **192–93, 315**
Mitschke, Sue, **210, 314, 316**
Modale, 148
Mondale, Walter ("Fritz"), 183, 185–87,
    247
Moore, C. Edwin, 22, 100
Moose Lodge, 23
Mooty, W. L., 34
Mosher, Ronald, 225, 226, 232, **233–34,
    235,** 236, **260, 261,** 314, 318
Mowry, John, 34
Murray, John, **91, 92,** 97, **121–22,
    123–24,** 134, 205, 206, 273, **279**
Murray, William, **44,** 50, 55–56, 61
Mursener, Jerry, **84–85, 111, 194,
    205–6, 207, 210–11, 216, 220–
    221, 274–75, 286, 330**

Naden, Robert, 34
Nagel, Dennis, **129, 169–70, 170–71,
    174–75, 175–76, 189,** 225, **227,**
    228, 236, **278, 279–80, 289, 311**
Nagle, George, 35
National Conference of State Legislatures,
    288
National Governors' Association, 161, 163,
    164, 170, 182, 311
Navistar. *See* International Harvester
    Corporation
Nelson, Dale, 83
Neu, Art, **43, 87, 114–15, 115–16,
    117,** 133, 134, 136, 152, **154,** 205,
    206–7, 259–60, 267, **271,** 272,
    273, **284–85,** 296, 313, **326, 327,
    331–32, 339**

New Federalism programs, 255
New Guinea, 161
Nixon, Richard M., 37, 75, 100, 106, 109, 121, 126, 127, 137, 141–44, 148, 149, 151, 161–62, 182, 183, 196, 206, 243, 254, 255, 305, 309
Nixon Girls, 58
No-fault insurance, 106
Norland, Lowell, 214, 226, **230, 233, 263, 282–83**

Oakley, Brice, 206, 219, 220, **227**
Odell, Mary Jane, 11, **33,** 225, **310, 313**
O'Halloran, Mary, 170
Olson, Richard, **11**
Omaha World Herald, 61
Oman, David, **147,** 149, **155, 156–57, 158–59,** 165, 169, **182, 184,** 188, **191, 193–94, 195–96,** 205, 207, **210,** 211, **213, 215–16, 218–19,** 220, **221, 222,** 225, **231, 244–45, 245–46, 247, 271, 273, 292, 302–3, 304–5, 305–6, 314, 315**
Ombudsman, 158
Open-meetings law, 166
Orr, Joann, 283
Oxenberger, Leo, 17, 19, **20, 21, 22–23, 24–25, 27, 28–29, 30, 31–32, 32–33, 66,** 157, 192, 297, 298

Packwood, Bob, 216
Panama Canal, 219
Pardun, Pat, 40
Parkin, Jerry, **183, 273**
Payton, Don, 65
Peebler, Chuck, 61
Percy, Charles, 178
Pester, Jack, 126, 147, 177–78, **182–83,** 184, **185,** 188, 190, **191, 193, 257, 261,** 274
Petersen, H. Rand, 46, 50, 51, 52, 54, 55, **56,** 63, 67, 97, 120, **123, 145,** 192
Peterson, Keith, **79–80**
Philippines, 325
Pioneer Hi-Bred International, 90, 226
Political action committees, 293
Polk County Republican party, 18–21, 30–33
Pomerantz, Marvin, **5,** 126, 177, 182, **183,** 184, **186,** 188, **189–90, 191,** 202, **203–4,** 205, **209, 210,** 215, 216, **217,** 219, 220, 225, 246, 250, 254, **272**
Pope, Larry, 147, **148–49, 206, 235, 238, 284, 303–4, 313, 344**
Pork Producers Council, 105
Prayers, in public schools, 177
Preferred Risk Insurance Company, 318
Preisser, Vic, 153, **339, 344**

Press, freedom of, 310
Principal Mutual Life. *See* Bankers Life Insurance Company
Prison conditions, 106
Property tax relief laws, 166

Quinn, Ken, 237, **238, 239–40,** 242, **322–23**

Rampton, Calvin, 163, 255
Ramsey, Richard, **172–73**
Rankin, Gerry, **96,** 99, **101, 115, 204, 229**
Rasdal, Harry, **43,** 54, 55, **57, 62–63, 66, 71**
Rasmussen, Clark, **44–45, 96,** 139, 144, **334**
Ray, Billie Lee (wife), 6, **8–9, 10, 13,** 14, **15, 19, 36,** 46, 48, **52,** 60, 63, 65, **66–67, 67–68,** 74, **87–88, 91, 123, 141,** 148, **184–85,** 188, 192, 194–95, **196–97, 198, 199,** 200, **207,** 214, 238, 268, 269, 274, 292, **316,** 317, 318, **320–21,** 322, **323,** 344
Ray, Clark (father), 3–7, 9, 19
Ray, Mildred (mother), 3, **4, 5–6, 7, 10**
Ray Girls, 19, 58, 92, 94, 148, 330
Reagan, Ronald, 144, 163, 177–80, 185, 224, 243–44, 246–50, 254, 294, 298, 305, 308, 323
Reagen, Michael, 153, 312
Redfern, Ed, 120, **130, 220–21,** 298
Redman, Dick, **40, 41–42,** 50, **63,** 68, 209, 246, 250, 330
Reed's Ice Cream store, 3, 346
Refugees, Indochinese, resettlement in Iowa, 225, 237–42, 346
Rehmann, John Keith, 27, **30,** 51, 55, 58, 62, 192
Reppert, Howard, 23
Republican Governors' Association, 163
Retail Food Dealers Association, 169, 171, 173
Rhodes, James, 245, 266
Richardson, Elliot, 178
Richey, Wayne, 312
Rigler, Robert, 22, 34, 55, **116,** 313
Rinard, Park, 94, 188
Ringgenberg, Clayton, 79, 92, **276**
Ritchie, Albert, 266
Roberts, Steve, 41, **122,** 201, 220, **227, 244,** 267, **272,** 294, **295, 296, 297,** 298, 313, **325, 326, 328, 330**
Rockefeller, Nelson, 37, 38, 49, 91, 124, 163, 178, 181, 182, 266
Romney, George, 69
Roosevelt, Franklin D., 6
Roosevelt High School, 3

Rosenfield, Joe, 144
Ruan, John, 261, 298, 309
Ruan Group, 296
Russia, 161, 232, 234–35

Sandler, Norman, **305, 309**
Sargent, Fran, 163
Scalise, Larry, 48
Schaben, James, 106, 139, 144–50, 256
Scherle, William, 44, 77, 89, 114, 142, 151, 309
Schissel, Nichola, **340**
Schmidhauser, John, 45
School foundation plan. *See* Education, aid to
Schroeder, Jack, 21, **22,** 34
Schroeder, Laverne, 170, 280
Schweiker, Lowell, 247
Schwengel, Fred, **44,** 45, 77
Scott, John, **171–72, 173**
Scranton, William, 36–38
Sears, John, 245, **248–49**
Segretti, Donald, 149
Selden, Marvin, **80,** 81, **90, 93, 94,** 99, **100–101,** 102, **116,** 139, 164–65, 167, 225, 226, 236, 253, **255,** 282, **327**
Sellers, Michael, 79
Shaff, David, 22, 34, 55
Shaw, Betty, 43
Shearer, Colleen, 237, 238, 313
Sherman, Bill, **8**
Shimanek, Nancy, **160**
Shotwell, Walt, 46, 63, 66, 73, 124, 141, 207, 330
Shriners, 161
Shultz, George, 319
Sierra Club, 171
Sigma Alpha Epsilon (social fraternity), 10–11, 16
Simbro, Bill, 239
Simon, William, 178
Smith, Bill, 134
Smith, Lloyd, 77, 152, 225
Smith, Marvin, 34
Smith, Mary Louise, 52, 177, **178–79,** 180–81, 182, 184, 187, 188, **189,** 190, 202, **206,** 209, 216, **217,** 218, 219, 220, 291, 298, **343–44**
Smith, Neal, 45
Soap Box Derby, 25
Soorholtz, John, **83, 105, 258**
Soth, Lauren, **306, 310**
Sound Storms, Inc., 85
South Dakota, economic development in, 263
Soybean Association, 105
Spooner, John, 147, 148
Standard Club, 22

"Stand by Your Man," as campaign song, 94
Stanek, Edward, 137, **170,** 312
Stanley, David, 49, 62, 71, 116, 209, 262
"Step to the Rear, Let a Leader Lead the Way," as campaign song, 68–69, 73–74, 94, 202
Stetson, Roger, **147–48**
Stoner, Tom, 70, 120, **121, 122, 124,** 125, **127–28, 130, 131, 140, 141, 142–43,** 147, 148–49, 186, 188, **189, 190–91, 192, 195, 204,** 205, 206, 209, 215, **216,** 250, 251, 252, **256,** 267, **273–74, 294,** 295, 296, 330, **332, 339**
Story City, Air National Guard airplane crash (1968), 107
Stromer, Del, 43, **49–50, 82, 103, 160–61,** 206, 267, 278
Stuart, Bill, 22
Synhorst, Melvin, 34, 77, 118, 152, 225, **330–31, 333**

Tai Dam, refugees, 237–41
Taiwan, 165
Tapscott, John, 130
Tauke, Tom, 177, 178, 206, 271, **285–86,** 294, **295,** 339
Taxpayers Association, 214
Tax rebate (1979), 228–31
Terrace Hill (governor's mansion), 141, 152, 195, 198–99, 207, 320
Thailand, refugees from, 225, 237–41
Thompson, Bill, **79,** 97, **307, 343**
Thompson, Jim, 245, 247
Thoren, Tom, 92, **94–95, 111,** 120, **124, 130, 136**
Thornburg, Dick, 245
Thornton, Gerald F., **261,** 262, 263, **335**
Tiemann, Norbert, 61
Tjernagel, Marie, **107, 108, 109,** 110
Tjernagel, Peter, 107–8
Tolan, Msgr. Joseph E., 227
Trucks, double-bottomed, 262, 280
Turner, Richard, 77, 85, 98, 152, 165, 201
Tuthill, Sam, 137
Tyler, Jim, **13–14**
Tyler, Joann, **13, 14**
Tyson, Bob, vii–viii, 36, **37, 38, 39,** 40–41, 42, **45,** 49, 50, 51, **55–56, 59, 65, 97, 161–62, 183, 236,** 292–93, **342**

United Nations: conference on boat people, 238; special assistant to Jeanne Kirkpatrick, 319, 324–25
U.S. Agency for International Development (USAID), 319

U.S. Air Force, and the Iowa Air National Guard, 107–13
U.S. Farmers Home Administration (FHA), 226
U.S. Federal Bureau of Investigation (FBI), 324
U.S. Occupational Safety and Health Administration (OSHA), 337
United Way, 144
University Church, Des Moines, 6
University of Iowa, 85, 148, 225, 234; Institute of Public Affairs, 254
Urban, Thomas, **90, 91,** 226, 261, **275**
Usher, Earl, **161**
Utilities, sales tax on, 228

Van Horn, Del, **50, 67, 82–83,** 104–5, **149, 256, 268, 286, 326**
Van Nostrand, Maurice, **38, 49,** 55, **57,** 67, 80, 103, 137, 203, 215, 217–20, 225, 251
Van Note, Janet, **11, 19, 58–59,** 79, 92, **180, 185, 193,** 225, **243, 326**
Varley, Andrew, 43, **103,** 134, 136, **171,** 225, 267, 312
Vermeer, Elmer ("Dutch"), **51,** 54, **55,** 63, 79, 80, **82, 91,** 92, **94,** 105, 106, 109, **128,** 134, 182, 225, **270,** 279
Veto, item, 230, 332
Vietnam, refugees from, 225, 237–41
Vietnam War, 131, 338; veterans of, 106
Viguerie, Richard, 219
Vorhees, Don, 49
Voter registration, 106
Voting age, 87
Vredenburg, Dwight, 173

Wadena rock festival (1970), 85–87
Wallace, George, 163
Wallace (Henry A.) Building, Des Moines, 135

Warren, Jack, 293, 296
Watergate scandal, 137, 141–44, 152, 309
Watson, Randi Ray (daughter), 24, **316**
Webster, Ben, **28, 32,** 33, **57,** 292, 294, **296,** 297, 298
Weissenburger, Monte, 254
Welden, Dick, 43
West, Jim, **116, 124–25, 160,** 214, **229, 232**
West Branch, 60
Whitney, Tom, 21, **74, 90, 95, 147,** 202–3, **208, 336**
WHO-TV, 225
Willey, Wythe, **103, 105,** 106, 109, 110, 121, 128, 130, 134, 148, 149, **152–53,** 182, 183, **184,** 188, **204–5, 208, 209,** 219, 220, **222,** 225, 228, **231, 235–36,** 246, 247, 248, **263, 277, 279, 286, 291, 293, 295–96,** 298, 302, **344**
Wilson, George ("Pic"), **273, 338**
Wilson, Larry, 313
Wilson, Paul, **209, 210, 211**
Wiretapping, 87, 93, 338
Witcover, Jules, 267
Wittgraf, George, **206, 272, 324–25**
WMT-Radio, 319
Women's rights, 179. *See also* Equal Rights Amendment
Woods, Dick, 147
World Trade Center, 325
World War II, 7
Wynette, Tammy, 94

Yepsen, David, 187, **210,** 221, **227,** 266, 297, 303, **304, 305, 330, 339**
Yoder, Earl, 49
Young Republicans, 19
Younkers Inc., 7

Zarley, Don, **11, 12–13**
Zeigler, Ron, 109